# A Community of Readers

## A Thematic Approach to Reading

# A Community of Readers

## A Thematic Approach to Reading

**Sixth Edition**

**Roberta Alexander**

Professor Emerita,
San Diego City College

and

**Jan Jarrell**
San Diego City College

WADSWORTH
CENGAGE Learning™

Australia • Brazil • Japan • Korea • Mexico • Singapore • Spain • United Kingdom • United States

*21015*
*GB*
*$104.95*

**A Community of Readers: A Thematic Approach to Reading, Sixth Edition**
Roberta Alexander and Jan Jarrell

Senior Publisher: Lyn Uhl

Director of Developmental Studies: Annie Todd

Development Editor: Ann Hofstra Grogg

Assistant Editor: Beth Rice

Editorial Assistant: Matthew Conte

Media Editor: Amy Gibbons

Marketing Manager: Sophie Teague

Marketing Coordinator: Brittany Blais

Marketing Communications Manager: Courtney Morris

Content Project Manager: Dan Saabye

Art Director: Jill Ort

Print Buyer: Betsy Donaghey

Rights Acquisition Specialist: Don Schlotman

Production Service: MPS Limited, a Macmillan Company

Text Designer: Dare Porter

Cover Designer: Walter Kopec

Cover Image: The Gee's Bend Foundation @ www.quiltsofgeesbend.com

Compositor: MPS Limited, a Macmillan Company

For product information and technology assistance, contact us at
**Cengage Learning Customer & Sales Support, 1-800-354-9706**
For permission to use material from this text or product,
submit all requests online at **www.cengage.com/permissions**.
Further permissions questions can be emailed to
**permissionrequest@cengage.com**.

Library of Congress Control Number: 2011936335

Student Edition:
ISBN-13: 978-1-111-83457-9

ISBN-10: 1-111-83457-1

**Wadsworth**
20 Channel Center Street
Boston, MA 02210
USA

Cengage Learning is a leading provider of customized learning solutions with office locations around the globe, including Singapore, the United Kingdom, Australia, Mexico, Brazil and Japan. Locate your local office at **international.cengage.com/region**

Cengage Learning products are represented in Canada by Nelson Education, Ltd.

For your course and learning solutions, visit **www.cengage.com**.

Purchase any of our products at your local college store or at our preferred online store **www.cengagebrain.com**.

**Instructors:** Please visit **login.cengage.com** and log in to access instructor-specific resources.

Printed in Canada
1 2 3 4 5 6 7 15 14 13 12 11

# Brief Contents

# Detailed Contents

**Chapter 8**   Critical Thinking: Crime and Punishment   319

# Readings by Discipline

In addition to the following readings, examples in the text and excerpts in exercises draw from a variety of disciplines that students will encounter in college.

## BIOLOGY

Boyer et al., "The Pill"

Bukatko and Daehler, "Drug-Abusing Mothers-To-Be: Are They Criminals?"

Ellis, "Drugs: The Truth"

Insel et al., "Wellness: The New Health Goal"

Medina, "Looking into Your Brain"

National Institutes of Health, "Stressed Out?"

Vitello, "A Ring Tone Meant to Fall on Deaf Ears"

## BUSINESS

Beekman and Beekman, "The Robot Revolution"

Jackson, "The National Eating Disorder"

Schlosser, "Behind the Counter"

Schlosser, "Oh, the Flavor of Your Fries"

## COMPUTERS AND TECHNOLOGY

Beekman and Beekman, "The Robot Revolution"

James, "Can You Hold, Please? Your Brain Is on the Line"

MacDonald, "Cyber-Bullying Defies Traditional School Bully Stereotype"

Vitello, "A Ring Tone Meant to Fall on Deaf Ears"

## CRIMINAL JUSTICE AND LAW

Bukatko and Daehler, "Drug-Abusing Mothers-To-Be: Are They Criminals?"

Gish, "The Falsely Accused on Death Row"

Kristoff, "End the War on Pot"

Martin et al., "Lizzie Borden, Murderer"

The Pew Charitable Trusts, "One in a Hundred"

## ECONOMICS

Chiras, "Curitiba, Brazil—A City with a Sustainable Vision"

Jackson, "The National Eating Disorder"

Kristoff, "End the War on Pot"

The Pew Charitable Trusts, "One in a Hundred"

## EDUCATION

Davis et al., "The Pact"

Downing, "Success in College: You Decide"

Downing, "Understanding Emotional Intelligence"

Eudy, "Signing for a Revolution: Gallaudet University and Deaf Culture"

Haring-Smith, "What Is Collaborative Learning?"

Peifer, "Suburb High, USA"

## ENVIRONMENTAL STUDIES

Chiras, "Curitiba, Brazil—A City with a Sustainable Vision"

## ETHICS

Beekman and Beekman, "The Robot Revolution"

Bukatko and Daehler, "Drug-Abusing Mothers-To-Be: Are They Criminals?"

Chiras, "Curitiba, Brazil—A City with a Sustainable Vision"

Eudy, "Signing for a Revolution: Gallaudet University and Deaf Culture"

Gish, "The Falsely Accused on Death Row"

Kristoff, "End the War on Pot"

The Pew Charitable Trusts, "One in a Hundred"

## ETHNIC STUDIES

Ahmed, "Identity in Transformation"

Espada, "Rage"

Kotlowitz, "Colorblind: When Blacks and Whites Can See No Gray"

Reid, "Spanish at School Translates to Suspension"

Reynolds, "Celebrations of Thanksgiving: A Marriage of Contrasting Traditions"

Staples, "Black Men and Public Space"

## GENDER STUDIES

Ahmed, "Identity in Transformation"

Bukatko and Daehler, "Drug-Abusing Mothers-To-Be: Are They Criminals?"

Cisneros, "Sally"

Espada, "Rage"

MacDonald, "Cyber-Bullying Defies Traditional School Bully Stereotype"

Sanders, "The Men We Carry in Our Minds"

Staples, "Black Men and Public Space"

Tannen, "Sex, Lies, and Conversation"

Thompson and Hickey, "Sex and Gender"

# To the Instructor

*A Community of Readers*, Sixth Edition, provides college students with guided, in-depth instruction in all aspects of the reading and learning processes: reading, discussing, writing, and critical thinking.

Organized around high-interest, motivational, and contemporary themes, *A Community of Readers* is a reading text that emphasizes student involvement in the entire reading process: prereading activities, active reading, post-reading activities, and critical reflection. Each chapter presents an essential reading skill and challenges students to master it through readings and exercises with a unifying theme. The first chapter focuses on the reading process and on joining a community of readers in a college setting. Each of the following chapters presents a reading skill, such as building vocabulary, identifying main ideas, understanding inferences, identifying facts and opinions, and thinking critically.

As students progress through each chapter, they learn, practice, and review all the reading skills they need to succeed in their college courses. Because each chapter of the text builds on a single theme, students have the time to develop schema and exchange knowledge on a particular concept or issue, including living with technology; food and culture; staying well; where we live, our communities; dealing with gender; living in a diverse society; and crime and punishment. With its emphasis on collaborative learning, *A Community of Readers* is accessible to students from various language and academic backgrounds.

The sixth edition of *A Community of Readers* maintains the emphasis on student participation in the classroom community and on self-motivated learning. Mastery tests and cumulative mastery tests allow students to test themselves on all the skills covered in the text. In addition, recognizing the importance of student motivation and engagement, "A Reader's Toolkit" provides opportunities for students to work in their classrooms and by themselves to supplement in-class instruction. In the "Toolkit" section on "Reading Visual Aids," students can inform and test themselves on their visual aid interpretive skills, and instructors can refer to this section when teaching the visual aids sections throughout the text. "Evaluating and Navigating Websites" gives instruction in the increasingly important skill of using the Internet. Especially helpful in facilitating student-centered learning are the two sections on "Reading Circles" and "Poster Sessions."

## NEW TO THE SIXTH EDITION

- **NEW! Strengthened emphasis on critical thinking.** A streamlined definition of critical thinking is introduced in Chapter 1 and is carried through all the chapters, culminating in a refocused Chapter 8. New exercises and reflection questions encourage students to analyze readings at a deeper level. Students see how reading skills connect, interact, and build on each other. They are guided through the process of how to make their own well-informed opinions.

- **NEW! Chapter 8.** Chapter 8 has a new theme, "Crime and Punishment," and it has been redesigned to strengthen students' critical-thinking skills. The four new readings invite students to form their own opinions about issues such as the legalization of marijuana and the high incarceration rate in the United States. The readings promote reflection, debate, and informed decision making.

- **NEW! Book design.** The sixth edition of *A Community of Readers* has been completely redesigned to be more inviting and engaging. It appears for the first time in full color with new photographs, illustrations, graphs, and tables throughout. Margins have been increased to promote more student interaction with the readings and pedagogy. The new visual elements enhance the content of the book while at the same time generating more interest in the topics.

- **NEW! Readings.** Ten new readings build on high-interest themes and relevant topics that are the hallmarks of this book. They come from academic, public, and popular sources. Altogether, the book has 18 readings drawn from textbooks to acquaint students with the content of college courses in a variety of disciplines and to help them build their reading skills in the academic material they will need to master for success in college. All the readings encourage students to learn and practice their skills in the context of the ideas and issues presented in each chapter.

- **NEW! Updated topics.** Chapter 1 develops the theme of "Joining a Community of Readers" with two new readings. The first is an excerpt from a powerful autobiographical work, *The Pact,* that underscores the importance of collaboration to success. The second new reading encourages students to choose how they will live their lives, as victims or as creators. The revitalized theme of Chapter 2, "Living with Technology," has two new readings on technological developments that also have important social implications—robot technology and the problem of cyberbullying on social networks.

- **NEW! Visual aids.** The "Reading Visual Aids" section in Part II, "A Reader's Toolkit," has been updated with new visuals and questions that provoke analysis and critical thinking. Teaching tips throughout the textbook suggest when this instruction can be used to increase students' understanding of visual material.

- **NEW! Improved pedagogy and exercises.** Examples of concept mapping have been added to Chapter 4 to enhance students' understanding of text organization. The readings in Chapter 8 promote students' independence as learners by asking them to identify vocabulary to focus on and to complete extended exercises that require them to write their own detailed responses.

- **NEW! Separate mastery tests.** One mastery test follows at the end of each chapter. In recognition of the way these tests are used for instructor and student evaluation, a new section at the end of Part I provides an additional mastery test for each chapter.

- **NEW! Aplia™ for *A Community of Readers*.** The power of Aplia's innovative, easy-to-use technology has been matched with the tone, language, level, and structure in *A Community of Readers* to give students a seamless, interactive learning experience. Founded by a professor to enhance his own courses, Aplia provides automatically graded coursework with detailed, immediate feedback on every question, as well as innovative teaching materials.

  - Aplia's Student Engagement Page integrates multimedia content, compelling readings, and interactive problems to heighten student interest.

  - In-context vocabulary features new and challenging words with auditory reinforcement.

  - Interactive assignments offer students immediate, detailed explanations for every answer.

  - Diagnostic tests provide an overall picture of class performance and allow instructors to view class progress on a student-by-student and topic-by-topic basis.

Aplia can be accessed at **www.aplia.com/developmentalenglish**.

## HALLMARK FEATURES

The sixth edition of *A Community of Readers* continues to offer a number of innovative features to enhance students' learning experience:

- **Focus on the reading process.** The essential steps to reading—prereading activities, active reading, postreading tasks, and critical thinking—are built into each chapter. Students are led to apply the new skills within the context of the reading process.

- **Thematic organization.** Because each chapter focuses on one theme, students can work with the ideas long enough to begin to understand and use complex material. Readings, as well as the examples used for skills, explanations, and exercises, further explore the chapter theme.

- **Topics that are current and relevant to students.** The readings reflect contemporary concerns of American society, addressing issues of gender, diversity, crime and public policy, advances in and problems with technology, and the nature and consequences of eating habits and the fast-food industry.

- **Integration of reading, vocabulary, and learning strategies.** Chapter 2 focuses on vocabulary skills, and those skills are reinforced throughout the text. Learning strategies (including mapping, outlining, and summarizing) are introduced in Chapter 4, with ample practice material presented throughout the text.

- **Critical-thinking skills.** By concentrating on one theme at a time, students have the opportunity to apply sustained critical thinking skills in class discussions and assigned writings. Chapter exercises consistently encourage students to use their background knowledge and to evaluate ideas, reflect, and make connections among various approaches and points of view. Chapter 8 challenges students to think more deeply about critical questions facing our society and asks them to come to their own well-informed positions.

- **Preparation for freshman composition.** Because the theme-based approach corresponds closely to the organization of a wide range of freshman composition texts, students become better prepared for the material in their composition classes. Emphasis is given to the writing and thinking skills essential for composition: paraphrasing; summarizing; recognizing organizational patterns; and evaluating bias, point of view, purpose, opinion, and arguments. Composition skills are developed through the "Reflect and Write" exercises, as well as the featured longer writing assignments in "Write About It."

- **Collaborative work.** Exercises throughout the text encourage students to collaborate with their peers. Group problem-solving skills help students in their academic work as well as in their future careers.

- **Reader's Tips.** This feature helps students further develop important reading skills. "Reader's Tips" cover topics such as "How to Read a Textbook," "Identifying General and Specific Information," "Stating the Source and Main Idea in Summaries," "Transitions and Clues for Patterns of Organization," "Tone," and "Fallacies."

- **Teaching Tips.** Integrated throughout the text, these teaching suggestions provide fresh pedagogical suggestions as well as reminders for sound instructional practices.

- **Glossed vocabulary for thematic readings.** This additional student aid facilitates student comprehension of the content-based reading selections.

- **Original and meaningful web-based activities.** Each chapter includes a *current* web activity. These activities direct students to do interesting and relevant research on the Web throughout the text. With this practice, students will be more prepared for research tasks required in freshman composition and other disciplines.

- **Cumulative mastery tests.** The two cumulative mastery tests give students the opportunity to test themselves on all the skills covered in the text. They can be used for review at the end of the term or even as pre- and posttest instruments to measure student progress. Cumulative Mastery Test B, focusing on Americans' relationship with food, is new for this edition.

- **Reading circles for working together in a collaborative community.** This section on reading circles in "A Reader's Toolkit" guides students through the process of successfully working as a *community*. It establishes a sustained, student-centered collaborative setting while providing the instructor with the necessary tools to effectively facilitate the process and monitor student progress and participation.

- **Poster sessions.** The section on poster sessions in "A Reader's Toolkit" walks students through the process of developing oral presentations with visual aids. This technique reduces stress for shy students and ensures that the presentations are interactive and participatory. At the same time, students with diverse learning styles and strengths are recognized and rewarded.

- **Suggested reading for book projects.** This current list of a wide variety of outstanding, appropriate books allows instructors and students to select additional whole-book reading projects.

Also available in this series is *Joining a Community of Readers*, which includes these same features but is intended for students in the first reading course.

## ORGANIZATION

The sixth edition of *A Community of Readers* consists of two parts. Part I, "Skills Instruction and Thematic Readings," includes skills-based chapters as well as mastery tests and cumulative mastery tests. Part II, "A Reader's Toolkit," provides additional instruction in related skills and activities (note taking, test taking, writing tips, reading response journals, evaluating and navigating websites) that can be assigned to complement classroom instruction and activities or can be worked on individually by students. In addition, Part II includes instructions for students on working collaboratively in reading circles and making presentations in poster sessions. Finally, "A Reader's Toolkit" offers an updated list of suggested readings for book projects.

Each chapter in *A Community of Readers* is designed to teach specific reading and study skills within the context of learning about and reflecting on an issue and generating informed reactions, opinions, and possible solutions to that issue. To accomplish this progression, each chapter contains the following features:

- **An opening illustration and quotation** introduce the theme of the chapter and provide prereading as well as analytical and critical-thinking questions asking students to explore their background knowledge and opinions on the topic.

- **Skills instruction** is carefully interwoven with readings about the topic of the chapter. Examples, readings, and exercises all focus on the chapter theme.

- **A chapter review** summarizes the issues and skills of the chapter and suggests post-reading extension activities for collaborative group work.

- **Writing and the connection between the reading and writing processes** are reinforced with "Reflect and Write" and "Write About It" exercises that require more extensive writing in every chapter.

- **A mastery test** at the end of each chapter gives students further opportunities to demonstrate their proficiency in the skills they have learned. An additional mastery test for each chapter is located at the end of Part I.

## THE ANCILLARY PACKAGE

All of the following elements of the ancillary package can be located at **login.cengage.com.**

### Instructor's Manual

A downloadable, password-protected version of the Instructor's Manual, with teaching suggestions from the author. Also available in print format.

### PowerPoint Slides

Use these series of approximately 15 to 20 slides per chapter to better illustrate your lectures.

### Instructor Links

A collection of links to popular reading and study skills websites.

### Test Bank (PDF)

Downloadable, password-protected tests (two per chapter) with answer keys. Also available in print format.

### Aplia for *A Community of Readers*: Engage, Prepare, Educate

Aplia is an interactive learning tool, offering thematic reading skills practice online at **www.aplia.com/developmentalenglish.** Aplia provides automatically graded coursework, including diagnostic tests, as well as innovative teaching materials. In this engaging, multimedia learning experience, students get immediate feedback on every question.

# Acknowledgments

We are grateful to our families—Marley, Elena, Paul, Aasiya, Abdulla, Hassan, Carol, Elijah, and Luke—for their patience and assistance. We would also like to thank all our reading students and our colleagues and friends for their help and positive support, especially Jan Lombardi, Jennifer Boots, Enrique Dávalos, Heather Eudy, Elizabeth Flynn, Nadia Mandilawi, Kelly Mayhew, Jim Miller, and Elva Salinas.

A special thank you to Annie Todd for her continued support and enthusiasm for this project. Thank you to Ann Hofstra Grogg whose good ideas, diligence, perseverance, and editorial insights were invaluable to our successfully completing both past and present editions of the text.

Thank you to our reviewers across the country:

Lisa Bosley, Eastern Kentucky University
Regina E. Boyd, Itawamba Community College
Sylvia Boyd, Phillips Community College of the University of Arkansas
Khairunessa Dossani, De Anza College
Christi Duque, Tarrant County College
Brent Green, Salt Lake Community College
Mary Harper, Broward College
Karen Harrel, Tarrant County College
Pete Kinnas, San Juan College
Candace Komlodi, GateWay Community College
Patty Kunkel, Santa Fe College
Anna McWhirter, GateWay Community College
Laura Meyers, Hawkeye Community College
Roxanne Morgan, American River College
Karen Parrish, University of Alaska Anchorage
Donna Richardson-Hall, Mercer County Community College
Meralee Silverman, Westchester Community College
Peggy Walker, Foothill College
Jacquelyn Warmsley, Tarrant County College
Jim Wilkins-Luton, Clark College

*Roberta Alexander*
*Jan Jarrell*

# To the Student

## WELCOME TO *A COMMUNITY OF READERS*

You probably bought this book because you need to strengthen your reading skills and strategies to be ready for the demands of college reading. If you are prepared to take responsibility for your own learning, and if you are ready to commit yourself to the work involved, you will learn the strategies and skills that you need to become an effective, thoughtful reader. You will also develop your ability to think critically and formulate your own opinions about what you read. You need these skills not only to pass this course but also to succeed in college and, even more important, in the workplace of the twenty-first century.

## WHY IS READING SO IMPORTANT?

Read any newspaper today or talk to any employer or human resources manager and you will realize that the demands of today's society—not only of college study—require that you be a literate person, that you be able to learn new skills and even new jobs or professions. During your lifetime, you will probably face the need to change jobs or professions three, four, or more times. And even if you are one of the lucky few who stays in one position or is successful at creating your own business, you will constantly face the need to upgrade your skills. Professionals of all kinds must stay current in their fields. This is true of office professionals, medical professionals, teachers, engineers, auto mechanics, managers, computer programmers, and industrial workers.

Learning is a lifelong endeavor that doesn't stop when you get your degree. The ability to learn and grow never becomes outdated and will serve you for the rest of your life. This textbook addresses the basics that will help you become a strong reader and student, acquire the skills necessary to be successful in your composition classes, be prepared for the challenges of lifelong learning for the workplace, and be an effective, fulfilled adult and citizen of the twenty-first century.

The skills and strategies you need to become a proficient reader and successful student are the same skills you will need in the workplace. A Department of Labor survey concluded that students should learn these workplace basics:

1. **Learning to learn.** *A Community of Readers* shows you how to become active in your own reading and learning processes (Chapter 1 and "A Reader's Toolkit"). You learn how you study best and whether you are putting your study time to good use.

2. **Listening and oral communications.** As a college reader, you will learn that the act of reading is reinforced and made more meaningful when you listen to other people's ideas about a subject and when you orally express your own ideas to your peers. All chapters of the text emphasize these skills.

3. **Competence in reading, writing, and computation.** As you work through this course, your reading competence will constantly improve. You will learn, review, and

practice all the basic skills necessary to be a strong reader: prereading (Chapter 1); active reading (Chapter 1); building your vocabulary (Chapter 2); monitoring your comprehension and recognizing main ideas and supporting details (Chapters 3 and 4); reviewing and remembering what you have read (Chapters 4 and 5); making connections between what you know and what you read (all chapters); and organizing what you read so you can retain information and understanding for tests and future needs (Chapters 3 through 8).

4. **Adaptability based on creative thinking and problem solving.** As a member of your classroom and a community of readers, you will be involved in bringing what you already know and what you learn through reading and discussion to a variety of issues, and you will practice thinking creatively and solving problems (all chapters). You will learn how to take notes ("A Reader's Toolkit"), how to interpret what an author is saying and how to make inferences (Chapter 6), and how to think critically to evaluate an author's position (Chapters 7 and 8 and in the "Reflect and Write" exercises throughout the text).

5. **Group effectiveness characterized by interpersonal skills, negotiation skills, and teamwork.** You will learn to work with your peers—other students—sharing your strengths and learning from each other (all chapters and "A Reader's Toolkit").

6. **Organizational effectiveness and leadership.** You will develop your organizational and leadership skills in the process of working with classmates toward a common goal.

If you are ready to tackle the material of this course, you are taking a big step toward a successful college career.

Put a check in the boxes of the following key questions for which you can answer "yes":

☐ Are learning and practicing college reading skills priorities for you at this time?

☐ Are you willing to make the effort to be actively involved in your own learning?

☐ Have you decided that you can and will succeed, one small step at a time?

☐ Do you have the time to commit to being a student? Remember that as a student, you have a job. The payoff may seem to come with passing grades and a degree, but most important, the payoff of developing your reading and learning skills is for yourself and your future.

☐ Are you willing to share ideas and to work together with other students to reach your goals?

☐ Are you willing to learn new reading strategies, not just to pass this class but to use whenever you must learn something new?

☐ Are you willing to open your mind to new ideas and ways of thinking?

☐ Are you willing to reflect on ideas and arguments, and to make conclusions and form opinions for yourself and with others?

Did you answer "yes" to all or most of the questions? If so, this book will help you reach your goals by assisting you to become a lifelong reader and learner. Welcome to *A Community of Readers*!

# A Community of Readers

A Thematic Approach to Reading

# PART 1

# Skills Instruction and Thematic Readings

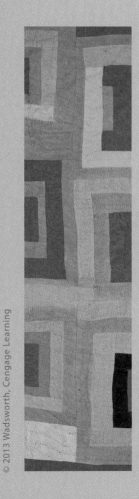

# 1 The Reading Process

## JOINING A COMMUNITY OF READERS

Hill Street Studios/Jupiter Images

*Love thy neighbor as thyself, but choose your neighborhood.*
*—Louise Beal*

1. What is happening in the photo? What might be the purpose of this activity?

2. What is the meaning of the quotation?

3. How do you think the messages of the photo and the quotation might be important to your success as a student?

4. What do *you* need to do to become a successful college student?

# Prepare to Read

When we chose the title of this book, *A Community of Readers*, we were thinking about the word *community* in a lot of ways. One way refers to the community of learners you have joined by enrolling in college. More specifically, we had in mind the community of readers in your class. It is important for you to be an active member of your classroom community. If you try to do everything on your own, you may end up feeling isolated and depressed. When you learn to work with other students or friends, to help them and to be helped by them, your chances of success in college (and in life) are much greater. When your classroom community is a friendly one, when you trust and respect each other, you feel comfortable and can participate in your own learning.

In this chapter, you will read about becoming a successful student and learn

- The PRO reading system:
  <u>P</u>reparing to read
  <u>R</u>eading actively and <u>R</u>eflecting
  <u>O</u>rganizing and using what you have read
- The importance of working with other students

In the process of acquiring these skills, you will read about joining a community of students and how to develop important qualities for becoming a successful learner. You will also read about college and school environments and learn memory techniques.

| **Reading 1** | # The Pact* — Dr. Sampson Davis, Dr. George Jenkins, |

### The Pact* — Dr. Sampson Davis, Dr. George Jenkins, and Dr. Rameck Hunt, with Lisa Frazier Page

**As teenagers from rough neighborhoods in New Jersey, the three authors made a pact—a pledge to each other—that they would become doctors. All three realized their dream. This selection, from their best-selling autobiography, highlights how friendships can make a powerful difference in an individual's life, the difference between success and failure or even life and death.**

1   We treat them in our hospitals every day.

2      They are young brothers, often drug dealers, gang members, or small-time criminals, who show up shot, stabbed, or beaten after a hustle gone bad. To some of our medical colleagues, they are just nameless thugs, perpetuating crime and death in neighborhoods that have seen far too much of those things. But when we look into their faces, we see ourselves as teenagers, we see our friends, we see what we easily could have become as young adults. And we're reminded of the thin line that separates us three twenty-nine-year-old doctors (an emergency-room physician, an internist, and a dentist) from these patients whose lives are filled with danger and desperation.

**perpetuating**
continuing; doing forever

**internist**
doctor who specializes in treating internal diseases and disorders

Saed Hindash/Star Ledger/Corbis News/Corbis

From left to right: Doctors Sampson Davis, George Jenkins, and Rameck Hunt

3      We grew up in poor, broken homes in New Jersey neighborhoods riddled with crime, drugs, and death, and came of age in the 1980s at the height of a crack epidemic that ravaged communities like ours throughout the nation. There were no doctors or lawyers walking the streets of our communities. Where we lived, hustlers reigned, and it was easy to follow their example. Two of us landed in juvenile-detention centers before our eighteenth birthdays. But inspired early by caring and imaginative role models, one of

**reigned**
ruled

*"Introduction," from *The Pact*, by Sampson Davis, George Jenkins, and Rameck Hunt, with Liza Frazier Page, copyright © 2002 by Three Doctors LLC. Used by permission of Riverhead Books, an imprint of Penguin Group (USA) Inc.

us in childhood latched on to a dream of becoming a dentist, steered clear of trouble, and in his senior year of high school persuaded his two best friends to apply to a college program for minority students interested in becoming doctors. We knew we'd never survive if we went after it alone. And so we made a pact: we'd help one another through, no matter what.

4    In college, the three of us stuck together to survive and thrive in a world that was different from anything we had ever known. We provided one another with a kind of positive peer pressure. From the moment we made our pact, the competition was on. When one of us finished his college application, the other two rushed to send theirs out. When we participated in a six-week remedial program at Seton Hall University the summer before our freshman year, each of us felt pressured to perform well because we knew our friends would excel and we didn't want to embarrass ourselves or lag behind. When one of us made an A on a test, the others strived to make A's, too.

**remedial program** classes and/or support services that prepare students with the skills necessary to be successful in college coursework

5    We studied together. We worked summer jobs together. We partied together. And we learned to solve our problems together. We are doctors today because of the positive influences that we had on one another.

6    The lives of most impressionable young people are defined by their friends, whether they are black, white, Hispanic, or Asian; whether they are rich, poor, or middle-class; whether they live in the city, the suburbs, or the country. Among boys, particularly, there seems to be some macho code that says to gain respect, you have to prove that you're bad. We know firsthand that the wrong friends can lead you to trouble. But even more, they can tear down hopes, dreams, and possibilities. We know, too, that the right friends inspire you, pull you through, rise with you.

7    Each of us experienced friendships that could have destroyed our lives. We suspect that many of the young brothers we treat every day in our hospitals are entangled in such friendships—friendships that require them to prove their toughness and manhood daily, even at the risk of losing their own lives. The three of us were blessed. We found in one another a friendship that works in a powerful way; a friendship that helped three vulnerable boys grow into successful men: a friendship that ultimately helped save our lives.

## Exercise 1

### Recall and Discuss

Based on Reading 1, answer the following questions and prepare to discuss them with your classmates.

1. Describe Davis's, Jenkins's, and Hunt's lives as teenagers. What challenges did they face?

_____

_____

_____

2. What made the difference for them? How were all three of them able to become successful doctors?

_____

_____

_____

_____

3. How might their story be important for you and your success in college?

_____

_____

**Exercise 2**

### Reflect: Introduce Yourself

To begin building your classroom community, you first need to do a little thinking about yourself and how you can become a part of this community. Answer the following questions about who you are and what your expectations are for this class. Be prepared to share your answers with other students.

1. What is your name, and how might we easily remember it? (Does your name have a special meaning? Is it readily associated with someone famous you admire? Does it sound like a word that might be used to describe you?)

_____

_____

2. What accomplishment are you most proud of?

_____

_____

3. Why are you going to college?

_____

_____

4. What kinds of things do you like to read for enjoyment?

_____

_____

## ✳The Reading Process: PRO

Reading is a *process*; that means reading is a series of small steps. We've divided the process into three basic steps. All good readers follow these steps, even though they may do so automatically. Depending on your purpose for reading and the type of material you are reading, you will vary your strategies for the three basic steps. You may find that you use some steps more than once in completing a reading task. Eventually, the reading process and the basic steps involved will become automatic: You won't even have to think about them most of the time. Until you form these good habits, you will need to be conscious of your reading strategies and apply them deliberately as you read and study.

**PRO reading system**
a process to follow for developing effective reading habits

The **PRO reading system** makes it easy for you to understand and remember the steps of the reading process so that you can approach your reading assignments more confidently and complete them more successfully. Each letter stands for an activity in the system.

P = <u>P</u>reparing to read
R = <u>R</u>eading actively and <u>R</u>eflecting
O = <u>O</u>rganizing and using what you have read

When you've mastered this system, you will be a reading pro!

## PREPARING TO READ

**prepare to read**
determine a purpose, preview, recognize previous knowledge, and predict what you will learn

The first step is preparing to read. Master readers **prepare to read**. They don't take a lot of time to prepare, but they are in the habit of completing certain activities as they begin the process of reading. Taking the time to get yourself ready to read is essential to understanding what you read. By preparing yourself to read, you can figure out what information will be coming and get ready to receive it. You can also develop curiosity about a subject, so that you will already be thinking as you begin to read. Have you ever read something and then not known what you had just read? One possible reason for this lack of focus is failure to prepare.

The first step in the PRO reading system, **P**, actually includes four p's, all of which are easy to understand and do. You may already include some of these in your reading approach. Preparing to read includes

- Determining a **purpose** for your reading
- **Previewing** what you are about to read
- Recognizing **previous knowledge** (what you already know about this topic)
- **Predicting** what you will learn from the reading

**purpose**
your reading goals

**Determining Your Purpose** Your **purpose** as a reader determines how carefully you will read, how much time you will need, and what reading strategies you will use. For example, you read the sports section of your daily newspaper very differently from the way you read a portion of your anatomy textbook, especially if you are preparing to take the state nursing exam. Your purpose in reading the sports page may be to find out the score in a particular game. You can scan the page quickly to find this information. If you are reading about anatomy, you have to read more slowly and methodically to understand, and you want to use strategies to help you remember the material.

As a college student, you will often have an obvious purpose: to learn as much as you possibly can about Native American poetry, about computer programming, or about the mechanics of laser graphics, for instance. At the same time, your purpose may be to master enough to do well on your exams. For example, in a reading class, you may need to demonstrate how well you can use your reading skills on a timed test. Whatever your immediate purpose, remember that the pleasure of learning should also influence how you read.

**previewing**
briefly looking over a section to find key points

**Previewing** **Previewing** is exactly what the word suggests. When you prepare to read, you should begin by "pre-viewing" the material you intend to read. In other words, look at what you're going to read before you read it. Get an overview of the material, and notice how interesting, as well as how difficult, it may be for you.

Once you have done this, you can predict what topics the reading will cover and choose the most effective reading strategies for that particular piece.

**Previewing a Section** When you begin to study for a specific class assignment, you should preview short sections as you are about to read them. Most people can deal with only one small block of reading material at a time. For each assignment, determine how much material to cover in your preview based on the level of difficulty of the material and your level of expertise as a reader.

For each section, read titles and headings, the introduction, the first sentences under the headings or the first sentence of each paragraph, italicized and bold-faced words, and the conclusion. Briefly study pictures, picture captions, charts, graphs, and any other unusual visual aids meant to "catch your eye." Keep in mind how this section fits with the information before and after it.

**Exercise 3**

## Preview a Section

Preview the material starting at the heading below, "Using Previous Knowledge," through page 11, to where Exercise 4 begins. This section covers the next steps in preparing to read. Fill in the following information as you preview.

1. List the headings in this section:

   _____

   _____

2. Read the first sentence under each heading. Briefly write what you learned from each.

   _____

   _____

   _____

3. What words are written in the margins with their definitions (glossed)?

   _____

4. What textbook features are bulleted that can help you form effective preview questions?

   _____

   _____

**Using Previous Knowledge** Part of preparing to read is considering what you already know about the topic. As you preview a section, you will probably recognize information about which you have some **previous knowledge**. This knowledge may come from your studies or your life experiences. If you already know a great deal about the subject of a reading, prepare to add any new information you find in this reading to your storehouse. Your brain has an extraordinary filing system,

**previous knowledge**
what you already know about a topic from prior reading and experience

more sophisticated than those of the most advanced computers. Sometimes you know as much as, or even more than, some authors about a given subject. In that case, prepare to compare your information and interpretation with theirs; you may even want to argue some points with them. At other times, you may know little about a topic. In that case, you can still relate the information to similar facts you already know. For example, when you read an article about health problems among preschool children in Rwanda, you may know nothing specific about Rwanda and its problems, but you probably do know—from your own experience, reading, and television—something about young children and about health problems. So you can relate the new information to what you already know.

Make thinking about your previously acquired knowledge part of preparing to read. You'll soon find you do it almost automatically, and your confidence in approaching new material will certainly increase. Also, it's easier to remember the new knowledge when you recognize its relationship to what you already know.

**predicting**
considering what you expect to learn from a reading

**Predicting What You Will Learn** Predicting what you think you will learn in the reading is the last step in preparing to read. Based on your preview of the reading and previous knowledge of the subject, you should have a good idea of what new information you will acquire. The preview gave you the framework or outline of the content. Now raise some questions that you think will be answered in the selection you are preparing to read. Asking questions based on your preview will prepare you to read actively, to be engaged with the material as you go through it. Actively seeking the answers to your questions will keep you alert and attentive and will help you understand what you are reading.

One simple way to create questions is to use the topics and concepts you noticed in your preview. For example, a section from a physical science textbook might have the following title and headings:

**Atomic Structure**
The Electron
The Atomic Nucleus
Protons and Neutrons

The title and headings give you clues to the content, and each subheading is about the makeup of an atom. In predicting what you will learn, you might come up with these preview questions first:

1. What is an electron? What is an atomic nucleus? What is a proton? What is a neutron?

The text includes a diagram of an atom. So your second question might combine the headings and the diagram:

2. What role does each part have in the functioning of the atom?

Besides these questions, which are fairly obvious, questions might arise from your previous knowledge and reading. You might ask a question like the following:

3. What does the structure of an atom have to do with the creation of the atomic bomb?

Thoughtful questions like this may not be answered in the text, but they can prepare you for the class lecture and discussion. Looking beyond the literal content to its implications can prepare you for critical thinking about the material you read.

© 2013 Wadsworth, Cengage Learning

In general, ask questions specifically related to the information in the textbook or other reading. To help you ask questions, look at features in your text such as

- Objectives
- Headings
- First sentences of each paragraph
- First and last paragraphs (if you are reading something long)
- Illustrations
- Questions in the back of the chapter

Other good ways to predict what you will be expected to learn from a reading are

- Questions your professors raise or points they emphasize in class
- Study guides your professors may give you

**Exercise 4**

## Prepare to Read a Textbook Section

Preview Reading 2 on pages 12 through 16 and answer the following questions.

1. What is the title of this reading?

   _____

2. What is your purpose for reading this piece?

   _____

   _____

3. What *previous knowledge* do you have about this topic? That is, what do you already know about it?

   _____

   _____

4. From your preview, write three questions that you predict the reading will answer.

   a. _____

   b. _____

   c. _____

# Success in School: You Decide*

— Skip Downing

**TEXT BOOK** **Skip Downing is the author of a popular student success textbook, *On Course: Strategies for Creating Success in College and in Life*. The textbook focuses on core principles, such as personal responsibility, self-motivation, and interdependence, which have been associated with success in school, work, and life. This selection from the chapter on accepting personal responsibility emphasizes the importance of choices we make. Are we accepting the role of Victim? Or are we choosing to be a Creator? Downing argues that the more we make Creator choices, the more we are able to achieve our goals and dreams.**

*I am the master of my fate; I am the captain of my soul.*

*—William E. Henley*

**passively**
not actively

The more we practice the habit of acting from a position of responsibility, the more effective we become as human beings, and the more successful we become as managers of our lives.

*—Joyce Chapman*

1   When psychologist Richard Logan studied people who survived ordeals such as being imprisoned in concentration camps or lost in the frozen Arctic, he found that all of these victors shared a common belief. They saw themselves as personally responsible for the outcomes and experiences of their lives.

2   Ironically, responsibility has gotten a bad reputation. Some see it as a heavy burden they have to lug through life. Quite the contrary, personal responsibility is the foundation of success because without it, our lives are shaped by forces outside of us. The essence of personal responsibility is responding wisely to life's opportunities and challenges, rather than waiting passively for luck or other people to make the choices for us.

3   Whether your challenge is surviving an Arctic blizzard or excelling in college, accepting personal responsibility moves you into cooperation with yourself and with the world. As long as you resist your role in creating the outcomes and experiences in your life, you will fall far short of your potential.

4   I first met Deborah when she was a student in my English 101 class. Deborah wanted to be a nurse, but before she could qualify for the nursing program, she had to pass English 101. She was taking the course for the fourth time.

5   "Your writing shows fine potential," I told Deborah after I had read her first essay. "You'll pass English 101 as soon as you eliminate your grammar problems."

6   "I know," she said. "That's what my other three instructors said."

7   "Well, let's make this your last semester in English 101, then. After each essay, make an appointment with me to go over your grammar problems."

8   "Okay."

9   "And go to the Writing Lab as often as possible. Start by studying verb tense. Let's eliminate one problem at a time."

10   "I'll go this afternoon!"

11   But Deborah never found time: *No, really . . . . I'll go to the lab just as soon as I . . . .*

12   Deborah scheduled two appointments with me during the semester and missed them both: *I'm so sorry . . . . I'll come to see you just as soon as I . . . .*

13   To pass English 101 at our college, students must pass one of two essays written at the end of the semester in an exam setting. Each essay, identified by social security number only, is graded by two other instructors. At semester's end, Deborah once again failed English 101. "It isn't fair!" Deborah protested. "Those exam graders expect us to be professional writers. They're keeping me from becoming a nurse!"

*"Success in College: You Decide," by Skip Downing from ON COURSE, STUDY SKILLS PLUS EDITION, 1st Edition. © 2011 Wadsworth, a part of Cengage Learning, Inc. Reproduced by permission. www.cengage.com/permissions

14    I suggested another possibility: "What if *you* are the one keeping you from becoming a nurse?"

15    Deborah didn't like that idea. She wanted to believe that her problem was "out there." Her only obstacle was *those* teachers. All her disappointments were *their* fault. The exam graders weren't fair. Life wasn't fair! In the face of this injustice, she was helpless.

16    I reminded Deborah that it was *she* who had not studied her grammar. It was *she* who had not come to conferences. It was *she* who had not accepted personal responsibility for creating her life the way she wanted it.

17    "Yes, but . . . ." she said.

## VICTIMS AND CREATORS

18    When people keep doing what they've been doing even when it doesn't work, they are acting as *Victims*. When people change their beliefs and behaviors to create the best results they can, they are acting as *Creators*.

19    When you accept personal responsibility, you believe that you create *everything* in your life. This idea upsets some people. Accidents happen, they say. People treat them badly. Sometimes they really are victims of outside forces.

20    This claim, of course, is true. At times, we *are* all affected by forces beyond our control. If a hurricane destroys my house, I am a victim (with a small "v"). But if I allow that event to ruin my life, I am a Victim (with a capital "V").

21    The essential issue is this: Would it improve your life to act *as if* you create all of the joys and sorrows in your life? Answer "YES!" and see that belief improve your life. After all, if you believe that someone or something out there causes all of your problems, then it's up to "them" to change. What a wait that can be! How long, for example, will Deborah have to wait for "those English teachers" to change?

22    If, however, you accept responsibility for creating your own results, what happens then? You will look for ways to create your desired outcomes and experiences despite obstacles. And if you look, you've just increased your chances of success immeasurably!

23    The benefits to students of accepting personal responsibility have been demonstrated in various studies. Researchers Robert Vallerand and Robert Bissonette, for example, asked 1,000 first-year college students to complete a questionnaire about why they were attending school. They used the students' answers to assess whether the students were "Origin-like" or "Pawn-like." The researchers defined *Origin-like* students as seeing themselves as the originators of their own behaviors, in other words, Creators. By contrast, *Pawn-like* students see themselves as mere puppets manipulated by others, in other words, Victims. A year later, the researchers returned to find out what had happened to the 1,000 students. They found that significantly more of the Creator-like students were still enrolled in college than the Victim-like students. If you want to succeed in college (and in life), then being a Creator gives you a big edge.

## RESPONSIBILITY AND CHOICE

24    The key ingredient of personal responsibility is *choice*. Animals respond to a stimulus because of instinct or habit. For humans, however, there is a brief, critical moment of decision available between the stimulus and the response. In this moment, we make the choices—consciously or unconsciously—that influence the outcomes of our lives.

25    Numerous times each day, you come to a fork in the road and must make a choice. Even not making a choice is a choice. Some choices have a small impact: Shall I get my hair cut today or tomorrow? Some have a huge impact: Shall I stay in college or drop out? The sum

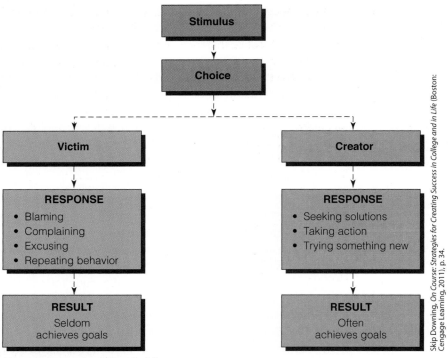

Skip Downing, *On Course: Strategies for Creating Success in College and in Life* (Boston: Cengage Learning, 2011), p. 34.

**Figure 1.1** Responsibility Model

of the choices you make from this day forward will create the eventual outcome of your life. The Responsibility Model (Figure 1.1) shows what the moment of choice looks like.

26    In that brief moment between stimulus and response, we can choose to be a Victim or a Creator. When we respond as a Victim, we complain, blame, make excuses, and repeat ineffective behaviors. When we respond as a Creator, we pause at each decision point and ask, "What are my options, and which option will best help me create my desired outcomes and experiences?"

27    The difference between responding to life as a Victim or Creator is how we choose to use our energy. When I'm blaming, complaining, and excusing, my efforts cause little or no improvement. Sure, it may feel good in that moment to claim that I'm a poor Victim and "they" are evil persecutors, but my good feelings are fleeting because afterward my problem still exists. By contrast, when I'm seeking solutions and taking actions, my efforts often (though not always) lead to improvements. At critical forks in the road, Victims waste their energy and remain stuck, while Creators use their energy for improving their outcomes and experiences.

28    But, let's be honest. No one makes Creator choices all of the time. I've never met anyone who did, least of all me. Our inner lives feature a perpetual tug of war between the Creator part of us and the Victim part of us. My own experiences have taught me the following life lesson: The more choices I make as a Creator, the more I improve the quality of my life. . . .

29    Here's an important choice you can make immediately. Accept, as Creators do, this belief: *I am responsible for creating my life as I want it.* Of course sometimes you won't be able to create the specific outcomes and experiences you want. The reality is that some circumstances will defy even your best efforts. But, believing that you always have a way to improve your present situation will motivate you to look for it, and by looking you'll often discover options you would never have found otherwise. For this reason, choosing to accept personal responsibility is the first step toward your success.

*Sidebar notes:*

I do think that the greatest lesson of life is that you are responsible for your own life.

—*Oprah Winfrey*

**fleeting**
short-lived

**perpetual**
ongoing

When you make the shift to being the predominant creative force in your life, you move from reacting and responding to the external circumstances of your life to creating directly the life you truly want.

—*Robert Fritz*

I am a Shawnee.
My forefathers
were warriors.
Their son is a
warrior. . . . From
my tribe I take
nothing. I am the
maker of my own
fortune.

—*Tecumseh*

30    Here's a related choice. Set aside any thought that Creator and Victim choices have any-thing to do with being good or bad, right or wrong, smart or dumb, worthy or unworthy. If you make a Victim choice, you aren't bad, wrong, dumb, or unworthy. For that matter, if you make a Creator choice, you aren't good, right, smart, or worthy. These judgments will merely distract you from the real issue: *Are* you getting the outcomes and experiences that *you* want in *your* life? If you are, then keep making the same choices because they're work-ing. But, if you're not creating the life you want, then you'd be wise to try something new. We benefit greatly when we shift our energy from defending ourselves from judgments and put it into improving the outcomes and experiences of our lives.

31    "Oh, I get what you mean!" one of my students once exclaimed as we were exploring this issue of personal responsibility, "You're saying that living my life is like traveling in my car. If I want to get where I want to go, I better be the driver and not a passenger." I appreciate her metaphor because it identifies that personal responsibility is about tak-ing hold of the steering wheel of our lives, about taking control of where we go and how we get there.

**folly**
foolishness

32    Ultimately each of us creates the quality of our life with the wisdom or folly of our choices.

---

**Exercise 5**

## Check Your Understanding

Based on Reading 2, choose the best answer to each of the following multiple choice questions.

1. The story about Deborah, the student who had failed English 101 four times, shows that
   a. she should get a job rather than go to college.
   b. some teachers do not have realistic expectations of their students.
   c. she did not accept personal responsibility for her failure.

2. Victims
   a. keep acting in the same way even if they do not get the results they want.
   b. change their response every time they encounter a problem.
   c. never get what they want.

3. Creators
   a. are never the victims of outside forces.
   b. are willing to change their beliefs and try different strategies.
   c. have an easier life than victims.

4. Researchers Robert Vallerand and Robert Bissonette found that
   a. *Origin-like* students acted like Victims.
   b. *Pawn-like* students thrived on manipulating others.
   c. *Origin-like* students were more likely to stay in college.

5. If you make a Creator choice, you
   a. seek options and solutions.
   b. will definitely get the outcome you want.
   c. are demonstrating intelligence and good values.

## Exercise 6

### Reflect and Write

Think about what you read in Reading 2 and what you already know about college success strategies. Answer the following questions, and prepare to discuss them with your classmates. Question 5 requires you to write a longer answer on a separate sheet of paper.

1. How did the activity of preparing to read help you when you proceeded to read this selection?

   _____

   _____

   _____

2. What do you think are the three most important strategies for student success in college? Give reasons and examples.

   _____

   _____

   _____

   _____

   _____

3. Look at the figure on p. 14. How do Victims usually respond to a difficult choice? How do Creators respond?

   _____

   _____

   _____

4. Think about what you learned about Victims and Creators. How might a Victim and Creator respond to each of the following situations?
   A. There is a lot of construction on campus, and parking is extremely tight. Juan is late to class for the second time in two weeks. His instructor counts two tardies as an absence. He will get a lower grade if he has more than two absences. How might Juan respond?

   Juan as Victim:_____

   _____

   _____

   _____

   Juan as Creator:_____

   _____

   _____

   _____

B. Sara had a fight with her boyfriend last night. Then her best friend told her to "get over it." Sara felt extremely hurt and angry. Sara has a math mid-term tomorrow night. Right now, she has a D+ in the class. How might Sara respond?

Sara as Victim: _____

_____

_____

Sara as Creator: _____

_____

_____

5. Think of a situation in which a person you know experienced challenges or setbacks as he or she tried to reach a school, work, or personal goal. Did he or she accept personal responsibility for the situation? Did he or she act as a Victim or as a Creator? On a separate piece of paper, write two or three paragraphs describing the person, the situation, the challenges, and the result. Make sure you include specific examples of what that person did or said that represents how he or she acted as a Victim or Creator. If the person was not successful, what other choices could he or she have made in order to change the outcome?

## READING ACTIVELY AND REFLECTING

Successful readers are actively involved in the process of reading. They interact with the text and think about what they are reading. These activities are part of the next step in the PRO system.

**active reading**
an involved, focused search for meaning while reading

**communication**
the art of sharing thoughts and feelings between people

**Reading Actively** The second major step in the **PRO** reading system is **R**, which stands for reading. Probably the most important advice we can give you about reading is that you must be an active reader. To remind you of this, we'll usually refer to reading in this text as **active reading**. Active reading is involved reading. What are you involved in doing? You are searching for the meaning of the author's words.

Reading is an act of **communication**. Reading allows you to share the thoughts and feelings of people you've never met, even people who lived hundreds or thousands of years ago or in a country you've never visited. Reading the printed word—in a book or magazine or on the computer—is a remarkably efficient way to communicate ideas across time and distance. Remember that there is a real human being on the other end—the writer—who is trying to share facts, ideas, and feelings with you. You are trying to decode his or her words and discover their meaning. When you understand the writer's message, the communication is complete.

So what do you need to do to be an active reader? First, you must become *involved* in what you are reading. Preparing to read, as you have learned in this chapter, will make that easier. In fact, careful preparation for reading may make active reading almost automatic. Once you have a purpose, previewing provides a framework for what you are about to read. Thinking about your previous knowledge of the subject helps you make connections between new and old information. Predicting helps you anticipate what you will learn as you read.

Second, you must be *interested* in what you are reading. It is not always easy to be interested in a topic, particularly if you know nothing about it. Allow yourself to be endlessly curious, to be open-minded about all kinds of information and all viewpoints. Books are a bit like people—the ones who seem unexciting at first may someday become your best friends. Also, keep your reading purpose in mind. Pleasure may sometimes have to take second place to necessity. What initially appears to be an uninspiring book may be required reading for the career you are pursuing. You may have to motivate yourself to stay attentive. Set yourself a goal of reading attentively for 50 minutes, and then reward yourself by doing something different for 10 or 15 minutes (for example, shooting hoops, calling a friend, or exercising). With a positive outlook, you can stay interested enough to profit from even the dullest books.

Third, you must be *alert and attentive* while reading. Choose a time and a place that allow you to concentrate. Most people try to establish a special setting where the habit of focusing becomes natural and is not a constant struggle. Your brain must have a chance to work uninterrupted for you to interpret the meaning of what you are reading. If you're too tired or distracted, you can't concentrate on reading.

**monitor comprehension** regular checks for involvement in, and understanding of, what you read

Lastly, you should **monitor**, or check, your involvement and **comprehension** periodically. Does your attention wander? How soon or how often does your attention wander? Can you determine why your attention wanders? Ask yourself, "Am I understanding what I'm reading?" Test yourself at intervals by asking, "What have I just read?" and "What seems to be important?" Or stop and try to answer the predicting questions you asked while you were preparing to read. Some people mark their texts—by underlining, highlighting, numbering, or checkmarking—to help their understanding. It's usually best to mark a section of a text during a second reading, when you are organizing to learn. Otherwise, you may mark too much. You'll practice techniques for marking texts in Chapter 4.

**reflecting** thinking about the concepts, ideas, interpretations, and emotions you've read about

**Reflecting** When you read actively, you also reflect as you read. **Reflecting** is thinking about the concepts, ideas, interpretations, and emotions you've read about. At times, we may become so involved in a reading that we stop to think about what we've just discovered. Reading is a *discovery process*. Certainly one of the greatest pleasures in reading comes from these discoveries. We are constantly learning new information about our world and gaining insight and understanding about ourselves and other people through our reading. It's not surprising that these insights make us stop and think. Every author hopes that will happen when we read his or her work. If a reading provides a lot of discovery stops for you, remember to allow yourself enough time to complete the work—and then enjoy your reading!

Reflecting on what you read does happen naturally, but it's often necessary to consciously plan to reflect on what you've been reading. You need to think not only about what you're learning now but also about how these ideas *connect* or relate to what you already know. People understand and learn new information best by connecting it with what they already know. Placing new knowledge in the context of what you already know requires time and thoughtful analysis.

There are a number of ways to actively organize your reflections. You might first ask yourself, "How does this information fit with what I've already learned and experienced?" If the information is new, you might simply insert it in the appropriate category in your "idea files." For example, if you recently learned the location of Dubuque, Iowa, you can place that information in your category of current information on U.S. geography. Sometimes, though, it's not so simple to add new information to your files. When you reflect on the new information, you will also have to decide how it connects with your previous knowledge. Reflecting on the relationships between old and new knowledge will help you to develop greater depth as a thinker. As you move forward in your college and work careers, reflection will be an invaluable tool for dealing with increasingly complex ideas, concepts, and problems.

Reflecting is also known as **critical thinking**. Critical thinking requires you to do more than collect large masses of data on a topic. It challenges you to combine what you learn in meaningful ways, to weigh facts against opinions, and to evaluate the significance and usefulness of ideas and solutions to problems ultimately, it is the ability to make an informed opinion about what you read. You'll get plenty of chances in the following chapters to develop and practice your critical reading and thinking skills.

**critical thinking**
the ability to make an informed opinion about what you read

**Exercise 7**

### Prepare to Read, Read Actively, and Reflect

Preview the following passage on page 20 about self-esteem from a health textbook, and complete items 1 through 4. Then follow the instructions in item 5 as you read. Finally, answer questions 6 and 7.

1. Preview the reading and list two or more things that you noted in your preview.

   a. _____

   b. _____

   c. _____

2. What do you already know about self-esteem?

   _____

3. What might be your purpose for reading textbook material like this?

   _____

4. Write three questions you predict this selection will answer.

   a. _____

   b. _____

   c. _____

5. To monitor your active reading, write two reflections (thoughts, comments, or questions) in the margins as you read.

## SELF-ESTEEM

*Self-esteem* refers to one's sense of self-respect or self-worth. It can be defined as how one evaluates oneself and values one's own personal worth as an individual. People with high self-esteem tend to feel good about themselves and have a positive outlook on life. People with low self-esteem often do not like themselves, constantly demean themselves, and doubt their ability to succeed.

### Tips for Improving Your Self-Esteem

- **Finding a Support Group**. The best way to maintain self-esteem is through a support group—peers who share your values and offer the nurturing that your family can no longer provide (or no longer provide on a daily basis). The prime prerequisite for a support group is that it makes you feel good about yourself and forces you to take an honest look at your actions and choices. Although the idea of finding a support group seems to imply establishing a wholly new group, remember that old ties are often among the strongest. Keeping in contact with old friends and with important family members can provide a foundation of unconditional love that may help you through the many life transitions ahead.

  Try to be a support for others, too. Join a discussion, political action, or recreational group. Write more postcards and "thinking of you" notes to people who matter. This will build both your own self-esteem and that of your friends.

- **Completing Required Tasks**. A way to boost your self-efficacy is to learn how to complete required tasks successfully and develop a history of success. You are not likely to succeed in your studies if you leave term papers until the last minute, fail to keep up with the reading for your courses, and do not ask for clarification of points that are confusing to you. Most college campuses provide study groups and learning centers for various content areas. These groups offer tips for managing time, understanding assignments, dealing with professors, and preparing for test-taking. Poor grades, or grades that do not meet expectations, are major contributors to diminished self-esteem and self-efficacy and to emotional distress among college students.

- **Forming Realistic Expectations**. Having realistic expectations for yourself is another method of boosting self-esteem. College is a time to explore your potential. The stresses of college life may make your expectations for success difficult to meet. If you expect perfect grades, a steady stream of Saturday-night dates and a soap-opera-type romantic involvement, and the perfect job, you may be setting yourself up for failure. Assess your current resources and the direction in which you are heading. Set small, incremental goals that are possible to meet.

- **Taking and Making Time for You**. Taking time to enjoy yourself is another way to boost your self-esteem and psychosocial health. Viewing each new activity as something to look forward to and an opportunity to have fun is an important part of keeping the excitement in your life. Wake up focusing on the fun things you have to look forward to each day, and try to make this anticipation a natural part of your day.

- **Maintaining Physical Health**. Maintaining physical health also contributes to self-esteem and self-efficacy. Regular exercise fosters a sense of well-being. Nourishing meals can help you avoid the weight gain experienced by many college students.

- **Examining Problems and Seeking Help**. Knowing when to seek help from friends, support groups, family, or professionals is another important factor in boosting self-esteem. Sometimes life's problems are insurmountable; sometimes you can handle them alone. Recognizing your strengths and acting appropriately are keys to psychosocial health.

**self-efficacy** belief in one's ability to perform a task successfully

*Donatelle, Access to Health*

6. Answer your questions from question 4 on page 19.

   a. _____

   b. _____

   c. _____

7. How well were you able to read actively and reflect? Did the two reflections that you wrote down while you were reading help you read actively? Explain your answer.

_____

_____

## Reader's Tip:
## Form a Study Group

One day an angel took a man to hell. When he got there, he saw a banquet table that was full of delicious food, but the people at the banquet were starving. Their elbows would not bend, so they could not place the food in their mouths. Even though they were surrounded by abundance, the people of hell were hungry.

The next day, the angel took the man to heaven. It was exactly the same as hell. There was a banquet table full of delicious food, but this time the people looked healthy and were happy. Their elbows also would not bend, but there was a crucial difference from the situation in hell: The people of heaven were feeding each other.

The lesson is clear, and it works for people in most situations, including at school: People do better working together and helping one another than working alone. Research has proven that if you collaborate with other students, you are more likely to be successful in your studies, and you are more likely to have a good time as well! Here are some guidelines:

1. Choose the right people. Look for students who

   - attend class regularly
   - come prepared
   - actively participate
   - do well on their assignments and tests

2. Choose your group goals, and team up with others who have similar or higher goals.

3. Choose group rules and decide

   - where, what time, and how often you will meet
   - what you will do during your meetings

**Exercise 8**    Reflect on Study Groups

1. Think about your class schedule. For which of your classes do you think it would be most helpful for you to form a study group? Briefly explain your reasons for picking each class.

_____

_____

_____

2. Brainstorm a list of people in this class that you think would be good to include in a study group. Briefly explain your reasons for picking these people. (If you don't know people in this class, write a plan for getting to know them.)

_____

_____

_____

3. List some possible specific goals for the study group.

_____

_____

_____

## ORGANIZING AND USING WHAT YOU HAVE READ

**organizing what you have read**
selecting, using, reciting, and examining yourself on what you have learned from your reading so you will retain it for tests and work applications in the future

Once you have successfully completed the **P** and **R** steps of the PRO system, you will be ready for **O**, **organizing and using what you have read**. You will have already prepared to read, read actively, and reflected on what you read. Actually, you will probably have done some organizing of your new knowledge already. All the steps in the reading process are interrelated and sometimes overlap, so it is a pleasant surprise when you arrive at the next step to find that you may have already done some of the work.

The purpose of organizing what you've read is to be sure that you can use your new information for exams and future assignments. The following steps, which spell the word *SURE*, will provide many ways to organize your material. Once you've practiced the different methods, you can decide which ones work best for you.

**S: Selecting the Facts and Concepts You Need to Know** You need a great deal of skill to *select* the important points to study. You must first understand what you've read. You must also be flexible in applying your skills to the expectations of different fields of study—such as biology, math, and sociology—and to the different approaches of individual instructors. This text provides you with reading experience in many subject areas. The following skills will help you select the facts and concepts you need to know. Each of these skills is explained in greater detail in later chapters, and you will practice each of them, some of them many times.

- Identifying the topic, main ideas, and important supporting points
- Identifying patterns of organization and relationships among ideas
- Recognizing the author's purpose
- Understanding inferences
- Evaluating fact versus opinion

**U: Using the Material You've Selected** To understand the new ideas you're learning, you must use the material in some way. Good readers know that it's easy to be overconfident. It's tempting to stop after you've read something and feel you understand it, but really mastering new information requires that you do something with it. You might use any of the following activities. You'll have plenty of chances in this book to practice these methods with readings from different content areas. You'll probably find that some methods are more effective for you than others.

- Summarizing
- Underlining and annotating texts
- Answering questions (your preview questions, questions you write in the margins as you actively read, instructor questions, questions at the end of each chapter, and others)
- Outlining
- Concept mapping
- Completing charts, graphs, and timelines
- Discussing (in your classroom, in a study group, with a tutor, or with a friend)

You will learn these skills in Chapters 3, 4, and 5.

**R: Reciting the Information** Once you have selected what you need to know and you've organized the information in a manageable format, you need to *recite*. Reciting is self-testing. Ask yourself the following questions:

- Do I really know the material? Have I memorized the essential concepts, definitions, and facts?
- Do I understand the important relationships and interpretations?
- Could I explain the information to someone else?
- Could I apply what I've learned in similar situations?
- Can I analyze, synthesize, and evaluate what I've learned?
- Can I use this knowledge to propose solutions to problems?

To help you, each chapter in this text ends with a Put it Together chart.

**E: Examining Your Learning Periodically** This is where the real work of being a student happens. You must recite, or self-test, periodically to remember what you need to know for exams and/or your future career. You need to *examine* yourself at regular intervals to reinforce what you have learned. A nursing student, for example, needs to know the names of muscles and bones in the body to pass exams—and to practice nursing in the years to come. Examining yourself helps you memorize the material and usually helps you to keep it in your long-term memory, not just to pass exams. To help you examine how well you've learned the skills and concepts in this textbook, there are two mastery tests, one at the end of the chapter and one in a section called "Additional Mastery Tests" at the end of Part I.

Educational psychologists know that regular reviews are the key to long-term retention of what we have learned. Most forgetting occurs immediately. That is, what you read today and what you learn in class lectures today will be almost totally forgotten within 24 hours, unless you review it. When you learn new information, try reviewing it on a schedule like this:

- Immediately
- Within 24 hours
- In two or three days
- In a week
- In two or three weeks
- In a month
- In increasingly wider-spaced intervals

After the first review, you can spread your reviews further and further apart and still remember what you need to know. Keep in mind that probably the most enjoyable and effective way to review is in study groups. Study groups can be your key to success as a student.

**Exercise 9**

## Prepare to Read

Preview Reading 3 on pages 25 through 27 and complete items 1 through 4. Then follow the instructions in item 5 as you read.

1. List three or more things that you noted in your preview.

   a. _____

   _____

   b. _____

   c. _____

2. What do you already know about how public high schools function?

   _____

   _____

3. What might be your purpose for reading material like this?

   _____

   _____

4. Write three preview questions you predict this selection will answer. Remember that in this essay, the author will be giving his opinions about high schools, so your questions might be about his ideas.

   a. _____

   _____

   b. _____

   c. _____

5. Write two reflections (thoughts, comments, or questions) in the margins as you read, using what you know about schools and the atmosphere that helps people learn. You can base these reflections on your own experiences or on the experiences of people you know.

---

**Reading 3**

# Suburb High, USA: School or . . . ?*

— MARLEY PEIFER

**The following reading, written by a high school senior, presents his opinions about the deterioration of the learning environment in suburban high schools in the United States. Prepare yourself to read actively and to reflect on what you read. As you read, make connections to what you already know about U.S. high schools and about learning situations. Also, to assist yourself in reading actively, think about whether or not you agree with the author's point of view.**

1  After eating a quick breakfast, taking a shower, and brushing my teeth, I hoist my 20-pound backpack and leave my house. Living only a few blocks from school, I hear the first bell sound. As the school comes into sight, I see crowds of students walking to their classes. The daily traffic jam in front of the school is as bad as usual. Sixteen-year-olds with fresh licenses in their wallets haphazardly honk and maneuver their way toward the full parking lot. Many live closer to school than I do. Security guards direct cars into the lot. The standard two cop cars are parked on the sidewalk in front of the gates. The two officers stand by their cars, arms crossed, faces stern, and emotionless as statues. The dean, vice principal, and other miscellaneous staff patrol the sidewalk wearing sunglasses and trench coats that make them seem almost inhuman. I stop at the crosswalk, push the button and wait to cross the street. Other kids standing around talk and joke with each other. Then the one-minute bell rings. People start running to their classes. Students carelessly park their cars, jump out, and start running. Just in case the students didn't seem hurried enough, or maybe to make themselves feel important, the previously described staff members whip electronic bullhorns out of their trench coats and remind them. Remarks such as "Get moving!" "Hurry it up, Missy!" and "Come on, one minute!" are how these staff greet the students and welcome them to another day of learning.

*diminutive*
*tiny*

2  The students with me on the other side of the street have stopped talking and now shuffle nervously, eyeing the crosswalk light and the second hand on their watches. A diminutive freshman next to me whose backpack is nearly bigger than he is has started a countdown on his digital watch. He looks at his friend next to him who is tightening his shoe laces. "Forty-five seconds." He looks up at the crosswalk, which still displays a red hand. "Thirty-five seconds." Further down the street I see students jaywalking, favoring dodging cars to being late. I look back at the tiny freshman, who's nearly trembling. "Twenty-five seconds," he stutters. Finally, the light turns green, and it's as if someone just fired the gun for a race. The top-heavy freshman sprints off, wobbling precariously. Everyone else is close behind.

---

*"Suburb High, USA: School or . . . ?" by Marley Peifer. Used by permission.

The bullhorn-toting staff spur them on. I run across the front lawn of the school toward the closest building. "Fifteen seconds," I hear from the bullhorn as I charge through the door, narrowly missing another student. Now, sprinting down the hallway, I see all the teachers lined up next to their open doors. My teacher is at the end of the hall. Her eyes make contact with mine. I'm only twenty yards away. Then the last bell rings. Up and down the hallway, the teachers shut and lock the doors. Exhausted and defeated, I walk the last few steps to my class and look in the window. The students are sitting down, and the teacher is taking roll. I try the doorknob even though I know it is locked. I look down the hallway and see the other students who didn't make it. A few, who have never been late before, look noticeably scared. Just then, the doors at the end of the hallway swing open and three security guards come in. They fan out, one coming toward me and the other students near me. "Let's go! ISS Room," he says, and begins escorting us out of the building. On our way there, I see other late students being taken away on golf carts. The staff members lock the gates, take off their trench coats, and return to their desk jobs. I spend an hour in the In-School Suspension Room because I was caught in the "Tardy Sweep."

## SCHOOL OR PRISON?

3    The previous account is of an average morning at my suburban high school. Much of it could have come from the pages of a prison inmate's journal. Even though a prison should be the last thing that one thinks of to describe a school, the school-prison analogy is quite commonly used by my fellow students these days. Unfortunately, my school is losing qualities of a high school and gaining more and more qualities of a prison. The administration increasingly emphasizes controlling students and ignores educational matters. In many cases, quality of education is sacrificed for increased "security." The administration seems to be more concerned with getting students in class on time than they are with whether students are learning once they are inside. This has been a steady trend since I was a freshman, and the future of the school doesn't look too good.

## THE EROSION OF FREEDOMS

4    When I was in eighth grade I was amazed at how much freedom the high school students had. I saw how they had "open campus" and could leave school for lunch. Many seniors who had jobs or were studying at a community college weren't even required to stay at school for all six periods. For these reasons I couldn't wait to go to high school. I wanted to be treated more like an adult. All the restrictions of middle school made me long for the new responsibilities and freedoms of high school. However, during the summer before I started high school, the administration got rid of the "open campus" system, saying it was causing too many truancies. So I wouldn't be able to eat my lunch at local fast food restaurants as I had dreamed of in eighth grade. That same summer, the lockers were removed, which meant that students had to carry absurdly heavy backpacks. Since I have been at the school, I have watched the number of security guards double, and I have seen how the nice ones have been replaced with stern ones. At the same time, I have witnessed the increased presence of uniformed police. Currently, two officers are assigned to our school, and on occasion there are more. They make no attempt to interact positively with the students or even to smile. The officers are in fact very intimidating. They wear dark glasses and walk around the school with scowls on their faces. They don't seem to realize they are at a school, or at least they don't show it. Instead, they walk around looking like prison guards with guns in their holsters. In my four years at the high school, I have watched countless new rules put into place as well as numerous regulations. Not only have most of these regulations been unnecessary, but many have in fact been detrimental to students' learning.

## OVERREACTING

5    In light of the recent shootings at high schools and colleges across the United States, it's easy to see why parents and school officials might be interested in increased security. They obviously want to prevent more shooting incidents. However, many of the measures being taken at my school would not help prevent a shooting, but they do slow the learning process and make students feel uncomfortable. Penalizing students who are ten seconds late by sending them to spend an hour doing nothing in the In-School Suspension Room is not going to prevent a school shooting or make the school safer. In fact, it creates more disruption to learning than being a little late. Not letting students wear hats on campus is not going to stop the next shooting; nor will not letting students go to the bathroom during a class period. Since the wave of school shootings, parents and teachers have been afraid to question new regulations imposed in the name of "security." I feel a few administrators have taken advantage of this to make the school as bureaucratically efficient and easy to manage as possible, regardless of the effects on education.

6    One of the adverse effects of these changes is psychological. Students are like sponges: we pick up what the staff are feeling and what the environment is like. If the school is an open, happy place where we feel like we can just walk up to the staff and talk to them, we will feel comfortable and probably even enjoy going to school and be enthusiastic about learning. If the school is a place where all the doors lock at the sound of a bell, and our interactions with the staff are limited to the times they yell at us through bullhorns, we will be unenthusiastic, sullen, and withdrawn. If the school is run like a school, students will act like students; but if the school is run like a prison, students will act like prisoners.

7    I need to say that I have had some teachers who know what school is about. They treat us like young people who will soon be making our way in life, either working or continuing our studies. They teach us to think critically and also to take responsibility for our actions, not simply to follow rules. They see that the way that our school is trying to provide order and security for students is frequently, or even most of the time, detrimental to learning. Most students know that if we are treated with respect rather than like prisoners, we will be better learners and thinkers.

8    Making our schools more like prisons negates what schools are supposed to be all about.

---

**Exercise 10**

## Read Actively

Briefly answer the following questions about how you applied the active reading process as you read Reading 3.

1. Did your attention wander as you read this short selection? When? Why?

   _____

2. If you were distracted, how could you have avoided this interruption to your reading?

   _____

3. How did you continue predicting and asking questions as you read?

   _____

4. How well did you monitor your comprehension?

   _____

5. What reflections did you write in the margins? Did your reflections trigger other connections and ideas? Explain.

_____

_____

**Exercise 11**

## Check Your Understanding

Based on Reading 3, write your answers to the following questions.

1. What do you learn about Peifer's school in paragraphs 1 and 2?

_____

_____

2. Why do you think Peifer says his school is like a prison?

_____

_____

_____

_____

_____

3. List at least three events or situations at Peifer's school that he doesn't like. (par. 4)

a. _____

b. _____

c. _____

d. _____

e. _____

4. Why have so many new security measures been put into place? (par. 5)

_____

_____

5. Why does Peifer say the students will act like prisoners?

_____

_____

_____

**Exercise 12**

## Reflect and Write

Think about what you read in Reading 3 and what you already know about this topic. Answer the following questions, and prepare to discuss them with your classmates. Question 5 requires you to write a longer answer on a separate piece of paper.

1. What was high school like when you attended?

   _____

   _____

2. Do you think Peifer's description of schools becoming more like prisons is accurate? Explain.

   _____

   _____

3. What do you think administrators and teachers can do to make high schools healthy places to learn and safe places for young people?

   _____

   _____

4. What do you think students can do to create a positive learning environment?

   _____

   _____

5. On a separate piece of paper, write two to three paragraphs about what you think is most important in shaping students' attitudes about learning. Be sure to give examples from your own experience and/or from the experience of people you know. For the title of your paragraphs, write "Shaping Students' Attitudes About Learning."

# Reader's Tip: Use a Textbook

Most textbooks are now written to make your job as a student easier. When studying for your classes, it's very important that you take advantage of all the learning assistance that your textbook can give you.

**Step One: Know Your Book**. Look at your textbook to find out what special features it has to make learning the material easier for you. Some of the possible features are:

- Table of contents—a list of the book's major topics and subtopics in the order they'll be presented; organized in chapters, sections, or units, with page numbers

- Epigraphs—appropriate quotations, often from well-known writers and thinkers; usually found at the beginning of a book or as a regular feature at the beginning of each chapter
- Footnotes—extra explanations, data, sources of information; may be at the bottom of the page, at the end of the chapter, or listed by chapter at the end of a book
- Appendix—additional useful information, such as maps, lists, charts, and tables; located at the end of a book
- Glossary—a list of important terms and their definitions; usually located in a special section at the end of a book
- Bibliography or references—a list of additional information on a topic, including books, journals, audiovisual materials, and websites; located at the end of each chapter or in a special section at the end of a book
- Answer keys—sometimes included in a special section at the end of a book, or in an appendix, to assist students
- Index—a list, usually alphabetical, of all important topics and terms found in the text, with page numbers for each; located at the end of a book

**Step Two: Understand the Textbook Aids within the Chapters.**

- Title and subtitle—the subject and important sections of the chapter, usually in larger print and boldface type
- Objectives—goals to be accomplished in the chapter
- Introduction—background information and main ideas to be covered in the chapter
- Headings, subheadings, and sub-subheadings—indicate the subject being covered
- Pictures—visual aids for understanding the focus and content of the chapter
- Charts and graphs—visual interpretations of information in the text that sometimes present additional facts and figures
- *Italicized* and **boldfaced** words—important terms the author wants to emphasize. Sometimes terms are defined in the margins, as they are in this book. Other times they are defined in a glossary at the end of a book
- Review questions—key questions that help you focus on the chapter's most important concepts
- Review or summary—a brief overview of the essential information covered in the chapter. Located at the end of the chapter, it is an aid for studying and retaining what you have learned

**Step Three: USE Your Textbook Aids as You Read!** Be sure to stop as you are reading each chapter in your textbooks to check out the aids that it might have.

- Look at the lists of chapter goals, and check out the questions in the back. These will help your brain get ready to focus on the material.
- Look at the pictures and maps, and think about how they further explain the content of the chapter.
- Figure out the charts. They often help you understand and remember material that is difficult to grasp.
- Check out the information in the margins. Sometimes there will be definitions of important words that you need to know. Other times there will be brief explanations of the material that may be all you need to remember.
- Pay special attention to *italicized* and **boldfaced** words. The authors wrote them this way to emphasize that they are important words that you probably will want to remember.
- Notice if there is a glossary in the back of the book or at the end of the chapter. It is the best place to check for definitions of words you don't know.
- Find out if your textbook has an answer key. That way, you can check your own work to find out immediately if you're on the right track.

**Exercise 13**   Check Out Your Textbooks

Answer the following questions about *A Community of Readers* and any other textbook that you might have for another class.

1. List five features, or textbook aids, that you can find in *A Community of Readers* that can make studying this book easier for you. List them here and explain why they are helpful.

   a. _____

   _____

   b. _____

   _____

   c. _____

   _____

   d. _____

   _____

   e. _____

   _____

2. List five features, or textbook aids, that you find in another textbook that can make studying that book easier for you. List them here.

a. _____

b. _____

c. _____

d. _____

e. _____

**Exercise 14**

## Preview a Chapter in *A Community of Readers*

Look at Chapter 7 and answer the following questions.

1. What can you learn about the chapter from the first page, which has the title, subtitle, a quotation, and a graph?

_____

_____

_____

_____

2. What are the main headings of the chapter?

_____

_____

_____

_____

_____

3. What skills will you learn?

_____

_____

4. What subjects will you be reading about as you practice these skills?

_____

_____

5. What kinds of charts and photos are there?

_____

_____

_____

_____

## Write About It

1. Answer A and B to prepare for writing an essay about how you can be successful as a student this semester.
   A. What goals do you want to set for yourself this semester?

   _____

   _____

   _____

   B. What are some steps you can take to ensure that you can accomplish your goals this semester?

      1. _____

      2. _____

      3. _____

      4. _____

   C. Write a paragraph or short essay that answers the question, "How can I be successful as a student this semester?" Be specific, and give examples of what you will do. Some things to consider include making sure you set up study times when you can concentrate, making friends and studying with other students in the class, and using techniques for remembering, such as reviewing regularly.

2. In what ways was the learning atmosphere in your high school similar to and different from the learning atmosphere you are now experiencing in college? Write two to three paragraphs comparing the two experiences.

# Chapter Review

| Put It Together: The Reading Process | |
| --- | --- |
| Skills and Concepts | Explanation |
| **PRO Reading System** (see pages 7–8) | A process to follow for developing effective reading habits |
| **P = Prepare to Read** (see pages 8–11) | Get *ready* to read.<br>1. Purpose (know what your goal is for reading)<br>2. Preview (quickly look at the material before you start to read)<br>3. Previous knowledge (recognize what you already know about the subject)<br>4. Predict (ask questions about what you think you will learn) |
| **R = Read Actively** (see pages 17–18) | Stay *focused* as you read.<br>1. Become involved<br>2. Be interested<br>3. Be alert and attentive<br>4. Monitor your involvement and comprehension |
| **R = Reflect** (see pages 18–19) | *Think* as you read.<br>1. Discover new ideas<br>2. Connect new knowledge to previous knowledge<br>3. Use critical thinking skills to evaluate your new knowledge |
| **O = Organize: SURE** (see pages 22–24) | *Do* something with what you have read.<br>S = <u>S</u>elect the facts and concepts you need to know<br>U = <u>U</u>se the material you've selected<br>R = <u>R</u>ecite the information (self-test)<br>E = <u>E</u>xamine your learning periodically (review) |
| **Reader's Tip: Form a Study Group** (see pages 21–22) | Students who are in study groups do better in school. When you form your study group:<br>• Choose the right people<br>• Decide as a group on your goals and rules |
| **Reader's Tip: Use a Textbook** (see pages 29–32) | Remember to check out and *use* the special features that textbooks have, such as the following:<br>• Chapter introductions, which sometimes list goals<br>• Information in the margins<br>• Italicized and boldfaced words<br>• Charts and graphs, and illustrations<br>• Review questions<br>• Glossaries<br>• Appendices |

## CRITICAL REFLECTIONS IN THE CLASSROOM COMMUNITY

Answer the following questions, and prepare to discuss them with your classmates.

1. Who are your friends at college? Are they people who share your goals and help you be successful?

2. Who are your friends away from college? Do they share goals and values similar to yours? Will being friends with them be a good influence on you?

3. Go visit at least two learning resources on your campus (for example, tutoring centers, academic advising or counseling centers, computer labs, or library). Find out what services they offer and their hours of operation. Using this information, write up a short description to explain these resources to other students.

 ## WORK THE WEB

College websites usually have a section devoted to skills students need to succeed. After completing the exercise below, you may want to check out your own college's website or the website of any colleges you are interested in, and find out which tips and support services these schools provide.

Do a web search for the Dartmouth College Academic Skills Center Lecture Notes. Complete the following task about listening habits—a skill essential for success in college that was not covered in Chapter 1 of *A Community of Readers*.

1. Scroll down to the section on listening. Click on and read "Ten Bad Listening Habits."

2. List four listening habits that you will change based on this reading.

    a. _____

    b. _____

    c. _____

    d. _____

## Prepare to Read and Read Actively

Answer the following questions. They will help you prepare to read "Take Your Memory Out of the Closet," which begins on page 37.

1. Which of the following might you do as you prepare to read? (Circle all that apply.)
   a. Determine your purpose for reading.
   b. Carefully start reading, beginning with the first sentence.
   c. Preview the reading.
   d. Ask questions the reading might answer.
   e. Try to determine what words you need to know and look them up in the dictionary.
   f. Consider your previous knowledge about the subject.

2. What is your purpose for reading this text? (Circle all that apply.)
   a. To complete a homework assignment
   b. To answer your questions about remembering material better
   c. To demonstrate that you can read and understand a textbook excerpt and respond to questions within a limited time
   d. To remember the information for a future test
   e. To get some information because you are interested in the subject

3. What previous knowledge do you have about memory? Write what you already know about how memory works.

   _____

   _____

4. Very quickly, preview the reading. What did you notice in your preview?

   _____

   _____

   _____

5. Write two questions you predict might be answered in this reading.

   a. _____

   b. _____

6. As you read, write two questions or comments in the margins that you might have as an active reader.

   _____

© 2013 Wadsworth, Cengage Learning

# Take Your Memory Out of the Closet*

— DAVE ELLIS

**TEXT BOOK** The following reading, from the textbook *Becoming a Master Student* by Dave Ellis, offers some good ways to remember information you encounter while reading. As you read, consider what you learned about this topic in exercise 1 as you prepared to read.

1    Once upon a time, people talked about human memory as if it were a closet. You stored individual memories there like old shirts and stray socks. Remembering something was a matter of rummaging through all that stuff. If you were lucky, you found what you wanted.

2    This view of memory creates some problems. For one thing, closets can get crowded. Things too easily disappear. Even with the biggest closet, you eventually run out of space. If you want to pack some new memories in there—well, too bad. There's no room. Brain researchers have shattered this image to bits. Memory is not a closet. It's not a place or a thing. Instead, memory is a *process*.

3    On a conscious level, memories appear as <u>distinct</u> and unconnected mental events: words, sensations, images. They can include details from the distant past—the smell of cookies baking in your grandmother's kitchen or the feel of sunlight warming your face through the window of your first-grade classroom. On a biological level, each of those memories involves millions of nerve cells, or <u>neurons</u>, firing chemical messages to each other. If you could observe these exchanges in real time, you'd see regions of cells all over the brain glowing with electrical charges at speeds that would put a computer to shame.

4    When a series of cells connects several times in a similar pattern, the result is a memory. Psychologist Donald Hebb uses the <u>aphorism</u> "Neurons which fire together, wire together" to describe this principle.[1] This means that memories are not really "stored." Instead, remembering is a process in which you *encode* information as links between active neurons that fire together and <u>*decode*</u>, or reactivate, neurons that wired together in the past. Memory is the probability that certain patterns of brain activity will occur again in the future. In effect, you re-create a memory each time you recall it.

encode
arrange

5    Whenever you learn something new, your brain changes physically by growing more connections between neurons. The more you learn, the greater the number of connections. For all practical purposes, there's no limit to how many memories your brain can encode.

6    There's a lot you can do to wire those neural networks into place. . . . Step out of your crowded mental closet into a world of infinite possibilities.

## THE MEMORY JUNGLE

7    Think of your memory as a vast, overgrown jungle. This memory jungle is thick with wild plants, exotic shrubs, twisted trees, and creeping vines. It spreads over thousands of square miles—dense, tangled, forbidding. Imagine that the jungle is <u>encompassed</u> on all sides by towering mountains. There is only one entrance to the jungle, a small meadow that is reached by a narrow pass through the mountains.

8    In the jungle there are animals, millions of them. The animals represent all of the information in your memory. Imagine that every thought, mental picture, or <u>perception</u> you ever had is represented by an animal in this jungle. Every single event ever perceived by any of your five senses—sight, touch, hearing, smell, or taste—has also passed through

*"Take Your Memory Out of the Closet" by David Ellis from BECOMING A MASTER STUDENT, 11th Edition. Copyright © 2006. Reprinted by permission of Houghton Mifflin Company.

meadow
grassland

the meadow and entered the jungle. Some of the thought animals, such as the color of your seventh-grade teacher's favorite sweater, are well hidden. Other thoughts, such as your cell phone number or the position of the reverse gear in your car, are easier to find.

9   There are two rules of the memory jungle. Each thought animal must pass through the meadow at the entrance to the jungle. And once an animal enters the jungle, it never leaves.

10   The meadow <u>represents</u> short-term memory. You use this kind of memory when you look up a telephone number and hold it in your memory long enough to make a call. Short-term memory appears to have a limited capacity (the meadow is small) and disappears fast (animals pass through the meadow quickly).

11   The jungle itself represents long-term memory. This is the kind of memory that allows you to recall information from day to day, week to week, and year to year. Remember that thought animals never leave the long-term memory jungle. The following <u>visualizations</u> can help you recall useful concepts about memory.

## VISUALIZATION #1: A WELL-WORN PATH

12   Imagine what happens as a thought, in this case we'll call it an elephant, bounds across short-term memory and into the jungle. The elephant leaves a trail of broken twigs and hoof prints that you can follow. Brain research suggests that thoughts can wear paths in the memory.[2] These paths are called neural traces. The more well-worn the neural trace, the easier it is to <u>retrieve</u> (find) the thought. In other words, the more often the elephant retraces the path, the clearer the path becomes. The more often you recall information, and the more often you put the same information into your memory, the easier it

Santosh Saligram/Alamy

is to find. When you buy a new car, for example, the first few times you try to find reverse, you have to think for a moment. After you have found reverse gear every day for a week, the path is worn into your memory. After a year, the path is so well-worn that when you dream about driving your car backward, you even dream the correct motion for putting the gear in reverse.

## VISUALIZATION #2: A HERD OF THOUGHTS

13   The second picture you can use to your advantage is the picture of many animals gathering at a clearing—like thoughts gathering at a central location in the memory. It is easier to retrieve thoughts that are grouped together, just as it is easier to find a herd of animals than it is to find a single elephant.

14   Pieces of information are easier to recall if you can <u>associate</u> them with similar information. For example, you can more readily remember a particular player's batting average if you can associate it with other baseball statistics.

## VISUALIZATION #3: TURNING YOUR BACK

15   Imagine releasing the elephant into the jungle, turning your back, and counting to 10. When you turn around, the elephant is gone. This is exactly what happens to most of the information you receive.

16   Generally, we can recall only 50 percent of the material we have just read. Within 24 hours, most of us can recall only about 20 percent. This means that 80 percent of the material has not been encoded and is wandering around, lost in the memory jungle.

17   The remedy is simple: Review quickly. Do not take your eyes off the thought animal as it crosses the short-term memory meadow, and review it soon after it enters the long-term memory jungle. Wear a path in your memory immediately.

## VISUALIZATION #4: YOU ARE DIRECTING THE ANIMAL TRAFFIC

18   The fourth picture is one with you in it. You are standing at the entrance to the short-term memory meadow, directing herds of thought animals as they file through the pass, across the meadow, and into your long-term memory. You are taking an active role in the learning process. You are paying attention. You are doing more than sitting on a rock and watching the animals file past into your brain. You have become part of the process, and in doing so, you have taken control of your memory.

**Notes**

1.  Donald Hebb, quoted in D. J. Siegel, "Memory: An Overview," *Journal of the American Academy of Child and Adolescent Psychiatry* 40, no. 9 (2001): 997–1011.

2.  Holger Hayden, "Biochemical Aspects of Learning and Memory," in *On the Biology of Learning*, ed. Karl H. Pribram (New York: Harcourt, Brace & World, 1969).

| **Exercise 2** |
|---|

Check Your "Prepare to Read and Read Actively"

Briefly answer the following questions about how you applied the active reading process as you read "Take Your Memory Out of the Closet."

1. Which of your preview questions were answered?

_____

2. What strategies did you use to be an active reader? In what ways did these strategies help you remain involved, interested, and attentive?

_____

_____

_____

3. List the important information in the reading that was new for you.

_____

**Exercise 3**

## Work with Words

Choose the best definition for each of the following words underlined in the reading. The paragraph number is provided in case you want to check the context.

1. *Distinct* (par. 3)
   a. interesting
   b. separate
   c. unusual

2. *Neurons* (par. 3)
   a. nerve cells
   b. chemical messages
   c. electrical charges

3. *Aphorism* (par. 4)
   a. joke
   b. principle
   c. brief saying

4. *Decode* (par. 4)
   a. reactivate neurons that are wired together, or remember
   b. change the memory process of the brain
   c. figure out the secret message after careful study

5. *Encompassed* (par. 7)
   a. included
   b. opened
   c. surrounded

6. *Perception* (par. 8)
   a. point of view
   b. awareness
   c. taste

7. *Represents* (par. 10)
   a. stands for
   b. looks like
   c. speaks for a group of people

8. *Visualizations* (par. 11)
   a. eyesight
   b. hallucinations
   c. imaginary pictures

9. *Retrieve* (par. 12)
   a. get back, or find
   b. salvage, or recycle
   c. relate to batting averages

10. *Associate* (par. 14)
    a. socialize
    b. separate
    c. connect

Exercise 4

## Check Your Understanding

Based on the reading "Take Your Memory Out of the Closet" by Dave Ellis, choose the best answer to each of the following multiple-choice questions.

1. Talking about human memory as if it were a closet
   a. makes it easier to understand how the memory process really works.
   b. creates problems in understanding how the memory process really works.
   c. is useful for understanding how the human brain stores memories.

2. Memory is a
   a. place.
   b. thing.
   c. process.

3. Neurons fire chemical messages to each other
   a. at the same rate as the fastest computers.
   b. more slowly than the fastest computers.
   c. a lot faster than the fastest computers.

4. Your brain can encode
   a. millions of memories.
   b. a limitless number of memories.
   c. the same number of memories as you have neurons.

5. Short-term memory is
   a. the type of memory you should use to store information away for the future.
   b. used when you want to remember a number for many years to come.
   c. compared to a small meadow, because your brain only has a limited capacity for it.

6. The more often you recall information, and the more often you put the same information into your memory, the more likely
   a. you will be able to find, or remember, that information when you need it.
   b. your neural pathways will become entangled, and you will confuse new information with old information.
   c. you will actually learn to enjoy the process of memorizing information.

7. The author discusses the neural traces in your brain as a kind of path to
   a. make it easier to imagine that the more often you think about something, the more likely you are to remember it.
   b. eliminate the questions you might have about how the memory process works.
   c. define neural traces.

8. The author compares picturing many animals together with the information in your memory to help you understand that
   a. animals usually stay together.
   b. when information is grouped with other information, it is easier to remember.
   c. it is easier to recall information if you concentrate on not allowing your brain to be cluttered.

9. The example of "releasing the elephant into the jungle, turning your back, and counting to 10" illustrates the
   a. importance of associating information with other information which is similar.
   b. importance of thinking about something different immediately after receiving new information, which will allow the brain to relax and remember the new information more effectively.
   c. idea that if we don't quickly review what we have read, we will forget 80 percent of it within 24 hours.

10. The author tells you to visualize yourself "directing the animal traffic" to emphasize the
   a. importance of relying on your short-term memory when all else fails.
   b. importance of paying attention and actively participating in the process of deciding what to put into your long-term memory, and doing the work that it takes.
   c. need to try to remember all the information you are exposed to.

**Exercise 5**

### Reflect

Think about what you read in "Take Your Memory Out of the Closet" and what you already know about this topic. Then answer the following questions.

1. How can this reading help you study more effectively?

_____

_____

_____

_____

_____

2. What are you supposed to think about when you look at the elephant in the path through the jungle? What does this picture have to do with memory?

_____

_____

_____

_____

_____

_____

_____

# Working with Words

## LIVING WITH TECHNOLOGY

Sean Justice/Taxi/Getty Images

*It is only when they go wrong that machines remind you how powerful they are. — Clive James*

1. What do you think the woman in the picture is trying to do? What do you think the children want her to do?

2. Have you ever been in a similar situation? In what way?

3. What do you think the quotation means? Give an example of when a machine has gone wrong in your experience or that you know about. What happened?

4. In what ways does technology affect your life? How do you think it will affect you in 10 or 20 years?

# Prepare to Read

New technological developments affect us in many ways. Computers influence everything from bus schedules, bank statements, and grocery shopping to air traffic control, medical equipment, and weapons of war. Other technological advances, such as cell phones, the Internet, iPods, iPads, and thousands of apps, increase and enhance communication. The almost-daily explosion of new technologies has become a normal part of modern life. Yet these innovations have also brought new concerns. Are we losing our ability to communicate face-to-face? Are there too many interruptions and distractions? How can we prevent our personal information from being stolen? Clearly, technology has a profound impact on our lives. Reading about new technological developments from a variety of sources is a good way of learning about vocabulary because so many technology-related words have been introduced into the language in the last 20 years.

In this chapter, you will learn a variety of approaches for learning new vocabulary, such as

- Figuring out the meaning of words from the context
- Figuring out the meaning of words by using word parts
- Using the dictionary
- Using textbook aids to learn specialized vocabulary

In the process of acquiring these skills, you will read about the constantly evolving technology and how it influences our lives.

**Reading 1**

# Can You Hold, Please? Your Brain Is on the Line* — Elijah James

**Recently, psychologists, neuroscientists, and business management professors have been studying the phenomenon of multitasking. With cell phones, instant messages, digital assistants, MP3 players, e-mail, and the Internet available virtually anytime and anywhere, we often find ourselves doing two—or more—things at the same time. However, recent research indicates that attention, health, productivity, and profits can suffer as a result of too much multitasking.**

1    In today's fast-paced world, it seems as if we get much more done than our parents and grandparents did. After all, we can talk and text, drive and talk or listen to tunes, respond to e-mail, and write a report all at the same time. But how does all this juggling affect us? Are we really better off?

**multitasking**
performing more than one task at the same time

2    Recent research suggests good reasons for limiting multitasking. Substantial evidence shows that driving while talking on a cell phone—even hands-free—is dangerous. Many states have already restricted cell phone use while driving, and others are in the process of doing so. During work or study, it is recommended that we check personal e-mail just once an hour and minimize other distractions such as listening to songs with lyrics, instant messaging, surfing the web, or watching television. In other words, we need to learn how to manage technology, not just succumb to it every time we hear a beep or ring.

**succumb**
give in

**neuroscientist**
a scientist who studies the brain and nervous system

3    With its millions of neurons and firing synapses, the human brain has an amazing capacity to adapt. Yet psychologists and neuroscientists have discovered that cognition (mental processes) slow down when people try to do two tasks simultaneously. As René Marois, a neuroscientist and director of the Human Information Processing Laboratory at Vanderbilt University, states, "A core limitation is an inability to concentrate on two things at once."[1]

4    Mr. Marois and other Vanderbilt researchers conducted a study that involved two tasks—responding to sounds and responding to images. In the first task, participants had to punch a key on a keyboard when they heard a certain sound. In the second task, they had to give an oral response when they saw a particular image. The researchers found that when participants were asked to do both tasks at about the same time, their ability to complete the second task was delayed by up to one second. Although one second doesn't seem critical, it could mean the difference between life and death when trying to avoid a road hazard or an oncoming car.

**renowned**
well-known

5    Other studies have more direct implications for studying and working. Dr. Russell Poldrack, associate professor of psychology at the University of California at Los Angeles, studied volunteers in their twenties, an age group that is renowned for its multitasking abilities. Through the use of magnetic resonance imaging, he found that when participants focused on a task, a different part of their brain was activated than when they did the same task while engaging in multitasking. That the part of the brain used for memory and recall—the hippocampus—was not active while multitasking is a concern to Poldrack because young people's brains are still developing. "They develop a more superficial style of study and may not learn material as well. What they get out of their study might be less deep," he said.[2]

---

*"Can You Hold Please? Your Brain is on the Line" by Elijah James.

6    In another study, researchers at Microsoft found that when workers replied to an e-mail or checked a website, it took them an average of 15 minutes to return to a task that required focus, such as writing a report or computer code. "I was surprised by how easily people were distracted and how long it took them to get back to the task," said Eric Horvitz, a Microsoft research scientist.[3] As a result, worker productivity and company profits go down.

7    Most researchers acknowledge that multitasking in certain situations is not only necessary; it can also be beneficial. Interruptions can spark creativity and collaboration. However, they caution that more is not always better and that individuals should make choices about how and when they multitask. Otherwise, they will be missing out on some of the brain's power and losing time rather than saving it.

**Notes**

1. Steve Lohr, "Slow Down Brave Multitasker, and Don't Read This in Traffic," *New York Times,* March 25, 2007.

2. Lori Aratani, "Teens Can Multitask, But What Are the Costs?" *Washington Post,* February 26, 2007.

3. Quoted in Lohr, "Slow Down Brave Multitasker."

**Exercise 1**

## Recall and Discuss

Based on Reading 1, answer the following questions and prepare to discuss them with your classmates.

1. According to this article and your own experience, what are some typical ways that people multitask?

   _____

   _____

   _____

   _____

   _____

2. What are some potential disadvantages of multitasking? What, in your opinion, are the advantages?

   _____

   _____

   _____

   _____

   _____

3. In what situations do you multitask? What technologies do you use? Do you feel that multitasking is a benefit or distraction for you? Explain your answers.

_____

_____

_____

_____

# Working with Words

Computers are a relatively new invention, and they are even changing our language. We have added words to English such as *hardware, software, email, chat room, listserv, social networking, cloud computing,* and many others because we need them to talk about computers. Everyone in our society today needs to know these words.

As a student, you will encounter new words in your college courses, and it is important for you to have a variety of strategies for dealing with them. In this chapter, you will learn some of the most basic ways of building your vocabulary and dealing with words that you may not know.

## READING AND VOCABULARY

Probably the one activity that will most improve your vocabulary is reading. The more you read, the more words you will learn. It's as simple as that. The more words you know, the easier it is for you to read and the more you will enjoy reading for its own sake. So maybe instead of watching a rerun of a TV program, try to set aside about half an hour a day to read for fun. Pick anything that you enjoy reading—sports magazines, fashion magazines, mystery novels, the newspaper. It doesn't matter what you read at first, as long as you get into the habit. Then gradually push yourself to read material that is a little more challenging and that expands the type of reading you do. Still, you want to enjoy this reading, so pick things that interest you. You will find that developing the lifelong habit of reading a lot will help you build your general vocabulary. And having a large vocabulary will help you in many ways: in school, at work, and whenever you want to communicate. A strong vocabulary is a powerful tool that you can put to work for you.

## CONTEXT CLUES

When you are reading college textbooks, you may run into many words that you do not know. One important skill you need to develop is figuring out the meaning of those words from the context of the reading itself. **Context** refers to the rest of the statement in which a particular word appears. It may include the entire sentence or even a paragraph or more.

**context**
the sentence or paragraph in which a word appears

For practice in understanding context clues, read the following paragraph, which has some words that you don't know but will understand because you understand the context.

> Yesterday, when I went to the *osmotle* to buy some *wattish* for dinner, I saw a *slampfer* I knew when I was 10 years old. He smiled and was very *ovish* to see me, but I was *amvish* to see him because I had some bad *dosilums* from the last time I had seen him.

Of course, the italicized words in this passage are not really words, but they could be. From the context, you know that *osmotle* is probably a store, *wattish* is some kind of food, and *slampfer* is a friend or acquaintance, or at least a person. Why were you able to understand these "words"? You could do so because you understood the meaning of the rest of the sentence and paragraph. You understood the context in which the words appeared. You may not know precisely what each word means, but you have a pretty good idea.

In this next section, you will work on figuring out the approximate meaning of words using context clues. The context provides basically four kinds of clues that might help you understand a word. They are

- Definition and synonym clues
- Example clues
- General information clues
- Contrast clues

**Definition and Synonym Clues** When you first encounter a word that you don't understand, don't immediately go to the dictionary. Often the actual definition of a word is provided for you in what you are reading. Sometimes the definition is an explanation of the word, and sometimes it is a synonym for the word. A **synonym** is a word that means the same as another word. Sometimes the definition or synonym is provided for you in different ways. Consider the following possibilities and the examples of each.

**synonym**
a word that has a similar meaning to another word

- **Between or after commas.** Notice how the comma sets off the actual definition of a word in the following sentence:

> The brain is made up of billions of *neurons*, nerve cells, which enable human thought, memory, and imagination.

In this example, we know that *neurons* are "nerve cells." The definition, set off by commas, is our clue.

- **After certain words.** The words *is, are, means, refers to, consists of, is called,* or *that is* can alert you to a definition. Notice how this kind of clue works in the following sentence:

> A technique that takes pictures of internal parts of the body, including the brain, is called *magnetic resonance imaging,* or MRI.

We know then that *magnetic resonance imaging* is "a technique that takes pictures of internal parts of the body" because of the words *is called.*

- **Between dashes.** In the following sentence, the synonym of a word appears between dashes:

  > The *hippocampus*—the part of the brain used for memory and recall—is not active during multitasking.

  The dashes tell us that "the part of the brain used for memory and recall" is the definition of *hippocampus*.

- **In parentheses.** In the following sentence, the synonym of a word appears in parentheses:

  > Psychologists and neuroscientists have discovered that *cognition* (mental processes) slows down when people try to do two tasks simultaneously.

  The parentheses tell us that the definition of *cognition* is "mental processes."

| Exercise 2 |
| --- |

### Understand Words Using Definition and Synonym Clues

Read the following sentences and write the definition or synonym of the italicized word or words, using the language used in the sentences themselves. Then write down what definition and synonym clue(s) helped you find the meaning. Be sure to use only the definitions provided in these sentences. The first one has been done for you.

1. Older people think more slowly than young people, but they have a faster *fluid intelligence* (ability to use information), so they can ignore interruptions and focus better.

   *Fluid intelligence*: **ability to use information**

   Clues: **parentheses**

2. The *information age* refers to the period of time since the 1980s when access to information started to increase rapidly.

   *Information age*: _____

   _____

   Clues: _____

3. Multitasking beyond the *optimal*, or best, level negatively affects one's work.

   *Optimal*: _____

   Clues: _____

4. The *findings*—results of the research—suggest that multitasking while driving is especially dangerous.

   *Findings*: _____

   Clues: _____

5. Google was the hugely popular search engine that had gone from obscurity in the mid-1990s to a point where it responded, more or less instantly, to 200 million *queries* per day from around the world—almost 40 percent of all Internet search requests. (Norton et al., *A People and a Nation*)

*Queries:* _____

Clues: _____

6. Researchers found that *productivity* (amount of work produced) decreased when multitasking moved beyond an ideal level.

*Productivity:* _____

Clues: _____

**Example Clues** Sometimes you can figure out the meaning of a word because you understand the examples or because both a definition and examples are provided in the reading. Look for the examples and the definitions for the italicized word in the following sentences.

> Today, most young people use a variety of electronic *devices* on a daily basis. It would be a hardship for many to go even a day without a cell phone, iPod, iPad, BlackBerry, or the computer and its access to the social universe of MySpace, Facebook, and YouTube.

In these sentences, examples the author gives for devices are "cell phone," "iPod," "iPad," "BlackBerry," and "computer." We know from this list that *device* must mean something like "electronic machine or tool."

**Exercise 3**

Understand Words Using Example Clues

Read the following sentences and write the definition or synonym of the italicized word or words, using the context provided in the sentences. Then write down what example clue helped you find the meaning.

1. During work or study, it is recommended that we check personal e-mail just once an hour and minimize other *distractions* such as listening to songs with lyrics, instant messaging, surfing the web, or watching television.

*Distractions:* _____

Example Clues: _____

_____

2. Thanks to technological advances and to the new forms of "broadband" access, [computer] users could do an astonishing *array* of things online. They could send and receive email, join online discussion groups, read newspapers, book vacations, download movies and music, purchase everything from

books to private jets, even do their banking—all through a small computer in their home. (Norton et al., *A People and a Nation*)

*Array:* _____

Example Clues: _____

_____

_____

**General Information Clues** Often you can understand an unfamiliar word because you already comprehend the rest of the information in the surrounding sentence or group of sentences. It was from this type of context clue that you were able to understand the example using the "words" *osmotle* and *wattish* on page 48. The contexts for the italicized words in the following example are a little more complicated, but you will probably be able to figure out what the words mean because you will understand the context. Sometimes you can understand a new word because the text explains what the word means. Often in the context of technology, the text explains what something does, and that helps you understand the meaning of the new term. Consider the following example:

> *Input devices* accept data or commands in a form that the computer can use; they send the data or commands to the processing unit. (Capron, *Computers*)

From this sentence, we know that input devices accept data and send them to the processing unit. So we can write a definition using this information: "Input devices are the parts of the computer that accept data in a form that the computer can use and send the data to the processing unit." Our clue is the explanation of what input devices do.

**Exercise 4**

## Understand Words Using General Information Clues

Read the following examples and write the definition or synonym of the italicized word or words, using the context provided in the sentences. Then write down what general information clue(s) helped you find the meaning.

1. As a result, worker productivity and company profits decline. Individuals' health may *deteriorate* as well. As the brain is pushed to perform beyond its normal capacity, adrenaline and other stress hormones are released. Over time, this stress can negatively affect memory and one's ability to concentrate.

   *Deteriorate:* _____

   Clues: _____

2. To be *technologically literate* means more than knowing how to use the Internet. It also means that you are aware of developments in such fields as biotechnology. For example, the use of biologically engineered cells and tissues has led to important scientific and medical breakthroughs such as lab-grown blood vessels for kidney dialysis patients. Most newspapers and newsmagazines have a technology section where you can keep up with new trends and developments such as this one. (Kanar, *The Confident Student*)

*Technologically literate*: _____

_____

Clues: _____

_____

_____

3. People often turn to the Internet with the hope of saving time—not wasting it. You can accommodate their desires by typing *concise* messages. Adopt the habit of getting to your point, sticking to it, and getting to the end. (Ellis, *Becoming a Master Student*)

*Concise*: _____

Clues: _____

_____

**Contrast Clues** Sometimes you can figure out the meaning of a word by understanding what it is *not*. Occasionally a context indicates that a word is different from or the opposite of another word. These words can be clues that there is a contrast: *but, in contrast to, although, on the other hand, however,* and *unlike*.

Consider the following example. Using the contrast clue, we can determine the meaning of *public domain software*.

> Unlike *public domain software,* copyrighted software must be purchased and cannot be copied.

We know that public domain software is different from copyrighted software. The information given about copyrighted software is that it must be purchased and cannot be copied. We can conclude, then, that the definition of *public domain software* is "software that is free and can be copied."

| **Exercise 5** | ## Understand Words Using Contrast Clues |

Use contrast clues to explain the meanings of the italicized words.

1. Although many of the early software packages were *cumbersome*, software packages today are quite easy to use.

   *Cumbersome:* _____

   Clues: _____

2. Using multiple electronic gadgets at the same time may reduce your brain's ability to retain information. On the other hand, technology can also *supplement* your brain and help you keep track of important appointments, assignments, and meetings.

   *Supplement:* _____

   Clues: _____

| **Exercise 6** | ## Understand Words Using Context Clues |

The following excerpt is from *Computers: Tools for an Information Age*, an introductory computer science textbook by H. L. Capron. It describes the Internet to students. As you read, you will notice that most of this excerpt is dedicated to the special vocabulary of the Internet. When you are done reading, define the terms underlined in the exercise using the context clues in the excerpt itself. Identify which words helped you define the vocabulary terms.

> The Internet, sometimes called simply the Net, is the largest and most far-flung network system of them all, connecting users worldwide. Surprisingly, the Internet is not really a network at all but a loosely organized collection of about 25,000 networks. Many people are astonished to discover that no one owns the Internet; it is run by volunteers. It has no central headquarters, no centrally offered services, and no comprehensive index to tell you what information is available.
>
> Originally developed and still subsidized by the United States government, the Internet connects libraries, college campuses, research labs, businesses, and any other organization or individual who has the capacity to hook up.

### Getting Connected

> How are all kinds of different computers able to communicate with one another? To access the Internet, a user's computer must connect to a computer called a server. Each server uses the same special software called TCP/IP (for Transmission Control Protocol/Internet Protocol); it is this consistency that allows different types of computers to communicate.... The supplier of the server computer, often called an Internet service provider (ISP), charges a fee, usually monthly, based on the amount of service provided. Once a user has chosen a service provider, he or she will be furnished with the information needed to connect to the server and, from there, to the Internet.

## Getting Around

**arcane**
old, out-of-date

Since the Internet did not begin as a commercial customer-pleasing package, it did not <u>initially</u> offer attractive options for finding information. The arcane commands were invoked only by a hardy and determined few. Furthermore, the vast sea of information, including news and trivia, can seem an overwhelming challenge to navigate. As both the Internet user population and the available information grew, new ways were developed to tour the Internet.

The most attractive method used to move around the Internet is called browsing. Using a program called a browser, you can use a mouse to point and click on screen icons to explore the Internet, particularly the Web, an Internet <u>subset of text, images, and sounds linked together</u> to allow users to <u>peruse</u> related topics. Each different location on the Web is called a web site or, more commonly, just a site. You may have heard the term home page; this is just the first page of a web site.

The Internet is an <u>important</u> and <u>complex</u> topic. Although it is easy to use once you know how, there is much to learn about its use and its place in the world of computers. (Capron, *Computers*)

1. *Far-flung:* _____

   Clues: _____

2. *Server:* _____

   _____

   Clues: _____

   _____

   _____

3. *Consistency:* _____

   Clues: _____

4. *Initially:* _____

   Clues: _____

   _____

5. *Peruse:* _____

   Clues: _____

   _____

6. *Complex:* _____

   Clues: _____

**Reading 2**

# Cyber-Bullying Defies Traditional School Bully Stereotype* — Gregg MacDonald

**Digital technology has made it faster and easier to communicate as well as to do tasks such as researching and word processing. Yet there are disadvantages to the increasing use of technology—problems that we could not have imagined 20 years ago. In this article published in 2010 in *The Washington Post*, Gregg MacDonald discusses the issue of cyber-bullying in the schools in Fairfax County, Virginia, and solutions that some community members are proposing to help reduce its negative effects on young people.**

**cyber**
relating to computers

**social networking sites**
websites such as Facebook and MySpace in which users share information via the Internet

**innuendos**
statements which have a negative meaning that is hinted at rather than said directly

**proliferation**
increase

1   The advent of social networking sites and text messaging has allowed young girls the opportunity to take on a role traditionally reserved for boys, experts say. The girls have become bullies—or, more specifically, cyber-bullies. The Virginia Department of Education defines cyber-bullying as "using information and communication technologies such as e-mail, cell phones, text messaging, instant messaging, and Web sites to support deliberate, hostile behavior intended to harm others."

2   Cyber-bullying in Fairfax County public schools seems to occur primarily in middle schools, said Sgt. William H. Fulton of Fairfax County police, school resource officer supervisor. "There are lots of threats and innuendos made through social networking sites, such as Facebook," he said. "A boy may break up with a girl, and sides may begin to form against one of the two parties. Before you know it, exchanges are made online and can potentially lead to trouble back at school."

3   Social networking sites allow teenagers to post events in their lives in real time, said Ilana Reyes, a counselor at Annandale High School. "It is so easy to say negative things through texting and online because you are not face-to-face with the person you're talking about," Reyes said. "Bullies say things and feel all big and bad because they are at home behind a computer, or on a phone, and aren't there to see the ramifications or the impact that it has on the other person."

4   Research suggests that girls are more likely than boys to engage in cyber-bullying but that both can be perpetrators and victims. "Without question, the nature of adolescent peer aggression has evolved due to the proliferation of information and communications technology," said Sameer Hinduja of the Cyber-bullying Research Center at Florida Atlantic University. "There have been several high-profile cases involving teens taking their own lives in part because of being harassed and mistreated over the Internet." The center's research has shown that adolescent girls are significantly more likely than boys to partake in and experience cyber-bullying. Girls also are more likely to report cyber-bullying to a parent or teacher. The center's research also suggests that the type of cyber-bullying tends to differ by gender; girls are more likely to spread rumors, while boys are more likely to post hurtful pictures or videos. A survey by the center found that cyber-bullying victims were almost twice as likely to have attempted suicide compared to youth who had experienced no cyber-bullying.

5   According to Virginia Department of Education guidelines, cyber-bullying can include sending "mean, vulgar or threatening" messages or images; posting sensitive or private information about another person; or intentionally excluding someone from an online

**Class 6 felony**
a serious crime
whose punishment
is either one to five
years in prison, or up
to 12 months in jail
and a maximum fine
of $2,500, or both

6  group. In Virginia, making a written threat, including those via texting, e-mail, instant messaging and the Internet, is a Class 6 felony.

Lucinda Crabtree of Falls Church knows the effects of cyber-bullying. When a friend's teen daughter committed suicide last year, potentially as a result of cyber-bullying, Crabtree decided she needed to act. She began researching ways to make parents more aware of their teen's online language and behavior. "I felt there was a cyber-communications gap between parents and their teens," she said. "We've all had a sort of secret language growing up, and kids today are no different. They have their own online and texting lingo. I felt that a better understanding of this cyber communication by my friend may have helped her recognize the warning signs in her daughter's behavior." Crabtree formed a volunteer panel of teens, parents, teachers, health care workers, and law enforcement professionals. The group researched the meanings of popular texting codes, Internet terminology, and emoticons—[such as] smiley faces in messages that impart meanings. "It was a serious education," Crabtree said. "For example, I had no idea that a percent sign can mean being high or drunk" or that a "four-pounder" is code for a .45-caliber Colt pistol.

7  Crabtree unveiled a software application, LRNtheLingo, last month that parents can use in the same way they might an online dictionary of cyber and slang terms. She wants to make the application available to public safety and school professionals. "Teachers and school resource officers need to learn to identify this secret online language as well as parents," she said. "If this helps just one cyber-bullying victim, it will be very rewarding." "Parents do need to get more involved and monitor what their kids are writing online," Reyes said. "Cell phone use in Fairfax County schools is prohibited. So most cyber-bullying occurs off school grounds, outside the reach of teachers or school resource officers."

**Exercise 7**

## Work with Words: Vocabulary in Context

The following sentences appear in Reading 2. Use context clues to choose the best definition or synonym of each italicized word in the sentences. The paragraph number is provided in case you want to check the context.

1. The *advent* of social networking sites and text messaging has allowed young girls the opportunity to take on a role traditionally reserved for boys, experts say. The girls have become bullies—or, more specifically, cyber-bullies. (par. 1)

   *advent*
   a. look
   b. hardware
   c. arrival

2. "Bullies say things and feel all big and bad because they are at home behind a computer, or on a phone, and aren't there to see the *ramifications* or the impact that it has on the other person." (par. 3)

   *ramifications*
   a. reasons
   b. attacks
   c. effects

3. "Without question, the nature of adolescent peer aggression has *evolved* due to the proliferation of information and communications technology," said Sameer Hinduja of the Cyber-bullying Research Center at Florida Atlantic University. (par. 4)

*evolved*
a. developed
b. shrunk
c. combined

4. The center's research has shown that adolescent girls are significantly more likely than boys to *partake* in and experience cyber-bullying. (par. 4)

*partake*
a. succeed
b. participate
c. result

5. Crabtree *unveiled* a software application, LRNtheLingo, last month that parents can use in the same way they might an online dictionary of cyber and slang terms. (par. 7)

*unveiled*
a. requested
b. introduced
c. maintained

**Exercise 8**

## Work with Words: More Vocabulary in Context

For the following italicized words, write the definitions on the lines provided. Write the context clue(s) you used to find the definition (*definition, synonym, example, general information, contrast*).

1. The Virginia Department of Education defines *cyber-bullying* as "using information and communication technologies such as e-mail, cell phones, text messaging, instant messaging and Web sites to support deliberate, hostile behavior intended to harm others." (par. 1)

*cyber-bullying*: _____

_____

_____

_____

Clues: _____

2. Research suggests that girls are more likely than boys to engage in cyber-bullying but that both can be *perpetrators* and victims. (par. 4)

*perpetrator*: _____

Clues: _____

3. "There have been several high-profile cases involving teens taking their own lives in part because of being harassed and *mistreated* over the Internet." (par. 4)

*mistreated:* _____

Clues: _____

4. "We've all had a sort of secret language growing up, and kids today are no different. They have their own online and texting *lingo*. (par. 6)

*lingo:* _____

Clues: _____

5. The group researched the meanings of popular texting codes, Internet terminology and *emoticons*—[such as] smiley faces in messages that *impart* meanings. (par. 6)

*emoticons:* _____

_____

Clues: _____

6. *impart:* _____

Clues: _____

---

**Exercise 9**

## Check Your Understanding

Based on Reading 2, choose the best answer to each of the following multiple-choice questions.

1. Which of the following statements would the author consider true?
   a. Only girls are cyber-bullies.
   b. We usually think of boys as bullies.
   c. Schools should take more responsibility for stopping bullies.

2. According to the article, the age group most affected by cyber-bullying is
   a. 10–14 year olds.
   b. 14–18 year olds.
   c. 19–23 year olds.

3. According to the author,
   a. girls are usually too embarrassed to admit that they have been the victim of a cyber-bully.
   b. girls act as cyber-bullies and are the victims of cyber-bullies more frequently than boys are.
   c. boys do not use social networking sites to spread rumors.

4. Which of the following statements would the author *disagree* with?
   a. Parents need to accept more responsibility in understanding and preventing cyber-bullying.
   b. Cyber-bullies are hiding behind a computer screen and do not have to face the consequences of their actions in person.
   c. There will always be bullies, and the Internet is a fact of modern life. In reality, there is little we can do to stop cyber-bullying.

5. The focus of Linda Crabtree's research is
   a. to design effective parental control software.
   b. to develop parents' awareness of online language and communication practices.
   c. to inform parents and teachers about the connection between cyber-bullying and suicide.

6. The author believes
   a. cyber-bullying is a fad that will go away.
   b. there should be more research about the causes of cyber-bullying.
   c. cyber-bullying is a serious problem that families and communities should address.

---

**Exercise 10**

### Reflect and Write

Think about what you read in Reading 2 and what you already know about social networking sites, texting, and cyber-bullying. Answer the following questions, and prepare to discuss them with your classmates.

1. What are the advantages and disadvantages of social networking sites and texting? Give some examples.

   _____

   _____

   _____

   _____

   _____

2. Why is cyber-bullying considered to be a serious problem? How does it differ from traditional bullying? On a separate piece of paper, write two or three paragraphs explaining your thoughts about cyber-bullying. Give examples to support your opinion from this article, other articles or TV programs, or personal experience (your own or that of someone you know). In your final paragraph, write about some possible ways to reduce cyber-bullying. For the title of your paragraphs, write "Cyber-Bullying: The Problem and Some Solutions."

# WORD PARTS

word parts
prefixes, roots,
and suffixes

Probably one of the most difficult aspects of studying any new subject is the vocabulary. The specialized vocabulary of a college discipline, for example, may be new to you. While you are often going to have to learn a lot of new words for certain subjects, certain techniques can help you. In addition to using the clues to understand the meaning of words from the context, recognizing word parts can make this job much easier for you.

Many thousands of words in the English language are made up of **word parts.** As a reader, you can greatly increase your vocabulary simply by learning some of the most common word parts. Knowing them will help you "take apart" a word to figure out its meaning. There are three types of word parts:

1. *Prefixes*, which appear at the beginning of a word
2. *Roots*, which can be at the beginning, middle, or end of a word
3. *Suffixes*, which appear at the end of a word

Each of these parts contributes to the meaning of a word. For example, *concurrent*, from *concurrent processing*, is actually a combination of two word parts, *con* (meaning *with*) and *current* (meaning *in progress*). So, *concurrent processing* means processing more than one thing at the same time—a large computer works on several jobs at one time.

You can add a suffix to *concurrent* to get *concurrently*. The *ly* on the end turns the word into an adverb, which describes how something is done; in this case, it describes how the processing is done. You could say, "A large computer can process several jobs *concurrently*." This means that the computer can do several jobs at the same time.

Tables 2.1, 2.2, and 2.3 list some of the most common Greek and Latin word parts used in English words and some more specialized word parts used in this chapter.

prefix
an addition at the
beginning of a word
that changes the
word's meaning

**Prefixes** A **prefix** is an addition at the beginning of a word that changes the word's meaning. Many prefixes serve similar functions. In this table, you will find prefixes that indicate *number*, *negation*, *time*, and *place* or *position* as well as other common prefixes. Look at the list of prefixes in Table 2.1. Notice the meaning and example word given for each prefix, and then write an example of your own in the box provided.

| Table 2.1 | Prefixes | | |
|-----------|----------|-----------|-----------|
| Number Prefixes | Meaning | Example 1 | Example 2 |
| mono- | one | monotonous | |
| uni- | one | unify | |
| bi- | two or twice | biweekly | |
| tri- | three | triangle | |
| quad- | four | quadratic | |
| multi- | many | multipurpose | |

| Table 2.1 *(continued)* | | | |
|---|---|---|---|
| **Number Prefixes** | **Meaning** | **Example 1** | **Example 2** |
| poly- | many | polygamy | |
| semi- | half, part | semicircle | |
| dec- | ten | decade | |
| **Negation or Negative Prefixes** | **Meaning** | **Example 1** | **Example 2** |
| ab- | away from, from | abnormal | |
| contra- | against | contradict | |
| de- | reverse, undo | deactivate | |
| dis- | apart from, reversal of | disapprove | |
| il- | not | illegible | |
| im- | not | immortal | |
| in- | not | incomplete | |
| un- | not | unimportant | |
| mal- | bad, wrong | malfunction | |
| mis- | wrong | mistake | |
| **Time Prefixes** | **Meaning** | **Example 1** | **Example 2** |
| post- | after, behind | postpone | |
| pre- | before | prefix | |
| proto- | first | prototype | |
| re- | again | rewrite | |
| **Place or Position Prefixes** | **Meaning** | **Example 1** | **Example 2** |
| circum- | around | circumference | |
| peri- | around | perimeter | |
| co- | with, together | cooperate | |
| col- | with, together | collaborate | |
| com- | with, together | communicate | |
| con- | with, together | connect | |
| sym- | with, together, similar | sympathetic | |
| syn- | with, together, similar | synonym | |
| en- | in, put into | enclose | |
| e- | out, from | evade | |

*(continued)*

| Table 2.1 (continued) | | | |
|---|---|---|---|
| **Place or Position Prefixes** | **Meaning** | **Example 1** | **Example 2** |
| ex- | out, from | expel | |
| inter- | between, among | international | |
| sub- | follow, under, below | submarine | |
| tele- | far off, distant | telepathy | |
| trans- | across, over | transfer | |
| **Other Common Prefixes** | **Meaning** | **Example 1** | **Example 2** |
| bene- | good, well | benefit | |
| hyper- | over, excessive | hyperactive | |
| micro- | very small or basic | microscope | |
| pro- | in favor of, forward | progress | |

**Exercise 11**

## Understand Words Using Prefixes

Using Table 2.1 as well as context, define each italicized word in the following sentences. Then identify the prefix and its meaning. The first one has been done for you.

1. By donating millions of dollars to charities, Bill Gates is hoping to be remembered as a *beneficent* man.

   *Beneficent*: __doing good (charitable)__

   Prefix and its meaning: __bene, "good"__

2. The *binary* number system uses two symbols, the digits 0 and 1.

   *Binary*: _____

   Prefix and its meaning: _____

3. Software programs make it possible to *compose* music on the computer without even playing an instrument.

   *Compose*: _____

   Prefix and its meaning: _____

4. If you make an error on the computer, you can *delete* it, so documents are really very easy to correct.

   *Delete*: _____

   Prefix and its meaning: _____

5. *Hypermedia* is an exciting new combination of text, numbers, music, sound, and visuals.

   *Hypermedia:* _____

   Prefix and its meaning: _____

6. Computerized programs for translating languages are very likely to *misinterpret* the meanings of some words.

   *Misinterpret:* _____

   Prefix and its meaning: _____

7. Using *multimedia* presentations in the classroom really helps the lessons come alive for the students.

   *Multimedia:* _____

   Prefix and its meaning: _____

8. Because they are not limited to black and white images, *polychromatic* screens are especially important for visual artists.

   *Polychromatic:* _____

   Prefix and its meaning: _____

9. Today computer *synthesizers* are used to put the sounds of many instruments together to get the effect the composer wants.

   *Synthesizers:* _____

   Prefix and its meaning: _____

10. *Telecommunication* through computers could well be one of the most important ways we link up with the outside world in the future.

    *Telecommunication:* _____

    Prefix and its meaning: _____

© 2013 Wadsworth, Cengage Learning

**root**
the core part of a word to which prefixes and suffixes may be added

**Roots** The **root** is the core part of a word. It provides the essential meaning that prefixes and suffixes modify. Look at the list of roots in Table 2.2. Notice the meaning and example word given for each root, and then write an example of your own in the box provided.

## Table 2.2   Roots

| Root | Meaning | Example 1 | Example 2 |
| --- | --- | --- | --- |
| auto | self-propelled, acting from within | automobile | |
| bio | life | biology | |
| cede, ceed | go | proceed | |
| cept | receive | intercept | |
| chrom | color | monochromatic | |
| chron | time | chronicle | |
| cogi, cogni | think, know | recognize | |
| cyber | having to do with computers | cyberspace | |
| data | numerical information in the form a computer can read | data processing | |
| digit | a single Arabic numeral, such as 1, or 2, or 0, or 3 | digital clock | |
| duct | lead | conduct | |
| equi | equal | equidistant | |
| gen | kinds, types | generalization | |
| homo | same | homogeneous | |
| log[y] | study of, reason, thought | psychology | |
| mit, mis | let go, send | missile | |
| mort | death | mortality | |
| neuro | nerve | neurosis | |
| phobia | fear | arachnophobia | |
| port | harbor (a place to come to), having to do with carry | portable | |
| psych | mind, soul | psychological | |
| sequi, seque | follow | sequence | |
| vers | turn | reverse | |
| vid, vis | see | vision | |

## Exercise 12   Understand Words Using Roots and Prefixes

Using Tables 2.1 and 2.2, on prefixes and roots, as well as the context, define each italicized word in the following sentences. Then identify the word part and its meaning. The first one has been done for you.

1. *Automated* factories require very little human input; instead they use robots for the assembly-line jobs, and computers for keeping inventory and taking care of the machines.

   *Automated:* **Automated means something that works with little human input.**

   Word part and its meaning: **auto, "acting from within" or "self-propelled"**

2. Online *databases* that give you access to updated encyclopedias or university libraries are a rich source of information when you are doing research.

   *Databases:* _____

   _____

   Word part and its meaning: _____

   _____

3. Before information can be input into a computer, it must be in a *digital* form.

   *Digital:* _____

   Word part and its meaning: _____

4. You have to be careful not to buy computer software that is *incompatible* with your specific computer system. You cannot use Macintosh software on an IBM computer.

   *Incompatible:* _____

   Word part and its meaning: _____

5. The *Internet* is an incredible resource that millions of people use to connect with each other and with a vast quantity of information.

   *Internet:* _____

   Word part and its meaning: _____

6. Keyboards, printers, and monitors are essential computer *peripherals*. Without them, we would not be able to do much with the computer itself.

   *Peripherals:* _____

   _____

   Word part and its meaning: _____

7. The beginning of the twenty-first century is going to see incredibly fast technological advances. It is not a good time to be *technophobic*.

   *Technophobic:* _____

   Word part and its meaning: _____

8. Early computers that could "speak" only did so in *monotone* so they sounded very strange.

   *Monotone*: _____

   Word part and its meaning: _____

9. *Sociologists* are very interested in analyzing the impact of computers on social interactions and on society in general.

   *Sociologists*: _____

   Word part and its meaning: _____

10. *Portable* laptop computers have become increasingly popular with people who frequently need to travel and work.

    *Portable*: _____

    Word part and its meaning: _____

**suffix**
an addition to the end of a word that often indicates the part of speech

**part of speech**
designation of the function of a word— that is, noun, verb, adjective, adverb

**verb**
a word that usually indicates action, but some verbs refer to states or conditions (for example, *to be* or *to seem*)

**noun**
a word that names a person, place, thing, emotion, or idea

**adjective**
a word that modifies or describes a noun; it usually answers questions such as "What kind?" or "How many?"

**adverb**
a word that describes how, when, or where an action occurs

## SUFFIXES AND PARTS OF SPEECH

**Suffixes**  A **suffix** is the ending of a word. Suffixes frequently tell us what **part of speech** the word is—that is, whether it is a noun, a verb, an adjective, or an adverb. Parts of speech tell you how words work in a sentence. Dictionaries identify the part of speech for a word and each of the word's various forms. For example, consider the word *conspire*; which means to secretly plan to commit a crime or do something evil. It has many forms, and each is used in a different way, depending on its function in a sentence:

- *To conspire* is a **verb**. *The students* conspired *against their teacher.* (It tells you what the students *did.*)

- *Conspiracy* is a **noun**. *There was a* conspiracy *to overthrow the president.* (It tells you *what* something is.)

- *Conspirator* is another noun, meaning someone who conspires. *The police estimated that there were at least four* conspirators *involved in the crime.* (It tells you *what* or *who* someone is.)

- *Conspiratorial* is an **adjective**. *The atmosphere in the room was* conspiratorial. (It *describes* something for you.)

- *Conspiratorially* is an **adverb**. *The boys discussed their plans* conspiratorially *in the bathroom.* (It tells you *how* the boys discussed their plans.)

Look at the list of suffixes in Table 2.3. Notice the meaning and example given for each suffix, and then write an example of your own in the box provided.

## Table 2.3   Suffixes

| Noun suffixes | Meaning | Example 1 | Example 2 |
|---|---|---|---|
| -or, -er, -ist, -ee, -ian | a person | conspirator | |
| | | teacher | |
| | | futurist | |
| | | referee | |
| | | physician | |
| -acy | an act, form of government | conspiracy | |
| | | democracy | |
| -ance, -ation, -tion, -sion, -ment | an act, a state, a condition | attendance | |
| | | computation | |
| | | restriction | |
| | | tension | |
| | | resentment | |
| -ism | a belief, form of government | socialism | |
| -ship, -hood, -ness | having to do with, referring to | relationship | |
| | | neighborhood | |
| | | friendliness | |
| **Adjective suffixes** | | | |
| -able, -ible, -al, -ic, -ing, -ive, -ous, -orial, -ant, -an | having a characteristic | reliable | |
| | | responsible | |
| | | practical | |
| | | antagonistic | |
| | | insulting | |
| | | inventive | |
| | | serious | |
| | | dictatorial | |
| | | hesitant | |
| | | authoritarian | |
| **Adverb suffixes** | | | |
| -ly | describes how something is done (sometimes added to the endings of adjectives) | efficiently responsibly insultingly | |

Exercise 13

## Understand Words Using Suffixes

Read the following two paragraphs from Beekman's *Computer Confluence*. Circle all the words with suffixes you recognize. Then list ten of those words in the space provided and identify the part of speech of each. Two have been done for you.

dossiers
files

1  In George Orwell's *1984*, (information) about every citizen was stored in a (massive) database controlled by the ever-vigilant Big Brother. As it turns out, this kind of central computer is no longer necessary for producing computerized dossiers of private citizens. With networked computers it's easy to compile profiles by combining information from different database files. As long as the files share a single unique field, like Social Security number, record matching is trivial and quick. And when database information is combined, the whole is often far greater than the sum of its parts.

2      Sometimes the results are beneficial. Record matching is used by government enforcement agencies to locate criminals ranging from tax evaders to mass murderers. Because credit bureaus collect data about us, we can use credit cards to borrow money wherever we go. But these benefits come with at least three problems:

- *Data errors are common.* A study of 1,500 reports from the three big credit bureaus found errors in 43 percent of the files.
- *Data can become nearly immortal.* Because files are commonly sold and copied, it's impossible to delete or correct erroneous records with absolute certainty.
- *Data aren't secure.* A *Business Week* reporter demonstrated this in 1989 by using his computer to obtain then Vice President Dan Quayle's credit report. Had he been a skilled criminal, he might have been able to change that report.

(***Beekman, Computer Confluence***)

| Word | Part of Speech |
|---|---|
| 1. information | noun |
| 2. massive | adjective |
| 3. | |
| 4. | |
| 5. | |
| 6. | |
| 7. | |
| 8. | |
| 9. | |
| 10. | |

**Exercise 14**

## Word Parts

Based on the reading in Exercise 13, define each italicized word, using the word part and context clues. Then identify the word part and its meaning.

1. With networked computers it's easy to *compile* profiles combining information from different database files. (par. 1)

   *Compile*: _____

   Word part and its meaning: _____

2. Sometimes the results are *beneficial*. Record matching is used by government enforcement agencies to locate criminals ranging from tax evaders to mass murderers. Because credit bureaus collect data about us, we can use credit cards to borrow money wherever we go. But these *benefits* come with at least three problems: (par. 2)

   *Beneficial*: _____

   Word part and its meaning: _____

3. *Benefit*: _____

   Word part and its meaning: _____

4. Data can become nearly *immortal*. Because files are commonly sold and copied, it's impossible to delete or correct erroneous records with absolute certainty. (par. 2)

   *Immortal*: _____

   Word part and its meaning: _____

## THE DICTIONARY

As a reader and as a student, you will find that the dictionary is a valuable tool to use when you don't understand a word. However, before you go to the dictionary, ask yourself these questions.

- Is it essential to understand the exact meaning of the word to understand the reading? You should consider your purpose as a reader: Do you need to understand the term completely because you will be tested on it or because you need it for your work?
- Is the word important? Is it key to understanding the subject or material you are reading?
- Have you tried to figure out the meaning from the context clues and from using what you know about word parts, but you are still not sure about the meaning?

If you answered "yes" to all three of these questions, then go to the dictionary.

**Parts of a Dictionary Entry** In your reading about computer science, you may encounter sentences like this:

> Email can be a dangerous time bomb because litigators argue that, more than any other kind of written communication, email reflects the real, unedited thoughts of the writer. This candid form of corporate communication increasingly has provided the most incriminating evidence used against companies in litigation.

In the first sentence, you find the word *litigators*. When you look it up in the dictionary (*American Heritage Talking Dictionary*, CD-ROM, 1998), you notice that *litigator* doesn't appear as an independent entry. So you will have to find another form of the word—in this case, by dropping the suffix to get *litigate*.

Notice that the dictionary entry gives you some very specific information. There are many different types of dictionaries, including books, online applications, and CD-ROMs. Many digital dictionaries have audio portions to help you with the pronunciation of the word. With some variations, good dictionaries should provide the following information:

Source: *American Heritage Dictionary of the English Language*, 3d ed., Talking Dictionary CD (Boston: Houghton Mifflin, 1998). Learning Company Properties © 1995 by Inso Corporation.

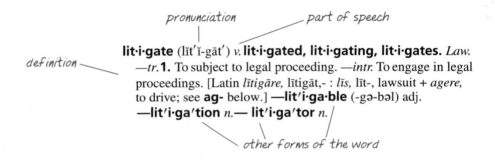

- Pronunciation (in parentheses after the word).
- Part of speech (after each form given for the word). Notice how the suffixes work in helping you understand the part of speech.
- Definition(s)—usually numbered. Often there is more than one meaning for a word. The dictionary shows this by giving additional definitions using both numbers and letters (for example, *1a* and *1b*).
- Other forms of the word.
- Origins of the word (in brackets after the definition). Frequently, you will find explanations of the Latin or Greek word parts that form the word.
- Examples of how the word has been used. Some dictionaries provide a quotation in which the word has been used by a famous author. Some simply include a sentence that illustrates how to use the word.

Altogether, there are four forms of *litigate* in the dictionary:

1. *litigate* is the base form of the word, and it is a verb.
2. *litigable* has the suffix *-able*, which forms the adjective meaning "can be litigated."

3. *litigation* has the suffix *-tion*, which forms the noun meaning "the act of litigating."
4. *litigator* has the suffix *-or*, which forms the noun meaning "someone who litigates."

**Exercise 15**

## Understand Dictionary Entries

Look at the following dictionary entries for two additional words, and answer the questions.

**can·did** (kan-dəd) *adj.* **1.** Free from prejudice; impartial. **2.** Characterized by openness and sincerity of expression; unreservedly straightforward: *In private, I gave them my candid opinion.* See Synonyms at **frank¹**. **3.** Not posed or rehearsed: *a candid snapshot.* —**can·did** *n.* An unposed informal photograph. [Latin *candidus*, glowing, white, pure, guileless, from *candere*, to shine. See **kand-** below.] —**can·did·ly** *adv.* —**can·did·ness** *n.*

*(American Heritage Dictionary)*

**in·crim·i·nate** (ĭn-krĭm'ə-nāt') *tr.v.* **in·crim·i·nat·ed, in·crim·i·nat·ing, in·crim·i·nates.** **1.** To accuse of a crime or other wrongful act. **2.** To cause to appear guilty of a crime or fault; implicate: *testimony that incriminated the defendant.* [Late Latin *incrīmināre, incrīmināt-* : Latin *in-*, causative pref.; see IN-²+ Latin *crīmen, crīmin-*, crime; see CRIME.] —**in·crim'i·na'tion** *n.* —**in·crim'i·na·to'ry** (-ne-tôr'ē, -tor'e) *adj.*

*(American Heritage Dictionary)*

1. What is the adverb form of *candid*? _____

2. What are the definitions of *candid* and what part of speech is it?

   _____

   _____

   _____

3. How many noun forms of *candid* are in this entry? _____

4. What are the definitions of *incriminate* and what part of speech is it?

   _____

5. What other forms of *incriminate* are provided? What part of speech is each?

   _____

   _____

**Choosing the Correct Meaning from the Dictionary** Dictionaries frequently list several meanings for words. Learning to use a dictionary and to find the definition for the word that you need as it is used in the context of your reading is a very important skill. If you are reading a college textbook, you should first look to see whether your text has a **glossary** at the end of the book. If it does, this is definitely the best place to look up the meanings of words that you don't know, because the definitions will correspond to the meanings of the words as they are used in the discipline you are studying. However, if your textbook does not come with a glossary of terms, you will need to use a dictionary.

Read the following sentence, taken from a computer science textbook, and think about the word *convey*.

> Companies may fail to convey the message that email, as a company conduit, is not private. (Capron, *Computers*)

When you look up the word *convey* in the dictionary, you cannot just pick the first definition that you find. You must look through all the definitions to find the one that matches the way your text uses the word. Study this dictionary entry:

**con·vey** (ken-vā') *tr.v.* **con·veyed, con·vey·ing, con·veys. 1.** To take or carry from one place to another; transport. **2.** To serve as a medium of transmission for; transmit: *wires that convey electricity.* **3.** To communicate or make known; impart: *"a look intended to convey sympathetic comprehension"* (Saki). **4.** *Law.* To transfer ownership of or title to. **5.** *Archaic.* To steal. [Middle English *conveien,* from Old French *conviār,* from Medieval Latin *conviare,* to escort: Latin *com-,* com- + *via,* way; see **wegh-** below.] —**con·vey' a·ble** *adj.*

*(American Heritage Dictionary)*

Note that *convey* has five definitions. The first definition has to do with transporting something from one place to another. The second has to do with serving as a medium for transmission. The third means to communicate or make known. The fourth refers to a legal transfer of ownership, and the fifth means to steal. Notice that the fourth and fifth definitions have italicized words in front of them. *Law* before the fourth definition gives the legal meaning of *convey. Archaic* before the fifth definition means that "to steal" is an old use of the word, and something written today would probably not be using that meaning. So which is the best definition for *convey* as it is used in the sentence?

> Companies may fail to *convey* the message that email, as a company conduit, is not private.

Clearly the only meaning from the list of definitions that works is the third, "to communicate or make known."

## Choose the Correct Dictionary Definitions

Read the following excerpt from a computer science textbook, paying special attention to the *underlined* words. Then find the correct definition for each underlined word using the dictionary definitions that follow. Write the definition and the part of speech (noun, verb, adjective, adverb) on the lines provided. As you do this exercise, take the time to look at the origins of the word (in brackets); you may notice some of the word parts that you learned earlier.

1   You have no privacy whatsoever. No privacy on the company email, that is. Your employer can snoop into messages you send or receive even if you think you erased them. You have only erased them from their <u>current</u> hard drive location; copies are still in the company computer files. In fact, most companies <u>archive</u> all such files on tape and store them for the foreseeable future. Companies may fail to convey the message that email, as a company <u>conduit</u>, is not private. Employees are often startled, after the fact, to discover that their messages have been invaded.

2       Furthermore, some people specialize in extracting deleted messages for use as evidence in court. Email can be a dangerous time bomb because litigators argue that, more than any other kind of written communication, email reflects the real, unedited thoughts of the writer. This candid form of corporate communication increasingly is providing the most incriminating evidence used against companies in litigation.

3       What to do? It is certainly <u>degrading</u> to have something you thought was private waved in front of you as evidence of <u>malingering</u>. As one computer expert put it, if nothing is private, just say so. Companies have begun doing exactly that. The company policy on email is—or should be—expressed in a clear, written document and routinely <u>disseminated</u> to all employees. However, even that step is probably insufficient. People tend to forget or get <u>complacent</u>. Reminders should be given through the usual company conduits—bulletin boards, posters, and so forth.

4       What about the email you send and receive at home—do you at least have privacy in your own home? Maybe not. You certainly cannot count on it if the computer of the party at the other end is in an office. Further, keep in mind that messages sent across the Internet hop from computer to computer, with (depending on the service used) the sender having little say about its route. There are many <u>vulnerable</u> spots along the way.

*(Capron, Computers)*

| Word | Definition | Part of Speech |
|---|---|---|
| 1. *Current*: | _____ | _____ |
| 2. *Archive*: | _____ | _____ |
| 3. *Conduit*: | _____ | _____ |
| 4. *Degrading*: | _____ | _____ |
| 5. *Malingering*: | _____ | _____ |
| 6. *Disseminated*: | _____ | _____ |
| 7. *Complacent*: | _____ | _____ |
| 8. *Vulnerable*: | _____ | _____ |

**ar·chive** (är' kīv') *n.* **1.** Often **archives**. A place or collection containing records, documents, or other materials of historical interest: *old land deeds in the municipal archives; the studio archives, a vast repository of silent-film prints and outtakes.* **2.** A repository for stored memories or information: *the archive of the mind.* [From French *archives,* from Latin *archīva,* from Greek *arkheia,* pl. of *arkheion,* town hall, from *arkhē,* government, from *arkhein,* to rule.] —**ar' chive'** *v.*

**com·pla·cent** (kəm-plā' sənt) *adj.* **1.** Contented to a fault; self-satisfied and unconcerned: *He had become complacent after years of success.* **2.** Eager to please; complaisant. [Latin *complacēns*, complacent-, present participle of *complacēre*, to please : *com-*, intensive pref.; see COM- + *placēre*, to please; see **plāk-¹** below.] —**com·pla'cent·ly** *adv.*

**con·duit** (kŏn'dōō-ĭt, -dĭt) *n.* **1.** A pipe or channel for conveying fluids, such as water. **2.** A tube or duct for enclosing electric wires or cable. **3.** A means by which something is transmitted: *an arms dealer who served as a conduit for intelligence data.* **4.** *Archaic.* A fountain. [Middle English, from Old French, from Medieval Latin *conductus*, from Latin, past participle of *cond cere*, to lead together. See CONDUCE.]

**cur·rent** (kûr'ənt, kur'-) *adj.* **1.** *Abbr.* **cur. a.** Belonging to the present time: *current events; current leaders.* **b.** Being in progress now: *current negotiations.* **2.** Passing from one to another; circulating: *current bills* and *coins.* **3.** Prevalent, especially at the present time: *current fashions.* See Synonyms at **prevailing. 4.** Running; flowing. —**cur·rent** *n.* **1.** A steady, smooth onward movement: *a current of air from a fan; a current of spoken words.* See Synonyms at **flow. 2.** The part of a body of liquid or gas that has a continuous onward movement: *rowed out into the river's swift current.* **3.** A general tendency, movement, or course. See Synonyms at **tendency. 4.** *Symbol* **i, I** *Electricity.* **a.** A flow of electric charge. **b.** The amount of electric charge flowing past a specified circuit point per unit time. [Middle English *curraunt*, from Old French *corant*, present participle of *courre*, to run, from Latin *currere*. See **kers-** below.] —**cur′rent·ly** *adv.* —**cur'rent·ness** *n.*

**de·grade** (dĭ-grād') *tr.v.* **de·grad·ed, de·grad·ing, de·grades. 1.** To reduce in grade, rank, or status; demote. **2.** To lower in dignity; dishonor or disgrace: *a scandal that degraded the participants.* **3.** To lower in moral or intellectual character; debase. **4.** To reduce in worth or value: *degrade a currency.* **5.** To impair in physical structure or function. **6.** *Geology.* To lower or wear by erosion or weathering. **7.** To cause (an organic compound) to undergo degradation. [Middle English *degraden*, from Old French *degrader*, from Late Latin *dēgradāre* : Latin *dē-*, de- + Latin *gradus*, step; see **ghredh-** below.] —**de·grad'er** *n.*

**de·grad·ing** (dĭ-grā'dĭng) *adj.* Tending or intended to degrade: *"There is nothing so degrading as the constant anxiety about one's means of livelihood"* (W. Somerset Maugham). —**de·grad'ing·ly** *adv.*

**dis·sem·i·nate** (dĭ-sĕm'ə-nāt') *v.* **dis·sem·i·nat·ed, dis·sem·i·nat·ing, dis·sem·i·nates.** —*tr.* **1.** To scatter widely, as in sowing seed. **2.** To spread abroad; promulgate: *disseminate information.* —*intr.* To become diffused; spread. [Latin *dissēmināre*, *dissēmināt-* : *dis-*, dis- + *sēmināre*, to sow (from *sēmen*, *sēmin-*, seed; see **sē-** below).] —**dis·sem′i·na′tion** *n.* —**dis·sem'i·na'tor** *n.*

**dis·sem·i·nat·ed** (dĭ-sĕm'ə-nā'tĭd) *adj.* Spread over a large area of a body, a tissue, or an organ.

**ma·lin·ger** (mə-lĭng'gər) *intr.v.* **ma·lin·gered, ma·lin·ger·ing, ma·lin·gers.** To feign illness or other incapacity in order to avoid duty or work. [From French *malingre*, sickly.] —**ma·lin'ger·er** *n.*

**vul·ner·a·ble** (vŭl'nər-ə-bəl) *adj.* **1. a.** Susceptible to physical injury. **b.** Susceptible to attack: *"We are vulnerable both by water and land, without either fleet or army"* (Alexander Hamilton). **c.** Open to censure or criticism; assailable. **2. a.** Liable to succumb, as to persuasion or temptation. **b.** *Games.* In a position to receive greater penalties or bonuses as a result of having won one game of a rubber. Used of bridge partners. [Late Latin *vulnerābilis*, wounding, from Latin *vulnerāre*, to wound, from *vulnus*, vulner-, wound. See **welə-** below.] —**vul'ner·a·bil'i·ty** or **vul'ner·a·ble·ness** *n.*—**vul'ner·a·bly** *adv.*

(*American Heritage Dictionary*)

**Reading 3**

ethics
standards of right
and wrong

# The Robot Revolution*

— GEORGE BEEKMAN AND BEN BEEKMAN

**TEXT BOOK** Artificial intelligence, or AI, is a branch of computer science and engineering that deals with "smart" machines—machines that demonstrate human-like abilities and behaviors. Though researchers disagree about how intelligent robots will become in the future, it is clear that this technology is advancing rapidly. George Beekman and Ben Beekman begin this selection from their textbook, *Tomorrow's Technology and You*, by quoting the Three Laws of Robotics proposed by the famous science fiction writer, Isaac Asimov. Asimov first expressed these rules in the early 1940s to show how robots in his stories should behave. These laws have since been cited in many discussions about robots, smart machines, and ethics.

---

*First:* A robot may not injure a human being, or, through inaction, allow a human being to come to harm.

*Second:* A robot must obey the orders given it by human beings, except where such orders would conflict with the First Law.

*Third:* A robot must protect its own existence as long as such protection does not conflict with the First or Second Law.

—ISAAC ASIMOV'S THREE LAWS OF ROBOTICS

1   Nowhere are AI technologies more visible than in the field of robotics. Vision, hearing, pattern recognition, knowledge engineering, expert decision making, natural language understanding, speech—they all come together in today's robots.

## WHAT IS A ROBOT?

2   The term *robot* (from the root word *robota*, the Czech word for "forced labor") first appeared in a 1923 play called *R.U.R.* (for Rossum's Universal Robots) by Czech playwright Karel Capek. Capek's robots were intelligent machines that could see, hear, touch, move, and exercise judgment based on common sense. But these powerful machines eventually rebelled against their human creators, just as hundreds of fictional robots have done in succeeding decades. Today movies, TV, and books are full of imaginary robots, both good and evil.

---

*Beekman, George, and Beekman, Ben. TOMORROW'S TECHNOLOGY AND YOU, COMPLETE, 9th Edition, © 2010, pp. 570, 572, 573. Reprinted by permission of Pearson Education, Inc., Upper Saddle River, NJ.

3    As exotic as they might seem, robots are similar to other kinds of computer technology people use every day. While a typical computer performs mental tasks, a robot is a computer-controlled machine designed to perform specific manual tasks. A robot's central processor might be a microprocessor embedded in the robot's shell, or it might be a supervisory computer that controls the robot from a distance. In any case, the processor is functionally identical to the processor found in a PC, a workstation, or a mainframe computer.

**microprocessor**
a single computer chip which controls the functioning of an electronic circuit

molotovcoketail/iStockphoto.com

4    The most important hardware differences between robots and other computers are the input and output peripherals. Instead of sending output to a screen or a printer, a robot sends commands to joints, arms, and other moving parts. The first robots had no corresponding input devices to monitor their movements and the surrounding environment. They were effectively deaf, blind, and in some cases dangerous—at least one Japanese worker was killed by an early sightless robot. Most modern robots include input sensors. These sensing devices enable robots to correct or modify their actions based on feedback from the outside world.

**sensors**
devices that detect signals

**infrared light**
light waves that humans cannot see, but which are able to produce a reaction with certain elements

5    Industrial robots seldom have the human-inspired anatomy of Hollywood's science fiction robots. Instead, they're designed to accomplish particular tasks in the best possible way. Robots can be designed to see infrared light, rotate joints 360 degrees, and do other things that aren't possible for humans. On the other hand, robots are constrained by the limitations of AI software. The most sophisticated robot today can't tie a pair of shoelaces, understand the vocabulary of a three-year-old child, or consistently tell the difference between a cat and a dog.

## STEEL-COLLAR WORKERS

6    From a management point of view, robots offer several advantages:

- Obviously, many robots save labor costs. Robots are expensive to design, install, and program. But once they're operational, they can work 24 hours a day, 365 days a year, without vacations, strikes, sick leave, or coffee breaks.

- Robots can also improve quality and increase productivity. They're especially effective at doing repetitive jobs in which bored, tired people are prone to make errors and have accidents.

● Robots are ideal for jobs such as cleaning up hazardous waste and salvaging under-sea wreckage from downed planes—jobs that are dangerous, uncomfortable, or impossible for human workers.

7    For all these reasons, the robot population is exploding. Today hundreds of thousands of industrial robots do welding, part fitting, painting, and other repetitive tasks in facto-ries all over the world. In most automated factories, robots work alongside humans, but in some state-of-the-art factories, the only function of human workers is to monitor and repair robots. Robots aren't used just in factories. Robots also shear sheep in Australia, paint ship hulls in France, disarm land mines in the Persian Gulf, and perform precision hip operations and other surgery.

8    Commercial robots still can't compete with people for jobs that require exceptional perceptual or fine-motor skills. But robots in research labs suggest that a new genera-tion of more competitive robots is on the way. Honda's ASIMO is a humanoid robot that can walk, run, recognize gestures and faces, distinguish sounds, and display a variety of "intelligent" behaviors. In 2008, ASIMO conducted the Detroit Symphony Orchestra in a widely viewed public performance. Other researchers are taking a dif-ferent approach, using fleets of insect-sized robots to do jobs that larger robots can't easily do. The technologies used in these experimental robots will undoubtedly show up in a variety of machines, from automated servants for people with disabilities to flying robots for the military. One pioneering example: Wakamaru is a yellow, one-meter tall Japanese domestic robot designed to provide companionship for elderly and disabled people. It can recognize speech, connect to the Internet, and call for help if something is wrong.

**pioneering**
innovative;
first one to do
something

ASIMO conducts the Detroit Symphony Orchestra on May 14, 2008, in a performance of "The Impossible Dream" from *Man of La Mancha*. The orchestra members thought the robot was a little stiff, but otherwise surprisingly realistic.

AP Photo/Paul Sancya

9      The robot revolution isn't necessarily good news for people who earn their living doing manual labor. While it's true that many of the jobs robots do are boring, dirty, or dangerous, they're still jobs. The issues surrounding automation and worker displacement are complex, and they aren't limited to factories.

## AI IMPLICATIONS AND ETHICAL QUESTIONS

10     From the earliest days of AI, research has been accompanied by questions about the implications of the work. The very idea of intelligent machines is at the same time confusing, exciting, and frightening to many people. Even when they don't work very well, AI programs generate emotional responses in the people who use them. . . .

11     As it matures, AI technology finds its way out of the research lab and into the marketplace. A growing number of programs and products incorporate pattern recognition, expert systems, and other AI techniques. In the near future, we're likely to see more products with embedded AI, including intelligent word processors that can help writers turn rough drafts into polished prose or smart appliances that can recognize and obey their owners' spoken commands. We'll also see more distributed intelligence—AI concepts applied to networks rather than to individual computers.

**MIT**
Massachusetts
Institute of
Technology, an
important research
university that
specializes in
engineering and
design

12     Where will it all lead? Will intensive AI research result in computers capable of intelligent behavior outside narrow domains? Patrick Winston, director of MIT's Artificial Intelligence Laboratory, once said, "The interesting issue is not whether machines can be made smarter but if humans are smart enough to pull it off. A raccoon obviously can't make a machine as smart as a raccoon. I wonder if humans can."

**silicon**
a natural material that
is commonly used in
computer processors

13     Many AI researchers believe that sooner or later they will pull it off. Some think artificial intelligence is the natural culmination of the evolutionary process—that the next intelligent life-form on Earth will be based on silicon rather than the carbon that is the basis of human life. Danny Hillis, supercomputer designer and cofounder of Applied Minds, Metaweb, and The Long Now Foundation, exemplifies this point of view when he says, "We are not evolution's ultimate product. There's something coming after us, and I imagine it is something wonderful. But we may never be able to comprehend it, any more than a caterpillar can comprehend turning into a butterfly." . . .

14     If smarter-than-human beings come to pass, how will they relate to the less intelligent humans that surround them? And how will humans handle the change? . . . This kind of thinking isn't easy—it goes to the heart of human values and forces us to look at our place in the universe.

## Exercise 17

### Work with Words

Use context clues, dictionary skills, and your knowledge of word parts to write a definition for each of the following italicized words. The paragraph number is provided in case you want to go back to check the context.

1. But these powerful machines eventually rebelled against their human creators, just as hundreds of fictional robots have done in *succeeding* decades. (par. 2)

   *succeeding:* _____

2. While a typical computer performs mental tasks, a robot is a computer-controlled machine designed to perform specific *manual* tasks. (par. 3)

   *manual*: _____

3. The first robots had no *corresponding* input devices to monitor their movements and the surrounding environment. (par. 4)

   *corresponding*: _____

4. On the other hand, robots are *constrained* by the limitations of AI software. (par. 5)

   *constrained*: _____

5. They're especially effective at doing repetitive jobs in which bored, tired people are *prone* to make errors and have accidents. (par. 6)

   *prone*: _____

6. Robots also shear sheep in Australia, paint ship hulls in France, *disarm* land mines in the Persian Gulf, and perform precision hip operations and other surgery. (par. 7)

   *disarm*: _____

7. In the near future, we're likely to see more products with embedded AI, including intelligent word processors that can help writers turn rough drafts into polished *prose* or smart appliances that can recognize and obey their owners' spoken commands. (par. 11)

   *prose*: _____

8. Will intensive AI research result in computers capable of intelligent behavior outside narrow *domains*? (par. 12)

   *domains*: _____

9. Some think artificial intelligence is the natural *culmination* of the evolutionary process—that the next intelligent life-form on Earth will be based on silicon rather than the carbon that is the basis of human life. (par. 13)

   *culmination*: _____

10. Danny Hillis, supercomputer designer and *cofounder* of Applied Minds, Metaweb, and The Long Now Foundation, exemplifies this point of view when he says, "We are not evolution's ultimate product." (par. 13)

    *cofounder*: _____

    _____

**Exercise 18**

## Check Your Understanding

Based on Reading 3, choose the best answer to each of the following multiple-choice questions.

1. What did the root of the word *robot* originally mean?
   a. intelligent machine
   b. forced labor
   c. microprocessor

2. In the beginning, robots could be dangerous because
   a. the commands did not function properly and the wrong part would sometimes move.
   b. they did not have the ability to change their actions based on input from the environment.
   c. they were designed to replace human workers.

3. AI software
   a. is the program that determines what a robot can do.
   b. has made it possible for a robot to tie a person's shoelaces.
   c. is designed to be as similar to human intelligence as possible.

4. Robots can save companies money because
   a. they do not cost very much to design, install, and program.
   b. they can work all the time without a break.
   c. they can improve a company's product.

5. Today, most of the jobs robots perform involve
   a. intelligence.
   b. danger.
   c. repetition.

6. ASIMO is an example of
   a. a new generation of robot that is more human-like.
   b. an insect-sized robot.
   c. a robot designed for the music industry.

7. Which of the following statements would the authors agree with?
   a. Robots should be developed rapidly because managers want more workers who complain less.
   b. Robots should be monitored so that they do not develop the capacity to think and make their own decisions.
   c. The increasing number of robots in the workplace is a concern because of worker displacement.

8. According to the article, in the future robots will be capable of distributed intelligence. Distributed intelligence is the application of AI
   a. to create smart appliances.
   b. to networks of computers.
   c. in the marketplace.

9. Researchers such as Danny Hillis believe that
   a. humans do not want robots to be too intelligent.
   b. humans are not smart enough to create truly intelligent robots.
   c. robots will move beyond humans some day.

10. The authors believe that
   a. there are many serious questions about the role robots should play in our society.
   b. the ability of robots to exceed our intelligence is not something we need to worry about now.
   c. in the future, we will be able to co-exist with robots as if they are our brothers and sisters.

**Exercise 19**

### Reflect and Write

Think about what you read in Reading 3 and what you already know about artificial intelligence and robots. Answer the following questions, and prepare to discuss them with your classmates.

1. In your opinion, what are the two greatest benefits and dangers of robots?

_____

_____

_____

_____

_____

_____

2. What is an example of a robot that you would you like to see developed? Why?

_____

_____

_____

_____

_____

3. Read a short story that includes robots or another type of artificial intelligence. Isaac Asimov wrote many stories about robots. Or, watch a film about robots or artificial intelligence. Some popular films include *Blade Runner* (1982), *A.I. Artificial Intelligence* (2001), and *I, Robot* (2004). After you read the story or watch the film, write a one- or two-paragraph summary. Then write a one-paragraph response to the story, describing your reaction and analysis. Did the robots follow Asimov's laws? Did the story connect with other ideas in this reading? As an alternative, write your own science fiction story about AI or robots.

# Reader's Tip:
# Learn Specialized Vocabulary
# with Textbook Aids

Most academic disciplines have specialized vocabularies, and when you take courses in math, sociology, psychology, biology, business, computer science, and others, you will need to learn terms that are unique to those subjects. Textbooks usually explain these special terms when they are introduced. They also contain other aids for learning them.

- The use of **boldface** or *italics* to emphasize specialized or important words
- Definitions of specialized words in the margins
- Key Words and Concepts sections, often at the ends of chapters
- Vocabulary questions in Chapter Reviews
- Glossaries at the ends of chapters or the back of the book

**boldface**
a typeface that is extra wide and dark for emphasis

**italics**
a typeface that is sloped to the right for emphasis

Notice that this textbook, *A Community of Readers*, highlights reading skill terms by printing them in boldface, defining them in the text, repeating them with definitions in the margins, and reminding you about them in the Chapter Review.

When you come across a term in your reading that is crucial for understanding a chapter or a reading assignment, be sure to look in the text itself for the author's definition or explanation. If, after checking the vocabulary aids in your textbook, you still can't find the meaning of a new term, you may have to look it up in a dictionary.

To help you learn specialized terms, it is a good idea to keep an ongoing list of them in your notebook. You will eventually figure out a system that works for you, but when you make your list or start a file of three-by-five cards, you might want to use a format like this:

Word: **databases**

*Appropriate definition for computer science*: computerized information storage

*Sentence*: Libraries, banks, and other institutions use databases to store information.

*Your sentence*: I wonder if I need to learn how to use database software in order to increase my chances of getting a good job?

**Exercise 20**   Recognize Textbook Vocabulary Aids

Review two textbooks that you are using this semester or have used in the past. What kinds of vocabulary aids do they have?

| Textbook Title | Vocabulary Aids | | |
|---|---|---|---|
| 1. _____ | _____ | _____ | _____ |
| 2. _____ | _____ | _____ | _____ |

> **Exercise 21**	Develop Your System for Learning
> Specialized Vocabulary
>
> Choose ten words that you think are important to learn from *A Community of Readers* or from another textbook. On a separate piece of paper or on three-by-five cards, write each word, its appropriate definition, the original sentence in which it appeared, and your own sentence using the word. Follow the model in the Reader's Tip on page 82.

## Write About It

Write the answers to the following questions on a separate piece of paper.

1.	Think about the different settings in which technology is used: for example, home, school, business, military, or government. List three to five new ways you imagine computers and other forms of technology will be used in our lives ten years from now.

2.	Using your list, write a short essay titled "Technology in Our Future." Discuss how these new forms of technology will affect our lives.

# Chapter Review

| Put It Together: Working with Words | |
|---|---|
| **Skills and Concepts** | **Explanation** |
| **Context** (see pages 47–48) | The sentence or paragraph in which the word appears |
| **Context Clues** • Definition and Synonym Clue (see page 48) | A clue that provides a definition or gives a synonym (same or similar meaning) |
| • Example Clue (see pages 50–51) | A clue that uses examples |
| • General Information Clue (see pages 51–52) | A clue that uses surrounding information in sentence or paragraph |
| • Contrast Clue (see pages 52–53) | A clue that contrasts the word with another word or concept |

## Put It Together: Working with Words

| Skills and Concepts | Explanation |
|---|---|
| **Word Parts**<br>(see pages 60–69)<br>• Prefix<br>(see pages 60–63)<br>• Root<br>(see pages 63–66)<br>• Suffix<br>(see pages 66–69) | An addition at the beginning of the word that changes the word's meaning<br><br>The core part of the word to which prefixes and suffixes are added<br><br>A word ending that usually indicates its part of speech |
| **Four Main Parts of Speech**<br>(see page 66)<br>• Verb<br>• Noun<br>• Adjective<br>• Adverb | <br><br>A word that indicates an action, state, or condition<br>A word that indicates a person, place, thing, emotion, or idea<br>A word that describes or modifies a noun<br>A word that tells how, when, or where the action takes place |
| **Dictionary Skills**<br>(see pages 69–75) | • Knowing when to look up a word in the dictionary<br>• Understanding dictionary entries<br>• Identifying the appropriate definition for the context |
| **Reader's Tip: Learn Specialized Vocabulary with Textbook Aids**<br>(see pages 82–83) | Textbooks usually explain new terms when they are introduced. They may also emphasize important vocabulary by<br>• using **boldface type** or *italics*<br>• inserting definitions in the margins<br>• including Key Words and Concepts sections<br>• including vocabulary questions in the Chapter Reviews<br>• providing glossaries at the end of each chapter or the back of the book |

## CRITICAL REFLECTIONS IN THE CLASSROOM COMMUNITY

Answer the following questions, and prepare to discuss them with your classmates.

1. What is the *one* technological invention that you could not live without? Explain your thoughts.

   _____

   _____

   _____

2. Which technology or technologies have a negative impact on your life or on our society? Explain your thoughts.

   _____

   _____

   _____

 ## WORK THE WEB

A site devoted to technology, HowStuffWorks, explores in depth how a number of new and old technologies actually function. With a spirit of curiosity and attention to new vocabulary, complete the following tasks.

Do a new search to find the link to HowStuffWorks.

1. Preview the home page of HowStuffWorks.

2. After previewing the HowStuffWorks home page, notice a bar with a number of categories. Choose either Auto, Science, or Tech, whichever you are most interested in, and find one particular technology you would like to learn about. (Avoid going to the many shopping links.) You may want to surf the website for several minutes before choosing an article because each HowStuffWorks article will give several additional recommendations at the bottom of the page. After you have identified the article you would like to read, choose the *Print* menu option so you won't be too distracted by the many advertisements. Read about how the technology you have chosen works. Using your vocabulary skills—context clues, word parts, and dictionary usage—choose five new words that are important to your understanding of this technology. On a piece of paper, identify which technology you chose, and write down at least five new words you learned and their definitions. Also provide the sentences in which they were written on the website.

**Name** _____ **Date** _____

# Looking into Your Brain*

— Mauricio Medina

**In the following reading, Mauricio Medina summarizes some of the recent technological advances in brain research. He also poses possible problems in using this technology. As you read, notice that most of the vocabulary is explained in the reading itself.**

1    In the last decade of the twentieth century, the science of the brain, also known as neuroscience, advanced enormously. New developments in scanning technology, such as MRI (magnetic resonance imaging), have allowed scientists to "see" the inner workings of the living brain in ways never before imaginable. Being able to look into people's brains has given neuroscientists a better understanding of many mental disorders and diseases and allowed for breakthroughs in the treatment of psychiatric and neurological problems. With these impressive accomplishments, research and development in neuroscience is now moving beyond the prevention and treatment of disease and expanding into other <u>realms</u> of our public and private lives. Using new types of MRI scans, neuroscientists are learning how to "read" people's minds. Through this technology, they can get a lot of information about you, including information about your personality, your behavior, and even your history. And, whether you like it or not, there are many reasons why people out there would like to get that information.

2    This powerful technology brings up many questions. What will the moral, legal, and social consequences of this technology be? What should be considered an invasion of privacy? Who should be allowed to look into our brains, and for what reasons? Who will have access to this technology, and what will it cost? Will this kind of information be usable in court? Will this technology be used in job interviews, pre-marital counseling, or college applications? Society as a whole needs to start thinking about the moral aspects of these technologies. We need to be informed and involved in decisions about what is acceptable and what is not acceptable.

## ETHICAL ISSUES

3    When technology advances so rapidly, it takes time for <u>ethical</u> questions and concerns to catch up. In 2006, an organized group of philosophers, neuroscientists, lawyers, and psychologists formed the Neuroethics Society. This new field—neuroethics—can inform the discussion about ethical and philosophical <u>dilemmas</u> that the advances in neuroscience have created. The mission of the Neuroethics Society is "to promote the development and responsible application of neuroscience through better understanding of its capabilities and its consequences."[1] These neuroethicists can help enlighten the public and promote serious, thoughtful discussions about the applications of neuroscience in our society. In this way, all of us who will be affected by this technology will be able to have access to information about it, and hopefully have a say about it.

4    How will the new advances in brain scanning technology affect the average person? According to Judy Illes, a neuropsychologist at Stanford University, "It's not so futuristic to imagine an employer able to test for who is a good team player, who a leader or a follower."[2] There are plenty of private and government employers that already

© 2013 Wadsworth, Cengage Learning

*"Looking Into Your Brain" by Mauricio Medina. Reprinted by permission of the author.

use psychological tests on potential employees to find out what is going on inside their head. Brain-scanning techniques can give much more detailed information and have the potential for being much more accurate as well as being much more **invasive**. Employers could get a deeper "look" at potential employees with an MRI than they could in a normal job interview. By interpreting images of your brain, they could make assumptions about your intelligence, your personality, your behavior, your math skills, your honesty, and whether you smoked marijuana in high school. On the basis of this information they could decide which candidate to hire and for what job. Is scanning someone's brain really a good way to find out if someone is right for a job? Is there something undemocratic about this type of judging people on the basis of what their brain looks like instead of on the basis of their potential? How will these scans affect equal opportunity?

**invasive**
limiting one's privacy

## HOW MRI SCANS WORK

5    How *do* neuroscientists go about "reading" someone's brain? Neuroscientists use a type of magnetic resonance imaging, or MRI. During an MRI, a person lies flat and still and is placed inside of a tube-like machine that scans the targeted body part. These scans produce detailed images of the body including soft <u>tissue</u> such as the brain. Neuroscientists can therefore see different parts of the brain without having to cut open the skull. With these scans they can also see different levels of oxygen in different parts of the brain, showing which parts of the brain are active. That is all that they can actually see; the rest is interpretation. MRI researcher John Dylan Haynes makes it sound easier than it really is: "Every thought is associated with a characteristic pattern of activation in the brain. By training a computer to recognize these patterns, it becomes possible to read a person's thoughts from patterns of <u>cerebral</u> activity. In this way a person's brain activity can betray their thoughts and emotions, can give clues whether they are lying, or can even predict what they are about to do."[3] It is important to understand how this technology works to realize that it is not perfect. It is not as simple as just "reading your mind," even though many corporations and researchers are trying to make it seem that way.

## THE TRUTH ABOUT LIE DETECTION

6    One application of new brain-scanning technologies is in the field of lie-detection. Two enthusiastic corporations are confident that new advances in brain imaging will allow them to tell if people are telling the truth with **inarguable** accuracy. These companies are already offering commercial services and promising that their test should hold up in court, unlike other lie-detecting tests. Polygraphs are the classic "lie-detecting" machines. They measure body responses such as rises in blood pressure and sweating that might indicate a person is not telling the truth. While polygraphs have been much used by the police, the government, and even talk show hosts, psychologists estimated that they have about a 60 percent accuracy rate according to a 1997 study.[4] That is only slightly better than chance. Some people who are not lying appear to be lying, and those people who are especially skilled at lying can consciously avoid being detected. The system is also dependent on someone interrogating the suspect and reading the machine, therefore making the results even more subjective. For these reasons the Supreme Court does not accept polygraph test results as accurate evidence. However, Cephos Corp. and No Lie MRI both promote their computer-run brain-scanning tests as accurate enough to stand up in the highest courts.[5]

**inarguable**
without question

electrode
a device
that collects
electronic
charges

7       U.S. law is still unclear about whether brain scans can be performed without <u>consent</u>. Current law allows police to draw blood if an accident is caused by suspected drunkenness. But without a court order, it is still illegal to take DNA samples, take MRIs, or attach electrodes to someone's brain without permission from that person. Hank Greely, a law professor and member of the Neuroethics Society, says that prosecuting attorneys will probably begin to demand MRIs in court "like a search warrant for the brain."[6]

8       It is important that the public understand the limitations of these MRI-based lie detectors. These systems are still <u>subjective</u> and imperfect. They require human interpretation of complicated and <u>variable</u> brain functions. Neuroscientists who are not involved in commercial lie-detection seem to be less confident of this technology than the representatives from Cephos Corp. and No Lie MRI. Sean Spence of the University of Sheffield in Britain says, "On individual scans it's really very difficult to judge who's lying and who's telling the truth." Thomas Zoëga Ramsøy, a neuroscientist in Denmark and publisher of a blog on neuroethics, sounds even less confident about the accuracy of this technology: "The same problems with the polygraph <u>persist</u>: we don't know what a lie really is, why people lie, and we won't catch those who don't think that they are lying. Today, doing any kind of lie detection is a risky business. And I wouldn't put my buck at Cephos or No Lie MRI."[7] One of the major arguments that Spence and Ramsøy both make is that judging a person based on studies done on *groups* of people is not accurate considering the variability of individual human brain functions.

9       U.S. government agencies, such as the Central Intelligence Agency and the military, have higher hopes for the new neuroscience technology and are funding much of the current research in lie detection. The Neuroethics Society has already held conferences to specifically debate the pros and cons of the use of brain scans for the purpose of "national security."[8] Steven Laken, the CEO of Cephos Corp., is promoting his company's commercial brain-scanning services to individuals and companies, as well as the government. It is possible that parents with enough money could hire Cephos Corp. to find out if their teenager is having sex or drinking alcohol, though right now such a service does not exist. As this technology becomes cheaper and more <u>refined</u>, it could be used in more and more aspects of our lives.

## GET INVOLVED

10      Like all technology, the new advances in neuroscience have the potential for great harm as well as the potential for good. Brain-scanning techniques need to be directed in the right direction. The public needs to be involved in decisions about what should be legal and what shouldn't be legal. If we do not stay informed about neuroscience technology, and if we do not get involved in debating the ethical and legal dilemmas this technology raises, then one day we might have our brains scanned for reasons that we disagree with, or as technology advances, perhaps without our even being aware of it.

### Notes

1. Neuroethics Society, http://www.neuroethicssociety.org/index.html (accessed March 3, 2008).

2. Quoted in Francine Russo, "A User's Guide to the Brain: Who Should Read Your Mind?" *Time*, January 9, 2007.

3. Quoted in Thomas Ramsøy and Martin Skov, Brain Ethics Blog, http://brainethics. wordpress.com/ (accessed March 3, 2008).

4. Dan Vergano, "Telling the Truth about Lie Detectors." *USA Today*, September 9, 2002.

5. Cephos Corp., http://www.cephoscorp.com/ (accessed March 3, 2008); No Lie MRI, Inc., http://www.noliemri.com/ (accessed March 3, 2008).

6. Quoted in Russo, "User's Guide."

7. Ramsøy and Skov, Brain Ethics Blog.

8. Neuroethics Society, http://www.neuroethicssociety.org/index.html.

**Exercise 1**

## Work with Words

Use context clues, dictionary skills, and your knowledge of word parts to choose the best definition for each italicized word in the following sentences from the reading. The paragraph number is provided in case you want to check the context.

1. *realms* (par. 1)
   a. kingdoms
   b. areas
   c. realities

2. *ethical* (par. 3)
   a. having to do with right and wrong
   b. philosophical
   c. having to do with the study of abstract principles

3. *dilemmas* (par. 3)
   a. personal choices
   b. individual problems
   c. difficult choices

4. *tissue* (par. 5)
   a. fabric
   b. flexible parts of the brain
   c. structural material in the human body

5. *cerebral* (par. 5)
   a. having to do with the brain
   b. having to do with nervous system
   c. having to do with patterns

6. *consent* (par. 7)
   a. awareness
   b. agreement
   c. refusal

7. *subjective* (par. 8)
   a. relating to a subject
   b. personal, possibly prejudiced
   c. highly controlled

8. *persist* (par. 8)
   a. cease
   b. reveal
   c. remain

9. *variable* (par. 8)
   a. quantifiable
   b. changeable
   c. contrary

10. *refined* (par. 9)
    a. improved
    b. freed from impurities
    c. cultured

---

## Exercise 2    Check Your Understanding

Based on the reading, choose the best answer to each of the following multiple-choice questions.

1. Which of the following sentences expresses the author's opinion about the new technologies used for "reading" our brains?
   a. If we do not stay informed about neuroscience technology, and if we do not get involved in debating the ethical and legal dilemmas this technology raises, then one day we might be getting our brains scanned for reasons that we disagree with, whether we like it or not.
   b. Being able to look into people's brains gives neuroscientists a better understanding of many mental disorders and diseases.
   c. U.S. government agencies, such as the Central Intelligence Agency and the military, have higher hopes for the new neuroscience technology and are funding lots of the current research in lie detection.

2. When Medina writes a series of questions in paragraph 2, he wants
   a. the reader to answer them.
   b. neuroethicists to answer them.
   c. the reader to recognize that we need to be informed and involved in decisions about how this technology will be used.

3. The purpose of the Neuroethics Society is to
   a. make a reasonable list of what should and should not be done when scientists are studying human brains.
   b. promote the development and responsible application of neuroscience through better understanding of its capabilities and its consequences.
   c. promote widespread discussion of lie-detection techniques among the general public so that the people can choose which technologies are the most accurate.

4. According to the article, employers might be interested in using brain scans to determine
   a. who the best person is to hire for a particular job.
   b. who should be fired if the company needs to make layoffs.
   c. which employees are doing illegal drugs or drinking too much.

5. Medina is concerned about
   a. employers' misuse of brain-scanning technology.
   b. employers' ability to control employees' thoughts using brain-scanning technology.
   c. neuroethicists' lack of understanding of the new technology.

6. MRI brain scans
   a. indicate when someone is lying with 100 percent accuracy.
   b. show which part of the brain is active.
   c. read people's thoughts and emotions.

7. It is currently illegal for
   a. lawyers to use polygraph (lie-detector) tests in court cases.
   b. detectives to administer brain scans without a person's permission.
   c. police to take a blood sample if drunk driving is suspected.

8. Which of the following statements is true?
   a. Some government agencies are interested in how brain-scanning technology might be used to enhance national security.
   b. Rich parents can pay an agency to scan the brains of their teenage children to determine if they are having sex, drinking, or doing illegal drugs.
   c. MRI scans are going to increase in price in the future.

9. One concern that neuroscientists have about using MRI scans in lie detection is that
   a. we do not know enough about how each individual's brain functions.
   b. there is no such thing as "truth."
   c. MRI scans do not yet provide accurate pictures of the brain.

10. Based on this reading, we can conclude that the author
    a. is excited about the potential of neuroscience in the twenty-first century to improve national security.
    b. believes what the heads of the corporations are saying about their MRI-based lie detectors.
    c. does not trust the claims of the corporations about the accuracy of their MRI-based lie detectors.

**Exercise 3**

## Reflect

Think about what you read in "Looking into Your Brain" and what you already know about some of the uses of neurotechnology. Then answer the following questions.

1. Medina writes that MRI-based lie-detection technology could be used in the job application and hiring process, in pre-marital counseling, in national security, or in college applications. Choose one of these possibilities and explain why you think it would be a good idea or a bad idea to use this technology for this purpose. Give at least two reasons to support your opinion.

_____

_____

_____

_____

_____

_____

2. What are the concerns about lie-detection technology that Medina presents in this reading? Explain them in your own words.

_____

_____

_____

_____

_____

_____

# 3 Topics and Main Ideas

## OUR FOOD, OUR CULTURE

Corbis

*Since everyone must eat, what we eat becomes a most powerful symbol of who we are. —Robin Fox*

1. This painting is by Norman Rockwell (1894–1978), an artist famous for his images of American life and culture. What does this picture make you think about or feel? Does it remind you of holiday meals with your family? Why or why not?

2. What role does food play in your family or your culture?

3. Do you think food symbolizes who we are? Explain your answer.

# Prepare to Read

Most of us take food for granted. We eat every day, usually several times a day. We lead very busy lives and, unlike our ancestors, spend relatively little time gathering, preparing, and even eating food. As a group, Americans eat more processed and "instant" foods than ever before. We eat at fast-food restaurants or on the go with take-out meals. Most children don't even think about where the food in the packages comes from, and often adults don't either. But food is more than nourishment. It is also an important part of our social lives. It plays a role in our get-togethers with friends and family. And although our tastes may be different, people around the world like to eat good food. So how do our eating habits—what and where we eat—affect our relationships with others? How do they affect our nutrition and health? How do they interact with our culture?

In this chapter, you will read about many aspects of food and culture and learn to

- Recognize topics in readings
- Identify stated and implied main ideas in paragraphs and short passages
- Recognize thesis statements in longer passages
- Put main ideas and thesis statements into your own words

In the process of acquiring these skills, you will read about food: how the foods we eat have changed, how our foods are processed and prepared, what's in the food we eat, how our eating habits and expectations influence our lives, and how our food and eating habits reflect our culture.

**Reading 1**

# Oh, the Flavor of Your Fries* — ERIC SCHLOSSER

**The following reading is from Eric Schlosser's best seller, *Fast Food Nation*. This book examines many aspects of the fast-food industry: where the food comes from, how it is processed, what ingredients it contains, what the working conditions are at all stages of producing and serving the food, and how the fast-food culture fits into other parts of our lives. In this reading, Schlosser explains the source of much of the flavor of fast food.**

1    The taste of McDonald's French fries has long been praised by customers, competitors, and even food critics. James Beard loved McDonald's fries. Their distinctive taste does not stem from the type of potatoes that McDonald's buys, the technology that processes them, or the restaurant equipment that fries them. Other chains buy their French fries from the same large processing companies, use Russet Burbanks, and have similar fryers in their restaurant kitchens. The taste of a fast food fry is largely determined by the cooking oil. For decades, McDonald's cooked its French fries in a mixture of about 7 percent cottonseed oil and 93 percent beef tallow. The mix gave the fries their unique flavor—and more saturated beef fat per ounce than a McDonald's hamburger.

**tallow**
substance taken from the fat of sheep or cows

2    Amid a barrage of criticism over the amount of cholesterol in their fries, McDonald's switched to pure vegetable oil in 1990. The switch presented the company with an enormous challenge: how to make fries that subtly taste like beef without cooking them in tallow. A look at the ingredients now used in the preparation of McDonald's French fries suggests how the problem was solved. Toward the end of the list is a seemingly innocuous, yet oddly mysterious phrase: "natural flavor." That ingredient helps to explain not only why the fries taste so good, but also why most fast food—indeed, most of the food Americans eat today—tastes the way it does.

**innocuous**
harmless

3    Open your refrigerator, your freezer, your kitchen cupboards, and look at the labels on your food. You'll find "natural flavor" or "artificial flavor" in just about every list of ingredients. The similarities between these two broad categories of flavor are far more significant than their differences. Both are man-made additives that give most processed food most of its taste. The initial purchase of a food item may be driven by its packaging or appearance, but subsequent purchases are determined mainly by its taste. About 90 percent of the money that Americans spend on food is used to buy processed food. But the canning, freezing, and dehydrating techniques used to process food destroy most of its flavor. Since the end of World War II, a vast industry has arisen in the United States to make processed food palatable. Without this flavor industry, today's fast food industry could not exist. The names of the leading American fast food chains and their best-selling menu items have become famous worldwide, embedded in our popular culture. Few people, however, can name the companies that manufacture fast food's taste.

**palatable**
tasty

**embedded in**
part of

**Exercise 1**

## Recall and Discuss

Based on Reading 1, answer the following questions and prepare to discuss them with your classmates.

1. What gave McDonald's french fries their unique flavor before 1990?

_____

2. What gives McDonald's french fries their flavor now?

   _____

3. What kinds of foods have "natural flavor" or "artificial flavor" listed as ingredients? Check your cabinets and list the foods that you find that have those ingredients.

   _____

   _____

4. Where do you think the "natural" and "artificial" flavors come from?

   _____

   _____

   _____

5. What is your favorite food? What food do you most dislike?

   _____

6. What do you think of fast-food restaurants? How often do you eat fast food? Explain your answer.

   _____

7. What are your eating habits? Do you usually eat with other people or alone? Do you eat quickly or slowly? At home or out? Explain your answers.

   _____

# Topics and Main Ideas

As a college reader, you need to be able to identify topics and main ideas in the information you read. In this chapter, you will practice these skills in a variety of readings and identify topics as well as stated and unstated main ideas in paragraphs and longer passages.

## TOPICS

**topic**
subject of a reading; answers the question "what is it about?"

When your instructors ask "what is the **topic**?" of a paragraph or passage, they are asking "what is it about?" You can usually state the answer in just a few key words. For example, read the following paragraph and decide what the topic is:

The flavor industry is highly secretive. Its leading companies will not divulge the precise formulas of flavor compounds or the identities of clients. The secrecy is deemed essential for protecting the reputation of beloved brands. The fast food chains, understandably, would like the public to believe that the flavors of their food somehow originate in their restaurant kitchens, not in distant factories run by other firms. (Schlosser, *Fast Food Nation*)

If someone asked you what the topic of this reading was, you would readily say "the flavor industry." If you wanted to be more specific, you might say the topic is "the secrecy of the flavor industry." Usually, you express the topic of a paragraph or passage in a few words rather than a complete sentence.

## MAIN IDEAS

**main idea**
most important point of the reading; a general statement about the topic

To answer the question "What is the **main idea?**" of a paragraph or longer reading, you must decide what **generalization** the writer is making about the topic. The main idea is a general statement that covers all the important points the author makes about the topic. For example, in the paragraph about the flavor industry, Schlosser's topic is the flavor industry—specifically, the secrecy of the flavor industry. What point is the author trying to make? Schlosser presents three facts about the topic:

**generalization**
broad, general statement that covers all the important points about a topic

1. Leading companies will not divulge the formulas of flavor compounds or the names of their clients.
2. Secrecy is deemed essential for protecting the reputation of beloved brands.
3. The fast-food chains would like the public to believe that the flavors of their food somehow originate in their restaurant kitchens, not in distant factories.

These facts support the main idea, which the author stated in the first sentence: "The flavor industry is highly secretive."

**assertion**
statement of an opinion or an argument for a particular understanding of the topic

The main idea can also be an **assertion** about or an interpretation of the topic, because some authors do more than present generalizations and supporting points. They take a stand, state an opinion, or argue for a particular understanding of their topics. Essays and editorials use main ideas this way. For example, a writer could focus a paragraph on the same topic—the secrecy of the flavor industry—with a much more argumentative edge, such as the following:

> The flavor industry should not be allowed to operate in secret. The formulas of flavor compounds as well as the identities of clients should be made public. People have the right to know that the flavors of their food do not come from the restaurant kitchens but from factories run by other firms.

In this case, the point that the author wishes to make about the topic is stated in the first sentence: "The flavor industry should not be allowed to operate in secret."

To identify the topic and main idea in a reading, ask yourself the following questions:

1. What is the reading about? (Identify the topic.)
2. What is the general point that is being made about the topic? (Identify the main idea.)
3. Do all or most of the important ideas or information in the reading support the main idea you have identified?

## STATED MAIN IDEAS IN PARAGRAPHS

**stated main idea**
main idea that clearly appears in a reading, often near the beginning

Often you may find a **stated main idea** in a passage. That is, you might find a sentence you can simply identify as the main idea. If a main idea is specifically stated in the paragraph, it is usually located near the beginning or at the end. Less often, it appears in the middle of the paragraph. Remember to identify the topic of the reading first. The main idea is simply the point the author is making about the topic.

If you have already completed a writing class, it may also help to think about the reading from the writer's viewpoint. Ask yourself which sentence in the paragraph tells you what the author believes about the topic. In your writing classes, you usually call the main idea sentence for a paragraph the **topic sentence.**

**topic sentence**
name for a main idea sentence usually used in writing classes

Read the following paragraph about the policy the federal government has set for labeling foods and its consequences:

> In a policy that's beneficial to flavor companies, the Food and Drug Administration does not require that they reveal all the chemicals in their additives as long as those chemicals are "generally regarded as safe" (GRAS). This policy means companies can keep their chemical flavor formulas secret. The fact that some flavor compounds have more ingredients than the food itself is kept hidden. The familiar phrase "artificial strawberry flavor" doesn't tell us about the chemical "magic" and manufacturing skill that can make a highly processed food taste like a strawberry. (Adapted from Schlosser, *Fast Food Nation*)

1. What is the topic of this paragraph?_____

_____

2. Underline the sentence that you think most clearly states the main idea in this paragraph.

Your answers are probably similar to these:

1. The topic is "policy regarding flavor formulas" or "labeling secrecy of flavor formulas."
2. You probably underlined the first sentence: "In a policy that's beneficial to flavor companies, the Food and Drug Administration does not require that they reveal all the chemicals in their additives as long as those chemicals are 'generally regarded as safe' (GRAS)."

The two examples we've looked at so far both have stated main ideas, and the main ideas are conveniently located at the beginning of the paragraphs. In expository writing—writing that explains—and the typical English essay, the main idea frequently appears at or near the beginning of the paragraph or in the opening paragraph. Sometimes, however, the writer waits until the end of the passage to present the main point. He or she may feel that presenting the details first will draw the reader to the same conclusions as the writer.

Read the following paragraph about International Flavors and Fragrances (IFF):

> In addition to being the world's largest flavor company, IFF manufactures the smell of six of the ten best-selling fine perfumes in the United States, including Estée Lauder's Beautiful, Clinique's Happy, Lancome's Trésor, and Calvin Klein's Eternity. It also makes the smell of household products such as deodorant, dishwashing detergent, bath soap, shampoo, furniture polish, and floor wax. . . . The basic science behind the scent of your shaving cream is the same as that governing the flavor of your TV dinner. (Schlosser, *Fast Food Nation*)

1. What is the topic of this paragraph?_____

_____

2. Underline the sentence that you think most clearly states the main idea in this paragraph.

Your answers are probably similar to these:

1. The topic is "flavors and scents manufactured by IFF" or "the science of scents and flavors."
2. You probably underlined the last sentence: "The basic science behind the scent of your shaving cream is the same as that governing the flavor of your TV dinner." Notice that the first and second sentences are examples that support this main idea.

## Reader's Tip: Identify General and Specific Information

Recognizing the main idea in a paragraph or longer passage is a critical reading skill. It is easy to become overwhelmed with information when reading about a new or complex topic. Identifying the main idea helps you distinguish important information from less important information. One way to help you determine the main idea is to identify general and specific information. **General** information is broad and inclusive. **Specific** information is particular and often gives examples of the more general information. General information applies to all or most of the specific members of a group or category. Notice the relationship between the general and specific information in Table 3.1. Then add items of your own on the lines provided. In the first two boxes, you will need to add specific examples. In the last two boxes, you will need to identify the broad category.

| Table 3.1 | | |
|---|---|---|
| General Information | Specific Information | Example |
| cheese | swiss | _____ |
|  | cheddar | _____ |
|  | american | _____ |
| breakfast foods | eggs | _____ |
|  | pancakes | _____ |
|  | cereal | _____ |
| _____ | coffee | tea |
|  | soda | juice |
|  | milk | wine |
| _____ | lemongrass | basil |
|  | oregano | sage |
|  | mint | cilantro |

**general**
broad and inclusive

**specific**
particular, often examples of a more general idea

In a paragraph or longer text, general ideas usually relate to the main idea. In the following paragraph, notice general and specific ideas.

Today an ordinary American might eat a bagel for breakfast, a gyro sandwich for lunch, and wonton soup, shrimp creole, and rice pilaf for dinner, followed by chocolate mousse and espresso. An evening snack might consist of nachos and lager beer. These items, each identified with a particular ethnic group, serve as tasty reminders that immigrants have made important and lasting contributions to the nation's culinary culture. The American diet also represents one of the few genuine ways that the multicultural nation has served as a melting pot. (Norton et al., *A People and a Nation*)

Which sentences are general and which are specific? Underline the general sentences and circle the specific sentences.

You probably decided that the first two sentences are more specific and the last two sentences are more general.

Which sentence expresses the main idea? Think about which sentence states the broadest or largest idea. Write "Main Idea" next to that sentence.

You likely concluded that the final sentence is the main idea.

**Exercise 2**   Identify General and Specific

Read each group of sentences and decide which ones express general ideas and which give specific ideas (information). On the lines provided, write "G" for general and "S" for specific. There is only one general idea for each number.

1. S McDonald's has more than 30,000 restaurants in more than 100 countries.

   S When a McDonald's opened in Kuwait City last year, the drive-through line was more than six miles long.

   G American fast-food franchises have become popular all over the world.

   S The most common fast-food restaurant in China, however, is Kentucky Fried Chicken, with more than 1,000 locations.

   S There is even a Kentucky Fried Chicken restaurant in Damascus, Syria.

2. G Maize, or corn, was the main part of the diet in many indigenous cultures in the Americas.

   S They dried the corn kernels and then ground them into meal.

   ___ They prepared the maize like a hot cereal, or they shaped it into cakes and baked it.

   ___ Some groups placed the kernels in the fire until they popped open, just as we do today.

3. ___ Chocolate, which spread from Mexico to Spain in the sixteenth century, became the preferred drink of European aristocrats.

   G Throughout history, new beverages from exotic lands have played an important role in trade and culture.

   ___ First cultivated in Arabia, coffee became popular with English and colonial American businessmen in the seventeenth century.

> _ Tea, which originated in China, grew to be even more popular than coffee with elite British men and women.
>
> _ Sugarcane, produced on large plantations in the Caribbean, was the source for making rum, a drink favored by the working classes.

**Exercise 3**

## Identify Topics and Stated Main Ideas

Read the following paragraphs about food issues. For each paragraph, write the topic on the line provided, and then choose the sentence you think most clearly states the main idea.

1. The flavor industry is now huge and extremely profitable. According to Eric Schlosser, "It has annual revenues of about $1.4 billion. Approximately ten thousand new processed food products are introduced every year in the United States. Almost all of them require flavor additives. . . . The latest flavor innovations and corporate realignments are heralded in publications such as *Food Chemical News, Food Engineering, Chemical Market Reporter,* and *Food Product Design*. The growth of IFF [International Flavors and Fragrances] has mirrored that of the flavor industry as a whole. IFF was formed in 1958, through the merger of two small companies. Its annual revenues have grown almost fifteen-fold since the early 1970s, and it now has manufacturing facilities in twenty countries." (Adapted from Schlosser, *Fast Food Nation*)

   Topic: _____

   Main idea:

   a. The IFF was formed in 1958, through the merger of two small companies.
   b. IFF's annual revenues have grown almost fifteen-fold since the early 1970s, and it now has manufacturing facilities in twenty countries.
   c. The flavor industry is now huge and extremely profitable.

2. Over the past few decades, as the fast-food industry has grown, so have the waistlines of most Americans. Today almost two-thirds of the adults in the United States and about one-sixth of the children are overweight or obese. Almost 50 million Americans are now obese. An additional 6 or 7 million are "morbidly obese": they weigh about 100 pounds more than they should. Since the early 1970s, the rate of obesity among American adults has increased by 50 percent. Among preschoolers it has doubled. And among children aged six to eleven it has tripled. According to James O. Hill, a nutritionist at the University of Colorado, "We've got the fattest, least fit generation of kids, ever." (Schlosser and Wilson, *Chew on This*)

   Topic: _____

   Main idea:

   a. Almost 50 million Americans are now obese.
   b. "We've got the fattest, least fit generation of kids, ever."
   c. Over the past few decades, as the fast-food industry has grown, so have the waistlines of most Americans.

3. For thousands of years human beings had to struggle for food. Getting enough food to survive usually required hard work—hunting, farming, fishing. And when

food supplies ran low, people had to survive for days or weeks without eating much. For most of human history, getting too fat wasn't the problem; getting food was the problem. Scientists think that our bodies developed fat cells in order to store energy for those periods when food was hard to find. Today few of us have to hunt, farm, or fish for our daily meals. All we have to do is open the refrigerator, go to the supermarket, or stop at a drive-through. Our bodies, however, still function as though the food may run out at any moment. As a result, it's much easier to gain weight (and store energy as fat) than it is to lose it. (Schlosser and Wilson, *Chew on This*)

Topic: _____

Main idea:

   a. For thousands of years human beings had to struggle for food.
   b. Today few of us have to hunt, farm, or fish for our daily meals.
   c. For most of human history, getting too fat wasn't the problem; getting food was the problem.

4. The rise of suburbia, changes in the American workplace, and the triumph of the automobile have made it easier to grow obese. A hundred years ago, few people worked behind a desk. They worked outdoors on a farm or indoors at a factory. They worked hard and burned a great deal of energy throughout the day. Today many people work in offices, talking on the phone, typing at a computer, sitting on their butts for most of the day. They drive to work instead of walking. They drive to the mall. They sit on the couch and play video games instead of exercising. And they eat a lot of fast food. The inactivity of American kids has played a large role in the spread of obesity. Less than 30 percent of high school students in the United States attend daily physical education classes, and only 12 percent of students walk to school. (Schlosser and Wilson, *Chew on This*)

Topic: _____

Main idea:

   a. Less than 30 percent of high school students in the United States attend daily physical education classes, and only 12 percent of students walk to school.
   b. The rise of suburbia, changes in the American workplace, and the triumph of the automobile have made it easier to grow obese.
   c. Today many people work in offices, talking on the phone, typing at a computer, sitting on their butts for most of the day.

5. The fast-food chains encourage people not only to eat things full of fat, salt, and sugar but also to eat larger portions at every meal. If you went to a fast-food restaurant during the 1950s and bought a Coca-Cola, you'd probably get about eight ounces of soda. That was the adult portion: eight ounces. Today the smallest Coke that McDonald's sells (a child's Coke) is twelve ounces. That's a 50 percent increase in size. Many customers purchase a large Coke, which is thirty-two ounces—four times bigger than the Cokes that fast-food restaurants used to sell. One of these large Cokes has 310 calories and contains the equivalent of almost thirty teaspoons of sugar. (Schlosser and Wilson, *Chew on This*)

Topic: _____

Main idea:

   a. The fast-food chains encourage people not only to eat things full of fat, salt, and sugar but also to eat larger portions at every meal.

    b. Many customers purchase a large Coke, which is thirty-two ounces—four times bigger than the Cokes that fast-food restaurants used to sell.

    c. One of these large Cokes has 310 calories and contains the equivalent of almost thirty teaspoons of sugar.

6. The hamburgers have gotten bigger, too. In 1957 the typical fast-food burger patty weighed one ounce. Today the typical burger patty weighs six ounces. Indeed, fast-food chains are now proud of how big their hamburgers have become. At Hardee's, the Monster Thickburger contains two-thirds of a pound of beef, four strips of bacon, and three slices of cheese, with mayonnaise on top. That one hamburger has 1,410 calories. To put those numbers in perspective, the average person aged nine to thirteen should eat about 1,800 calories in a single day. (Schlosser and Wilson, *Chew on This*)

Topic: _____

Main idea:

    a. At Hardee's, the Monster Thickburger contains two-thirds of a pound of beef, four strips of bacon, and three slices of cheese, with mayonnaise on top.

    b. Indeed, fast-food chains are now proud of how big their hamburgers have become.

    c. The hamburgers have gotten bigger, too.

## RESTATING MAIN IDEAS

One valuable way to check your understanding of a main idea is to try to write it in your own words. Can you explain to a friend or fellow student the point the author is trying to make? If the instructor in a history or biology class rewords an important idea in a test question, will you immediately recognize it and be able to answer the question correctly? We retain information more easily if we can "translate" it into terms that connect with what we already know.

    Many college assignments in other classes require you to restate main idea sentences in your own words. Some instructors may use the term, "paraphrasing." **Paraphrasing** is another way to say restating an idea in your own words. For example, the stated main idea for paragraph 1 in Exercise 3 was "The flavor industry is now huge and extremely profitable." You could restate it as "The flavor industry makes a lot of money and has grown tremendously."

    Notice that the restated main idea is written as a complete sentence. A topic is written in only a few words or a single phrase, but a main idea has to be expressed as a complete thought about the topic.

**paraphrasing**
restating an idea in
your own words

**Exercise 4**

### Restate Main Ideas

Restate the following main idea sentences (from Exercise 3) in your own words.

1. Over the past few decades, as the fast-food industry has grown, so have the waistlines of most Americans.

_____

_____

2. For most of human history, getting too fat wasn't the problem; getting food was the problem.

_____

_____

_____

3. The rise of suburbia, changes in the American workplace, and the triumph of the automobile have made it easier to grow obese.

_____

_____

4. The fast-food chains encourage people not only to eat things full of fat, salt, and sugar but also to eat larger portions at every meal.

_____

_____

## IMPLIED MAIN IDEAS IN PARAGRAPHS

Sometimes the main idea is not directly stated in a paragraph. But all the ideas in the reading add up to a general point that the writer wants you to understand. In this case, the **main idea** is **implied**. Whether the main idea is stated or implied, you can construct a main idea sentence based on the wording of the topic that you have identified.

**implied main idea**
main idea that is suggested but not specifically stated by a reading

For example, read the following paragraph about the vegetarian diet:

> Studies show that vegetarians' cholesterol levels are low, and vegetarians are seldom overweight. As a result, they're less apt to be candidates for heart disease than those who consume large quantities of meat. Vegetarians also have lower incidences of breast, colon, and prostate cancer; high blood pressure; and osteoporosis. When combined with exercise and stress reduction, vegetarian diets have led to reductions in the buildup of harmful plaque within the blood vessels of the heart. (Hales, *An Invitation to Health*)

What is the topic? You probably decided "'vegetarians' health" or "the benefits of a vegetarian diet." You need to ask, "What is the point the author is trying to make about this topic? What is the main idea?" You might say that her overall point is, "The vegetarian diet is beneficial." Or, if you wanted to be more specific, you might say, "The vegetarian diet has a variety of proven health benefits."

**Exercise 5**

Identify Implied Main Ideas

Read the following paragraphs about food. For each paragraph, write the topic on the line provided, and then select the best statement of the main idea from the choices given. The first one has been done for you.

1. From 1859 until 1875, the annual per capita consumption of raw sugar in the United States had varied from a low of 18.6 pounds (during the Civil War) to a high of 42.6 pounds. By 1898, the year of the Spanish-American War, it had risen to 65.4 pounds per person per year. But ten years later, the figure was over 86 pounds or nearly four ounces daily. The consumption of *sucrose*—processed sugar from cane and beet—reached around 115 pounds in the 1920s; but the present-day consumption of *all* processed sugars in the United States is higher than that. In the last three decades, and due as much to political changes as anything else, a corn sweetener called high-fructose corn syrup has captured an important portion of the sweetener market. (Mintz, "Pleasure, Profit, and Satiation")

Topic: __American consumption of sugar__

Implied main idea:

a. Because of political pressures, corn sweeteners have captured an important portion of the sweetener market.
b. From 1859 until 1875, the annual per capita consumption of raw sugar in the United States went from a low of 18.6 pounds to a high of 42.6 pounds.
c. The consumption of sugar per person in the United States increased steadily from 1859 to the present.

The best statement of the main idea is c. Although a and b state important information from the paragraph, neither one is general enough to be the main idea.

2. The statistics about food additive consumption in the United States are interesting. The average American consumes over 140 pounds of sweeteners every year. We eat over 15 pounds of table salt. And by eating processed and fast-foods, we also put a number of chemicals in our bodies that we are not at all aware of—between 5 to 10 pounds. (Adapted from Hales, *An Invitation to Health*)

Topic: _____

Implied main idea:

a. We eat a huge quantity of additives, especially if we include the sugar and salt.
b. We eat between five and ten pounds of chemicals per year that we are not aware of.
c. The average American consumes more than 140 pounds of sweeteners every year.

3. Nitrites—additives used in bacon and lunch meats—add color and inhibit spoilage, but they have been identified as contributing to the development of cancer. Sulfites—additives used to prevent food such as dried apricots from turning brown—can cause severe allergic reactions. (Adapted from Hales, *An Invitation to Health*)

Topic: _____

Implied main idea:

a. Nitrites can cause cancer.
b. Sulfites can cause allergic reactions.
c. Some additives, such as nitrites and sulfites, pose health risks.

4. Because calcium intake is so important throughout life for maintaining a strong bone structure, it is critical that you consume the minimum required amounts each day. Over half of our calcium intake usually comes from milk, one of the highest sources of dietary calcium. New, calcium-fortified orange juice provides a good way to get calcium if you are not a milk drinker. Many green, leafy vegetables are good sources of calcium, but some contain oxalic acid, which makes their calcium harder to absorb. Spinach, chard, and beet greens are not particularly good sources of calcium, whereas broccoli, cauliflower, and many peas and beans offer good supplies (pinto beans and soybeans are among the best). Many nuts, particularly almonds, brazil nuts, and hazelnuts, and seeds such as sunflower and sesame contain good amounts of calcium. Molasses is fairly high in calcium. Some fruits—such as citrus fruits, figs, raisins, and dried apricots—have moderate amounts. (Donatelle, *Access to Health*)

Topic: _____

Implied main idea:

a. Calcium intake is important for maintaining a strong bone structure.
b. Fortified orange juice is a new way to get your calcium.
c. There are many good food sources of calcium.

5. The Spaniards gave the name "pepper" (pimienta) to the hot-tasting capsicums (called chili peppers today) they found in Mexico. But the "pepper" they were looking for was in Asia, not the newly found continent of America. Chili peppers, which can be various sizes, colors, and shapes, are used to flavor foods. They can be blistery hot, used for chili powder or cayenne pepper. They can be an ingredient in mild Tabasco sauce and are frequently added directly to a variety of bean and meat dishes. Bell peppers—green, yellow, or red—are often used in salads. And some types of bell peppers make the mild spice called paprika, which is not hot at all. (Johnson, "Peppers")

Topic: _____

Implied main idea:

a. The Spaniards mistakenly called capsicums peppers, or pimientas, when they discovered them in Mexico.
b. Chili peppers come in a variety of forms and are used in many different ways to flavor food.
c. The "pepper" that the Spaniards were looking for was not in America but in Asia.

6. Food can also bestow powerful feelings of comfort in times of need and create a sense of community and togetherness. It can be beautiful to look at, have a delicious smell, and offer exquisite tastes—whether the item in hand is a perfectly seared sirloin steak or a carne asada burrito dripping with freshly made guacamole. In our diverse culture, we have special foods for holidays, such as hard-boiled eggs at Easter and turkey with cranberry sauce at Thanksgiving, as well as ethnic specialties like *tamales* (Mexican and Central American), *pasteles* (Puerto Rican), and dishes made with sticky rice (Chinese and Southeast Asian). An important symbolic gesture in times of war can be seen in food drops—with the attacking country showering the civilians, caught between warring interests, with meals (as the United States did in Afghanistan in 2001 and 2002). And one way many people in the United States show their charity is by participating in meal programs such as Meals-On-Wheels, which delivers food to housebound folks, or soup kitchens, which provide meals for homeless or hungry people. (Mayhew, "Easy Bake Ovens and Fashion Magazines")

Topic: _____

Implied main idea:

a. Holiday foods are important to people of all cultures.
b. In many ways, food is important in culture.
c. An important symbolic gesture in times of war can be seen in food drops—with the attacking country showering the civilians, caught between warring interests, with meals.

7. In 1998, products made of Olean (also known by its generic name, olestra), the first calorie-free fat replacement ingredient that can be used to fry foods, entered the national marketplace. Because the ingredients of Olean are processed in a special way, the body doesn't break them down and so Olean doesn't add fat or calories to foods. On the basis of more than 150 research studies, the FDA (Food and Drug Administration) approved Olean for use in savory snacks, such as chips and crackers, and many medical organizations, including the American Dietetic Association, have supported its use as one way to reduce fat and calories in the diet. However, some participants in early tests have reported gastrointestinal side effects, and consumer advocacy groups, such as the Center for Science in the Public Interest, have warned that fat replacement products may pose potential risks that could outweigh their benefits. (Hales, *An Invitation to Health*)

Topic: _____

Implied main idea:

a. There is disagreement about the health benefits and risks of Olean, the calorie-free fat replacement.
b. Olean lets you enjoy the flavor without consuming the calories of fat.
c. Fat replacement products are risky.

8. The average American eats fast food or highly processed foods several times a week—an eating habit that in many ways is symptomatic of our lifestyle: we are in a hurry. At the same time, fast-food restaurants are now opening in countries all over the world. Many people, however, are not happy with the trend toward eating quickly and rushing through life. In reaction to this tendency, the Slow Food Movement has begun. The principles of the Slow Food Movement are simple. Its 65,000

members from 42 different countries believe it is important to take the time to enjoy life, and part of that enjoyment comes from spending hours working together preparing family meals and eating together leisurely. They advocate opposing the spread of American fast-food outlets and the growth of supermarkets. They support local farmers and food producers, and they believe that it is healthier to eat organic foods. The movement—perhaps led by their Italian members—advocates the consumption of excellent local wines.

Topic: _____

Implied main idea:

a. In response to the growth of the fast-food industry, people around the world have organized the Slow Food Movement, whose principles are to support the local production of food and to take the time to cook and enjoy healthy food together.
b. The Slow Food Movement has demonstrated its importance and its popular success by recruiting 65,000 members in 42 countries.
c. The average American eats fast food or highly processed foods several times a week—an eating habit that in many ways is symptomatic of our lifestyle: we are in a hurry.

## Exercise 6    Identify Stated and Implied Main Ideas

Read the following paragraphs about eating disorders taken from a variety of college textbooks. For each paragraph, write the topic on the line provided, and then select the best statement of the main idea from the choices given. Finally, to check your understanding, rewrite the main idea in your own words on the lines provided. The first one has been done for you.

1. When I was in high school, female figures that can only be described as well-rounded were in vogue. Beginning in the mid-1960s, however, this standard of beauty changed drastically, shifting toward a much slimmer shape. Puzzling as this is to me personally, the "thin is beautiful" image has persisted and is emphasized over and over again by television, films, and magazines. Despite this fact, a growing proportion of adults in the United States and other countries are actually overweight. . . . Given this increasing gap between physical reality and the image of personal beauty portrayed by the mass media, it is not surprising that feeding and eating disorders—disturbances in eating behavior that involve maladaptive and unhealthy efforts to control body weight—are increasingly common. . . . In addition, the trend in recent decades has been for these disturbing disorders to start at earlier and earlier ages—as young as age eight (Nietzel et al., 1998). (Baron, *Psychology*)

Topic: **beauty standards and eating disorders**

Main idea:

a. When I was in high school, female figures that can only be described as well-rounded were in vogue.
b. While the media sends the "thin is beautiful" message, many adults in the United States are overweight, so it is no surprise that eating disorders are becoming more common.

c. The trend in recent decades has been for disturbing eating disorders to start at earlier and earlier ages.

The main idea in your own words: <u>**One cause of eating disorders is the**</u>

<u>**difference between increasingly overweight Americans and the "thin**</u>

<u>**is beautiful" image they see in the media.**</u>

2. Anorexia nervosa involves an intense and excessive fear of gaining weight coupled with refusal to maintain a normal body weight. In other words, people with this disorder relentlessly pursue the goal of being thin, no matter what this does to their health. They often have distorted perceptions of their own bodies, believing that they are much heavier than they really are. As a result of such fears and distorted perceptions, they starve themselves to the point where their weight drops to dangerously low levels. (Baron, *Psychology*)

Topic: _____

Main idea:

a. People with anorexia nervosa have an excessive fear of gaining weight.
b. Because they have distorted perceptions of their own bodies, people with anorexia nervosa try to be excessively thin, no matter what it does to their health.
c. People with anorexia nervosa often have distorted perceptions of their own bodies, believing that they are much heavier than they really are.

The main idea in your words: _____

_____

3. Why do persons with this disorder have such an intense fear of becoming fat? Important clues are provided by the fact that anorexia nervosa is far more common among females than males. This has led researchers to propose that because many societies emphasize physical attractiveness for females far more than for males, adolescents and young women feel tremendous pressure to live up to the images of beauty shown in the mass media—to be as thin as the models who are held up as paragons of female desirability. If they are not this thin, they reason, they will be viewed as unattractive. Actually, such assumptions appear to be false: Research findings indicate that few men prefer the extremely thin figures that anorexics believe men admire (e.g., Williamson, Cubic, & Gleaves, 1993); rather, men find a fuller-figured, more rounded appearance much more attractive. (Baron, *Psychology*)

Topic: _____

Main idea:

a. Researchers propose that anorexia is more common among females because many societies emphasize physical attractiveness for women, and the media (television, magazines, etc.) define "attractive" as thin.

b. Actually, few men prefer the extremely thin figures that anorexics believe men admire.
c. Anorexics believe that if they are not extremely thin, they will be viewed as unattractive.

The main idea in your own words: _____

_____

_____

4. If you found anorexia nervosa disturbing, you may find a second eating disorder, bulimia nervosa, even more unsettling. In this disorder individuals engage in recurrent episodes of binge eating—eating huge amounts of food within short periods of time—followed by some kind of compensatory behavior designed to prevent weight gain. This can involve self-induced vomiting, the misuse of laxatives, fasting, or exercise so excessive that it is potentially harmful to the person's health. Amazing as it may seem, persons suffering from bulimia nervosa—again, mainly young women—report purging about twelve times per week, and many purge even more often than this. My daughter once had a roommate who was a recovered bulimic. She was no longer trapped in the binge-purge cycle and was of normal weight, as are most bulimics; but her repeated binge-purge cycles had done permanent harm to her digestive system, and she had to stick to a bland diet of boiled or steamed foods. (Baron, *Psychology*)

Topic: _____

Main idea:

a. Bulimia nervosa—an eating disorder that involves binge eating and then purging to prevent weight gain—can lead to permanent health problems.
b. Purging can involve self-induced vomiting, the misuse of laxatives, fasting, or exercise so excessive that it is potentially harmful to the person's health.
c. Persons suffering from bulimia nervosa report purging about twelve times per week or even more often.

The main idea in your own words: _____

_____

_____

5. Does binge eating have a biochemical basis? It has been suggested that both binge eaters—people who go through episodes of overindulgence in food—and bulimics tend to crave and binge on sugars and starchy foods—that is, simple carbohydrates. Laboratory animals have been observed to overeat and become obese when offered highly palatable foods that are high in sugar and fat and low in fiber, and perhaps the same is true with some humans. A possible explanation is that simple carbohydrates elevate the level of the brain chemical serotonin, which affects mood and emotion and which may be low in compulsive overeaters and bulimics. In other words, people with eating disorders may be self-medicating themselves against depression by responding to carbohydrate cravings. (Williams and Knight, *Healthy for Life*)

Topic: _____

Main idea:

   a. Laboratory animals have been observed to overeat and become obese when offered highly palatable foods that are high in sugar and fat and low in fiber, and perhaps the same is true with some humans.

   b. Simple carbohydrates elevate the level of the brain chemical serotonin.

   c. Binge eating may have a biochemical basis.

The main idea in your own words: _____

_____

6. Because anorexics frequently deny their symptoms, there is often powerful resistance to treatment. With therapy, about 70% of patients recover or are improved. Unfortunately, the disease may be fatal for those who are not able to seek treatment or don't respond to treatment. Clearly, an important goal of treatment is to improve nutrition. Other therapies include psychotherapy and behavior therapy to control food-consumption behavior. Some drug therapy has been successful, including the use of antidepressants and antipsychotic drugs. (Williams and Knight, *Healthy for Life*)

Topic: _____

Main idea:

   a. The goal of treatment for anorexics is to improve nutrition.

   b. It is important for anorexics to get treatment, and several options are available, although anorexics often resist treatment.

   c. Therapies include psychotherapy and behavior therapy to control food-consumption behavior.

The main idea in your own words: _____

_____

_____

**Exercise 7**

### Work with Words

Use context clues, dictionary skills, and your knowledge of word parts to determine the appropriate meaning of each italicized word in the following sentences from the paragraphs in Exercise 6. Write the meaning of the word on the lines provided. The paragraph number is provided in case you want to check the context.

1. Puzzling as this is to me personally, the "thin is beautiful" image has *persisted* and is emphasized over and over again by television, films, and magazines. (par. 1)

   *Persisted*: _____

2. Given this increasing gap between physical reality and the image of personal beauty portrayed by the mass media, it is not surprising that *feeding and eating disorders*—disturbances in eating behavior that involve . . . unhealthy efforts to control body weight—are increasingly common. (par. 1)

*Feeding and eating disorders:* _____

_____

3. In other words, people with this disorder *relentlessly* pursue the goal of being thin, no matter what this does to their health. (par. 2)

*Relentlessly:* _____

4. As a result of such fears and *distorted perceptions*, they starve themselves to the point where their weight drops to dangerously low levels. (par. 2)

*Distorted perceptions:* _____

_____

5. This has led researchers to propose that because many societies emphasize physical attractiveness for females far more than for males, adolescents and young women feel tremendous pressure to live up to the images of beauty shown in the mass media—to be as thin as the models who are held up as *paragons* of female desirability. (par. 3)

*Paragons:* _____

6. [Bulimia nervosa] can involve self-induced vomiting, the misuse of laxatives, fasting, or exercise so excessive that it is potentially harmful to the person's health. Amazing as it may seem, persons suffering from bulimia nervosa—again, mainly young women—report *purging* about twelve times per week, and many purge even more often than this. (par. 4)

*Purging:* _____

7. Laboratory animals have been observed to overeat and become *obese* when offered highly *palatable* foods that are high in sugar and fat and low in fiber, and perhaps the same is true with some humans. (par. 5)

*Obese:* _____

8. *Palatable:* _____

9. A possible explanation is that simple carbohydrates elevate the level of the brain chemical *serotonin*, which affects mood and emotion and which may be low in compulsive overeaters and bulimics. (par. 5)

*Serotonin:* _____

10. Some drug therapy has been successful, including the use of *antidepressants* and antipsychotic drugs. (par. 6)

*Antidepressants:* _____

# MAIN IDEAS IN SHORT PASSAGES

Sometimes the main idea is not presented in a single paragraph but across two or more connected paragraphs that are unified around one idea. For short passages, titles and subheads can often help you identify the topic and main idea.

Read the following passage, and then select the best topic and main idea from the choices given. Remember, consider the information in both paragraphs as you make your selections.

### Corn

Corn is the staple of the U.S. diet. Most of the American diet is affected by corn, although few Americans fully recognize its pervasiveness. In addition to being a vegetable, corn (in one form or another) appears in soft drinks, canned foods, candy, condensed milk, baby food, jams, instant coffee, instant potatoes, and soup, among other things.

Among the many colors of corn, only the yellow and white varieties are defined as edible in the dominant U.S. culture; the more exotic colors (blue, green, orange, black, and red) are considered fit only for decoration at Thanksgiving time (although blue corn chips and other blue corn products have become available in gourmet food stores and trendy restaurants). One might speculate that this arbitrary preference for some colors of corn reflects the early American immigrants' rejection of the "exotic" elements of Native American cultures. (Ferrante, *Sociology*)

What is the best topic for this passage?

   a. corn in the United States
   b. colors of corn
   c. immigrants and corn

The best choice is "a" because both paragraphs deal with corn in the United States. What is the best main idea for this passage?

   a. Americans prefer certain colors of corn because the early settlers rejected "exotic" elements of Native American culture.
   b. Corn is pervasive in the American diet, and our preferences in types of corn may reflect the preferences of early American immigrants.
   c. Corn is the staple of the U.S. diet.

The best choice is "b" because it covers the information in both paragraphs. The first paragraph deals with how pervasive corn is in the American diet, but the second paragraph is about the types and colors of corn and speculates about why we prefer certain varieties. Both ideas are included in "b."

**Exercise 8**

## Identify Topics and Main Ideas in Short Passages

Read the following short passages about food. For each passage, choose the best topic and main idea. Then write the main idea in your own words on the lines provided.

  1. **Water, an Essential Part of Your Food and Your Body**

Water is the major component in the human body: You are composed of about 60% water. Your need for other nutrients, in terms of weight, is much less than your need for water. You can live up to 50 days without food, but only a few days without water.

Water is distributed all over the body, among lean and other tissues and in blood and other body fluids. Water is used in the digestion and absorption of food and is the medium in which most of the chemical reactions take place within the body. Some water-based fluids like blood transport substances around the body, while other fluids serve as lubricants or cushions. Water also helps regulate body temperature. (Insel et al., *Core Concepts in Health*)

Topic:

a. water in the human body
b. dehydration
c. water and food

Main idea:

a. Water is distributed all over the body, among lean and other tissues and in blood and other body fluids.
b. Water is the major component in the human body, and it is essential for many bodily processes.
c. You are composed of about 60 percent water.

The main idea in your own words: _____

_____

2. **Immigrants and Food**

Early in the 1900s, as America struggled to digest yet another wave of immigrants, a social worker paid a visit to an Italian family recently settled in Boston. In most ways, the newcomers seemed to have taken to their new home, language, and culture. There was, however, one troubling sign. "Still eating spaghetti," the social worker noted. "Not yet assimilated." Absurd as that conclusion seems now—especially in this era of pasta—it aptly illustrates our long-standing faith in a link between eating and identity. Anxious to Americanize immigrants quickly, U.S. officials saw food as a critical psychological bridge between newcomers and their old culture—and as a barrier to assimilation.

Many immigrants, for example, did not share Americans' faith in large, hearty breakfasts, preferring bread and coffee. Worse, they used garlic and other spices, and mixed their foods, often preparing an entire meal in a single pot. Break these habits, get them to eat like Americans—to partake in the meat-heavy, super-abundant U.S. diet—and, the theory confidently held, you'd have them thinking, acting, and feeling like Americans in no time. (Roberts, "How Americans Eat")

Topic:

a. spaghetti and Italian immigrants in the early 1900s
b. immigrants' preferences for breakfast
c. immigrants and food in the early 1900s

Main idea:

a. Italian immigrants were still eating spaghetti and garlic in the early 1900s.

b. It was believed that if you could get immigrants to eat like Americans, you could get them to think, act, and feel like Americans.

c. Many immigrants did not share Americans' faith in large, hearty breakfasts, preferring bread and coffee.

The main idea in your own words: _____

_____

_____

## MAIN IDEAS AND THESIS STATEMENTS IN LONG PASSAGES

**thesis statement**
main idea in a long piece of writing, especially an essay, often intended to state an argument

You've already identified main ideas in paragraphs and short passages. You can use the same skills when reading essays, short articles, and long excerpts from textbooks. Essays often have a persuasive, assertive, or even argumentative main idea. In such cases, the main idea is called a **thesis statement**. A thesis statement is the main idea in a longer piece of writing, particularly an essay. Unlike the main idea of an article or a section of a textbook, which is usually based on facts and data, the thesis statement of an essay may be based on arguments and interpretations of information, events, or ideas. A longer piece of writing may contain several paragraphs or combinations of paragraphs, each of which has a main idea. All the main ideas combine to form the thesis statement of the entire article or essay. Whether you are identifying the main idea of a paragraph or looking for the thesis of an essay, the process is the same. Remember to consider the title when you are trying to determine the author's thesis. Frequently, the title itself gives you the clues you need to determine the thesis.

**Exercise 9**

### Identify Thesis Statements in Long Passages

Read the following long passages. Then choose the best topic and thesis statement, and write the thesis statement in your own words on the lines provided.

1. In this article, Rachel Garrett discusses the misleading food labeling in the United States compared with the labeling in other countries.

### Reading the Labels

When I shop, I rely on the nutrition information and the list of ingredients to tell me exactly what I'm getting. In certain countries, like Britain and Thailand, manufacturers are required to state the exact percentages of each ingredient.[1] This makes it easier for consumers to determine more accurately what's in the food they're buying. In the United States, on the other hand, food manufacturers are required only to list the ingredients in order from highest to lowest percentage. This sometimes makes it difficult to tell exactly how much of any given ingredient is really in the package. Also, it's easy to form an inaccurate impression of a food's ingredients from the larger design of the label. Sometimes certain words are emphasized, and other words—like "artificially flavored"—are barely visible. Also, pictures often misrepresent what's in the package. During a recent trip to the grocery store, I found a number of examples of this technically accurate but deliberately misleading packaging.

First up was a cup of Maruchan Instant Lunch Ramen Noodles with Vegetables. When I opened it (after paying for and taking it home, of course), I found very few vegetables. The ingredients label says there are carrots, garlic, and onions. But I found less than half a teaspoon of freeze-dried carrots, and the five green flecks are a far cry from the seventeen fresh-looking scallions on the box. "With chili piquin and shrimp," the box says. And indeed, the picture shows five shrimp and colorful red chilies. I found that there were only four shrimp (about half an inch across) in the whole container, and no sign of the chilies. Nissin Cup Noodles with Shrimp does not fare much better. The box features five plump shrimp along with an array of fresh peas and carrots. Inside, there were four freeze-dried shrimp even smaller than Maruchan's (three were less than half an inch across) and five sad-looking peas, split and cracked from the same freeze-drying process. There was also a third of a teaspoon of carrots.

In the same aisle, I found a box of Rice-a-Roni's Chicken and Broccoli. Below the large green box that says "Chicken and Broccoli," I noticed the word "Flavor"—but only because I was looking for it. It is in light brown lettering on a lighter brown background. In other words, I'm not getting a chicken and broccoli meal, I'm getting chicken and broccoli flavor. That is a big difference: There is more chicken fat, MSG, chicken broth, "natural flavors," and gelatin in this box than there is chicken.

In the juice section, Kerns All Nectar seems to be aiming for the "natural" look, with its colorful, fruit-covered cans and clean black and white lettering. I don't know what "All Nectar" means, but the Mango All Nectar says, in tiny lettering above the nutrition label, "Contains 20% Juice." The hummingbird hovering above those fresh mangoes on the can must be in for a nasty surprise. Instead of "nectar," which carries connotations of something naturally sweet, the poor bird will find mango puree concentrate in a solution of water and high fructose corn syrup. In fact, this product is distributed by Nestlé, a company I associate more with chocolate milk than healthy, natural fruit beverages. But it was not easy to find the Nestlé brand anywhere on the label. It's down at the bottom of the tiny print.

I found another healthy-sounding drink a few shelves down. Tropicana Twister Kinetic Kiwi Strawberry is covered with pictures of kiwi fruit and strawberries, which did lead me to believe those were significant ingredients. In fact, this beverage contains only 15 percent juice, most of which is made of pears and grapes. The main ingredients are, once again, water and high fructose corn syrup. The label says, "Now with FruitForce™ Energy Releasing B Vitamins Infused Into Bold Fruit Flavors For An Active Lifestyle!" This is a fancy way of saying that they added two B vitamins: niacin and pantothenic acid (they are the last two ingredients on the list). In the United States, herbal and dietary supplements must tell consumers that their claims are just that, claims. But because Tropicana Twister is a food and not a supplement, the label doesn't have to say, "This statement has not been evaluated by the FDA." I wonder what sort of "energy" is supposed to be released. Perhaps I would feel a "sugar rush" after drinking all that high fructose corn syrup, but medical science has not proved that B vitamins have a similar effect.

Kiwi Strawberry seems to be a popular flavor, and I was curious to see if I could find anything called "Kiwi Strawberry" in which there were real kiwi fruit and strawberries, with no other added flavors. I didn't find anything like that, but I did find TreeTop's Fruit Rocketz: Ztrawberry Kiwi. This is a fruit snack that comes in a tube. It doesn't require refrigeration or a spoon, which might make it appealing for school lunches. A regular apple would be a better—and cheaper—option. The tubes of fruit are covered with strawberries and kiwi fruit. So I expected to find strawberry or kiwi fruit at least among the ingredients. In fact, the three main ingredients are apples, high fructose corn syrup, and water, followed by "natural flavor" and Red 40 (food coloring). Essentially, I'm buying red-colored, artificially flavored applesauce.

Fed up with all the prepared food, I went to the baking aisle to see what sort of options are available if I wanted to step into the kitchen and make something myself. Betty Crocker's Blueberry Muffin Mix seems designed to let me do just that. "Blueberry" is the largest word on the label, but next to "Muffin Mix" I saw (in very thin pink letters on a red background), "Imitation Blueberries Artificially Flavored." Those delicious-looking muffins on the package are, in fact, full of "imitation blueberry nuggets" made of dextrose, soybean and cottonseed oil, bleached flour, cellulose gum, citric acid, and artificial colors and flavors. Among the other muffin ingredients is—surprise—dried corn syrup. (Garrett, "Reading the Labels")

**Note**

1. "Label Watch," *Nutrition Action Health Letter*, U.S. Edition, July/August 2001, Center for Science in the Public Interest, http://www.cspinet.org/nah/07_01/ingredients.html (accessed September 2, 2005).

Topic:

a. U.S. consumers and labels
b. dishonest and misleading food labeling in the United States
c. more is less

Thesis statement:

a. Processed foods in the United States are of a poorer quality than processed foods in other countries such as Thailand and the United Kingdom.
b. There are many kinds of processed foods such as Maruchan Instant Lunch Ramen Noodles with Vegetables, Nissan Cup Noodles with Shrimp, Rice-a-Roni Chicken and Broccoli, and Kerns All Nectar.
c. The labeling of processed foods in the United States is often deliberately misleading and dishonest.

The thesis statement in your own words: _____

_____

_____

2. In this excerpt from an article, Jim Spadaccina discusses some of the side effects of eating chocolate.

## The Sweet Lure of Chocolate

One of the most pleasant effects of eating chocolate is the "good feeling" that many people experience after indulging. Chocolate contains more than 300 known chemicals. Scientists have been working on isolating specific chemicals and chemical combinations, which may explain some of the pleasurable effects of consuming chocolate.

Caffeine is the most well known of these chemical ingredients, and while it's present in chocolate, it can only be found in small quantities. Theobromine, a weak stimulant, is also present, in slightly higher amounts. The combination of these two chemicals (and possibly others) may provide the "lift" that chocolate eaters experience. Phenylethylamine is also found in chocolate. It's related to amphetamines, which are strong stimulants. All of these stimulants increase the activity of neurotransmitters (brain chemicals) in parts of the brain that control our ability to pay attention and stay alert.

While stimulants contribute to a temporary sense of well-being, there are other chemicals and other theories as to why chocolate makes us feel good. Perhaps the most controversial findings come from researchers at the Neurosciences Institute in San Diego, California. They believe that "chocolate contains pharmacologically active substances that have the same effect on the brain as marijuana, and that these chemicals may be responsible for certain drug-induced psychoses associated with chocolate craving." (Spadaccina, "The Sweet Lure of Chocolate")

Topic:

a. reasons for the good feeling when you eat chocolate
b. chocolate and marijuana
c. chocolate and stimulants

Thesis statement:

a. Chocolate contains more than 300 known chemicals.
b. Researchers say that the good feeling people get when they eat chocolate may be due to the stimulants and other chemicals in chocolate.
c. Stimulants increase the activity of neurotransmitters (brain chemicals) in parts of the brain that control our ability to pay attention and stay alert.

Write the thesis statement in your own words. _____

_____

_____

**Reading 2**

# Celebrations of Thanksgiving: A Marriage of Contrasting Traditions* — APRIL REYNOLDS

**The following reading describes the familiar tastes and traditions of the author's African-American upbringing in the South and how she missed the Thanksgivings of her childhood when she moved to New York City. As you read, make connections to your own experience with food and celebrations, and notice how Reynolds uses specific information to support her main ideas.**

1    Thanksgiving was the one day of the year my father prayed. My memories of him looming over our dinner table are as fresh as paint, and I recall his big hands clasped together as he searched our family's collective past year for things to be thankful for. "Lord, this year . . ." his voice dwindled as he thought of something appropriate, and we watched him squirm. Our house was literally falling down around us; the plumbing didn't work; you couldn't turn on the vacuum and television at the same time; there were holes in the floor and ceiling because our home couldn't stand up to Texas weather. Too poor (according to him) or too cheap (according to my mother), my father hadn't hired someone to come in and fix everything that ailed our crumbling house. But every year at Thanksgiving, my dad was determined to tell the Lord that he and his were thankful for something. "Lord, I thank you for my children," he prayed, but we all knew we were a mixed blessing. We were five mouths to feed and clothe and house, and my parents were fond of telling us we were more trouble than we were worth.

**dwindled**
became less and less

2    What finally saved my father's yearly obligatory prayer were the small children and hungry relatives gathered around the dining room table. Starved and ready to eat, they would show their united impatience with overly loud coughs that always suspiciously sounded like, "Hurry up, man." Embarrassed by the silence, my father would inevitably state the obvious, "Lord, Lord, I want to thank you for the bounty on this table," recognizing that what a poor Southern family of seven could be grateful for lay right before him.

## A JOB WELL DONE

3    This holiday, in some ways, was like the Cadillac sitting in our driveway—a physical manifestation of my father's financial success. A black man who picked cotton during his childhood, who had not one but both parents die before he was 15, who didn't even complete the seventh grade, was able to provide enough food for as many as 20 uncles, aunts, and cousins. Though my father swore he never went into debt, clearly he spent at least two of his paychecks in order to provide such a bounty. In my family, Thanksgiving was a time to show your wealth, even if you didn't have very much of it. In essence, every year we gathered around the table to congratulate my father on a job well done and not succumbing to welfare.

4    And what a feast we had. The necessary turkey that over the course of the years had undergone a plethora of cooking techniques—from browned to the point of charred to a pale, almost translucent skin—that resisted the culinary advice my relatives gave my mother (cook it in a brown paper bag, it'll seal in the juice; blast it at five hundred degrees for an hour and then turn it down) was the table's centerpiece. It was surrounded by ham, chitterlings smothered in tomato gravy and hot sauce, collard greens with ham hocks,

**chitterlings**
hog intestines

*April Reynolds, "Celebrations of Thanksgiving: A Marriage of Contrasting Tradition," http://usinfo.state.gov/journals/itsv/0704/ijse/reynolds.htm

and the secret Reynolds ingredient: dill pickle juice. Then there were turnip greens, candied yams, Jiffy cornbread dressing, mashed potatoes, macaroni and cheese, and creamed spinach. For dessert: banana bread pudding, sweet potato pie, coconut cream pie, chocolate cake, cheesecake, and sometimes as many as seven pecan pies. I always skipped dessert, but how I loved the food. The family conversation, watching the intricacies of putting together a menu—my mother literally spent weeks thinking about food preparation—made it my favorite holiday. Without the responsibility of gift giving that Christmas and birthdays brought, the only thing my sisters and I had to worry about was how much would be left over after the meal and making sly bets about which cousin, despite being as full as a tick, would go back for a third helping of corn bread dressing.

**sly**
sneaky

5    When I left for college in New York, it was Thanksgiving that I missed the most. Too poor to travel back to home, I spent the short holiday in Brooklyn with friends. At the time, I chalked up their version of Thanksgiving to youthful ignorance. The only thing on the table I recognized was the mashed potatoes. None of my friends had heard of dressing and chitterlings. Gone was the giblet gravy and ham. Instead, David, my friend from California, Alicyn from Greece, and Penelope from France had cooked up vats of couscous and curried red lentils, yellow pepper and goat cheese tarts. We ate roasted capon in lieu of turkey. I'm no fool; capon is an old chicken. And to make matters worse, my sisters called me from Texas, spoon-feeding me family gossip and news on how the year's turkey turned out. I missed the familiarity of my family's food. Did moving to New York mean eating platters of tabouli and green falafel every Thanksgiving? Suddenly, I longed for my cacophonous relatives. What was Thanksgiving if my aunt Gladys wasn't there to yank off her wig and scratch her head, her personal signal that she loved the turkey? I decided I should make my own Thanksgiving. Maybe I couldn't have the numerous Reynolds clan, but certainly I was deserving of the once a year treat of giblet gravy.

**couscous**
North African type of pasta dish

**cacophonous**
unpleasantly noisy

## FROM GUEST TO HOST

6    It was a leap into adulthood, creating my own Thanksgiving meal. Suddenly, I had made the move from guest to responsible host all because of my favorite holiday. We invited friends and co-workers whose families were too far away. No more moussaka for me; I called my parents, taking copious notes on how to create moist dressing and my mother's world famous chitterlings. Everything was going to be wonderful, a true Southern Thanksgiving in East Harlem. There was only one problem: my husband.

7    Well, he's not really a problem, but he's certainly Italian. It seems I wasn't the only one aching for reminders of home during Thanksgiving. We weren't inviting enough people to justify every dish we agreed was essential for a proper Thanksgiving, nor did we have space to prepare so much food. Our Thanksgiving holiday, even now, is a complicated compromise, a negotiation of Northern taste buds, Southern desires, and Italian expectations. And so while we don't have chitterlings or spaghetti with red gravy, we did agree that without a rendition of Kenneth's grandmother's towering antipasti, Thanksgiving just wasn't Thanksgiving.

8    Capicolla, mortadella, prosciutto, sopressatta, Genoa salami—all sliced paper thin—are piled up to a dizzying height along with endive, tomatoes, roasted bell peppers, capers, and Italian tuna fish. This appetizer is so important, according to my husband, that the women gather around this cold antipasto and have their picture taken just before they all sit down to eat.

9    We don't take pictures of the antipasti in my house, but every year I faithfully follow Grandma Edith's recipe. And though I miss some of the dishes my family prepared, like my father, I'm grateful and happy with the bounty on the table. This marriage of mine,

a coming together of home cooking and celebration, of Italian and black Southern cuisine eaten by my many Northern friends, is distinctly American. And trust me, next year I'll get to make my chitterlings.

**Exercise 10**

## Work with Words

The following sentences appear in Reading 2, Reynolds's "Celebrations of Thanksgiving." Use context clues, dictionary skills, and your knowledge of word parts to determine the appropriate meaning of each italicized word in the sentences. Write the meaning on the lines provided. The paragraph number is provided in case you want to check the context.

1. My memories of him looming over our dinner table are as fresh as paint, and I recall his big hands clasped together as he searched our family's *collective* past year for things to be thankful for. (par. 1)

   *Collective*: _____

2. Our house was *literally* falling down around us; the plumbing didn't work; you couldn't turn on the vacuum and television at the same time; there were holes in the floor and ceiling because our home couldn't stand up to Texas weather. (par. 1)

   *Literally*: _____

3. What finally saved my father's yearly *obligatory* prayer were the small children and hungry relatives gathered around the dining room table. (par. 2)

   *Obligatory*: _____

4. Embarrassed by the silence, my father would *inevitably* state the obvious, "Lord, Lord, I want to thank you for the *bounty* on this table," recognizing that what a poor Southern family of seven could be grateful for lay right before him. (par. 2)

   *Inevitably*: _____

5. *Bounty*: _____

6. In essence, every year we gathered around the table to congratulate my father on a job well done and not *succumbing* to welfare. (par. 3)

   *Succumbing*: _____

7. The necessary turkey that over the course of the years had undergone a *plethora* of cooking techniques—from browned to the point of charred to a pale, almost *translucent* skin—that resisted the culinary advice my relatives gave my mother (cook it in a brown paper bag, it'll seal in the juice; blast it at five hundred degrees for an hour and then turn it down) was the table's centerpiece. (par. 4)

   *Plethora*: _____

8. *Translucent*: _____

9. The family conversation, watching the *intricacies* of putting together a menu—my mother literally spent weeks thinking about food preparation—made it my favorite holiday. (par. 4)

   *Intricacies:* _____

10. And so while we don't have chitterlings or spaghetti with red gravy, we did agree that without a *rendition* of Kenneth's grandmother's towering antipasti, Thanksgiving just wasn't Thanksgiving. (par. 7)

    *Rendition:* _____

---

**Exercise 11**

## Identify Topics and Main Ideas

For each of the following paragraphs from Reading 2, choose the best topic and main idea statement. Then write the main idea in your own words on the lines provided.

1. Paragraph 3

   Topic:

   a. the food we ate at Thanksgiving
   b. my parents' schooling
   c. my father's accomplishments

   Main idea:

   a. My father worked hard so that in spite of his difficult childhood he was able to share his wealth with many family members at Thanksgiving.
   b. Though my father swore he never went into debt, clearly he spent at least two of his paychecks in order to provide such a bounty.
   c. In my family, Thanksgiving was a time to show your wealth, even if you didn't have very much of it.

   The main idea in your own words: _____

   _____

2. Paragraph 4

   Topic:

   a. Thanksgiving feast
   b. how to cook a turkey
   c. the love of food

   Main idea:

   a. The family conversation, and watching the preparations for Thanksgiving made it my favorite holiday.
   b. Our Thanksgiving meal was a real feast.
   c. There are several ways to successfully cook a turkey.

   The main idea in your own words: _____

3. Paragraph 5

Topic:

a. meal preparation
b. Thanksgiving in the South
c. Thanksgiving in New York

Main idea:

a. The Thanksgiving in New York was not a good one for me; I missed home, the food, and family, and none of the things we ate were like the food for Thanksgiving back home.
b. I spent the short holiday in Brooklyn with my friends.
c. The wonderful food we had was from all over the world and was perfect for the occasion.

The main idea in your own words: _____

_____

_____

**Exercise 12**

### Check Your Understanding

Answer the following questions based on Reading 2.

1. Read the thesis statement of the reading and then restate it in your own words.

Thesis: "This marriage of mine, a coming together of home cooking and celebration, of Italian and black Southern cuisine eaten by my many Northern friends, is distinctly American." (par. 9)

_____

_____

2. In paragraph 5, Reynolds complains about the Thanksgiving meal she had in New York when she left home to attend college. She was especially upset about the kinds of food that were served. In this part of the paragraph, she provides a rich list of the *specific* foods that she did not think of as Thanksgiving food. List those foods here.

_____

_____

3. In paragraph 3, Reynolds writes about the challenges and successes of her father.

a. What were the *specific* challenges he had faced? _____

_____

_____

b. What were his *specific* accomplishments? _____

_____

_____

4. In paragraph 4, Reynolds gives examples of delicious foods the family shared at Thanksgiving. Underline the *specific* foods she includes in her description of the meal.

**Exercise 13**

## Reflect and Write

Think about what you read in Reading 2 and what you already know about holidays, special foods, and cultural traditions. Answer the following questions, and prepare to discuss them with your classmates.

1. What food has special significance to you? Describe the food with specific details and explain why it is important to you.

_____

_____

_____

_____

_____

2. What is your least favorite food? Why is it your least favorite? What memories are associated with this food? Explain.

_____

_____

_____

_____

3. On a separate piece of paper, write two or three paragraphs comparing and contrasting a holiday or special meal you ate as a child with the meal you typically eat at the same holiday or special occasion today. How are the meals similar? How are they different? Consider foods and their preparation as well as where, when, and with whom you ate or eat. Make sure to identify the holiday or special occasion. For the title of your paragraphs, write "A Special Meal: Then and Now."

## Reading 3

# Table Rituals*— Laurie Tarkan

**The following article by Laurie Tarkan appeared in the *New York Times*. In it, Tarkan discusses studies that support the importance of families eating together. As you read, consider your personal experience of eating meals with members of your family.**

**illicit**
illegal

1   The family dinner has long been an example of family togetherness. But recently, scientists have been coming up with compelling reasons—including a lowered risk of smoking, drinking, and doing illicit drugs among teenagers—for families to pull up a chair around the table.

2   The interest in the ritual may have been spurred by concerns that the number of families who do not dine together is increasing. According to several surveys, 30 to 40 percent of families do not eat dinner together five to seven nights a week, though most families eat dinner together some days a week. Families with older teenagers eat fewer dinners together than those with younger children. The two most common obstacles, parents say, are late working hours and activities that overlap with mealtime, like soccer games and Girl Scout meetings.

**carve out**
find

3   Many families that do dine together make a concerted effort to carve out the time. Some spend Sundays cooking meals for the week, some do prep work the evening before, some use takeout a couple of nights a week, and many parents of young children guiltily admit that they could not prepare a dinner if it were not for the TV, which gets turned on for 30 to 60 minutes while they cook. . . .

Many families do not regularly eat meals together. Studies have shown that more than 30 percent of American children eat dinner in front of the television every night.

4   Childhood memories often influence people's opinion about the importance of family dinners. Isabel Wurgaft, a member of a group for working mothers in Millburn, N.J., said: "Growing up, my father got home late, at 8 p.m., but my mother always made us wait to eat as a family no matter how much we complained. Now that my father has passed away over 10 years ago, dinner conversations are the strongest and best memories for me and my sisters." For others, though, the struggle is apparent. "I feel guilty because it's supposed to be very important for families to eat together, but it just doesn't work with our schedule," said Janette Pazer, another member of the

working mothers' group. "I'd have to leave work an hour early, and try to cook while they're hanging on me for attention and asking for homework help, rather than getting my full attention when I get home."

5    In past eras, the family meal was more of a practicality—people had to eat, and they turned up at the table, where food was being served. "In the contemporary world, we've made an icon of the dinner hour as a way to hold on to something, otherwise people would go off in different directions and never get together," said Barbara Haber, the author of *From Hardtack to Home Fries: An Uncommon History of American Cooks and Meals*.

icon
symbol

6    Recent studies have begun to shore up the idea that family dinners can have an effect. For example, a 2004 study of 4,746 children 11 to 18 years old, published in the *Archives of Pediatrics and Adolescent Medicine*, found that frequent family meals were associated with a lower risk of smoking, drinking, and using marijuana; with a lower incidence of depressive symptoms and suicidal thoughts; and with better grades. Another study last year, a survey of 12- to 17-year-olds by the National Center on Addiction and Substance Abuse at Columbia University, found that teenagers who reported eating two or fewer dinners a week with family members were more than one and a half times as likely to smoke, drink or use illegal substances than were teenagers who had five to seven family dinners. "We also noticed that the more often teens had dinner with their parents, the less likely they were to have sexually active friends, less likely girls were to have boyfriends two years older, and the less time teens spent with boyfriends or girlfriends," said Joseph A. Califano Jr., the center's chairman and president. A study from the University of Minnesota published last year found that adolescent girls who reported having more frequent family meals and a positive atmosphere during those meals were less likely to have eating disorders.

7    "The family dinner is an important time for families to be together and talk, it's important for family bonds having time together that's not stressful, enjoying each other's company and being around food," said Dr. Karen Weber Cullen, a behavioral nutritionist at the Children's Nutrition Research Center at Baylor College of Medicine in Houston. Family meals, experts say, also offer a predictable routine and an opportunity for parents to monitor their children's behavior. "That monitoring has been related to a host of positive physical and mental health outcomes in children and adolescents," said Dr. Barbara Fiese, who studies family routines and rituals at Syracuse University. She added that regular family meals also provide an opportunity to establish a sense of belonging to a family unit.

8    According to one study, family dinners may help improve the vocabulary of younger children. Researchers at Harvard in 1996 looked at the types of activities that promoted language development. Family dinners were more important than play, story time, and other family events. And those families that engaged in extended discourse at the dinner table, like story telling and explanations, rather than one-phrase comments, like "eat your vegetables," had children with better language skills, said Dr. Catherine Snow, professor of education at Harvard and the researcher of the study. "When there is more than one adult at the table, it tends to make talk richer, topics are established by adult interest and can be extremely valuable opportunities for children to learn," Dr. Snow said.

9    A handful of studies have also suggested that eating as a family improves children's consumption of fruits and vegetables, grains, fiber, and vitamins and minerals. Children who have family meals also eat less fried food, saturated fat, and soda, studies suggest.

**Exercise 14**

## Work with Words

The following sentences appear in Reading 3, Tarkan's "Table Rituals." Use context clues, dictionary skills, and your knowledge of word parts to determine the appropriate meaning of each italicized word in the sentences. Write the meaning of the word on the lines provided. The paragraph number is provided in case you want to check the context.

1. But recently, scientists have been coming up with *compelling* reasons—including a lowered risk of smoking, drinking, and doing illicit drugs among teenagers—for families to pull up a chair around the table. (par. 1)

   *Compelling:* _____

2. Many families that do dine together make a *concerted* effort to carve out the time. (par. 3)

   *Concerted:* _____

3. For others, though, the struggle is *apparent.* "I feel guilty because it's supposed to be very important for families to eat together, but it just doesn't work with our schedule," said Janette Pazer, another member of the working mothers' group. (par. 4)

   *Apparent:* _____

4. "In the *contemporary* world, we've made an icon of the dinner hour as a way to hold on to something, otherwise people would go off in different directions and never get together." (par. 5)

   *Contemporary:* _____

5. Recent studies have begun to *shore up* the idea that family dinners can have an effect. (par. 6)

   *Shore up:* _____

6. For example, a 2004 study of 4,746 children 11 to 18 years old, published in the *Archives of Pediatrics and Adolescent Medicine,* found that frequent family meals were associated with a lower risk of smoking, drinking, and using marijuana; with a lower *incidence* of depressive symptoms and suicidal thoughts; and with better grades. (par. 6)

   *Incidence:* _____

7. She added that regular family meals also provide an opportunity to establish a *sense* of belonging to a family unit. (par. 7)

   *Sense:* _____

8. Researchers at Harvard in 1996 looked at the types of activities that *promoted* language development. (par. 8)

   *Promoted:* _____

9. And those families that engaged in extended *discourse* at the dinner table, like story telling and explanations, rather than one-phrase comments, like "eat your vegetables," had children with better language skills, said Dr. Catherine Snow, professor of education at Harvard and the researcher of the study. (par. 8)

*Discourse*: _____

10. A handful of studies have also suggested that eating as a family improves children's *consumption* of fruits and vegetables, grains, fiber, and vitamins and minerals. (par. 9)

*Consumption*: _____

**Exercise 15**

## Identify Topics and Main Ideas

For each of the following paragraphs from Reading 3, choose the best topic and main idea statement. Then write the main idea in your own words on the lines provided.

1. Paragraph 2

   Topic:

   a. reasons for not eating together
   b. teenagers not at the dinner table
   c. decline in numbers of families eating together

   Main idea:

   a. For a variety of reasons, fewer families are eating meals together.
   b. According to several surveys, 30 to 40 percent of families do not eat dinner together five days a week.
   c. Working late and activities that overlap with mealtime are common problems.

   The main idea in your own words: _____

   _____

2. Paragraph 4

   Topic:

   a. fond childhood memories of eating together
   b. childhood memories and obstacles to eating together
   c. reasons for not eating together

   Main idea:

   a. Childhood memories influence people's opinions about the importance of family dinners.

    b. Some people just can't manage to get things organized to have meals together, even though for many people childhood meals are among their most important memories.

    c. It simply does not work out for people with small children to try to have meals together in the evening because the children need so much attention and homework help.

The main idea in your own words: _____

_____

_____

3. Paragraphs 1–9

Topic:

    a. making the effort to eat together
    b. practical family meals
    c. benefits of eating together

Main idea:

    a. Many families make a special effort to eat together at least a few times a week.
    b. In the past, the family meal was more of a practicality—people had to eat, and they turned up at the table, where food was being served.
    c. Recent studies demonstrate some important reasons for families to eat meals together, especially for the benefit of teenagers.

The main idea in your own words: _____

_____

_____

**Exercise 16**

### Check Your Understanding

Based on Reading 3, choose the best answer to each of the following multiple-choice questions.

1. Which of the following behaviors of teenagers seems to be encouraged when the family has meals together?
    a. performing well in athletics
    b. smoking
    c. getting good grades

2. Which of the following behaviors of teenagers seems to be discouraged when the family has meals together?
    a. good grades in school
    b. depression and illegal drug use
    c. language development

3. Family meals—with good interaction and conversation—tend to improve which of the following for young children?
   a. language skills
   b. math skills
   c. skills for getting along with people

4. It's important to remember that for family meals to have so many good effects
   a. the food should be nutritious.
   b. the atmosphere should not be stressful.
   c. the interaction should be exciting.

**Exercise 17**

### Reflect and Write

Think about what you read in Reading 3 and what you already know about the benefits of family meals. Answer the following questions, and prepare to discuss them with your classmates.

1. Why do you think many American families do not regularly eat together?

   _____

   _____

   _____

   _____

   _____

2. List the qualities you think families that eat together would have.

   _____

   _____

   _____

   _____

3. On a separate sheet of paper, write one or two paragraphs to answer the following questions. What eating habits does/did your family have? Do or did you eat together? Is or was it a pleasant experience? Make sure you provide specific examples to support your answer.

## Write About It

Find a short article (approximately two pages) from a magazine, newspaper, or Internet source about one of the following topics:

- Food and nutrition
- Eating disorders
- The fast-food industry
- A specific food or additive (such as salt, sugar, chocolate, hamburgers)
- American eating habits
- Diets

On a separate sheet of paper and in your own words, answer the following questions about the article you have chosen.

1. What is the title of the article, and who is the author?

2. Where does the article come from? (Write the name of the magazine or website and give the date, if possible.)

3. What is the topic of the article?

4. What is the thesis?

5. What points does the author make to help you understand or to convince you of the thesis of the article?

6. What is your reaction to the article? Was the article interesting to you? Why or why not? Was it convincing? Why or why not?

7. Would you recommend this article to other students? Explain.

8. What new information did you learn from the article?

# Chapter Review

| Put It Together: Topics and Main Ideas | |
|---|---|
| Skills and Concepts | Explanation |
| **Topic** (see pages 96–97) | Subject of a reading; answers the question "What is it about?" in a few words, not a full sentence |
| **Main Idea** (see pages 96–99) | Most important point of the reading; a general statement about the topic, written as a full sentence |
| **Generalization** (see page 97) | Broad, general statement that covers all the important points about a topic |
| **Assertion** (see page 97) | Statement of an opinion or an argument for a particular understanding of the topic |

## Put It Together: Topics and Main Ideas

| Skills and Concepts | Explanation |
| --- | --- |
| **Stated Main Idea** (see pages 97–99) | Main idea that clearly appears in a reading, often near the beginning |
| **Topic Sentence** (see page 98) | Name usually used in writing classes for a main idea sentence |
| **Paraphrasing** (see page 103) | Restating an idea in your own words |
| **Implied Main Idea** (see page 104) | Main idea that is suggested but not specifically stated by a reading |
| **Thesis Statement** (see page 115) | Main idea in a long piece of writing, especially an essay, often intended to state an argument |

## CRITICAL REFLECTIONS IN THE CLASSROOM COMMUNITY

As a group or individually, complete the following activities.

1. List at least four ways that convenience foods—fast foods and processed foods—have affected our lives. You may also want to think about and include how it has affected the way we work.

   _____

   _____

   _____

   _____

   _____

   _____

2. List the ingredients in five foods you find on store shelves or in your kitchen at home, and when you come to class, compare lists. Discuss which foods have the most additives and how much you can find out about the food from the label.

3. Go to a fast-food restaurant. Find out about, and then write a report on, the calories of the meals served, fat content, and price. If you are working with classmates, different students in your group should go to different fast-food restaurants. Present and compare your findings in class.

4. Follow the directions in Activity 3, but talk to the workers at the restaurant(s) about how the food is prepared, how much the workers earn, and what benefits they have. If possible, also interview the manager(s).

## 🌐 WORK THE WEB

1. Because so many American adults and children are overweight, researchers are investigating possible solutions to the problem. An article on the National Institutes of Health's (NIH) website describes how and why "mindless eating" can negatively affect your weight. Read "Hidden Persuaders: The Mindless Eating That Adds Pounds" and determine the topic and main idea of the article. On the lines provided, write the main idea in your own words. To find this article, do a web search for "NIH Hidden Persuaders."

_____

_____

_____

_____

_____

2. One tip that the article mentions is controlling portion size. Portions have increased dramatically over the last 20 to 50 years. Take the "Portion Distortion" quizzes (I and II) on the National Institutes of Health's website. To find these quizzes, do a web search for "NIH Portion Distortion." Which change in portion size surprised you the most? Based on this information, will you change the portion size of any foods or drinks that you consume? If so, what will you change? Why?

_____

_____

_____

_____

Name _____ Date _____

# Behind the Counter*

— ERIC SCHLOSSER

**TEXT BOOK** The following reading is from Eric Schlosser's best-seller, *Fast Food Nation*. Here he explains how work is organized in fast-food restaurants and the historical precedents for organizing work in this way. One of Schlosser's main assertions is that fast-food restaurants are really run like factory assembly lines. As you read, you might think about what it's like to work in one of these restaurants and the way assembly-line preparation affects the food you eat. Also, try to identify his thesis for the reading and the main idea of each paragraph.

1   The labor practices of the fast food industry have their <u>origins</u> in the assembly line systems adopted by American manufacturers in the early twentieth century. Business historian Alfred D. Chandler has argued that a high rate of "<u>throughput</u>" was the most important aspect of these mass production systems. A factory's throughput is the speed and volume of its flow—a much more crucial measurement, according to Chandler, than the number of workers it employs or the value of its machinery. With innovative technology and the proper organization, a small number of workers can produce an enormous amount of goods cheaply. Throughput is all about increasing the speed of assembly, about doing things faster in order to make more.

2   Although the McDonald brothers had never <u>encountered</u> the term "throughput" or studied "scientific management," they instinctively grasped the underlying principles and applied them in the Speedee Service System. The restaurant operating scheme they developed has been widely adopted and refined over the past half century. The ethos of the assembly line remains at its core. The fast food industry's obsession with throughput has <u>altered</u> the way millions of Americans work, turned commercial kitchens into small factories, and changed familiar foods into commodities that are manufactured.

**ethos**
philosophy or values

**conveyer belts**
belts that move products down a line

3   At Burger King restaurants, frozen hamburger patties are placed on a conveyer belt and <u>emerge</u> from a broiler ninety seconds later fully cooked. The ovens at Pizza Hut and at Domino's also use conveyer belts to ensure the standardized cooking times. The ovens at McDonald's look like commercial laundry presses, with big steel hoods that swing down and grill hamburgers on both sides at once. The burgers, chicken, french fries, and buns are all frozen when they arrive at a McDonald's; the shakes and sodas begin as syrup. . . . At Taco Bell restaurants the food is "assembled," not prepared. The guacamole isn't made by workers in the kitchen; it's made at a factory in Michoacán, Mexico, then frozen and shipped north. The chain's taco meat arrives frozen and precooked in vacuum-sealed plastic bags. The beans are dehydrated and look like brownish corn flakes. The cooking process is fairly simple. "Everything's add water," a Taco Bell employee told me. "Just add hot water."

**dehydrated**
dried

4   Although Richard and Mac McDonald introduced the division of labor to the restaurant business, it was a McDonald's executive named Fred Turner who created a production system of unusual thoroughness and attention to detail. In 1958, Turner put together an operations and training manual for the company that was seventy-five

pages long, specifying how almost everything should be done. Hamburgers were always to be placed on the grill in six neat rows; french fries had to be exactly 0.28 inches thick. The McDonald's operations manual today has ten times the number of pages and weighs about four pounds. Known within the company as "the Bible," it contains precise instructions on how various appliances should be used, how each item on the menu should look, and how employees should greet customers. Operators who disobey these rules can lose their <u>franchises</u>. Cooking instructions are not only printed in the manual; they are often designed into the machines. A McDonald's kitchen is full of buzzers and flashing lights that tell employees what to do.

5      At the front counter, computerized cash registers issue their own commands. Once an order has been placed, buttons light up and suggest other menu items that can be added. Workers at the counter are told to increase the size of an order by recommending special **promotions**, pushing dessert, pointing out the financial logic behind the purchase of a larger drink. While doing so, they are instructed to be upbeat and friendly. "Smile with a greeting and make a positive first impression," a Burger King training manual suggests. "Show them you are glad to see them. Include eye contact with the cheerful greeting."

**promotions**
offers

6      The strict <u>regimentation</u> at fast food restaurants creates standardized products. It increases the throughput. And it gives fast food companies an enormous amount of power over their employees. "When management determines exactly how every task is to be done ... and can impose its own rules about pace, output, quality, and technique," the sociologist Robin Leidner has noted, "[it] makes workers increasingly interchangeable." The management no longer depends upon the talents or skills of its workers—those things are built into the operating system and machines. Jobs that have been "de-skilled" can be filled cheaply. The need to <u>retain</u> any individual worker is greatly reduced by the ease with which he or she can be replaced.

7      Teenagers have long provided the fast food industry with the <u>bulk</u> of its workforce. The industry's rapid growth coincided with the **baby-boom** expansion of that age group. Teenagers were in many ways the ideal candidates for these low-paying jobs. Since most teenagers still lived at home, they could afford to work for wages too low to support an adult, and until recently, their limited skills attracted few other employers. A job at a fast food restaurant became an American rite of passage, a first job soon left behind for better things. The flexible terms of employment in the fast food industry also attracted housewives who needed extra income. As the number of baby-boom teenagers declined, the fast food chains began to hire other <u>marginalized</u> workers: recent immigrants, the elderly, and the handicapped.

**baby-boom**
referring to
the population
explosion
between 1946
and 1964

| Exercise 1 | Work with Words |

Use context clues, dictionary skills, and your knowledge of word parts to choose the best definition for each of the following words underlined in the reading. For some of the following words, dictionary definitions have been provided for you. The paragraph number is provided in case you want to check the context.

1. *Origins* (par. 1)
   a. beginnings, precedents
   b. ancestry, family tree
   c. connections

2. *"Throughput"* (par. 1)
   a. crucial measurement
   b. number of workers a factory employs and the value of its machinery
   c. speed and volume of flow in a mass production system

3. *Encountered* (par. 2)

**en·coun·ter** (ĕn-koun´tər) *n.* **1.** A meeting, especially one that is unplanned, unexpected, or brief: *a chance encounter in the park.* **2. a.** A hostile or adversarial confrontation; a contest: *a tense naval encounter.* **b.** An often violent meeting; a clash. **—en·coun·ter** *v.* **en·coun·tered, en·coun·ter·ing, en·coun·ters.—***tr.* **1.** To meet, especially unexpectedly; come upon: *encountered an old friend on the street.* **2.** To confront in battle or contention. **3.** To come up against: *encounter numerous obstacles.—intr.* To meet, especially unexpectedly. [Middle English *encountre,* from Old French, from *encontrer,* to meet, from Late Latin *incontrāre* : Latin *in-,* in; see EN-[1] + Latin *contrā,* against; see **kom** below.]

*(American Heritage Dictionary)*

   a. confronted in battle
   b. met, as in seen or heard
   c. came up against obstacles

4. *Altered* (par. 2)

**al·ter** (ôl´tər) *v.* **al·tered, al·ter·ing, al·ters.—***tr.* **1.** To change or make different; modify: *altered my will.* **2.** To adjust (a garment) for a better fit. **3.** To castrate or spay (an animal, such as a cat or a dog).*—intr.* To change or become different. [Middle English *alteren,* from Old French *alterer,* from Medieval Latin *alterāre,* from Latin *alter,* other. See **al-**[1] below.]

*(American Heritage Dictionary)*

   a. castrated or spayed
   b. adjusted for a better fit
   c. changed or made different

5. *Emerge* (par. 3)
   a. come out
   b. burn
   c. drop down

6. *Franchises* (par. 4)

**fran·chise** (frăn´chīz´) *n.* **1.** A privilege or right officially granted a person or a group by a government, especially: **a.** The constitutional or statutory right to vote. **b.** The establishment of a corporation's existence. **c.** The granting of certain rights and powers to a corporation. **d.** Legal immunity from servitude, certain burdens, or other restrictions. **2. a.** Authorization granted to someone to sell or distribute a company's goods or services in a certain area. **b.** A business or group of businesses established or operated under such authorization. **3.** The territory or limits within which immunity, a privilege, or a right may be exercised. **4.** *Informal.* A professional sports team.

*(American Heritage Dictionary)*

a. a privilege officially granted by a government
b. authorization granted to someone to sell or distribute a company's goods or services in a certain area
c. the constitutional right to vote

7. *Regimentation* (par. 6)

**reg·i·ment** (rĕj´ə-mənt) *n. Abbr.* **reg., regt. 1.** A military unit of ground troops consisting of at least two battalions, usually commanded by a colonel. **2.** A large group of people.—**reg·i·ment** *tr.v.* **reg·i·ment·ed, reg·i·ment·ing, reg·i·ments** (rĕj´ə-mĕnt´). **1.** To form into a regiment. **2.** To put into systematic order; systematize. **3.** To subject to uniformity and rigid order. [Middle English, government, rule, from Old French, from Late Latin *regimentum*, rule, from Latin *regere*, to rule. See **reg-** below.]—**reg´i·men´tal** (-mĕn´tl) *adj.*—**reg´i·men´tal·ly** *adv.*—**reg´i·men·ta´tion** *n.*

*(American Heritage Dictionary)*

a. formation of a military unit
b. a large group of people
c. the act of putting into systematic order and making uniform

8. *Retain* (par. 6)

**re·tain** (rĭ-tān´) *tr.v.* **re·tained, re·tain·ing, re·tains.** *Abbr.* **ret. 1.** To maintain possession of. See Synonyms at **keep. 2.** To keep or hold in a particular place, condition, or position. **3.** To keep in mind; remember. **4.** To hire (an attorney, for example) by the payment of a fee. **5.** To keep in one's service or pay. [Middle English *retainen*, from Old French *retenir*, from Latin *retinēre*: re-, re- + *tenēre*, to hold; see **ten-** below.]—**re·tain´a·bil´i·ty** *n.*—**re·tain´a·ble** *adj.*—**re·tain´ment** *n.*

*(American Heritage Dictionary)*

a. to maintain possession of
b. to keep in mind
c. to keep in one's service or pay

9. *Bulk* (par. 7)

**bulk** (bŭlk) *n.* **1.** Size, mass, or volume, especially when very large. **2. a.** A distinct mass or portion of matter, especially a large one: t*he dark bulk of buildings against the sky.* **b.** The body of a human being, especially when large. **3.** The major portion or greater part: "*The great bulk of necessary work can never be anything but painful*" (Bertrand Russell). **4.** See **fiber. 5.** Thickness of paper or cardboard in relation to weight. **6.** *Abbr.* **blk.** *Nautical.* A ship's cargo.

*(American Heritage Dictionary)*

a. size, mass, or volume
b. the major portion or greater part
c. thickness of paper or cardboard

10. *Marginalized* (par. 7)
a. baby-boom teenagers
b. fast-food workers
c. recent immigrants, the elderly, the handicapped

**Exercise 2**

## Check Your Understanding

Based on the reading, Schlosser's "Behind the Counter," choose the best answer to each of the following multiple-choice questions.

1. "Throughput" is probably
   a. the most important aspect of mass production systems.
   b. organizing work by following instincts.
   c. a term that has become obsolete in the beginning of the twenty-first century.

2. The McDonald brothers used the same ideas as "scientific management," even though
   a. they were never exposed to those ideas.
   b. they knew instinctively the ideas might not work.
   c. the ideas were obsolete.

3. The author argues that the fast-food industry's obsession with throughput has
   a. changed the nutritional value of food.
   b. changed the way millions of Americans work.
   c. improved the working conditions of millions of Americans.

4. Fred Turner was the first person to
   a. introduce a division of labor in the restaurant business.
   b. open a McDonald's restaurant.
   c. put together an operations and training manual for McDonald's.

5. When the author writes, "Hamburgers were always to be placed on the grill in six neat rows," he is giving an example of
   a. the regimentation of fast-food preparation.
   b. the need for longer operations manuals.
   c. the way cooking instructions are designed into the machines.

6. Workers at the counter are told to recommend special promotions to
   a. make the customers happy.
   b. increase the size of an order.
   c. help customers save money.

7. Fast-food workers tend to be upbeat and cheerful because they are
   a. satisfied with their jobs.
   b. chosen because they like to work with people.
   c. instructed to do so.

8. Robin Leidner noted that the organization of work at fast-food restaurants "makes workers increasingly interchangeable." This means that
   a. it is easy to replace a fast-food worker.
   b. managers will value the workers more because it takes time to train them.
   c. workers can use their talents and skills to contribute to the smooth running of the business.

9. Teenagers have provided the fast-food industry with most of its workforce for all the following reasons except
   a. the jobs are low paying.
   b. there are good possibilities for advancement.
   c. they didn't need to have skills and experience.

10. Eric Schlosser, the author of the reading "Behind the Counter," is
    a. very happy about the organization of the fast-food business because of the advantages it brings to the customers.
    b. interested only in analyzing how fast-food businesses work.
    c. critical of the way fast-food restaurants turn food preparation into assembly lines and make workers easily replaceable.

**Exercise 3**

## Identify Topics and Main Ideas

For each of the following paragraphs from the reading, choose the best topic and main idea statement.

1. Paragraphs 1 and 2

   Topic:

   a. the fast-food industry
   b. throughput and the fast-food industry
   c. the McDonald brothers and restaurant operating schemes

   Main idea:

   a. The fast-food industry bases its practices on throughput, an idea that was developed by American manufacturers in the early twentieth century and is about increasing the speed of assembly.
   b. Business historian Alfred D. Chandler has argued that a high rate of "throughput" was the most important aspect of mass production systems.
   c. A factory's throughput is the speed and volume of its flow.

2. Paragraph 3

   Topic:

   a. standardized cooking times
   b. how fast food is prepared
   c. the use of water to prepare food

   Main idea:

   a. The foods at fast-food restaurants may come from far away.
   b. At Taco Bell, the cooking process comes down to just adding water.
   c. At fast-food restaurants, food seems to be "assembled" (like putting pieces of something together) rather than prepared.

3. Paragraph 4

Topic:

a. operating instructions at McDonald's
b. the division of labor in the restaurant business
c. McDonald's franchises

Main idea:

a. Operations manuals specify exactly how everything is supposed to be done at McDonald's.
b. Fred Turner created a production system of unusual thoroughness.
c. Cooking instructions are often designed into the machines.

4. Paragraph 6

Topic:

a. workers at fast-food restaurants and the team approach
b. the talents of workers at fast-food restaurants
c. regimentation and easy replacement of employees at fast-food restaurants

Main idea:

a. The need to retain a worker is reduced because it is easy to replace them.
b. The management no longer depends on the talents or skills of its workers.
c. The strict regimentation at fast-food restaurants creates standardized products, increases throughput, and gives fast-food companies an enormous power over their workers.

5. Paragraphs 1–7

Topic:

a. source of food at fast-food restaurants
b. organization of work at fast-food restaurants
c. quality of food at fast-food restaurants

Main idea:

a. The regimented organization and de-skilling of tasks at fast-food restaurants have turned the work into very simple assembly and have made the employees easily replaceable and vulnerable.
b. The fast-food industry has gotten most of its techniques of organization from assembly-line systems of the early twentieth century.
c. Fast-food workers are mostly teenagers and other marginalized workers because the jobs are low paying and don't require skill.

**Exercise 4**

Reflect

Think about what you read in "Behind the Counter" and what you already know about different work situations. Then answer the following questions.

1. Why do you think fast-food restaurants have organized their food preparation systems like assembly lines? Explain your answer.

_____

_____

_____

_____

2. Have you or anyone you know ever worked in a fast-food restaurant or in a situation where the work was strictly regimented, as in a factory assembly line? Describe what it's like to work under those conditions. (If you don't have experience, use your imagination.) What kinds of satisfaction might workers get? What kinds of problems might they have? Explain your answers.

_____

_____

_____

_____

# 4 Support for Main Ideas

## STAYING WELL

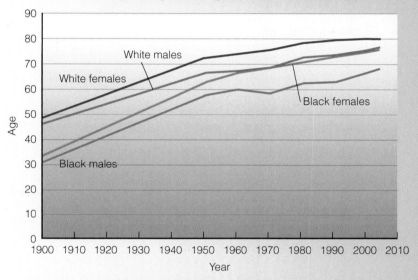

**Life Expectancy at Birth by Sex and Race, 1900–2004**

Source: U.S. National Center for Health Statistics, *Health*, United States, 2006, with *Chartbook on Trends in the Health of Americans* (Hyattsville, MD: Centers for Disease Control and Prevention, 2006).

*You can set yourself up to be sick, or you can choose to stay well.*
*—Wayne Dyer*

1. Why do you think life expectancy has increased over the last one hundred years?

2. What does this graph show about differences in life expectancy with respect to sex and race?

3. What do you think this quotation means? Does the graph support the quotation?

4. List some decisions people make in their day-to-day lives that affect their health and well-being.

# Prepare to Read

Today, according to health experts, we are living in the age of *wellness*. In the past century, human life expectancy has almost doubled. The average person born a hundred years ago could expect to live only into his or her 40s, while the average baby born now can expect to live well into his or her 70s. How can you take advantage of the information about health and wellness that has become available to us? How can you achieve optimal well-being and live a long, productive, and fulfilling life?

In this chapter, you will read about wellness and learn to

- Recognize how major and minor points support main ideas
- Organize your understanding of what you have read by
  Marking texts
  Making bulleted lists
  Mapping
  Outlining
  Summarizing

In the process of acquiring these skills, you will read about how your health is affected by factors such as exercise, diet, and stress.

## Reading 1    Wellness: The New Health Goal*

— Paul M. Insel, Walton T. Roth, L. McKay Rollins, and
Ray A. Peterson

**TEXT BOOK** The following reading from the college text *Core Concepts in Health* defines "wellness" as "the ability to live life fully—with vitality and meaning." The authors identify six dimensions of health and well-being that interact in all our lives.

1   *Wellness* is an expanded idea of health. Many people think of health as being just the absence of physical disease. But wellness transcends this concept of health, as when individuals with serious illnesses or disabilities rise above their physical or mental limitations to live rich, meaningful, vital lives. Some aspects of health are determined by your genes, your age, and other factors that may be beyond your control. But true wellness is largely determined by the decisions you make about how to live your life.... We will use the terms "health" and "wellness" interchangeably to mean the ability to live life fully—with vitality and meaning.

### THE DIMENSIONS OF WELLNESS

static
unchanging

2   No matter what your age or health status, you can optimize your health in each of the following six interrelated dimensions. Wellness in any dimension is not a static goal but a dynamic process of change and growth.

### Physical Wellness

3   Optimal physical health requires eating well, exercising, avoiding harmful habits, making responsible decisions about sex, learning about and recognizing the symptoms of disease, getting regular medical and dental checkups, and taking steps to prevent injuries at home, on the road, and on the job. The habits you develop and the decisions you make today will largely determine not only how many years you will live, but the quality of your life during those years.

### Emotional Wellness

fluctuates
changes

4   Optimism, trust, self-esteem, self-acceptance, self-confidence, self-control, satisfying relationships, and an ability to share feelings are just some of the qualities and aspects of emotional wellness. Emotional health is a dynamic state that fluctuates with your physical, intellectual, spiritual, interpersonal and social, and environmental health. Maintaining emotional wellness requires monitoring and exploring your thoughts and feelings, identifying obstacles to emotional well-being, and finding solutions to emotional problems, with the help of a therapist if necessary.

### Intellectual Wellness

hallmarks
distinctive features

5   The hallmarks of intellectual health include an openness to new ideas, a capacity to question and think critically, and the motivation to master new skills, as well as a sense of humor,

*"Wellness: The New Health Goal" from Paul M. Insel and Walton T. Roth, CORE CONCEPTS IN HEALTH, 9th Edition, pp. 2–3. Copyright © 2002. Reproduced with permission of the publisher, The McGraw-Hill Companies.

creativity, and curiosity. An active mind is essential to overall wellness, and for learning about, evaluating, and storing health-related information. Your mind detects problems, finds solutions, and directs behavior. People who enjoy intellectual wellness never stop learning. They relish new experiences and challenges and actively seek them out.

## Spiritual Wellness

**altruism**
unselfish concern for others

**antidote**
something that relieves or neutralizes

6    To enjoy spiritual health is to possess a set of guiding beliefs, principles, or values that give meaning and purpose to your life, especially during difficult times. Spiritual wellness involves the capacity for love, compassion, forgiveness, altruism, joy, and fulfillment. It is an antidote to cynicism, anger, fear, anxiety, self-absorption, and pessimism. Spirituality transcends the individual and can be a common bond among people. Organized religions help many people develop spiritual health. Many others find meaning and purpose in their lives on their own—through nature, art, meditation, political action, or good works.

## Interpersonal and Social Wellness

7    Satisfying relationships are basic to both physical and emotional health. We need to have mutually loving, supportive people in our lives. Developing interpersonal wellness means learning good communication skills, developing the capacity for intimacy, and cultivating a support network of caring friends and/or family members. Social wellness requires participating in and contributing to your community, country, and world.

## Environmental or Planetary Wellness

8    Increasingly, personal health depends on the health of the planet. Examples of environmental threats to health are ultraviolet radiation in sunlight, air and water pollution, secondhand tobacco smoke in indoor air, and violence in our society. Wellness requires learning about and protecting yourself against such hazards—and doing what you can to reduce or eliminate them, either on your own or with others.

9    The six dimensions of wellness interact continuously, influencing and being influenced by one another. Making a change in one dimension often affects some or all of the others. Maintaining good health is a dynamic process, and increasing your level of wellness in one area of life often influences many others.

**Exercise 1**

### Recall and Discuss

Based on Reading 1, answer the following questions and prepare to discuss them with your classmates.

1. What are the six dimensions of wellness that the authors identify? What others might you add?

    a. _____    e. _____

    b. _____    f. _____

    c. _____    g. _____

    d. _____    h. _____

2. The authors state that "true wellness is largely determined by the decisions you make about how to live your life." Do you agree or disagree with the authors? Explain your answer using examples from your own experiences or observations.

_____

_____

_____

_____

3. How do you think the six dimensions of wellness are affected by people's decisions?

_____

_____

_____

_____

# Supporting Points

Main ideas are explained by *supporting points*. In Chapter 3, when you learned to identify the main idea of a paragraph or longer passage, you were finding the most important idea in the reading. All the rest of the information supported the main idea. Recognizing how to distinguish between main ideas and supporting points is an important reading comprehension skill. This chapter focuses on the support that writers provide to back up their main ideas.

## MAJOR SUPPORTING POINTS

**major supporting points**
chief ideas or facts that support the main idea

Supporting points explain the writer's main idea in detail. **Major supporting points** are the chief ideas or facts that support the main idea. For example, in Reading 1, "Wellness," the authors' main idea is stated in the first sentence of the second paragraph: "No matter what your age or health status, you can optimize your health in each of the following six interrelated dimensions." The authors are alerting the readers to watch for six supporting points. The six subheadings that follow name the major supporting points:

| | |
|---|---|
| Physical Wellness | Spiritual Wellness |
| Emotional Wellness | Interpersonal and Social Wellness |
| Intellectual Wellness | Environmental or Planetary Wellness |

For each of these sections, you can identify a major supporting sentence. For example, under "Environmental or Planetary Wellness," the main idea of the paragraph is "Increasingly, personal health depends on the health of the planet."

Together, the main ideas of the paragraphs are major supporting points for the main idea of the reading. Identifying main ideas and their major supporting points can help you determine which points you need to know for tests or for work situations.

## MINOR SUPPORTING POINTS

**minor supporting points**
additional explanations, examples, facts, and statistics that develop the major supporting points

Besides major supporting points, readings contain many additional explanations that may be identified as **minor supporting points**. Minor supporting points are simply more detailed explanations, examples, facts, or statistics that back up the major points. For example, after asserting in paragraph 8 of the reading, "Increasingly, personal health depends on the health of the planet," the authors go on to provide examples of environmental threats to health

- Ultraviolet radiation in sunlight
- Air and water pollution
- Secondhand tobacco smoke in indoor air
- Violence in our society

For each of these examples, the authors could certainly have provided additional layers of details, such as statistics on skin cancer and identification of areas most affected by water pollution. However, writers judge how much detail to include based on their perceptions of readers' needs and purposes. For an introductory health text, they would include a lot less information on this topic than they would for a group of environmental scientists studying the relationship between health and the environment. In that case, several books of detailed information would be needed to discuss the topic thoroughly.

## DISTINGUISHING BETWEEN MAJOR AND MINOR SUPPORTING POINTS

Perhaps one of the most important skills for a reader to acquire is the ability to tell which parts of a reading are most important to remember. Certainly, identifying main ideas is crucial, but distinguishing between major and minor supporting points is also essential. For practice, read the following paragraph and determine the main idea. Then we'll take a look at the major and minor supporting points.

> Today, many people are striving for optimal health. A century ago, such a goal was unknown—people counted themselves lucky just to survive. A child born in 1890, for example, could expect to live only about 40 years. Killers such as polio, smallpox, diphtheria, measles, and mumps took the lives of a tragic number of infants and children in the days before vaccinations. Youngsters who escaped these threats still risked death from infectious diseases such as tuberculosis, typhus, or dysentery. In 1918 alone, 20 million people died in a flu epidemic. Millions of others lost their lives to common bacterial infections in the era before antibiotics. Environmental conditions—unrefrigerated food, poor sanitation, and air polluted by coal-burning furnaces and factories—contributed to the spread and the deadliness of these diseases. (Insel and Roth, *Core Concepts in Health*)

You probably came up with a statement for the main idea of this paragraph that is something like, "A hundred years ago, people were not concerned about optimal health; they felt lucky just to survive the many risks to their health at that time."

How do the authors go on to convince readers that their main idea is valid? First, they present the major *supporting points*: the major risks people faced, such as

- Childhood diseases
- Infectious diseases
- Common bacterial infections
- Environmental conditions

But the authors do not stop with a simple identification of each risk; they go on to give *minor supporting points*—explanations and examples for each. For example, under childhood diseases, the authors identify "killers such as polio, smallpox, diphtheria, measles, and mumps." Obviously, many books could be written on health issues in the early twentieth century, with a great deal more specific detail on this subject. The authors of this health text selected only the details they felt were most important for students to know in an introductory course on the subject.

## Exercise 2

### Identify Main Ideas and Major and Minor Supporting Points

Read the following summary of *Healthy People 2010*, and identify the major and minor supporting points for the entire reading. Then choose the best answer to each of the multiple-choice questions.

1   *Healthy People*, published by the U.S. Department of Health and Human Services (DHHS), set forth broad public health goals for the United States. Originally published in 1990, it was updated for the year 2010, and currently the government is developing objectives for *Healthy People 2020*. There are two main goals proposed in *Healthy People 2010*.

**life expectancy** the average number of years a person can expect to live

2   • *Increasing Quality and Years of Healthy Life.* Although life expectancy in the United States has increased since the beginning of the century, there is still room for improvement. Surprisingly, 18 countries have a longer life expectancy than the United States. In Japan, for example, women can expect to live an average of 82.9 years compared with 78.9 years for women in the United States. Japanese men have a life expectancy of 76.4 years compared with 72.5 years for American men.

3   Increasing the number of years of healthy life is another important goal. "Years of healthy life" refers to the time people spend in good health, with no acute or chronic limiting conditions. Although life expectancy increased by a full year from 1990 to 1996, years of healthy life only increased from 64.0 years to 64.2 years during the same time. This meant that although people were living longer, they were spending more time in poor health.

4   • *Eliminating Health Disparities.* Health disparities between different ethnic groups in the American population continue to be a source of concern. Some groups, such as African Americans, Hispanics, American Indians, and Alaska Natives, are disproportionately affected by certain diseases. For example, the death rates for heart disease, all forms of cancer, and HIV/AIDS are higher for African Americans than for whites. Hispanics, who made up 11 percent of the total population in 1996, accounted for 20 percent of the new tuberculosis cases. American Indians and Alaska Natives have a rate of diabetes that is more than twice that of whites.

5   There are also substantial differences in life expectancy among different economic groups in the United States. For example, people from households with an annual income of at least $25,000 live an average of 3 to 7 years longer than people

from households with annual incomes of less than $10,000. People with higher income levels generally can afford better care, are able to take time off work for medical reasons, and aren't limited by public transportation.

1. Which of the following is the best thesis statement for *Healthy People 2010*?
   a. There are large health disparities among various ethnic groups in the United States.
   b. A goal of *Healthy People 2010* is to increase life expectancy in the United States.
   c. *Healthy People 2010* proposes to improve the health of all Americans.

2. The statement "Japanese men have a life expectancy of 76.4 years compared with 72.5 years for American men" in paragraph 2 is a
   a. major supporting point.
   b. minor supporting point.

3. The statement "Increasing the number of years of healthy life is another important goal" in paragraph 3 is a
   a. major supporting point.
   b. minor supporting point.

4. The statement "Although life expectancy increased by a full year from 1990 to 1996, years of healthy life only increased from 64.0 years to 64.2 years during the same time" in paragraph 3 is a
   a. major supporting point.
   b. minor supporting point.

5. The statement "Health disparities between different ethnic groups in the American population continue to be a source of concern" in paragraph 4 is a
   a. major supporting point.
   b. minor supporting point.

6. The statement "Hispanics, who made up 11 percent of the total population in 1996, accounted for 20 percent of the new tuberculosis cases" in paragraph 4 is a
   a. major supporting point.
   b. minor supporting point.

7. The statement "There are also substantial differences in life expectancy among different economic groups in the United States" in paragraph 5 is a
   a. major supporting point.
   b. minor supporting point.

8. The statement "For example, people from households with an annual income of at least $25,000 live an average of 3 to 7 years longer than people from households with annual incomes of less than $10,000" in paragraph 5 is a
   a. major supporting point.
   b. minor supporting point.

| Exercise 3 | Restate Main Ideas and Major and Minor Supporting Points |
|---|---|

Based on the summary of *Healthy People 2010* on pages 149–150, complete the following.

1. Write, in your own words, the thesis of this reading.

   _____

   _____

   _____

2. List the four major supporting points in this excerpt.

   a. _____

   _____

   b. _____

   c. _____

   _____

   d. _____

   _____

3. List the three examples (minor supporting points) used to support the point "There are large disparities between different ethnic groups."

   a. _____

   _____

   b. _____

   _____

   c. _____

   _____

# Organizing to Learn

**organizing to learn**
last step in the PRO reading system; helps you understand and remember what you learned in a reading

**Organizing to learn** is the last major step in the PRO reading system. As you learned in Chapter 1, organizing helps you to understand what you read and remember the information for tests and for use in the future. There are a number of ways to organize the information you read, and identifying main ideas, major supporting points, and minor supporting points makes this part of the reading process much easier. In this section, you will practice five different ways to organize what you've read: marking texts, making bulleted lists, mapping, outlining, and summarizing.

## MARKING TEXTS

**marking texts**
highlighting and
using a system
of symbols and
annotations on
the text itself to
make review and
retention easier

**Marking texts** is probably the quickest way to organize what you have read. People use a variety of methods to mark texts, including the following:

- Highlighting or underlining important points
- Putting check marks beside important points
- Using numbers to identify lists of examples, steps in a process, and so on
- Drawing arrows to "connect" ideas
- Circling essential vocabulary (note that *essential vocabulary* consists of only the important words, not all the words that you don't know)
- Using different colors for different types of information
- Using question marks (???) to identify points where you need to ask questions of the instructor, a tutor, or someone in your study group
- Annotating—writing notes in the margin to draw your attention to a point in a paragraph, noting "causes," "definition," or "examples"
- Writing down your own reactions or comments, such as "good point," or "I don't agree," in the margins

There are probably as many ways to mark texts as there are individual students. You need to choose the ways that work best for you and then use them consistently so you can come back in a month, or three months, and still know what your marks mean. Use the knowledge you've already gained about main ideas and major supporting points to select the material to be marked. Also, be very conscious of what your professor emphasizes in lecture and discussion. If he or she makes a special effort to reinforce some concept or vocabulary in the text, you will probably need to know that material.

You need to mark ideas, concepts, and vocabulary in your text carefully and efficiently. You will return to these items many times for review. When you are studying for an exam about several chapters, you do not want to reread the chapters completely, so careful selection of the significant points to mark is important.

Perhaps the best advice to help you save time in marking texts is this: *When you read new material the first time, do not mark the text.* During a first reading, almost everything seems important, so you may mark too much. That's why you see so many used textbooks with whole pages "painted" with yellow highlighter.

Many texts have been designed to make the task very easy for you. Bullets, boldfaced print, italics, color changes, charts, graphs, and numerous inserts are already provided in many texts to highlight the concepts and vocabulary you need to learn. Efficient marking of texts is probably most important in books that don't provide as much assistance to the student.

In a second reading, mark passages and information you want to remember. After you have marked your text, you should have a clear understanding of what you have read, and you should have organized it in a way that's easy to learn and to remember.

Now let's take a paragraph about health issues in the United States and see how you might mark it for future review. Notice that the following paragraph is marked in a way that will make reviewing the main points easy. The main idea is underlined twice. The seven major supporting points are numbered and underlined. The annotations in the margin note some points the marker of the text wished to emphasize in her review.

Is good health just the absence of disease-causing organisms? In many

**causes**

big-city hospitals, <u>a great many health problems have nothing to do with germs</u>, points out medical-ethics consultant Bruce Hilton. Surgeons regularly practice "battlefield medicine," attending to the multiple gunshot and knife

**violence**
**accidents**

wounds of the (1) <u>victims of violence</u>. Or they sew up (2) <u>car-crash survivors</u>, many of whom (a) did not wear seatbelts, many of whose (b) accidents were alcohol-caused. In the psychiatric wing, a high proportion of patients have

**drugs**

(3) <u>cocaine or other drug-related problems</u>. In the nursery, (a) undersized crack-cocaine babies fight to survive. Other newborns won't live out the year

**lack of**
**prevention**

because their mothers (4) <u>didn't have access to prenatal health care</u>. Elsewhere cigarette (5) <u>smokers</u> await their turn for radiation treatment of their lung cancer or respiratory therapy for their emphysema. Indeed, if you were to walk around the hospital you would turn up many other reasons for poor health, says Hilton: "(6) skin cancer from <u>too many days on the beach</u>, or peo-

**bad health**
**habits**

ple whose disease was (7) <u>food—too much, not the right kind, or too little</u>."
(Williams and Knight, *Healthy for Life*)

---

**Exercise 4**

## Organize to Learn: Mark a Text

Read the following excerpt from Dianne Hales's *An Invitation to Health*, about maintaining health in sexual relationships. Underline main ideas and number major supporting points under each main idea. Use other marking and annotations as you wish. Do not mark too much!

1  Abstinence is the only guarantee of sexual safety—and one that more and more young people are choosing. The choice of an abstinent (or celibate) lifestyle offers many advantages, both in the present and the future. By choosing not to be sexually active with a partner, individuals can safeguard their physical health, their fertility, and their future.

2      For men and women who are sexually active, a mutually faithful sexual relationship with just one healthy partner is the safest option. For those not in such relationships,

**STD**
sexually
transmitted disease

safer-sex practices are essential for reducing risks. Some experts believe that condom use may be a more effective tactic than any drug or vaccine in preventing STDs.

3     How can you tell if someone you're dating or hope to date has been exposed to an STD? The bad news is, you can't. But the good news is, it doesn't matter—as long as you avoid sexual activity that could put you at risk of infection. Ideally, before engaging in any such behavior, both of you should talk about your prior sexual history (including number of partners and sexually transmitted diseases) and other high-risk behavior, such as the use of injection drugs. If you know someone well enough to consider having sex with that person, you should be able to talk about STDs. If the person is unwilling to talk, you shouldn't have sex.

4     Even if you do talk openly, you can't be sure a potential partner is telling you the truth. In various surveys of college students, a significant proportion of the men and women said they would lie to a potential partner about having an STD or testing positive for HIV. The only way of knowing for certain that a prospective partner is safe is through laboratory testing. Sex educators and health professionals strongly encourage couples to abstain from any sexual activity that puts them at risk for STDs until they both undergo medical examinations and laboratory testing to rule out STDs. This process greatly reduces the danger of disease transmission and can also help foster a deep sense of mutual trust and commitment. Many campus and public health clinics provide exams or laboratory testing either free of charge or on a sliding scale determined by your income. (Hales, *An Invitation to Health*)

**HIV**
human immunodeficiency virus, the virus that causes AIDS

## MAKING BULLETED LISTS

Another way to organize supporting points is to list them. When people make computer-aided presentations in school or at work, they often use **bulleted lists** to reinforce the main ideas and major supporting points. Textbooks very frequently use lists accented by bullets to attract the readers' attention to important supporting points. For example, read the following discussion on smokers' dependence on nicotine. Notice how the author uses bullets to emphasize the list of causes for dependence.

**bulleted list**
list accented by symbols called bullets to make supporting points easier to identify

Nicotine has a much more powerful hold on smokers than alcohol does on drinkers. Whereas about 10% of alcohol users lose control of their intake of alcohol and become alcoholics, as many as 80% of all heavy smokers have tried to cut down on or quit smoking but cannot overcome their dependence.
     Nicotine causes dependence by at least three means:

- It provides a strong sensation of pleasure.
- It leads to fairly severe discomfort during withdrawal.
- It stimulates cravings long after obvious withdrawal symptoms have passed. (Hales, *An Invitation to Health*)

**Exercise 5**

Organize to Learn: Make a Bulleted List

Using Reading 1 on pages 145–146, list the major supporting points on the bulleted lines provided. The main idea and the first supporting point have already been done for you.

**Wellness: The New Health Goal**

No matter what your age or health status, you can optimize your health in each of the following six interrelated dimensions.

- physical wellness _____
- _____
- _____
- _____
- _____
- _____

## MAPPING

**mapping**
organizing
information
graphically
to show
relationships
among facts and/
or ideas

**Mapping** is an excellent choice for organizing supporting details for a reading. For some people, this method is particularly helpful because it provides a visual way to learn and remember information. Notice how the information in a paragraph or in a longer passage can be organized graphically so that you immediately understand relationships between the main idea, the major supporting details, minor supporting details, and even more minor supporting details (additional details). Mapping is a good way to show these relationships. Now take a look at the sample map.

The following selection is adapted from the Centers for Disease Control's "Healthy Youth" link. Read the paragraphs, and then review the map to see one way of mapping information to make it easier to study.

## Your Education and Your Health

Health disparities are related to inequities in education. Dropping out of school is associated with multiple social and health problems. Overall, individuals with less education are more likely to experience a number of health risks such as obesity, substance abuse, and intentional and unintentional injury, compared to individuals with more education. Higher levels of education are associated with a longer life and an increased likelihood of obtaining or understanding basic health information and services needed to make appropriate health decisions.

At the same time, health problems are associated with academic difficulties. Health risks such as teenage pregnancy, poor dietary choices, physical and emotional abuse, inadequate physical activity, gang involvement, and chronic illness have a significant impact on how well students perform in school. (Centers for Disease Control, "Healthy Youth")

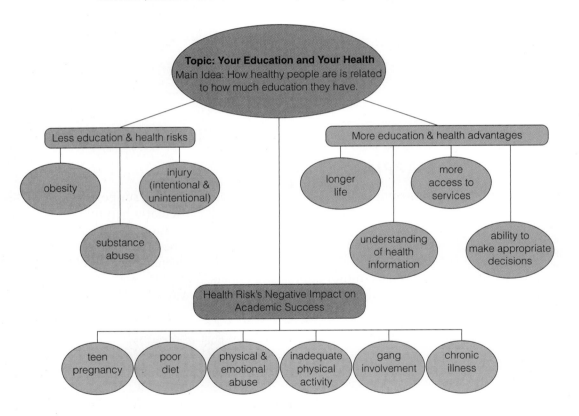

| Exercise 6 |

## Organize to Learn: Make a Map

Read the following selection, based on the government's Centers for Disease Control website. Then complete the map that is partially filled in.

Dating violence is a type of intimate partner violence. It occurs between two people in a close relationship. The nature of dating violence can be physical, emotional, or sexual.

- **Physical**—This occurs when a partner is pinched, hit, shoved, or kicked.
- **Emotional**—This means threatening a partner or harming his or her sense of self-worth. Examples include name calling, shaming, bullying, embarrassing on purpose, or keeping him or her away from friends and family.
- **Sexual**—This is forcing a partner to engage in a sex act when he or she does not or cannot consent. (Centers for Disease Control, "Teen Dating Violence")

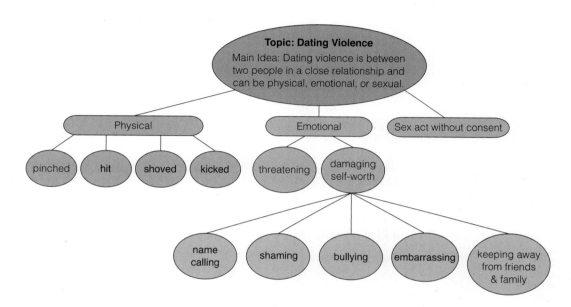

## OUTLINING

© 2013 Wadsworth, Cengage Learning

**outlining**
a formal strategy for organizing readings by divisions showing the relationships between main ideas and major and minor supporting points

**Outlining** is another strategy for thinking about and organizing information so that you can remember it for future use. Similar to mapping outlining requires you (1) to select the most important points in what you have read and (2) to decide how the various points are related.

Formal outlining requires you to follow an exact pattern. You may not always want to outline your study materials formally, but even when you are doing an informal outline for your own use, it's helpful to use this format as a basis. Also, you will find that a formal outline is required for many college research writing assignments.

Outlines may be constructed by topic (usually phrases) or in complete sentences. The format includes a title, which names the topic of the outline; a statement of the main idea (called a thesis statement in writing classes), which states the main point about the topic; and divisions of the support for the thesis, which are marked first by Roman numerals (I, II, III, IV, V), then by capital letters (A, B, C, D, E), next by Arabic numerals (1, 2, 3, 4, 5), and then by lowercase letters (a, b, c, d, e). Each division means that the information has been divided into still lower levels of support. Since each indentation and change of number and letter means you are dividing information, you must always have at least a I and II, A and B, 1 and 2, or a and b. If the Roman numerals indicate major divisions of the topic, then the capital letters are major supporting points, and numbers and small letters are minor and still more detailed points of support. Traditional topic outline format looks something like the following example:

## Title (Topic)

**Main Idea:** This is the main point about the topic.

    I. Major division
       A. Major supporting point
          1. Minor supporting point
             a. Still more minor supporting point and details
             b. Still more minor supporting point and details
          2. Minor supporting point
       B. Major supporting point
    II. Major division
       A. Major supporting point
          1. Minor supporting point
             a. Still more minor supporting point and details
             b. Still more minor supporting point and details
          2. Minor supporting point
       B. Major supporting point

The following is one example of an outline based on the summary of *Healthy People 2010* on pp. 149–150.

## Healthy People 2010

**Main Idea (thesis):** *Healthy People 2010* proposes to improve the health of *all* Americans.

    I. Increase years of life and quality of life
       A. Life expectancy is up but could be better (18 countries are better)
          1. Women in Japan, 82.9 years; women in U.S., 78.9 years
          2. Men in Japan, 76.4 years; men in U.S., 72.5 years
       B. Years of healthy life needs to improve

    II. Eliminate health disparities
       A. Among ethnic groups
          1. African American death rates higher than those for whites
             a. heart disease
             b. cancer
             c. HIV/AIDS
          2. Hispanics (higher rate of TB)
          3. American Indians and Alaska Natives (diabetes two times that of whites)
       B. Among economic groups
          1. People with incomes $25,000 and up live 3–7 years longer than those with incomes less than $10,000
          2. People with higher income can afford better care, time off work, transportation

**Exercise 7**

### Organize to Learn: Write an Outline

Read the following selection, which is adapted from the government's *Let's Move* website (http://www.letsmove.gov/learnthefacts.php). When you finish, complete the outline that is partially filled in for you. This information is familiar to you both from your prior knowledge and from the readings in Chapter 2.

# America's Move to Raise a Healthy Generation of Kids*

**The physical and emotional health of an entire generation and the economic health and security of our nation is at stake.**

—FIRST LADY MICHELLE OBAMA, FEBRUARY 9, 2010

## CHILDHOOD OBESITY BY THE NUMBERS

1   Over the past three decades, childhood obesity rates in America have tripled, and today, nearly one in three children in America are overweight or obese. One-third of all children born in 2000 or later will suffer from diabetes at some point in their lives; many others will face chronic obesity-related health problems like heart disease, high blood pressure, cancer, and asthma.

## THIRTY YEARS AGO

2   Thirty years ago, most people led lives that kept them at a pretty healthy weight. Kids walked to and from school every day, ran around at recess, participated in gym class, and played for hours after school before dinner. Meals were home-cooked with reasonable portion sizes, and there was always a vegetable on the plate. Eating fast food was rare and snacking between meals was an occasional treat.

## TODAY

3   While kids thirty years ago ate just one snack a day, they are now trending toward three—so they're taking in an additional 200 calories a day just from snacks. And one in five school-age kids has up to six snacks a day. Portion sizes have also exploded. Food portions are two to five times bigger than they used to be. Beverage portions have grown as well. In the mid-1970s, average sweetened drink portions were

FRENCH FRIES

20 Years Ago                    Today

210 Calories                    610 Calories
2.4 ounces                      6.9 ounces
        Calorie Difference: 400 Calories

U.S. Department of Health and Human Services

*"Learn the Facts," from http://www.letsmove.gov/

13.6 ounces. Today, kids think nothing of drinking 20 ounces of soda at a time. In total, we are now eating 31 percent more calories than we were forty years ago—including 56 percent more fats and oils and 14 percent more sugars and sweeteners. The average American now eats fifteen more pounds of sugar a year than in 1970.

4     Kids today lead a very different kind of life, and it involves less activity. Walks to and from school have been replaced by car and bus rides. Gym class and school sports have been cut and are often replaced now by afternoons with TV, video games, and the Internet.

5     And the average American child spends more than 7.5 hours a day watching TV and movies, using cell phones and computers for entertainment, and playing video games, and only a third of high school students get the recommended levels of physical activity.

6     That's the bad news. The good news is by making a few simple changes we can help our kids lead healthier lives—and we already have all of the tools we need to do it. We just need the will.

## THE SOLUTION

7   We can solve the challenge of childhood obesity within a generation so that children born today will reach adulthood at a healthy weight if we all work together. Through the *Let's Move!* campaign—a comprehensive, collaborative, and community-oriented initiative that addresses all of the various factors that lead to childhood obesity—we are engaging every sector of society that impacts the health of children to provide schools, families, and communities the simple tools they need to help kids be more active, eat better, and get healthy."

### America's Move to Raise a Healthy Generation of Kids

**Main idea:** _____

_____

_____

_____

I. Obesity by the numbers

  A.  Numbers tripled in 30 years; one in three children are obese

  B.  _____

  C.  Other chronic illnesses

    1. _____

    2. _____

    3. _____

    4. _____

II. Thirty years ago

    A. Kids were active

        1. _____

        2. ran around at recess

        3. _____

        4. _____

    B. _____

        1. _____

        2. reasonable portions

        3. included vegetables

        4. eating fast food was rare

        5. _____

III. Today

    A. _____

        1. _____

            a. six snacks instead of one

            b. _____

        2. bigger portion sizes (2–5 times bigger)

        3. bigger beverage portions

        4. _____

            a. 56% more fat,

            b. _____

    B. Activity Levels

        1. _____

        2. gym classes and sports cut

        3. _____

IV. The Solution: *Let's Move!*: A community-oriented initiative to address all factors leading to obesity and including schools, families, and communities to help kids become more active, eat good food, and be healthy

# SUMMARIZING

**summary**
a concise version, in your own words, of the main idea and major supporting points of a reading

A fifth important method of organizing information is writing a summary. Once you have identified the topic, the main idea or thesis statement, and the major supporting points in a reading, you are prepared to write a summary. A **summary** is a condensed version of a reading, much shorter than the original, that includes the main idea and the major supporting points. It must be written *in your own words*, and it should not include your opinions or details and examples not present in the original.

Summaries are useful in organizing information for studying, for answering essay questions on exams, for writing research papers, and for condensing large amounts of data for research assignments.

To write an effective summary, follow these steps:

1. Carefully read and make sure you understand the material you are going to summarize.
2. Determine the main idea or thesis (for readings that are written to persuade). Write that main idea in a sentence using your own words. (When you write the main idea sentence, you will give credit to the author whose work you are summarizing and will mention the title of the reading, article, or book. Giving information on the source is described in more detail later.)
3. Decide what major supporting details you need to include.
4. Decide whether to include minor supporting details. A summary is supposed to be brief, so you usually do not need to include this level of detail.
5. Write the summary in your own words, beginning with your main idea sentence and including the major supporting details. Use complete sentences.
6. Remember, it is easier to use your own words if you are not looking directly at the passage while you write. *Don't copy!* If you use the author's language, be sure to put quotation marks around those words.

In a summary, you are giving the information or opinion of another writer in an abbreviated form. You are not giving your own opinion. Unless your instructor asks you to do so, do not inject your ideas into your summary.

A full summary of Reading 1 might look like this:

According to Paul M. Insel and his coauthors, in the reading, "Wellness: The New Health Goal," wellness depends on the decisions each person makes about how to live. Wellness is more than not being sick. Included in this concept of health is the ability to live an active, full, and meaningful life. To achieve wellness, people need to address the six dimensions of wellness: (1) physical wellness, (2) emotional wellness, (3) intellectual wellness, (4) spiritual wellness, (5) interpersonal and social wellness, and (6) environmental or planetary wellness.

# Reader's Tip: State the Source and the Main Idea in Summaries

The first sentence of your summary should include not only the main idea but also some basic information about the source.

1. The name of the author or of the group or institution responsible for the reading
2. The title of the reading or the article
3. The main idea (or thesis statement if the reading is trying to persuade you)

One way to write your first sentence is to start with "According to [author's name], in the [type of publication], "[title of article]," [complete main idea sentence in your own words].

For example, this is the thesis statement for Reading 1, Insel and Roth's "Wellness": "True wellness is largely determined by the decisions you make about how to live your life." So the first sentence of a summary might say this:

> According to Paul M. Insel and his coauthors, in the article, "Wellness: The New Health Goal," wellness depends on the decisions each person makes about how to live.

**Exercise 8** State the Source and the Main Idea in Summaries

The following are main idea sentences. Rewrite them in your own words, give credit to the author, and give the title of the reading. Use the format "According to . . ." Other than the sentences from *Healthy People 2010*, these are not real authors or real texts. We've created them to give you practice writing strong first sentences for summaries.

1. Smoking is a behavior that increases a variety of health risks, including death. (From an article entitled "Break the Habit," by Elizabeth Jones)

_____

_____

2. Inequalities in income and education lead to health disparities in the United States. (From *Healthy People 2010*, a publication of the Department of Health and Human Services)

_____

_____

3. African Americans are at a greater risk for heart disease and high blood pressure. (From the article "Disparities in Health Care," by Joe Davis)

_____

_____

_____

4. Even though the United States is one of the wealthiest nations in the world, it doesn't mean that we eat well. (From Nellie Jones's book *Eat Right to Stay Fit*)

_____

_____

_____

5. Recent health gains for the U.S. population as a whole appear to reflect achievements among the high socioeconomic groups; low socioeconomic groups continue to lag behind. (From *Healthy People 2010*, a publication of the Department of Health and Human Services)

_____

_____

_____

**Exercise 9**

### Organize to Learn: Write a Summary

Using the outline you made in Exercise 7, on pages 160–161, write a summary in your own words on a separate sheet of paper of the information in "America's Move to Raise a Healthy Generation of Kids."

**Reading 2**

# Understanding Emotional Intelligence*

— Skip Downing

**TEXT BOOK** Emotional intelligence is a key dimension in overall wellness and important for success in many aspects of our lives. After teaching college students for twenty years, Skip Downing realized that too often students who don't succeed have as much (or more) academic potential as their successful classmates. He concluded that "people who are successful (by their own definition) consistently make wiser choices than people who struggle." The following reading is from his college textbook, *On Course*. It is used in college success seminars that focus on empowering students from the "inside out" rather than focusing primarily on study skills.

## FACING LIFE'S CHALLENGES WITH OR WITHOUT EMOTIONAL INTELLIGENCE

1   For most of us, life presents a bumpy road now and then. We fail a college course. The job we want goes to someone else. The person we love doesn't return our affections. Our health gives way to sickness. How we handle these distressing experiences is critical to the outcomes of and experiences of our lives.

2   During final exam period one semester, I heard a shriek from the nursing education office. Seconds later, a student charged out of the office, screaming, scattering papers in the air, and stumbling down the hall. A cluster of concerned classmates caught up to her and desperately tried to offer comfort. "It's all right. You can take the exam again next semester. It's okay. Really." She leaned against the wall, eyes closed. She slid down the wall until she sat in a limp heap, surrounded by sympathetic voices. Later, I heard that she dropped out of school.

3   At the end of another semester, I had the unpleasant task of telling one of my hardest-working students that she had failed the proficiency exams. Her mother had died during the semester, so I was particularly worried about how she would handle more bad news. We had a conference, and upon telling her the news, I began consoling her. For about a minute, she listened quietly and then said, "You're taking my failure pretty hard. Do you need a hug?" Before I could respond, she plucked me out of my chair and gave me a hug. "Don't worry," she said, patting my back. "I'll pass next semester," and sure enough, she did.

## EMOTIONAL CONTROL AND SUCCESS

4   An experiment during the 1960s shows just how important emotional control is to success. Four-year-old children at a preschool were told they could have one marshmallow immediately, or if they could wait for about twenty minutes, they could have two. More than a dozen years later, experimenters examined the differences in the lives of the one-marshmallow (emotionally impulsive) children and the two-marshmallow (emotionally intelligent) children. The adolescents who as children were able to delay gratification were found to be superior to their counterparts as high school students and to score an average of 210 points higher on their SAT's (Scholastic Aptitude Tests). Additionally, the two-marshmallow teenagers had borne fewer children while unmarried and had

*"Understanding Emotional Intelligence" by Skip Downing from ON COURSE, 5th Edition, pp. 212–214. Reprinted by permission of Houghton Mifflin Company.

experienced fewer problems with the law. Clearly the ability to endure some emotional discomfort in the present in exchange for greater rewards in the future is a key to success.

## FOUR COMPONENTS OF EMOTIONAL INTELLIGENCE

5   As a relatively new field of study, emotional intelligence is still being defined. However, Daniel Goleman, author of the book *Emotional Intelligence*, identifies four components that contribute to emotional effectiveness. The first two qualities are personal and have to do with recognizing and effectively managing one's own emotions. The second two are social and have to do with recognizing and effectively managing emotions in relationships with others.

### 1. Emotional Self-Awareness: Knowing your feelings in the moment

6   Self-awareness of one's own feelings as they occur is the foundation of emotional intelligence and is fundamental to effective decision making. Thus, people who are keenly aware of their changing moods are better pilots of their lives. For example, emotional self-awareness helps you deal effectively with feelings of being overwhelmed instead of using television (or some other distraction) as a temporary escape.

### 2. Emotional Self-Management: Managing strong feelings

> Every great, successful person I know shares the capacity to remain centered, clear and powerful in the midst of emotional "storms."
>
> —Anthony Robbins

7   Emotional Self-Management enables people to make wise choices despite the pull of powerful emotions. People who excel at this skill avoid making critical decisions during times of high drama; instead they wait until their inner storm has calmed and then make considered choices that contribute to their desired outcomes and experiences. For example, emotional self-management helps you resist dropping an important class simply because you got angry at the teacher. It also helps you make a choice that offers delayed benefits (e.g., writing a term paper) in place of a choice that promises instant gratification (e.g., attending a party).

### 3. Social Awareness: Empathizing accurately with other people's emotions

8   Empathy is the fundamental "people skill." Those with empathy and compassion are more attuned to the subtle social signals that reveal what others need or want. For example, social awareness helps you notice and offer comfort when someone is consumed by anxiety or sadness.

### 4. Relationship Management: Handling emotions in relationships with skill and harmony

9   The art of relationships depends, in large part, upon the skill of managing emotions in others. People who excel at skills such as listening, resolving conflicts, cooperating, and articulating the pulse of a group do well at anything that relies on interacting smoothly with others. For example, relationship management helps a person resist saying something that might publicly embarrass someone else.

## KNOWING YOUR OWN EMOTIONS

10   The foundation of emotional intelligence is a keen awareness of our own emotions as they rise and fall. None of the other abilities can exist without this one. Here are some steps toward becoming more attuned to your emotions:

## Build a vocabulary of feelings

11    Learn the names of emotions you might experience. There are dozens. How many can you name beyond anger, fear, sadness, and happiness?

## Be mindful of emotions as they are happening

12    Learn to identify and express emotions in the moment. Be aware of the subtleties of emotion, learning to make fine distinctions between feelings that are similar such as sadness and depression.

## Understand what is causing your emotion

**irrational**
unreasonable

13    Look behind the emotion. See when anger is caused by hurt feelings. Notice when anxiety is caused by irrational thoughts. Realize when sadness is caused by disappointments. Identify when happiness is caused by immediate gratification that gets you off course from your long-term goals.

## Recognize the difference between a feeling and resulting actions

14    Feeling an emotion is one thing; acting on the emotion is quite another. Emotions and behaviors are separate experiences, one internal, one external. Note when you tend to confuse the two, as a student did who said, "My teacher made me so angry I had to drop the class." You can be angry with a teacher and still remain enrolled in a class that is important to your goals and dreams.

**enhance**
improve

15    You will never reach your full potential without emotional intelligence. No matter how academically bright you may be, emotional illiteracy will limit your achievements. Developing emotional wisdom will fuel your motivation, help you successfully negotiate emotional storms (yours and others'), and enhance your chances of creating your greatest goals and dreams.

---

**Exercise 10**

### Work with Words

Use context clues, dictionary skills, and your knowledge of word parts to choose the best definition for each italicized word in the following sentences from Reading 2. The paragraph number is provided in case you want to check the context.

1. We had a conference, and upon telling her the news, I began *consoling* her. (par. 3)

   *Consoling*
   a. explaining something
   b. kindly reassuring
   c. criticizing

2. The adolescents who as children were able to delay *gratification* were found to be superior to their *counterparts* as high school students and to score an average of 210 points higher on their SAT's (Scholastic Aptitude Tests). (par. 4)

*Gratification*
a. hunger
b. procrastination
c. pleasure

3. *Counterparts*
a. others in the same category
b. teammates
c. competitors

4. *Empathy* is the fundamental "people skill." (par. 8)

*Empathy*
a. understanding someone else's feelings
b. analyzing someone else's feelings
c. soothing someone else's hurt feelings

5. People who excel at skills such as listening, resolving conflicts, cooperating, and *articulating* the pulse of a group do well at anything that relies on interacting smoothly with others. (par. 9)

*Articulating*
a. analyzing
b. expressing clearly
c. expressing oneself eloquently

**Exercise 11**

## Check Your Understanding

Based on Reading 2, choose the best answer to each of the following multiple-choice questions.

1. Which of the following sentences best expresses the most important idea of the entire reading?
   a. You will never reach your full potential without emotional intelligence.
   b. It is essential to understand what causes your emotions.
   c. Testing children when they are four years old can help predict who will be successful in the future.

2. The author tells the story of the student who failed his class telling him "Don't worry, I'll pass next semester" as an example of someone who
   a. has excellent academic preparation.
   b. possesses a high level of emotional intelligence.
   c. is probably not realistic.

3. According to this reading, academic success requires you to have
   a. a high IQ.
   b. emotional intelligence as well as academic capability.
   c. empathy for others in a variety of college settings.

4. The basic components of emotional intelligence include
   a. being aware of one's own feelings and changing moods.
   b. the ability to empathize and comfort others, especially in times of crisis.

    c. recognizing and managing one's own emotions and recognizing and
       effectively managing emotions in relationships with others.

5. Skills such as listening, resolving conflicts, and cooperating are examples of
   a. emotional self-awareness.
   b. emotional self-management.
   c. relationship management.

**Exercise 12**

### Organize to Learn: Outline

Complete the following outline for Reading 2.

## Understanding Emotional Intelligence

**Main Idea:** _____

_____

_____

  I. Life's challenges and outcomes are better if we have emotional intelligence

    A. _____

      1. Drama over not passing test

      2. Drops out

    B. _____

      1. Shows self-confidence

      2. Passes class following semester

  II. Emotional control and success (experiment with 4-year-old children)

    A. Choices

      1. _____

      2. wait 20 minutes, get two marshmallows

    B. Those who could wait became better students and made better choices

      1. _____

      2. _____

 III. Four Components of Emotional Intelligence

    A. Emotional self-awareness

    B. Emotional self-management

    C. _____

    D. _____

IV. _____

    A. _____

    B. Be mindful of emotions

    C. Understand causes of emotions

    D. _____

**Exercise 13**

### Organize to Learn: Write a Summary

Using the outline that you completed in Exercise 12, on pages 169–170, write a brief summary of Reading 2 on a separate sheet of paper. Be sure to put the main idea sentence in your own words on a separate piece of paper. Be sure to include the author's name and the title of the reading.

**Exercise 14**

### Reflect and Write

Think about what you read in Reading 2 and what you already know about your emotions and emotions generally. Then answer the following questions in your own words.

1. What example does the author give at the beginning of the reading of someone who probably made a poor choice because of a lack of emotional intelligence? Which component of emotional intelligence did she lack according to the author?

_____

_____

_____

_____

_____

_____

2. On a separate piece of paper, write two paragraphs. In the first, give an example of an incident in which you or someone you know displayed strong emotional intelligence skills. Explain the situation and which components of emotional intelligence were used. In the second paragraph, give an example of an incident in which you or someone you know displayed weak emotional intelligence skills. Explain the situation and which components of emotional intelligence were lacking. Give your paragraphs a title such as, "Examples of Emotional Intelligence."

| Reading 3 | # Stressed Out?* |

— NATIONAL INSTITUTES OF HEALTH

**In today's world, stress is a fact of life. Recent studies have consistently shown that stress is more than just an annoying aspect of modern society. Rather, it can severely damage one's health and well-being. This article, published in the January 2007 edition of the National Institutes of Health's newsletter *News in Health*, describes the impact of stress on our bodies and brains and suggests how we can manage it more effectively.**

1   Maybe it's money trouble or the burden of caring for a sick relative. Maybe it's your job. Maybe it's the traffic. Whatever the cause, everyone seems stressed out these days. People once hotly debated the idea that stress can affect your body, but we now know that stress can cause both short- and long-term changes to your body and mind. The more we understand how stress affects us, the more we learn about how to cope better.

2   Long before we humans learned how to drive cars to work and check in with the office on handheld computers, our bodies evolved to be finely attuned to a predator's attack. When we sense danger, our bodies quickly release hormones like adrenaline into our bloodstream that increase our heart rate, focus our attention, and cause other changes to quickly prepare us for coming danger. Stress was—and still is—crucial to our survival. The stress that we're adapted to deal with, however, is the short, intense kind—like running away before a bear can make a lunch of us. Modern life frequently gives us little time between periods of stress for our body to recuperate.

**predator**
animal that kills and eats other animals

3   This chronic stress eventually takes both a mental and physical toll.

4   The effects of stress on the body are well documented. It's long been known that blood pressure and  cholesterol levels go up in people who are stressed. Studies have now linked chronic stress with cardiovascular problems like hypertension, coronary heart disease, and stroke. The immune system is also affected by stress. Dr. Esther M. Sternberg at NIH's National Institute of Mental Health says it makes sense for the immune system to gear up and get ready to heal potential wounds. But chronic stress can cause the system to backfire. Research has shown that wounds in people under chronic stress heal more slowly. Caregivers of people with Alzheimer's disease, who are often under great stress, are more likely to get the flu or a cold—and when they take vaccines to protect their loved ones from getting flu, their bodies don't respond as well.

**cardiovascular**
the system of heart and vessels that circulates blood throughout the body

**immune system**
the system that protects your body from invading viruses, bacteria, and other microscopic threats

*"Stressed Out?" by National Institutes of Health. America's Move to Raise a Healthier Generation of Kids from http://newsinhealth.nih.gov/pdf/NIHNiH%20January07.pdf

**hormones**
molecules sent through the bloodstream to signal another part of the body to grow or react a certain way

Certain hormones that are released when you're stressed out, such as cortisol and cate-cholamines, have been tied to these long-term effects of stress. Sternberg says, "If you're pumping out a lot of cortisol and your immune cells are bathed in high levels of stress hormones, they're going to be tuned down."

5    Animal studies and brain imaging studies in people have shown that chronic stress can have a similar effect on the brain. Dr. Bruce S. McEwen of Rockefeller University explains, "Hyperactivity of the stress response results in changes over time in the circuitry of the brain." Brain cells bombarded by stress signals have little recovery time and eventually start to shrink and cut connections to other brain cells. The network that coordinates our thoughts, emotions and reactions thus starts to rearrange. Over time, entire regions of the brain can grow or shrink. That may explain why studies have linked higher levels of stress hormones with lower memory, focus, and problem-solving skills.

**circuitry**
wiring

6    Not everyone deals with stress the same way, however, and why some people seem to cope better is a major area of research. McEwen says studies in animals show that early life experiences and the quality of maternal care affect how curious an animal is when it's older and how stressed it gets in a new environment. Dr. Teresa Seeman of the University of California at Los Angeles School of Medicine points out that studies have also linked poverty and deprivation in childhood with how well people deal with stress. "There does appear to be a lingering impact," Seeman says, but adds that it's difficult to know the exact cause. In addition, two factors that affect how much stress people feel are self-esteem and a sense of control. Workers who feel more in control at their jobs tend to feel less stress. People with low self-esteem produce more cortisol when they're asked to do something that's not easy for them, like speak in front of other people. They also don't become accustomed to the stress even after doing something several times and continue to produce high levels of cortisol.

7    It's not easy to change things like self-esteem and your sense of control at work, but there are other causes of stress which can be more easily addressed. "Sleep deprivation is a major issue," McEwen says. People who are stressed out tend to get less quality sleep. And sleep deprivation affects your ability to control your mood and make good decisions. It also throws the stress hormones in your body off balance. "If you're sleep deprived," McEwen explains, "blood pressure and cortisol don't go down at night like they should." McEwen sees people who work night shifts as a window into what chronic stress does to the body over time. "They're more likely to become obese and to have diabetes, cardiovascular disease, and depression," he says.

© 2013 Wadsworth, Cengage Learning

8    People who are stressed out tend to do other things that make their body less healthy and more vulnerable to the effects of stress. Many eat more fatty comfort foods, which can lead to obesity and diabetes. They may smoke or drink more, raising the risk for cancer and other diseases. And they often feel they're just too busy to exercise. Seeman says, "Being physically active helps keep the body's systems in better shape and thus better able to deal with any demands from other stressful conditions." Another element of modern life which can contribute to higher stress is the tendency to isolate oneself from others. Sometimes it seems like the only time we interact with our family or co-workers is when we're having a conflict. Seeman says it's important to develop a network of people you can go to and talk with when you're confronted with difficulties in your life. "Large studies have clearly shown," she says, "that people who have more social relationships, a larger network of people they interact with on a regular basis, live longer. Research suggests they're less likely to show declines as they're older."

9    All this research highlights the fact that healthy practices can complement mainstream medicine to help treat and prevent disease. Do things that make you feel good about yourself, mentally and physically. Get enough sleep. Eat a healthy diet and exercise regularly. Develop a network of people you can turn to in difficult times. If you still find yourself too stressed out, talk to your health care professional. There are many therapies they may recommend to help you deal with stress and its consequences. The effects of being chronically stressed are too serious to simply accept as a fact of modern life.

**Exercise 15**

## Work with Words

Use context clues, dictionary skills, and your knowledge of word parts to determine the meaning of each italicized word in the sentences from Reading 3. Write the meaning of the word on the lines provided. The paragraph number is provided in case you want to check the context.

1. Stress was—and still is—*crucial* to our survival. (par. 2)

   *Crucial*: _____

2. This *chronic* stress eventually takes both a mental and physical toll. (par. 3)

   *Chronic*: _____

3. Dr. Teresa Seeman of the University of California at Los Angeles School of Medicine points out that studies have also linked poverty and *deprivation* in childhood with how well people deal with stress. (par. 6)

   *Deprivation*: _____

4. People who are stressed out tend to do other things that make their body less healthy and more *vulnerable* to the effects of stress. (par. 8)

*Vulnerable*: _____

5. Seeman says it's important to develop a network of people you can go to and talk with when you're *confronted with* difficulties in your life. (par. 8)

*Confronted with*: _____

6. All this research highlights the fact that healthy practices can *complement* mainstream medicine to help treat and prevent disease. (par. 9)

*Complement*: _____

**Exercise 16**

## Check Your Understanding

Based on Reading 3, decide whether each of the following statements is true or false.

_____    1. Stress causes only temporary changes in our bodies.

_____    2. Stress is a natural part of our lives.

_____    3. Stress can produce physical and psychological effects.

_____    4. Chronic stress has been linked with a weakened immune system.

_____    5. Dr. McEwen believes that the effects of stress on the body are more serious than the effects it has on the brain.

_____    6. High levels of stress hormones are related to an inability to focus.

_____    7. All people react to stress in the same predictable way.

_____    8. Dr. Seeman believes that early childhood experiences may affect one's ability to handle stress.

_____    9. Sleep deprivation and stress have similar effects on the body.

_____    10. If you are experiencing high levels of stress, researchers suggest that you spend some time alone.

**Exercise 17**

## Organize to Learn

1. Mark the text in Reading 3 on pages 171–173.

2. Now outline the material you marked in paragraphs 3 through 9.

3. Briefly summarize the reading. Remember to put the main idea sentence in your own words and include the author and title of the reading.

**Exercise 18**

### Reflect and Write

1. What is the relationship between stress and hormones?

_____

_____

_____

_____

_____

2. According to the article, why is sleep so important?

_____

_____

_____

_____

3. Choose the stressor that is most important in your life *now*. In three or four paragraphs, (1) state the most important source of stress for you, (2) explain its causes, (3) describe its impact on your life, and (4) develop and explain a plan for managing this stress. Be sure to include sufficient major and minor supporting points to make your ideas clear and to back up your main idea. Be prepared to share your writing with classmates. For the title of your paragraphs, write "A Major Stressor in My Life."

• • • • • •

## Write About It

Find an article on the National Institutes of Health website, *newsinhealth.nih.gov/* that relates to health, wellness, stress, exercise, or alternative medicine. Read the article. Identify the main idea and major supporting points. Develop a map or an outline of the article. Write a summary of the article. In your first sentence, identify the title, author, and source and restate the main idea in your own words. For your title, write "Summary of "[name of article]_____."

# Chapter Review

| Put It Together: Support for Main Ideas | |
| --- | --- |
| Skills and Concepts | Explanation |
| **Supporting Points** | Support for main idea |
| **Major supporting points** (see pages 147–149) | Chief ideas or facts that support the main idea |
| **Minor supporting points** (see pages 148–149) | Additional explanations, examples, facts, and statistics that develop the major supporting points |
| **Organizing to Learn** (see pages 151–158) | Last step of the PRO reading system; helps you understand and remember what you learned in a reading |
| **Marking Texts** (see pages 152–153) | Highlighting and using a system of symbols and annotations on the text itself to make review and retention easier |
| **Making Bulleted Lists** (see page 154) | Lists accented by symbols called bullets to make supporting points easier to identify |
| **Mapping** (see pages 155–156) | Organizing information graphically to show relationships among facts and/or ideas |
| **Outlining** (see pages 157–158) | A formal strategy for organizing readings by divisions showing the relationships between main ideas and major and minor supporting points |
| **Summarizing** (see page 162) | Writing a concise version of the main idea and major supporting points of a reading in your own words |
| **Reader's Tip:** **Stating the Source and Main Idea in Summaries** (see pages 163–164) | Include: 1. The name of the author or of the group or institution responsible for the reading 2. The title of the reading or the article 3. The main idea (or thesis statement if the reading is trying to persuade you) in your own words |

## CRITICAL REFLECTIONS IN THE CLASSROOM COMMUNITY

Answer the following questions, and prepare to discuss them with your classmates.

1. List at least four positive aspects of your life that enhance the quality of your life and could increase your life expectancy.

   a. _____

   b. _____

c. _____

d. _____

e. _____

2. List two or three areas of your life that you would like to change to make your life healthier and more enjoyable.

a. _____

b. _____

c. _____

 **WORK THE WEB**

Many sites on the Web are devoted to wellness. One site developed by doctors and researchers that provides information on and tools for improving health is that of the Mayo Clinic. Do an Internet search for Mayo Clinic and complete the following tasks.

1. Once you've arrived at the home page, click on "Health Information" at the top of the page. Then click on "Healthy Living." (If the website has been reorganized, explore it to find the "Healthy Living" section.)

2. There you will find a number of links, such as "Nutrition," "Fitness," "Quit Smoking," and "Consumer Health."

3. From the list, pick an aspect of healthy living that interests you and continue to narrow your search until you find an article you like.

4. Read the article, paying attention to the main idea and supporting details.

5. Using the guidelines for writing summaries in this chapter, write a summary of your article.

Name _____ Date _____

# Drugs: The Truth*

— DAVE ELLIS

**TEXT BOOK** The following reading from the college textbook, *Becoming a Master Student* by Dave Ellis, deals openly with why substance abuse is appealing, what the characteristics of addiction are, and why it is difficult to break an addiction. Finally, he makes suggestions about how to break a substance abuse habit. As you read, notice how the author uses supporting details to support the main ideas.

## THE FUN

1   The truth is that getting high can be fun. In our culture, and especially in our media, getting high has become <u>synonymous</u> with having a good time. Even if you don't smoke, drink, or use other drugs, you are certain to come in contact with people who do.

2   For centuries, human beings have <u>devised</u> ways to change their feelings and thoughts by <u>altering</u> their body chemistry. The Chinese were using marijuana five thousand years ago. Herodotus, the ancient Greek historian, wrote about a group of people in Eastern Europe who threw marijuana on hot stones and inhaled the vapors. More recently, during the American Civil War, customers could buy opium and morphine across the counter of their neighborhood store. A few decades later, Americans were able to buy soft drinks that contained coca—the plant from which cocaine is derived.

3   Today we are still a drug-using society. Of course, some of those uses are therapeutic and lawful, including drugs that are taken as prescribed by a doctor or psychologist. The problem comes when we turn to drugs as *the* solution to any problem, even before seeking professional guidance. Are you uncomfortable? Often the first response is "Take something."

4   We live in times when reaching for instant comfort via chemicals is not only condoned—it is approved. If you're bored, tense, or anxious, you can drink a can of beer, down a glass of wine, or light up a cigarette. And these are only the legal <u>options</u>. If you're willing to take risks, you can pick from a large selection of illegal drugs on the street.

5   There is a big payoff in using alcohol, tobacco, caffeine, cocaine, heroin, or other drugs—or people wouldn't do it. The payoff can be direct, such as relaxation, self-confidence, comfort, excitement, or other forms of pleasure. At times, the payoff is not so obvious, as when people seek to avoid rejection, mask emotional pain, win peer group acceptance, or reject authority.

6   Perhaps drugs have a timeless appeal because human beings face two <u>perennial</u> problems: how to cope with unpleasant moods, and how to deal with difficult circumstances such as poverty, loneliness, or the prospect of death. When faced with either problem, people are often tempted to ignore potential solutions and go directly to the chemical fix.

## THE COSTS

7   In addition to the payoffs, there are costs. For some people, the cost is much greater than the payoff. That cost goes beyond money. Even if illegal drug use doesn't make you broke, it can make you crazy. This is not necessarily the kind of crazy where you dress up like Napoleon. Rather, it is the kind where you care about little else except finding more drugs—friends, school, work, and family be damned.

**opium**
drug made from pods of the opium poppy, the same flower from which heroin is made

**condoned**
accepted

*"Drugs: The Truth" by David Ellis from BECOMING A MASTER STUDENT, 11th Edition. Copyright © 2006. Reprinted by permission of Houghton Mifflin Company.

compulsive
relating to an
irresistible urge

8    Substance abuse—the compulsive use of a chemical in alcohol or drugs resulting in negative consequences—is only part of the picture. People can also relate to food, gambling, money, sex, and even work in compulsive ways.

9    Some people will stop abusing a substance or activity when the consequences get serious enough. Other people don't stop. They continue their self-defeating behaviors, no matter the consequences for themselves, their friends, or their families. At that point the problem goes beyond abuse. It's addiction.

10   With substance addiction, the costs can include overdose, infection, and lowered <u>immunity</u> to disease—all of which can be fatal. Long-term excessive drinking damages every organ system in the human body. Each year, almost 400,000 people die from the effects of cigarette smoking.

11   Lectures about why to avoid alcohol and drug abuse and addiction can be pointless. <u>Ultimately</u>, we don't take care of our bodies because someone says we should. We might take care of ourselves when we see that the costs of using a substance outweigh the benefits. You choose. It's your body.

12   Acknowledging that alcohol, tobacco, and other drugs can be fun infuriates a lot of people who might assume that this is the same as condoning their use. The point is this: People are more likely to abstain when they're convinced that using these substances leads to more pain than pleasure over the long run.

## THE FULL SCOPE OF ADDICTION

13   Here are some guidelines that can help you decide if addiction is a barrier for you right now. Most addictions share some key features, such as the following:

- *Loss of control*—continued substance use or activity in spite of <u>adverse</u> consequences.
- *Pattern of relapse*—vowing to quit or limit the activity or substance use and continually failing to do so.
- *Tolerance*—the need to take increasing amounts of a substance to produce the desired effect.
- *Withdrawal*—signs and symptoms of physical and mental discomfort or illness when the substance is taken away.

14   The same basic features can be present in anything from cocaine use to compulsive gambling. All of this can add up to a continuous cycle of abuse or addiction. These common features prompt many people to call some forms of addiction a disease. The American Medical Association formally recognized alcoholism as a disease in 1956. Some people do not agree that alcoholism is a disease or that all addictions can be labeled with that term. You don't have to wait until this question is settled before examining your own life. If you have a problem with addiction, consider getting help. The problem might be your own addiction or perhaps the behavior of someone you love. In any case, consider acting on several of the following suggestions.

### Admit the problem

15   People with active addictions are a varied group—rich and poor, young and old, successful and unsuccessful. Often these people do have one thing in common: They are masters of denial. They deny that they are unhappy. They deny that they have hurt anyone. They are convinced that they can quit any time they want. They sometimes become so <u>adept</u> at hiding the problem from themselves that they die.

## Pay attention

16  If you do use a substance compulsively or behave in compulsive ways, do so with awareness. Then pay attention to the consequences. Act with <u>deliberate</u> decision rather than out of habit or under pressure from others.

## Look at the costs

**tradeoff**
exchange of one
thing for another

17  There is always a tradeoff. Drinking 10 beers might result in a temporary high, and you will probably remember that feeling. No one feels great the morning after consuming 10 beers, but it seems easier to forget pain. Often people don't notice how bad alcoholism, drug addiction, or other forms of substance abuse make them feel.

## Take responsibility

18  Nobody plans to become an addict. If you have pneumonia, you can recover without guilt or shame. Approach an addiction in yourself or others in the same way. You can take responsibility for your recovery without blame, shame, or guilt.

## Get help

19  Many people find that they cannot treat addiction on their own. Addictive behaviors are often symptoms of an illness that needs treatment.

20  Two broad options exist for getting help with addiction. One is the growing self-help movement. The other is formal treatment. People recovering from addiction often combine the two.

21  Many self-help groups are modeled after Alcoholics Anonymous. AA is made up of recovering alcoholics and addicts. These people understand the problems of abuse first-hand, and they follow a systematic, 12-step approach to living without it. This is one of the oldest and most successful self-help programs in the world. Chapters of AA welcome people from all walks of life, and you don't have to be an alcoholic to attend most meetings. Programs based on AA principles exist for many other forms of addiction as well.

22  Some people feel uncomfortable with the AA approach. Other resources exist for these people, including private therapy and group therapy. Also investigate organizations such as Women for Sobriety, the Secular Organizations for Sobriety, and Rational Recovery Systems. Use whatever works for you.

23  Treatment programs are available in almost every community. They might be residential (you live there for weeks or months at a time) or outpatient (you visit several hours a day). Find out where these treatment centers are located by calling a doctor, a mental health professional, or a local hospital.

24  Alcohol and drug treatments are now covered by many health insurance programs. If you don't have insurance, it is usually possible to arrange some other payment program. Cost is no reason to avoid treatment.

## Get help for a friend or family member

25  You might know someone who uses alcohol or other drugs in a way that can lead to serious and sustained negative consequences. If so, you have every right to express your concern to that person. Wait until the person is clear-headed and then mention specific incidents. For example: "Last night you drank five beers when we were at my apartment, and then you wanted to drive home. When I offered to call a cab for you instead, you refused." Also be prepared to offer a source of help, such as the phone number of a local treatment center.

© 2013 Wadsworth, Cengage Learning

**Exercise 1**

## Work with Words

Use context, clues, dictionary skills, and your knowledge of word parts to choose the best definition for each of the following words underlined in the reading. The paragraph number is provided in case you want to check the context.

1. *Synonymous* (par. 1)
   a. opposite meaning
   b. same meaning
   c. dictionary definition

2. *Devised* (par. 2)
   a. invented
   b. discouraged
   c. allowed

3. *Altering* (par. 2)
   a. improving
   b. rejecting
   c. changing

4. *Options* (par. 4)
   a. choices
   b. chances
   c. requirements

5. *Perennial* (par. 6)
   a. short-term
   b. eventual
   c. continual

6. *Immunity* (par. 10)
   a. susceptibility
   b. resistance
   c. cooperation

7. *Ultimately* (par. 11)
   a. finally
   b. occasionally
   c. fortunately

8. *Adverse* (par. 13)
   a. contrary
   b. unnecessary
   c. harmful

9. *Adept* (par. 15)
   a. skillful
   b. inconsiderate
   c. clumsy

10. *Deliberate* (par. 16)
    a. compulsive
    b. careful
    c. organized

**Exercise 2**

## Check Your Understanding

Based on the reading, choose the best answer to each of the following multiple-choice questions.

1. What is the best topic for paragraph 2?
   a. ways people have changed their feelings and thoughts over centuries
   b. why people have changed their feelings over centuries
   c. minimal use of drugs over centuries

2. What is the best main idea statement for paragraph 2?
   a. The Chinese were using marijuana five thousand years ago.
   b. For thousands of years, people have found ways to alter their feelings and thoughts by altering their body chemistry.
   c. A group of people in Eastern Europe threw marijuana on hot stones and inhaled the vapors.

3. What is the best topic for paragraph 10?
   a. substance abuse
   b. the costs of substance abuse
   c. death rates caused by cigarette smoking

4. What is the best main idea statement for paragraph 10?
   a. The costs can include overdose and infection.
   b. Each year, almost 400,000 people die from the effects of cigarette smoking.

    c. Substance addiction causes many problems for the human body, many of which can be fatal.

5. According to Ellis,
    a. there's no problem taking drugs, as long as they're legal.
    b. people are encouraged to take something when they need comfort and this leads us to believe that drugs can solve any problem.
    c. the only reason people start using drugs is to get acceptance from their peer group.

6. When people have tolerance to a drug, it means
    a. they can't quit.
    b. they get sick when they try to quit.
    c. they need to take increasing amounts to get the desired effect.

7. Withdrawal refers to
    a. the physical and mental symptoms that occur when a substance is taken away.
    b. lack of control.
    c. the barrier to stopping substance abuse.

8. According to Ellis,
    a. alcoholism was declared a disease so people who are addicted to it need to consider getting help.
    b. there is disagreement about whether alcoholism is a disease, so until this debate is settled, people should wait to find out the best form of treatment.
    c. regardless of whether alcoholism is recognized as a disease by everyone, people who are addicted to it need to try to break their addiction.

9. Which of the following statements does Ellis agree with?
    a. Recovering from an addiction should not involve blame, shame, or guilt.
    b. The best treatment for alcoholics is to join Alcoholics Anonymous.
    c. Alcoholics should feel guilty for the pain they have caused themselves and other people; accepting guilt is the first step toward recovery.

**Exercise 3**

### Organize to Learn: Outline and Summarize

Complete the following outline for the reading. Then, using your outline, write a brief summary of the reading on a separate sheet of paper. In your first sentence, put the main idea in your own words, and include the title and the author of the reading.

Main idea: According to Dave Ellis in his reading "Drugs: The Truth," substance use can be fun, but the emotional and physical costs of addiction are usually so high that people need to seek ways to break their habit.

I. The Fun—Reasons people get high

   A. Synonymous for having fun

   B. _____

   C. _____

    D. Expectation of instant comfort

    E. Direct payoff

       1. _____

       2. Self-confidence

       3. _____

       4. _____

    F. Not obvious payoff

       1. _____

       2. Mask emotional pain

       3. _____

       4. _____

    G. Appeal of drugs due to two perennial problems

       1. Coping with unpleasant moods

       2. Dealing with difficult circumstances

          a. _____

          b. _____

          c. _____

II. _____

    A. Money

    B. _____

    C. _____

    D. Physical risks

       1. _____

       2. _____

       3. _____

    E. More likely to stop when understand costs are greater than pleasure

III. _____

    A. Features of addiction

       1. _____

       2. _____

       3. _____

       4. _____

B. Suggestions for quitting

1. _____

2. _____

3. _____

4. _____

5. _____

   a. _____

   b. Formal treatment like therapy

**Exercise 4**

## Reflect

Think about what you read in "Drugs: The Truth" and what you already know from your experience and observations about drugs (legal and illegal) and addiction. Then answer the following questions in complete sentences.

1. Other than "for fun," what do you think are the three most important reasons that people use drugs?

_____

_____

_____

_____

2. What do you think are the three most important "costs" of addiction?

_____

_____

_____

_____

3. Think about someone you know or someone you have read about who attempted to recover from an addiction. What was his or her process of recovery and how long did it take? Why do you think he or she was successful or unsuccessful?

_____

_____

_____

_____

# 5 Patterns of Organization

## WHERE WE LIVE, OUR COMMUNITIES

Visions of America/SuperStock

Condor 36, 2009/Used under license from Shutterstock.com

*It is our task—our essential, central, crucial task—to transform ourselves from mere social creatures into community creatures.—M. Scott Peck*

1. What observations can you make about each of the photos? Where do you think each is? Who you think lives there? Does your neighborhood look like either of them?

2. How would you describe the city, town, or neighborhood where you grew up? Where you live now?

3. What do you think the quotation means? How does it relate to the picture?

4. What does community mean to you? What communities are you a part of?

## Prepare to Read

Americans have always been a people on the move. Our mobility has a profound impact on where and how we live in the twenty-first century. The history of the United States and many changes in this country today are largely based on people moving here from other countries in search of a better life. During the nineteenth and early twentieth centuries, we moved from the countryside to the cities. Then, especially after World War II, we moved to the suburbs, where we thought we could escape the hassles, crowds, and crime of the cities. But new trends have emerged—toward the far suburbs, or "edge cities," and into gated communities, where more than seven million Americans live today. Where we live affects our lives in every way. However, when we think of "community," we don't always think about where we live. Most of us also belong to communities based on our interests or other things we have in common with people. Many of us now belong to virtual communities where the people we interact with live far away and we never see. What are the effects of these trends in where Americans live and the communities we belong to?

In this chapter, you will read about our cities, neighborhoods, and communities and learn to

- Recognize a variety of patterns of organization
- Identify transitions and other clues that signal each pattern
- Use patterns to organize what you read into timelines, maps, circle diagrams, flow charts, and other visual forms to aid your comprehension and retention

In the process of acquiring these skills, you will read about the history of cities and trends in the places and spaces in which we live and spend our time.

# American Cities One Hundred Years Ago*

—ROBERT A. DIVINE, T. H. BREEN, GEORGE M. FREDRICKSON,
AND R. HAL WILLIAMS

**TEXT BOOK** **The following reading from an American history textbook, *America, Past and Present,* describes what life was like for poor immigrants in American cities at the beginning of the twentieth century. As you read, compare the living conditions of the people described here to how you and your family live today.**

1    One day around 1900, Harriet Vittum, a settlement house worker in Chicago, went to the aid of a young Polish girl who lived in a nearby slum. The girl, aged 15, had discovered she was pregnant and had taken poison. An ambulance was on the way, and Vittum, told of the poisoning, rushed over to do what she could.

2    Quickly, she raced up the three flights of stairs to the floor where the girl and her family lived. Pushing open the door, she found the father, several male boarders, and two or three small boys asleep on the kitchen floor. In the next room, the mother was on the floor among several women boarders and one or two small children. Glancing out the window, Vittum saw the wall of another building so close she could reach out and touch it.

**boarders**
people who
receive meals
where they
live

Mother and her children in a Chicago tenement, 1910

**tenement**
apartment
building with
substandard
conditions

3    There was a third room; in it lay the 15-year-old girl, along with two more small children who were asleep. Looking at the scene, Vittum thought about the girl's life in the crowded tenement. Should she try to save her? Vittum asked herself. Should she even try to bring the girl back "to the misery and hopelessness of the life she was living in that awful place"?

---

* "American Cities One Hundred Years Ago" by Divine, Robert A., Breen, T. H., Fredrickson, George M.; and Williams, R. Hal, from AMERICA PAST AND PRESENT, 6th Edition, © 2002, pp. 549–550. Reprinted by permission of Pearson Education, Inc., Upper Saddle River, NJ.

4     The young girl died, and in later years, Vittum often told her story. It was easy to see why. The girl's life in the slum, the children on the floor, the need to take in boarders to make ends meet, the way the mother and father collapsed at the end of a workday that began long before sunup—all reflected the experiences of millions of people living in the nation's cities.

lured
attracted

5     People poured into cities in the last part of the nineteenth century, lured by glitter and excitement, by friends and relatives who were already there, and, above all, by the greater opportunities for jobs and higher wages. Between 1860 and 1910, the rural population of the United States almost doubled; the number of people living in cities increased sevenfold.

6     Little of the increase came from natural growth, since urban families had high rates of infant mortality, a declining fertility rate, and a high death rate from injury and disease. Many of the newcomers came from rural America, and many more came from Europe, Latin America, and Asia. In one of the most significant migrations in American history, thousands of African Americans began in the 1880s to move from the rural South to northern cities. By 1900, there were large black communities in New York, Baltimore, Chicago, Washington, DC, and other cities. Yet to come was the even greater black migration during World War I.

7     Two major forces reshaped American society between 1870 and 1920. One was industrialization; the other was urbanization, the headlong rush of people from their rural roots into the modern urban environment. By 1920, the city had become the center of American economic, social, and cultural life.

**Exercise 1**

## Recall and Discuss

Based on Reading 1, answer the following questions and prepare to discuss them with your classmates.

1. What story does this reading begin with, and why do you think the authors begin with it?

   _____

   _____

   _____

   _____

2. How did the rural and urban populations of the United States change between 1860 and 1910?

   _____

   _____

   _____

3. Where did the people come from who were moving to the cities?

   _____

   _____

4. What were the two major forces that reshaped American society between 1870 and 1920?

_____

_____

_____

5. Describe the house or apartment you live in. What is each room used for? How many people live together? Are they related? Are they friends? Are they former strangers sharing living space? Does the space feel crowded? Compare and contrast where you live to where the young girl in the story lived.

_____

_____

_____

# Patterns of Organization

As you learned in Chapter 4, separating supporting points from main ideas is an important reading skill. Identifying the different ways writers organize their supporting points is another essential skill for improving reading comprehension. The various arrangements authors use are called **patterns of organization.** Recognizing them helps you to

**patterns of organization**
the way a writer chooses to organize his or her material to help us understand the relationships among ideas

- *See how the writer thinks* about the topic and understand the relationships among ideas as the writer perceives them
- *Organize to learn,* using the patterns to improve your comprehension and make it easier for you to remember the information for tests and other uses in the future

Some of the most common patterns of organization are

- Chronological order and narration
- Definition and classification
- Exemplification
- Cause and effect
- Comparison and contrast
- Process
- Problem and solution
- Argument

You will be introduced to each one in this chapter. Sometimes one pattern will clearly be dominant in a paragraph or in an essay. But writers often combine patterns of organization to express their ideas. As a reader, you need to decipher the writer's patterns. In composition classes, you will learn to use many of these same patterns for organizing your own writing into effective essays. As a student, you need to recognize patterns used frequently in various disciplines, such as sociology, biology, math, and anthropology. In history, for example, much of the information is organized chronologically. In biology, textbooks often emphasize classifications of plants and animals. Introductory sociology may provide you with many definitions of important terms, and math will require you to analyze and solve problems.

The different organizational patterns are easier to identify if you are aware of the transitions and other clues that usually accompany each pattern. **Transitions** are words or phrases that link ideas, such as *for example, second, in contrast, on the other hand, because,* and *therefore.* They establish relationships between clauses, between sentences within a paragraph, and between paragraphs and longer sections. They provide you with clues for identifying which pattern is being used in a selection.

**transitions**
words or phrases that link ideas and/or identify relationships

## CHRONOLOGICAL ORDER AND NARRATION

**chronological order**
information organized in time order

**Chronological order** is a pattern of organization commonly used in history and other disciplines. It answers the questions "when did it happen?" and "in what order?" This pattern presents information according to the order that it occurred in time. For example, in the following excerpt from a sociology textbook, the authors state the main idea in the first sentence: "the United States is becoming increasingly urbanized." Then they explain in chronological order that this urbanization has occurred over a long period. In the following excerpt, italics have been added to emphasize the transitions and clues related to time organization.

> Many Americans have romantic notions of moving to the country to escape the hustle and bustle of city life, but the United States is becoming increasingly urbanized. *In 1790,* only about 5 percent of Americans lived in cities and fewer than 25 cities had a population of more than 25,000. *Two hundred years later* those figures had substantially changed. Over three-fourths of the U.S. population *now* lives in towns or cities, and another 20 percent live within the sphere of influence of a city. (Thompson and Hickey, *Society in Focus*)

The phrases "in 1790" and "two hundred years later," and the word *now* keep you aware of the movement of Americans over time.

**narration**
information organized to tell a story

**Narration** is a similar pattern that uses chronological or time order. It answers the question "what happened?" It uses a story, or a narrative, to communicate information. In a narrative, the reader is always wondering what will happen next. Narrative is commonly used in short stories and novels, but some textbooks use narrative as well. For example, the history textbook from which Reading 1 was taken used the story of an impoverished pregnant girl and the social worker who tried to rescue her as a way to tell students about the experiences of those who lived in America's cities 100 years ago. Here's a story of a different period of American history: the Depression of the 1930s, when a drought forced tens of thousands of farmers off their land. Having lost everything they had, thousands headed to California, where they had heard jobs were plentiful. This mass migration movement was called the Dust Bowl Migration. The following narrative is told in retrospect: a grown woman now, the narrator tells her story of that period as she experienced it as a young girl.

> The year was 1936 when Daddy set me on his knee, looked me in the eye, and said, "Ruby, you ever heard o' California?" His voice was shaky but sure, if that's possible, and I knew right then we wouldn't be in Gavin County, Oklahoma, much longer. I was born in Gavin County, in a farmhouse, just like the ones you may have seen in the pictures, and so was my three older brothers and two big sisters. At that time—actually, for the five years or so before that—all anybody could talk about was "Black Sunday" and all the wind and dust that had took away our wheat.

It took away my granddaddy's entire house, too, and all the while my daddy was clipping out advertisements in the papers saying they needed hands in some place called San Joaquin. We were always hungry, and Mama cried a lot, especially after Aunt Rose died. So I didn't fuss much when we loaded up the truck with everything we could fit—mattresses, pots, pans, trunks of clothes, you name it—and made our way onto the Mother Road, the street they call U.S. Highway 66. (Meyer, "Dust Bowl Days")

Many clues in this narrative passage tell you that it is organized in time order. Ruby says father let her know they were leaving Oklahoma when "The year was 1936," and the reader learns how long the troubles had been going on when the author says, "for five years or so." We learn that her father had been considering moving the family when Ruby states, "while my daddy was clipping out advertisements." We know things got worse for the mother "after Aunt Rose died" and the daughter's reaction "when we loaded up the truck . . . and made our way." If you were to read the rest of this story, you would find out what happened on the journey to California and what life was like for migrant farmworkers there.

The narration of a story does not always move forward in a straight line. Stories, novels, and movies sometimes reorganize the time order and employ techniques like flashbacks—narratives that take place in the past—to enhance the effect of the storytelling. Textbooks, on the other hand, are much more likely to use strict chronological order to present information. An American history text, for example, might start at the time before Columbus and continue through the Revolutionary War, westward expansion, the Civil War, and up to the present time.

**Transitions and Clues** As you've seen, chronological order and narration often use dates and times to specify when something happened. Besides actual dates and times, transitional words such as *then, when, after, before, while, during, earlier, meanwhile, until, now, immediately, finally, as soon as, next, last,* and *later* signal you to be aware of time relationships between the ideas or events.

**Organizing to Learn: Creating a Time Line** One way to learn events in the proper chronological order as you study and review for a test is to prepare a **time line.** For example, the information in the following paragraph from *Sociology: A Down-to-Earth Approach* by James Henslin could be organized in a time line like the one that appears like the one that follows.

**time line**
a graphic representation that uses lines and dates to illustrate the time order of events

It took all of human history [about 250,000 years] for the world's population to reach its first billion around 1800. It then took about one hundred thirty years (until 1930) to add the second billion. Just thirty years later (1960), the world population hit 3 billion. The time it took to reach the fourth billion was cut in half, to only fifteen years (1975). It then took just twelve more years (1987) for the total to hit 5 billion, and another twelve for it to reach 6 billion (in 1999). (Henslin, *Sociology*)

*Population Growth in Human History*

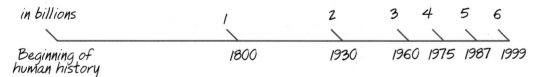

**Exercise 2**

Organize to Learn: Create a Time Line

Use the following paragraph on world urbanization to complete the time line. Italics have been added to the paragraph to emphasize the transitions and clues related to time organization. Add the correct percentage of urban population for each period. The first entry has been made for you.

> *Around the year 1800,* perhaps 3 percent of the world's population lived in urban places of 5,000 people or more. *By 1900* the proportion had risen to over 13 percent and by 1990 the percentage had increased to over 43. According to statistical data provided by the United Nations, *by the year 2025,* 60 percent of the world's population will live in urban places. *Within the past century* the city has thus become the dominant center of modern civilization. (Brunn and Williams, *Cities of the World*)

*Growth in World Urban Population, 1800–2025*

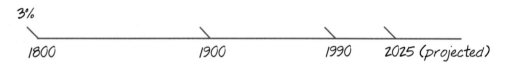

3%

1800          1900          1990     2025 (projected)

## DEFINITION AND CLASSIFICATION

**definition**
information organized to answer the question "what is it?"

**Definition** is the pattern of organization that attempts to answer the question "what is it?" A definition of a term or concept may be short—just a few words—or it may be quite long—a paragraph or more. Textbooks often print key terms in boldface and include definitions in the body of the text, in the margins, and/or in a glossary at the end of the book. In this textbook, we show the definitions in the margins.

Sometimes a definition places an item in a class, or category, and then distinguishes it from the other items in that category. For example, a Siamese is a cat, but *Webster's II New Riverside University Dictionary* does much more than place Siamese in the category of cats. According to *Webster's,* a Siamese cat is "a short-haired cat originally bred in the Orient, having blue eyes and a pale fawn or gray coat with darker ears, face, tail, and feet."

**classification**
information organized into categories or groups

Definition is closely related to another organizational pattern, **classification.** Classification is information organized into categories or groups. This pattern answers the questions "what kinds or types are there?" and "how can we group items into classes or categories?" It is common to see definition and classification used in combination, because they are closely related. For example, an article might classify all the major breeds of cats and define the characteristics of each specific breed. Here is an example that defines the term *community* and includes categories of communities.

> Any group or collection of individuals living in the same place and sharing certain behaviors, interests, and needs can be called a community. The term is used in different academic disciplines ranging from developmental psychology to plant ecology. Human communities can be broken down into three main categories: location-based communities, cultural communities, and community organizations. A different kind of community is the virtual community, whose members do not live in the same place but interact through technology of some sort.

**Transitions and Clues** Authors frequently use the words *is* or *are* to connect a term to a definition. For example, "A location-based community *is* a group of individuals living in the same place." Definitions might also be introduced with commas or with phrases such as *could be defined as, refers to, means, signifies, can be considered,* or *consists of.* Classifications may use clues like the *first type, second kind, third variety, fourth category,* or *another group* to introduce elements in a classification.

**Organizing to Learn: Creating a Vocabulary List** One way to organize definitions for studying is to create a *vocabulary list* or prepare vocabulary cards for terms to be memorized, as you did for specialized vocabulary in Chapter 2, page 82. For example, for the previous excerpt, you might make the following list, or vocabulary cards, for terms it introduces and defines.

- *Community*: A group of individuals living in the same place and/or sharing certain behaviors, interests, and needs.
- *Virtual community*: A community whose members do not share a place but interact through technology.

Outlining is also a good way to study information that has already been organized as a classification. See pages 157 through 158 in Chapter 4 for directions.

**Exercise 3**

Organize to Learn: Identify Definition and Classification

Read the following paragraphs that further explain community, then complete the two activities that follow.

> *Location-based communities* are primarily *defined by* their location, such as the residents of a particular city or members of a neighborhood gang. Groups of people that share food traditions, religion, and/or ethnic background *can be considered cultural communities.* Even fans of the same football team could be considered part of a cultural community. Such communities share cultural ideas, beliefs, and behaviors. *Community organizations are* political, economic, or kinship-based communities such as extended families or trade unions. In the real world, communities are more complicated and difficult to classify. All three forms of community may overlap or be combined in different ways, and individuals usually belong to and move between different communities.

1. Circle two transitions or clues that this paragraph is organized by definition.
2. Define the following terms and categories from the context of the excerpt.
   a. Location-based communities

   _____

   _____

   b. Cultural communities

   _____

   _____

   c. Community organizations

   _____

# EXEMPLIFICATION

**exemplification**
a pattern of
examples used to
support ideas

One of the most common patterns of organization is **exemplification**, the use of examples to support ideas. It answers the question "what examples support the main idea?" Examples can support other patterns of organization. Notice how the following paragraph uses examples to reinforce the explanation of virtual communities.

> The term *virtual community* has been created to refer to communities that do *not* share a location; members of these communities might never communicate face-to-face. Instead, *virtual communities* are based on forms of communication such as letters, telephones, or the Internet. Examples of clubs, magazines, and organizations that depend on letters for their members to interact have existed since the 1700s. However, the most common virtual communities today are online communities such as chat rooms, blogs, forums, message boards, social networking sites, and role-playing games.

Notice that the author mentions examples of communication for virtual communities—letters, telephones, and Internet. Then, further examples are given for some types of Internet virtual communities—chat rooms, blogs, forums, message boards, social networking sites, and role-playing games.

**Transitions and Clues** The words *and, or, for example, such as, for instance, in fact, in addition, furthermore, moreover, and also are* often used to introduce examples. In textbooks, a string of examples may even be numbered or bulleted to make it easier for you to identify them. The words *and* or *or* are commonly used to link the final examples in a series. The use of *commas* for a *series of items,* as in the last line of the paragraph, indicates a list of examples.

**Organizing to Learn: Using an Outline and Map** Outlining and mapping help you understand the relative importance of the detailed information that examples provide. For example, the above paragraph could be outlined as follows.

## Virtual Communities

**Main idea:** Virtual communities do not share a location and do not communicate face to face.

  I. Forms of communication
     A. Letters
     B. Telephones
     C. Internet

  II. Historical examples of virtual communities that depended on letters
     A. Clubs
     B. Magazines
     C. Organizations

  III. Most common virtual communities today
     A. Chat rooms
     B. Blogs
     C. Forums
     D. Message boards
     E. Social networking sites
     F. Role-playing games

Some people find mapping more helpful than outlining, and it is an excellent choice for organizing examples and other patterns. The outlined information from the paragraph about virtual communities could be organized in a map like the one below. Compare the map to the outline. The principles are basically the same.

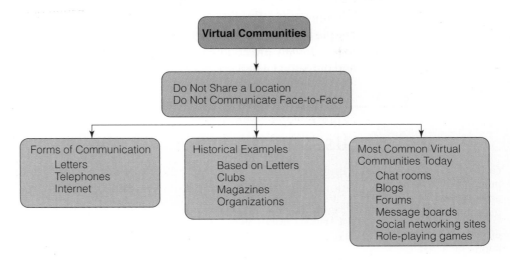

**Exercise 4**

Organize to Learn: Mark Examples in Text

In the following excerpt about the central downtown park in Tijuana, Mexico, number the examples that support the main idea stated in the first sentence.

> You can get a taste of the more traditional features of Mexican cities if you visit the central downtown park, or *la plaza central*. Usually, this plaza is in the middle of the Mexican city or town. It is a place where people go to take a walk, to see friends, or just to enjoy themselves and socialize. The central plaza is home to the government palace and the major church. Frequently, you find many small stores and markets in and around the plaza. Bus and minivan routes often begin and end here as well, so it's easy to get there. (Dávalos, "Tijuana and San Diego")

**Exercise 5**

Organize to Learn: Create a Map

Read the following paragraph about belonging to communities. Then, create a map showing how the author fits into different communities and how some of these communities overlap.

I was born and raised in a suburban neighborhood in Chicago, Illinois. However, I feel like I identify with many things that go beyond the boundaries of my neighborhood and the boundaries of the United States. Both my parents were born in El Salvador, and a lot of my family still lives there. I grew up eating Salvadorian food, speaking Spanish, and practicing Catholicism at home. At the same time I was making friends in elementary school with people from different backgrounds. When I got to high school, I had learned to love Indian and Ethiopian food, and I was already a big fan of reggae music and old Kung Fu movies.

## CAUSE AND EFFECT

**cause**
information that answers the question "why?"

**effect**
information that explains results or outcomes

Readings organized using the pattern of **cause** and **effect** usually answer the questions "*why* did something happen?" and "what were the *results* of a particular event?" For example, a reading on urbanization from a college sociology textbook might try to explain why cities have grown so rapidly and the effects, or results, of that rapid growth. Cause-and-effect relationships are often very complicated. Usually there is not simply one cause-and-effect relationship to explain a situation. Sometimes there are underlying causes and immediate causes. Sometimes there are immediate effects and long-term effects. All these layers of relationships require considerable analysis by the writer and then by the reader to reach reasonable conclusions.

For example, read the following paragraph about housing.

While the number of poor people has been growing, the supply of affordable housing has been shrinking. Rents for the least expensive apartments are rising much faster than the income of the tenants. The average poor family now spends about 65 percent of its income on housing—more than double the maximum amount the Department of Housing and Urban Development says they should have to spend. An increasing number of people are being forced to move in with relatives and friends or are living in converted garages, old cars and vans, tents, or on the streets. Estimates of the number of homeless people in the United States vary widely, but virtually everyone agrees that their numbers have soared in the last decade. (Coleman and Cressey, *Social Problems*)

This paragraph analyzes one of the basic causes for the increase in homelessness: The cost of housing is increasing much faster than poor people's incomes.

**Transitions and Clues** Many transitions are commonly associated with cause-and-effect reasoning, making this pattern easy to identify. Causal relationships are indicated by words such as *the reason why, because, and since*, and by verbs such as *lead to, cause, result in, influence, give rise to,* and *contribute to*, and verbs that show a trend, such as *accelerate, intensify,* and *increase.* Effects may be introduced by transitions such as *therefore, as a result, subsequently, consequently, so,* and *hence.*

**Organizing to Learn: Creating a Chart** One way to organize cause-and-effect relationships among facts and/or ideas is to create a chart. For example, the information in the above paragraph might be organized like this:

| Shrinking Supply of Affordable Housing | | |
| --- | --- | --- |
| Cause | | Effects on Poor Families |
| Rent rising faster than income | ⇒ | Spend 65% of income on housing |
| | ⇒ | Forced to move in with relatives |
| | ⇒ | Moving into old cars, tents |
| | ⇒ | Number of homeless has soared |

In this case, only one cause is identified—the rising cost of housing—but it is obvious that that one cause has multiple effects.

**Exercise 6**

## Organize to Learn: Identify Cause and Effect

Read the following paragraph about urbanization from a sociology textbook. Circle all the transitions and other words indicating that the reasoning used here is primarily cause and effect. Then complete the cause-and-effect chart.

> Because cities have tended to grow rapidly, very little planning has gone into their physical shape, and their social structure has also given rise to occasional problems. The large concentration of people in cities requires buildings that are close together and many stories high. Without proper planning, this necessity can lead to ugliness, to lack of green and open spaces, to the often-mentioned "asphalt jungle" look. Modern city planners are much more aware of the need to pay special attention to a pleasing appearance, so that the cities of the future will probably be much more attractive than those of the past. (Perry and Perry, *Contemporary Society*)

| Lack of Urban Planning | | |
| --- | --- | --- |
| Cause | | Effects |
| 1. Cities have grown rapidly | ⇒ | 1. _____ |
| 2. _____ | ⇒ | 2. Buildings are close together and many stories high |
| 3. Without proper planning | ⇒ | 3. _____  _____ |
| 4. _____  _____ | ⇒ | 4. Cities of the future will probably be more attractive |

**Exercise 7**

## Organize to Learn: Identify Cause and Effect

Read the following paragraph about urbanization from a sociology textbook. Circle all the transitions and other words indicating that the reasoning used here is primarily cause and effect. Then complete the cause-and-effect chart.

> The stunning increase in the cost of buying a private home has been a major contributor to the growing division between the haves and the have-nots in our society. Those who already own a home have received windfall profits, but first-time home buyers are often shut out of the market. And even though the recent pace of real estate inflation seems to have slowed, the cost of an average home more than doubled in the last decade and a half. And as a result, the average buyer is now older and more likely to need two incomes to make the payments. (Coleman and Cressey, *Social Problems*)

| Higher Housing Prices | |
|---|---|
| Cause | Effects |
| _____  ⇒ | a.  Growing division between haves and have-nots |
| ⇒ | b.  _____ |
| ⇒ | c.  _____ <br> _____ |

## COMPARISON AND CONTRAST

**comparison**
information that explains how two things are similar

**contrast**
information that explains how two things are different

Another common pattern of organization is comparison and contrast. **Comparison** answers the question "how are two items similar?" **Contrast** answers the question "how are two items different?" The items being compared or contrasted can be almost anything: people, ideas, cities, trees, buildings, processes, and so on. The items being considered usually fit into the same general category or have something in common.

Many times, authors use both comparison and contrast in an article, but usually their examination focuses primarily on either similarities or differences. The term *compare* is sometimes used to mean both comparison and contrast. For example, on an essay test, a professor may ask students to compare the economies of Chicago and Tokyo. A complete answer would need to include the significant similarities and differences between the two cities' economies.

**Transitions and Clues** Transitional words and phrases used for comparisons include *similarly, likewise, also, alike, same,* and *in comparison.* For contrasts, *yet, nevertheless, in contrast, on the other hand, however, but,* and *conversely* are some of the transitional words used.

**Organizing to Learn: Creating a Circle Diagram** An effective way to organize a comparison and contrast is to use circles to form a diagram sometimes called a Venn diagram. If two items being compared share a common trait, the circles overlap. Read the following excerpt about grocery stores, and then study the accompanying diagram.

The grocery stores in low-income neighborhoods and those in the better-off sections of cities have a couple of things in common: They sell food, and people shop and spend money in them. But the similarities end there. Big grocery stores in low-income areas are few and far between. Most residents have to take buses or drive at least 10 miles to get to one. The few stores in the "hood" are stark contrasts to those found in more affluent areas. Only people who have no choice go to "poor stores" because their prices are generally higher, the quality of the food is usually poorer, and the selection is meager.

The conveniently located "rich stores" frequently have bright lights highlighting delicious-looking produce, beautiful refrigerated cases of freshly cooked "homemade" foods that can be picked up for the evening dinner, and cheery folks all around the store offering the shoppers samples of tasty tidbits. In contrast, the poor stores have fluorescent bulbs that don't do much to make the wilted produce look very appetizing, no display areas offering freshly prepared foods, and certainly no samples for shoppers to take.

The poor stores do have at least one feature not found in their upscale counterparts across town: they accept WIC (Women-Infants-Children) coupons for poor families. Many low-income shoppers use WIC coupons, and the program has excessively complicated rules, so checkout lines are almost always painfully long. The result is more restless children, more frustration, and more humiliation for the shoppers.

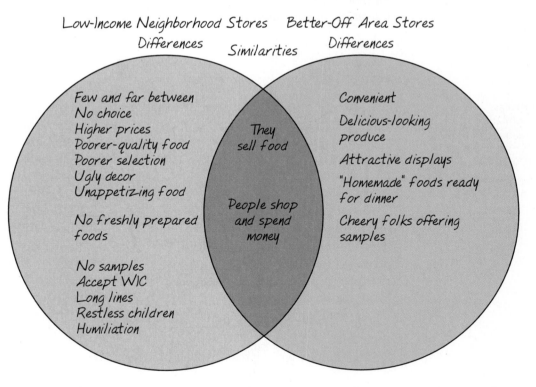

Low-Income Neighborhood Stores          Better-Off Area Stores
        Differences        Similarities        Differences

**Low-Income (left circle):**
Few and far between
No choice
Higher prices
Poorer-quality food
Poorer selection
Ugly decor
Unappetizing food

No freshly prepared foods

No samples
Accept WIC
Long lines
Restless children
Humiliation

**Similarities (center):**
They sell food

People shop and spend money

**Better-Off (right circle):**
Convenient
Delicious-looking produce
Attractive displays
"Homemade" foods ready for dinner
Cheery folks offering samples

Notice that in the diagram, there are many differences and only two similarities. Sometimes you might map two elements that are completely different, completely contrasting. In that case, the circles would be completely separate.

**Exercise 8**

## Organize to Learn: Create a Circle Diagram

Read Yi-Fu Tuan's contrast of American and Chinese attitudes toward where we live. Then, on a separate sheet of paper, create circles that identify the main points of comparison and contrast. According to the author, are there any points where the attitudes of the two cultures are similar? If so, you can allow the circles to overlap at that point.

Americans have a sense of space, not of place. Go to an American home in exurbia, and almost the first thing you do is drift toward the picture window. How curious that the first compliment you pay your host inside his house is to say how lovely it is outside his house! He is pleased that you should admire his vistas. The distant horizon is not merely a line separating earth from sky, it is a symbol of the future. The American is not rooted in his place, however lovely: his eyes are drawn by the expanding space to a point on the horizon, which is his future.

By contrast, consider the traditional Chinese home. Blank walls enclose it. Step behind the spirit wall and you are in a courtyard with perhaps a miniature garden around the corner. Once inside the private compound you are wrapped in an ambiance of calm beauty, an ordered world of buildings, pavement, rock, and decorative vegetation. But you have no distant view: nowhere does space open out before you. Raw nature in such a home is experienced only as weather, and the only open space is the sky above. The Chinese is rooted in his place. When he has to leave, it is not for the promised land on the terrestrial horizon, but for another world all together along the vertical, religious axis of his imagination. (Tuan, "American Space, Chinese Place")

## PROCESS

**process**
information organized to show how something is done step-by-step

**Process** is the organizational pattern that answers the questions "how?" and "What was the sequence of steps?" For example, a reading organized around process might explain how to write an essay, how to replace brake shoes on a car, or how to earn money on the stock market. A process is usually explained in steps. If you are learning to bake a cake, you will follow the recipe directions in order, step by step. Often success depends on completing each step in the proper sequence; thus, the steps in a process are often labeled *first, second, third,* and so on. Frequently, the process for doing something is written as a numbered list. For instance, a cookie recipe might start like this:

1. Heat the oven to 350 degrees.
2. Mix together the flour, baking powder, salt, and sugar.
3. Melt the butter.

The recipe would continue to list the steps the cook would follow to make the final product.

Another kind of writing that involves process is a description of how something takes place. You will encounter this kind of organizational pattern in many college courses, including sociology, biology, physics, and history. Read the following paragraph. Once you understand the process of gentrification, you will understand the meaning of the word if it's not familiar to you.

The gentrification of a neighborhood is usually a gradual process. Some recent examples of neighborhoods in different stages of the gentrification process are Harlem in New York and the Mission District in San Francisco. The process begins in a neighborhood where low-income and blue-collar people have lived for years. Slowly, the area becomes interesting and desirable to people with extra money to spend. The neighborhood is usually convenient, close to downtown and entertainment districts. It has beautiful, old homes, some divided up into apartments. The homes are cheap, and young professional people with lots of money and energy for renovation are attracted to them.

As the gentrification process continues, more people buy and remodel homes or rent upscale space in these areas, and prices go up. A natural part of the process is that the residents who do not make a lot of money eventually are forced to move out because they can no longer afford to stay in the neighborhood. Homeowners decide to move because they can no longer afford the property taxes and selling their houses for substantially more than they paid for them seems like a good idea. Throughout the process, services that cater to the upper-middle class begin to appear: fancy coffee shops, upscale restaurants, and specialty stores such as bakeries, bistros, and delicatessens. In the end, the neighborhood is completely transformed. People whose families may have lived there for generations are no longer there.

**Transitions and Clues** The transitions commonly used to identify process as an organizational pattern include *how to, in the process of, the steps to follow, stages,* and terms that identify steps, such as *begin, continue,* and *end* or *first, second,* and *third.* Some of these transitions overlap with those used in chronological order because both patterns of organization arrange points in time, although for different purposes.

**Organizing to Learn: Creating a Flowchart** Because a process consists of clearly defined steps, making a numbered list of them is one way to organize ideas to be sure you understand them. Another way is to create a **flowchart,** which is a graphic organizer popular among businesses and computer applications. A flowchart uses arrows to show sequence, or directions. For example, the stages of the gentrification process could be represented in a simple flowchart like the one shown below.

**flowchart**
a graphic
representation of
a process, usually
using arrows

**The Gentrification Process**

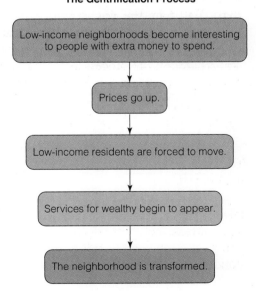

Low-income neighborhoods become interesting to people with extra money to spend.

Prices go up.

Low-income residents are forced to move.

Services for wealthy begin to appear.

The neighborhood is transformed.

**Exercise 9**

## Organize to Learn: Create a Flowchart

Read the following excerpt. Watch for the stages in the process of migration that help to explain the ethnic concentrations in some urban and rural neighborhoods. Then, on a separate sheet of paper, create a flowchart that illustrates the process of chain migration and the growth of ethnic groups.

### Chain Migration

In the United States, people are considered ethnic if they are not part of the majority. Mexicans in Mexico are generally not part of an ethnic group, but when they immigrate to the United States, they become part of an ethnic group. Chain migration describes the process by which people migrate to a specific community of a foreign country and become members of an ethnic group.

First, usually one person or a few people decide to move in search of a better life. Then, after establishing themselves in a new place, these people write letters and make phone calls back home telling people they should move too. Eventually, the idea catches on, and many people from the same area decide to migrate. Finally, large numbers of people move from one village or from neighboring villages to join the first pioneers in their new home. In this way, neighbors in the old country become neighbors in a new country. And each person who moves encourages other people from back home to follow. Thus the process of chain migration continues, and the ethnic groups grow. (Adapted from Jordan-Bychkov and Domosh, *Human Mosaic*)

**Exercise 10**

## Organize to Learn: Write a Summary

In your own words, *briefly* summarize "Chain Migration." Start with a sentence that states the main idea and gives credit to the source (the author and title of the excerpt). Then list, in sentence form, the steps in the process.

_____

_____

_____

_____

_____

_____

**Exercise 11**

Organize to Learn: Create a Vocabulary List

Define the following terms from the context of the excerpt.

1. *Ethnic* _____

2. *Chain migration* _____

   _____

**Exercise 12**

Reflect

Think about what you read in "Chain Migration" and what you already know about the topic. Answer the following questions, and prepare to discuss them with your classmates.

1. How long have you lived where you are now? Where does your immediate family live?

   _____

   _____

2. Has your family migrated from one state to another or from one country to another? Did your grandparents or great-grandparents migrate here from somewhere else?

   _____

   _____

3. How did the members of your family end up living where they are now? What were the steps in the *process* of their migration?

   _____

   _____

4. Why did your family migrate? If you don't know, interview a family member. If there is no one in your family who migrated, interview a neighbor or a classmate.

   _____

   _____

**Reading 2**

# Gated Developments: Fortresses or Communities?* —Heather Eudy

**The following reading studies the upsurge in what are known as gated communities—their characteristics and history as well as the reasons why they appeal to a growing number of people. As you read, think about the gated communities in your area, and notice the patterns of organization that Eudy uses.**

1     A sea-breeze-kissed, Italian-style, 2,500-square-foot home at the Royal Palm Yacht and Country Club in Boca Raton, Florida, will provide you with a waterfront villa, yacht dockage, and a private lap pool for approximately $29.5 million. Also in Italian style, a home in Beverly Park in Los Angeles, California, can be had for between $10 million and $26 million, where you can bask in the "privacy" and "prestige" of 24-hour security, your own park, and a golf course. Or perhaps you would prefer to live in Cobblestone, also known as "The Toughest Gate," in Tucson, Arizona, for $13.5 million and enjoy your very own indoor gun and archery range fortressed from the outside world.

2     Gated communities such as these are not all that new to America; however, their numbers are rising, and not just as ostentatious and elaborate walled cities—hideouts for the

**affluent**
wealthy

affluent—but also as planned developments for the middle class. In fact, people of all economic standing are seeking closed communities with controlled access—entry available only to residents usually requiring a key, code, or electronic device—and the protection of walls or fences. Where did this propensity for restricted-entry neighborhoods begin?

3     Walled cities could first be found in ancient Rome and areas occupied by the Romans. In particular, walled settlements built by Roman soldiers around 300 AD guarded the Roman families in England. In the Middle Ages, English kings followed the Roman example by creating barriers to protect their castles against invaders. Later, Spanish fort towns were built in the Caribbean, and as early as the 1850s, gated developments could be found in major U.S. cities like New York and St. Louis. These communities functioned as solace for the very wealthy well into the twentieth century. In the 1960s and 1970s, the appeal of protected communities grew as retirement developments arose, and increased rapidly for prestige, leisure, and safety reasons in the 1980s. The majority of these developments are in the Sun Belt states (the Southeast and Southwest), where most resort and retirement areas are located because of the weather. California, Florida, and Texas have particularly high numbers of gated communities. But these exclusive neighborhoods have now sprung up everywhere, except in rural states. And although in the past they were restricted to the elite, they are now primarily settled by the middle and upper-middle classes.

**elite**
the wealthiest
and most
powerful group
of people

4     The types of gated communities vary depending on the economic status of the residents and the purpose the residents have for living there. In their book entitled, *Fortress America: Gated Communities in the United States*, Edward J. Blakely and Mary Gail Snyder categorize gated communities according to people's reasons for moving into them. The three categories are Lifestyle Communities, Prestige Communities, and the Security Zone. Lifestyle Communities are those centered around leisure activities. Here you find private golf courses, athletic clubs, riding trails, parks, rivers, and sometimes beaches. A planned community in Las Vegas, Nevada, known as Green Valley, for example,

© 2013 Wadsworth, Cengage Learning

---

*"Gated Developments: Fortresses or Communities?" by Heather Eudy.

centers around swimming pools, a cinema, restaurants, and an upscale athletic club where made-to-order smoothies come fresh from the bartender's blender. Prestige Communities, the second category, exist for distinction and status—a place where the rich and famous can separate themselves from the less rich and less famous. Finally, Security Zone communities are marketed as havens from crime, with gates, guards, and barricades to keep out uninvited people. In all of the communities, walls serve as dividers from the outside. Most have round-the-clock security, private guards, surveillance, controlled access, video monitors, and streets and parks for residents only.

**havens**
safe areas

5    Demographers and sociologists—scientists who study the characteristics of populations and those who study social developments and institutions—are scrutinizing the causes for the rise in popularity of gated communities. They are finding that many people move to homes within gates in order to feel safe. Some enjoy the cleanliness, the shared values, status, exclusiveness, seclusion, and quiet. They also appreciate the high property values gated communities ensure and the private access to leisure areas such as beaches and parks.

**status**
social position

6    To fully understand this trend toward gated communities in the United States, one must study the country's history of suburbanization. Suburbanization—the development of areas just outside of city boundaries—began when transportation improvements, such as rail lines and automobiles, allowed upper-class and middle-class people to escape city life. At that time, suburbia seemed to be a utopia—a harmonious environment free of the tensions of the city. Even the names of the suburban developments suggest features of the natural landscape, such as River Forest and Forest Park, both suburbs of Chicago. Middle-class Americans relocated to the suburbs to get away from real and perceived urban problems. The suburbs, they thought, were safe and clean, had good schools, and were inhabited by like-minded people. But then the suburbs began to get crowded and run down, and racial minorities and immigrants began moving in. So now new communities are being built with gates to provide privacy and safety, once and for all.

7    But, safety from what? There seem to be growing fears in America about the future, fears about physical and economic security. Fulbright scholar Renaud Le Goix claims that urban fear and social paranoia have pushed Americans inside the gates. According to the U.S. Census Bureau's 2001 American Housing Survey, more than 7 million households live in walled or fenced developments, and 4 million of those have controlled access. Homeowners (predominantly white) and renters (more ethnically diverse and less affluent) alike are living behind gates. But are gated communities really safer? Research has uncovered very little evidence that gating reduces crime. There have been cases in which gated communities have been deliberately, and successfully, targeted for burglary, and cases in which the residents of gated communities have themselves been the criminals. In fact, firefighters and police officers even question gated developments' efficiency during emergencies, since access to the properties is difficult.

**illusion**
false appearance

8    Even if the illusion of safety is enough to ease residents' fears, there is a negative impact on the individual and society. Many demographers and sociologists have concluded that controlled-access living accelerates socioeconomic segregation, even isolation. For example, in "Gates and Ghettoes," Anita Rice asserts that gating increases the polarization of social classes and highlights inequality. People living inside gated communities are, on average, wealthier and more likely to be property owners than the general population. Additionally, gated communities intensify exclusion. That means there is less public space available to people on the outside. When public resources like beaches, parks, and nature trails are private spaces, not public places, those who

**polarization**
increased
separation

are excluded lose. And while those in gated communities find their property values rising, people outside the gates find theirs dwindling. Finally, the social segregation that comes with gated communities breeds a culture of distrust. People of different backgrounds are less likely to interact. Fellow citizens become intruders. If we don't know each other and trust each other, if we continue to isolate ourselves from one another, will we ever be able to genuinely solve social problems? At what cost do the barriers rise?

**Sources**

Blakely, Edward J., and Mary Gail Snyder. *Fortress America: Gated Communities in the United States.* Washington, DC: Brookings Institution Press, 1999.

El Nasser, Haya. "Gated Communities More Popular, and Not Just for the Rich." *USA Today,* December 15, 2002.

Le Goix, Renaud. "The Suburban Paradise or the Parceling of Cities?" *UCLA International Institute.* http://www.international.ucla.edu/article.asp?parentid=4664 (accessed September 7, 2005).

Rice, Anita. "Gates and Ghettoes: A Tale of Two Britains?" *BBC News.* March 18, 2004. http://news.bbc.co.uk/1/hi/programmes/if/3513980.stm.

U.S. Census Bureau. *American Housing Survey for the United States: 2001.* http://www.huduser.org/datasets/ahs.html (accessed September 25, 2005).

**Exercise 13**

## Work with Words

The following sentences appear in Reading 2. Use context clues, your knowledge of word parts, and if necessary, your dictionary skills to determine the meaning of each italicized word in the sentences. Write the meaning of the word in the lines provided. The paragraph number is provided in case you want to check the context.

1. Gated communities such as these are not all that new to America; however, their numbers are rising, and not just as *ostentatious* and elaborate walled cities—hideouts for the affluent—but also as planned developments for the middle class. (par. 2)

   *Ostentatious*: _____

2. Where did this *propensity* for restricted-entry neighborhoods begin? (par. 2)

   *Propensity*: _____

3. These communities functioned as *solace* for the very wealthy well into the twentieth century. (par. 3)

   *Solace*: _____

4. *Demographers and sociologists*—scientists who study the characteristics of populations and those who study social developments and institutions—are *scrutinizing* the causes for the rise in popularity of gated communities. (par. 5)

   *Demographers*: _____

5. *Sociologists*: _____

6. *Scrutinizing*: _____

7. *Suburbanization*—the development of areas just outside the city boundaries—began when transportation improvements, such as rail lines and automobiles, allowed upper-class and middle-class people to escape city life. (par. 6)

   *Suburbanization*: _____

8. At that time, suburbia seemed to be a *utopia*—a harmonious environment free of the tensions of the city. (par. 6)

   *Utopia*: _____

9. Fulbright scholar Renaud Le Goix claims that urban fear and social *paranoia* have pushed Americans inside the gates. (par. 7)

   *Paranoia*: _____

10. For example, in "Gates and Ghettoes," Anita Rice asserts that gating increases the *polarization* of social classes and highlights inequality. (par. 8)

    *Polarization*: _____

**Exercise 14**

## Check Your Understanding

Based on Reading 2, write your answers to the following questions on the lines provided.

1. What is the topic of Reading 2?

   _____

2. What is the main idea of the reading?

   _____

   _____

   _____

3. Where and when did gated communities begin, and where in the United States are they most popular today?

   _____

   _____

   _____

4. What are the three categories of gated communities Blakely and Snyder discuss in their book?

   _____

   _____

5. What is the topic of paragraph 5?

_____

_____

6. What is the main idea of paragraph 5?

_____

_____

_____

7. What connection between suburbia and gated communities does the author make in paragraph 6?

_____

_____

8. What has research shown about the safety of gated communities?

_____

_____

9. What is the main idea of paragraph 8?

_____

_____

_____

10. List three ways that gated communities intensify the divisions between classes.

    a. _____

    b. _____

    c. _____

**Exercise 15**

## Identify Patterns of Organization

Based on Reading 2, choose the best answer to each of the following multiple-choice questions. Then write the transitions or clues that helped you select the pattern of organization.

1. What is the dominant pattern of organization for paragraph 1?
   a. Cause and effect
   b. Process
   c. Exemplification

   Transitions and clues: _____

2. What is the dominant pattern of organization for paragraph 3?
   a. Problem and solution
   b. Chronological order
   c. Comparison and contrast

   Transitions and clues: _____

   _____

3. What is the dominant pattern of organization for paragraph 4?
   a. Classification
   b. Narration
   c. Chronological order

   Transitions and clues: _____

4. What is the dominant pattern of organization for paragraph 5?
   a. Process
   b. Comparison and contrast
   c. Cause and effect

   Transitions and clues: _____

5. What are the dominant patterns of organization for paragraph 6?
   a. Definition and chronological order
   b. Narration, comparison and contrast
   c. Exemplification and classification

   Transitions and clues: _____

   _____

**Exercise 16**

### Organize to Learn: Create an Outline, Map, or Flowchart

On a separate sheet of paper, organize what you read in Reading 2 to help you learn it.

1. Create a map or flowchart of the information in paragraph 4.

2. Prepare an outline or map of the information in paragraph 8.

**Exercise 17**

### Reflect and Write

Think about what you read in Reading 2 and what you already know about gated communities. Then answer the following questions.

1. Were you aware that some homes cost millions of dollars, like the ones mentioned in paragraph 1 of the reading? Describe the wealthy homes you have seen in your region.

_____

_____

_____

2. On a separate piece of paper, write an essay asserting your opinion of gated communities. Do you believe that they are positive entities, negative, or both? Your position (opinion) should be your thesis statement. Explain the reasons for your opinion. Be sure to develop your paper with specific examples, possibly considering advantages and disadvantages of living within a gated community as well as the effects of gated communities for people who don't live within them. Give your paper an appropriate title that reflects your opinion.

# Combined Patterns of Organization

Most of the time, an author uses a combination of organizational patterns to express ideas, rather than just one pattern. There may be one primary pattern, but to explain an idea or concept thoroughly, the author may need to use other patterns, too. A paragraph can have almost any combination of organizational patterns. For example, you might find comparison and contrast combined with exemplification and cause and effect. Two more patterns of organization that you should be able to recognize and analyze are *problem and solution* and *argumentation*. Authors of essays and editorials frequently use these patterns when they write about controversial topics.

## PROBLEM AND SOLUTION

**problem**
an issue that needs to be resolved

In problem-and-solution organization, a writer first presents a significant **problem** and explains in detail the issue that needs to be resolved. Often, the writer uses a cause-and-effect approach to explain the problem. But other patterns of organization can also be used effectively within the problem-and-solution organization. The following paragraph from a U.S. history textbook uses exemplification and cause and effect to list the problems made worse by the growth of cities.

> The growth of urban areas exacerbated many problems, including the absence of clean drinking water, the lack of cheap public transportation, and most importantly, poor sanitation. Sanitation problems led to heavy urban mortality rates and frequent epidemics of typhoid, dysentery, typhus, cholera, and yellow fever. (Martin et al., *America and Its Peoples*)

**solution**
a way of resolving issues or solving problems

A textbook in sociology or a government analysis of urban problems might conclude a discussion of urban problems with a series of possible **solutions**, or ways that the problems can be solved. Here is a paragraph from the U.S. Department of Housing and Urban Development's publication *The State of the Cities, 1999.* Notice that it uses the exemplification and comparison-and-contrast patterns of organization to explain both problems and solutions.

> *St. Louis, MO.* The East-West Gateway Coordinating Council—the planning body for the St. Louis metropolitan area—is engaged in a variety of regional efforts to address the economic, social, and environmental issues facing the region. A major concern is the mismatch between where unemployed workers in the central city live and where jobs are proliferating in the metro area. The Council launched the St. Louis Regional Jobs Initiative to try to address these imbalances and better align the region's workforce development, economic development, transportation, and social service programs to help low-income job seekers. The initiative provides funding and support for community-based initiatives that help the workers, especially young people, find meaningful jobs that can support a family. The council also coordinates the local HUD-funded *Bridges to Work* demonstration, which is testing the effectiveness of jobs initiatives that coordinate placement, transportation, and career-building services that connect inner-city neighborhoods to job-rich suburbs. (U.S. Department of Housing and Urban Development, *The State of the Cities, 1999*)

**Transitions and Clues** To identify a problem, writers use terms like *problem, need, difficulty, dilemma, challenge,* and *issue.* When they present possible solutions, writers use terms like *propose, suggest, indicate, solve, resolve, improve, rectify, plan,* and *respond to a need.*

**Organizing to Learn: Using a Chart and a Bulleted List** One way to organize problem-and-solution relationships is to create a chart. Study how the information in the paragraph from *State of the Cities, 1999* has been organized into a chart with arrows and bulleted lists. Arrows connect the problems with the solutions, and bullets signal supporting points.

| Solving Problems in St. Louis | | |
| --- | :---: | --- |
| Problem | ⇒ | Solution |
| Mismatch between where unemployed workers live and where the jobs are | ⇒ | Formation of St. Louis Regional Jobs Initiative to better align<br>• Workforce development<br>• Economic development<br>• Transportation<br>• Social services<br>and help low-income job seekers find meaningful jobs that can support a family |
| Need to connect inner-city neighborhoods to job-rich suburbs | ⇒ | *Bridges to Work* demonstration—job-rich suburbs testing effectiveness of job initiatives that coordinate<br>• Placement<br>• Transportation<br>• Career-building services |

## Identify Combined Patterns of Organization

Read the following paragraphs about rural–urban migration in general, but especially in Mexico. Then complete the activities that follow.

**rural**
related to the countryside

**surplus**
excess

> During the Industrial Revolution, economists viewed rural–urban migration as a natural and beneficial process. The countryside had a surplus of labor and a lack of jobs while cities had surplus jobs and a lack of labor; therefore, workers moved naturally to where they were needed. This perspective continues to be influential today as most trade organizations and governments believe that the only way for a nation to develop is by abandoning rural, agriculturally based economies in favor of urban, industrially based economies.
>
> One example of this development perspective being put into practice can be seen on the Mexican–U.S. border where the North American Free Trade Agreement has promoted the *maquiladora* industry. Maquiladoras are factories that import materials from the United States, assemble the product in Mexico with cheap labor, then export the product back to the United States where it can be sold for a high price or sent to another country. Many of the workers in the maquiladoras of Mexico's border cities have left the countryside in search of jobs.

1. How many patterns of organization can you find in these two paragraphs? List them.

   _____

   _____

2. Circle the words that are clues for the patterns of organization that you listed.

# ARGUMENT

**argument**
information intended to convince a reader through logical reasoning

**Argument** is a pattern of organization writers often use to convince you to believe or act in a certain way. As an extension of the problem-and-solution pattern, the argument pattern presents evidence that a problem exists or is serious. Sometimes a writer wants to persuade you that one or more of the proposed solutions is the best. Writers whose intention is to persuade often incorporate emotional appeals into the argument. On the other hand, some writers rely on logic alone. They don't want to persuade you that one solution is better than any other. Instead, they present facts to help you draw your own conclusions, which they hope match their own.

**Transitions and Clues** Arguments use terms like *argue, strongly recommend, in support of, therefore, thus, convince,* and *persuade.*

**Organizing to Learn: Using Many Options** Since an argument can be used in combination with any organizational pattern as a way to support its points, you will need to decide, based on the nature of the argument, which is the best way to organize to learn. Like the problem-and-solution pattern of organization, an argument is well organized in a chart.

**Exercise 19**

## Organize to Learn: Create a Chart or Map, and Write a Summary

Read the following paragraphs. Then complete the activities that follow.

**maquiladoras**
factories that
import materials
from the United
States, assemble the
product in Mexico,
then export the
product back to the
United States

Enthusiasts of the North American Free Trade Agreement (NAFTA) say that rural–urban migration and the *maquiladora* industry are natural and necessary steps on Mexico's road to development. However, critics of NAFTA point out many problems with this form of development. These problems include uncontrolled urban growth, the mistreatment of urban workers, and the decay of the rural economy.

As people abandon the poverty of the countryside, they are often forced into worse conditions in the shantytowns on the edges of Mexican cities. These slums and cities are growing so fast that the government could not provide basic services even if it wanted to. Many who come to the cities get jobs in the maquiladoras where they are paid low wages, work long hours, and are often exposed to dangerous materials. The workers have few enforceable rights because they are so replaceable; there are always newly arrived, even more desperate people willing to take their job.

Scholars in Mexico and the United States have pointed out that the Mexican government has neglected and probably deliberately worsened the economic crisis in the countryside. In this way, jobless, poor, rural people are forced into the cities, providing a surplus of cheap labor. Although this development strategy might create a good place to assemble cheap hair dryers and televisions for the United States, it also creates all the problems mentioned above. Instead, the government could provide technical and financial support for peasants and small farmers. This would strengthen the foundation of the rural economy so that people would not be desperate and forced to move to shantytowns in the cities to work in the maquiladoras. The smaller numbers of people who *did* move into the cities would be able to find decent jobs, and the slow growth of urban areas would mean that basic services such as sanitation and electricity could be provided.

1. On a separate sheet of paper, make a chart or map in which you show the problems caused by rural–urban migration and the maquiladora industry.

2. Now, write a summary of the excerpt, using your chart or map to help you.

## Reading 3

# Curitiba, Brazil—A City with a Sustainable Vision* —DANIEL D. CHIRAS

**TEXT BOOK** The following reading is from the college textbook, *Environmental Science*. It appears in a special feature of the text entitled "Sustainable Development" and describes how urban development in a city in Brazil has been done well.

---

1    Most modern cities have grown up around the automobile. City planners have literally shaped their cities around major transit corridors. Thus, the location of subdivisions, industrial facilities, and services has been largely determined by roads and highways, access routes primarily traveled by people in automobiles.

2    Proving that there is an alternative path is a city that's gaining wide recognition: Curitiba, Brazil. Lying near the east coast in the southernmost part of Brazil about 500 miles south of Rio de Janeiro, Curitiba is a showcase of wise planning and sustainable design principles that have served the city and the planet well.

**sustainable** organized in a way that doesn't damage the environment

**principles** basic rules

3    Since 1950, Curitiba's population has grown from 300,000 to over 2.1 million. For most cities, this rate of growth, combined with poor planning, would have been a prescription for disaster. Poverty, pollution, crime, and highway congestion would have been the inevitable results—not so in Curitiba.

4    The city was blessed with a visionary mayor in the 1970s, Jaime Lerner, who adopted proposals first made in the 1960s to plot a future for the city based on mass

Curitiba's extensive bus system, with its raised boarding tubes, is a main reason why Curitiba is studied as a model for sustainable urban development.

Ron Giling/PhotoLibrary

© 2013 Wadsworth, Cengage Learning

---

**ecological**
considering the relationship to the natural environment

**vision**
ability to consider the future

5    transit, ecological design, appropriate technology, and public participation—all essential elements of sustainability. Lerner was an architect and planner of extraordinary vision.

As witness to his foresight, consider this: Today, 1.3 million commuters travel into Curitiba each day to go to work. Three quarters of these people travel by bus. This remarkable feat is made possible by an extensive, privately operated bus system that transports people in and out of the city with remarkable speed.

6    In most cities, bus systems are notoriously slow. Although they move large numbers of people, they bog down in heavy traffic on city streets. In Curitiba, however, buses move passengers into and out of the city at such rapid speeds for several reasons. First, the city has constructed five major roadways that penetrate into the heart of the city. Each of these roadways has two lanes designated for buses. In addition, bus stops are equipped with special devices called raised tubes, which allow passengers to pay before they get on the bus. This greatly speeds up the boarding process that slows down many a bus in the United States and other countries. Extra-wide doors also contribute to the speed of boarding. Double- and triple-length buses increase the system's capacity. Together, these innovations reduce the transit time by one third.

7    Curitiba has made it possible to move in other directions as well. Many smaller bus routes connect residential areas with the main transit corridors so that one can travel about freely. Commuters can take a bus to the main route, hop on an express bus, and be downtown in record speed.

8    This system of transit not only makes good sense from an environmental standpoint—because buses transport people with fewer resources and much less pollution than the automobile—it also makes sense from an economic standpoint. It's much cheaper than a subway system.

9    So that the less fortunate, Curitiba's poor, can gain access to the system, the city purchased land along major corridors, which was developed for low-income families.

**boast**
brag

10   Curitiba has more to boast about than its mass transit system. It has established an extensive network of parks along natural drainages. This not only provides residents with someplace to escape from the buildings and roadways, it reduces damage from flooding. Prior to the establishment of this system, developers often built homes and other structures in drainage areas. When floods came, many a home was damaged. Today, this system of parks with specially constructed ponds has nearly eliminated flooding and saved the city millions of dollars in engineering and construction costs. Low-tech solutions work and save money.

11   Curitiba promotes participation and cooperation, too. The city recognizes that solutions require the participation of many sectors, including business, government, community groups, and others. Fortunately, other cities are beginning to learn from Curitiba.

**Exercise 20**

## Work with Words

Identify words in Reading 3 that are unfamiliar to you and that are important for understanding the reading. Choose three to five of these words to add to your personal vocabulary. On a separate sheet of paper, or on 3 × 5 cards, write each word and its appropriate meaning, the original sentence in which it appeared, and your own sentence using the word.

**Exercise 21**

## Check Your Understanding

Based on Reading 3, write your answers to the following questions.

1. What is the topic of this reading?

   _____

   _____

2. What is the main idea of this reading?

   _____

   _____

3. What problems was Curitiba working to solve?

   _____

   _____

   _____

4. What were the solutions Curitiba implemented to solve problems?

   _____

   _____

   _____

   _____

   _____

   _____

**Exercise 22**

## Identify Patterns of Organization

Based on Reading 3, choose the best answer to each of the following multiple-choice questions.

1. What are the dominant patterns of organization for paragraph 1?
   a. Chronological order and process
   b. Cause and effect
   c. Narration

2. What are the dominant patterns of organization for paragraphs 3 and 4?
   a. Chronological order and problem and solution
   b. Definition and comparison and contrast
   c. Narration and description

3. Which pattern of organization is not in paragraph 6?
   a. Exemplification
   b. Comparison and contrast
   c. Definition

4. What is the dominant pattern of organization for the whole reading?
   a. Problem and solution
   b. Comparison and contrast
   c. Exemplification

**Exercise 23**

## Reflect and Write

Think about what you read in Reading 3 and what you already know about cities, their transportation systems, and organization. Answer the following questions, and prepare to discuss them with your classmates.

1. Write a four- or five-sentence summary of Reading 3. Your first sentence should identify the author, the title of the reading, and the main idea. The following three of four sentences should focus on the major supporting points.

2. Write two or three paragraphs in which you include the following information. (1) Describe the transportation system in place where you live. Explain the positive and/or negative aspects of this system. (2) Explain how the transportation system works for you or people that you know. (3) Make some suggestions for how your local transportation system could be improved.

## Reader's Tip:
## Summary Chart of Transitions
## and Clues for Patterns of Organization

| Patterns | Transitions and Clues |
| --- | --- |
| Chronological order and narration | *then, when, after, before, while, during, earlier, meanwhile, until, now, immediately, finally, as soon as, next, last, later,* plus *dates* and *times* |
| Definition and classification | **Definition:** *is, could be defined as, refers to, means, signifies, can be considered, consists of* **Classification:** *kinds, types, varieties, categories, groups* |

| Exemplification | *and, or, for example, such as, for instance, in fact, in addition, furthermore, moreover, also,* plus a series of items, set off by many commas |
|---|---|
| Cause and effect | **Cause:** *the reason why, because, since, lead to, cause, result in, influence, give rise to, contribute to, accelerate, intensify, increase* **Effect:** *therefore, as a result, subsequently, consequently, so, hence* |
| Comparison and contrast | **Comparison:** *similarly, likewise, also, alike, same, in comparison* **Contrast:** *yet, nevertheless, in contrast, on the other hand, however, but, conversely* |
| Process | *how to, in the process of, the steps to follow, stages, begin, continue, end, first, second, third* |
| Problem and solution | **Problem:** *problem, need, difficulty, dilemma, challenge, issue* **Solution:** *propose, suggest, indicate, solve, resolve, improve, rectify, plan, respond to a need* |
| Argument | *argue, strongly recommend, in support of, therefore, thus, convince, persuade* |

## Write About It

1. Write a short essay about your neighborhood. Describe your neighborhood, including things that make living there pleasant and things that make living there difficult. Explain your feelings about where you live. Consider the physical characteristics of your neighborhood (for example, location, convenience, play areas, shopping) as well as the relationships between and among the people who live there (such as the connectedness of neighbors, friendliness, helpfulness). Then, in a final paragraph, state what you think would contribute to making your neighborhood a better place. Include what you as an individual (or in combination with your family or friends) could do to improve your neighborhood. Give your essay an appropriate title.

2. Write a paragraph about a "community" you belong to other than your neighborhood. You may discuss your membership in a church, a union, a sports team, a fan club, a learning community, an Internet group, or any other "community" you participate in. What do you have in common with other members of your community? What do you do with them? You might want to also discuss whether your community has a positive or negative influence on your life, and why.

# Chapter Review

| Put It Together: Patterns of Organization | |
|---|---|
| Skills and Concepts | Explanation |
| **Patterns of Organization** (see pages 189–190) | The way a writer chooses to organize his or her material to help us understand the relationships among ideas |
| **Transitions** (see page 190) | Words or phrases that link ideas and/or identify relationships |
| **Chronological Order** (see page 190) | Information organized in time order |
| **Narration** (see page 190) | Information organized to tell a story |
| **Time Line** (see page 191) | A graphic representation that uses lines and dates to illustrate the time order of events |
| **Definition** (see page 192) | Information organized to answer the question "what is it?" |
| **Classification** (see page 192) | Information organized into categories or groups |
| **Exemplification** (see page 194) | A pattern of examples used to support ideas |
| **Cause** (see page 196) | Information that answers the question "why?" |
| **Effect** (see page 196) | Information that explains results or outcomes |
| **Comparison** (see page 198) | Information that explains how two things are similar |
| **Contrast** (see page 198) | Information that explains how two things are different |
| **Process** (see page 200) | Information organized to show how something is done step-by-step |
| **Flowchart** (see page 201) | A graphic representation of a process, usually using arrows |

| Put It Together: Patterns of Organization | |
|---|---|
| Skills and Concepts | Explanation |
| **Problem** (see page 210) | An issue that needs to be resolved |
| **Solution** (see pages 210–211) | A way of resolving issues or solving problems |
| **Argument** (see page 212) | Information intended to convince a reader through logical reasoning |

## CRITICAL REFLECTIONS IN THE CLASSROOM COMMUNITY

Answer the following questions, and be prepared to discuss them with your classmates.

1. List three things in your college community that you think make going to school there enjoyable and pleasant.

   a. _____

   b. _____

   c. _____

2. List three things in your college community that make going to school there difficult.

   a. _____

   b. _____

   c. _____

3. List three things that you think would contribute to making your college community a better place to go to school.

   a. _____

   b. _____

   c. _____

 ## WORK THE WEB

Now that you have examined some issues related to place, take this time to use the Internet as a tool to understand more about where you live.

   Do an Internet search for the U.S. Census Bureau. Once you've done a preview of the site, look for information about the city, county, and state you live in. You can check out statistics about things like the cost of housing, family income, and the ethnic background of people living there. You can compare some of those statistics with nationwide statistics. You can also see how certain things have changed over time. Find five facts that you find interesting. Write your information in the form of complete sentences. Your answers will often be in the comparison-and-contrast or chronological order pattern of organization.

a. _____

_____

b. _____

_____

c. _____

_____ .

d. _____

_____

e. _____

_____

Name _____ Date _____

# Life and Death in an Indian City*

—JOAN FERRANTE

**TEXT BOOK** The following reading from the college textbook *Sociology: A Global Perspective* describes conditions in Bhopal, India, after one of the most disastrous industrial accidents in history took place in 1984. The fate of the poor people who lived in that city raises questions of how where we live affects the quality of our lives, affects our health, and can even be the cause of death. As you read, try to identify the various patterns of organization used to present this information.

## AN INDUSTRIAL ACCIDENT

1   On December 3, 1984, approximately 40 tons of methylisocyanate (MIC), a highly toxic, <u>volatile</u>, flammable chemical used in making <u>pesticides</u>, escaped from a Union Carbide storage tank and blanketed the densely populated city of Bhopal, India. Investigators determined that between 120 and 140 gallons of water somehow had entered the storage tank containing MIC. The combination <u>triggered</u> a violent chemical reaction that could not be contained. As a result, approximately 800,000 residents awoke coughing, vomiting, and with eyes burning and watering. They opened their doors and joined the "largest unplanned human <u>exodus</u> of the industrial age":

2       Those able to board a bicycle, moped, bullock car, bus, or vehicle of any kind did. But for most of the poor, their feet were the only form of transportation available. Many dropped along the way, gasping for breath, choking on their own vomit and, finally, drowning in their own fluids. Families were separated; whole groups were wiped out at a time. Those strong enough to keep going ran three, six, up to twelve miles before they stopped. Most ran until they dropped. (Weir 1984, p. 17)

3       Although exact numbers are not known, the most conservative estimates are that the chemical accident killed at least 2,500 people immediately and injured another 250,000. Since the accident, 22,149 deaths related to it have been officially registered. More than 17 years later, 10 to 15 people continue[d] to die each month from accident-related injuries, and most of the injured (an estimated 200,000 people) live with the long-term and <u>chronic</u> side effects of their exposure, which include lung and kidney damage, visual impairment, skin diseases and eruptions, neurological disorders, and gynecological damage (Everest 1986; Sharma 2000). Survivors also include a generation of Bhopal residents born around the time of the disaster, many of whom suffer lung and liver-related problems (Sharma 2000). These injuries have affected their capacity to earn a living.

**impairment** limitation

4   In 1989, Union Carbide agreed to pay $470 million to the Indian government as <u>compensation</u> to the victims and their families. The victims of Union Carbide were prevented by law from suing Union Carbide in U.S. courts (*The Economist* 1994). Depending on how one determines victim status, the <u>settlement</u> breaks down to about $3,000 per family affected. However, legal complications have delayed these payments. It also

* "Life and Death in an Indian City" by Joan Ferrante from SOCIOLOGY: A GLOBAL PERSPECTIVE, 5th Edition. Reprinted by permission of the author.

appears that government initiatives aimed at vocational rehabilitation of accident vic-tims have failed. Only a few thousand survivors have received such services.

## INDIA'S PROBLEM OF URBANIZATION

compounded
complicated

5    In India, the problem of urbanization is compounded by the fact that many migrants who come to the cities depart from some of the most economically <u>precarious</u> sec-tions of India. In fact, most rural-to-urban migrants are not pulled into the cities by employment opportunities, but rather are forced to move there because they have no alternatives. When these migrants come to the cities, they face not only unem-ployment, but also a shortage of housing and a lack of services (electricity, running water, waste disposal). One distinguishing characteristic of cities in labor-intensive poor countries is the <u>prevalence</u> of slums and squatter settlements, which are much poorer and larger than even the worst slums in core economies.

6    One vivid and dramatic example concerns the city of Bhopal, India. . . . The popula-tion of Bhopal stood at 102,000 in 1966. After Union Carbide and other industries settled there in the 1960s, the population grew to 385,000 in 1971, 670,000 in 1981, and 800,000 in 1984.[1] At the time of the accident, approximately 20 percent of Bhopal's 800,000 residents lived in squatter settlements. The location of two of these squatter camps—directly across from the Union Carbide plant—explains why the deaths occurred <u>disproportionately</u> among the poorer residents. The people who lived in these camps were paid poverty-level wages, which prevented them from acquiring decent living quarters.[2]

**Notes**

1. In 2001, Bhopal's population was 1.6 million. It has doubled in size in less than 20 years.

2. Only a small percentage of people who lived in the camps were employees of Union Carbide.

**Exercise 1**

## Work with Words

Use context clues, dictionary skills, and your knowledge of word parts to choose the best definition for each of the following words underlined in the reading. The paragraph number is provided in case you want to check the context.

1. *Volatile* (par. 1)
   a. characterized by violence
   b. stable
   c. easily turning into vapor

2. *Pesticide* (par. 1)
   a. chemical to control pests
   b. chemical to kill pests
   c. free of pests

3. *Triggered* (par. 1)
   a. fired
   b. started
   c. shot

4. *Exodus* (par. 1)
   a. departure, flight
   b. departure of Israelites from Egypt
   c. second book of the Bible

5. *Chronic* (par. 3)
   a. habitual
   b. weakness and disability
   c. continuing and recurring

6. *Compensation* (par. 4)
   a. psychological mechanism to overcome a personal deficiency
   b. something received to pay for a loss or injury
   c. improvement of a defect by overusing something else

7. *Settlement* (par. 4)
   a. neighborhood of squatters
   b. legal agreement
   c. colony in its early stages

8. *Precarious* (par. 5)
   a. violently dangerous
   b. stable
   c. insecure

9. *Prevalence* (par. 5)
   a. superiority
   b. inferiority
   c. condition of being widespread

10. *Disproportionately* (par. 6)
    a. out of proportion, more often
    b. in small numbers, less often
    c. wrong shape, size, and figure

---

**Exercise 2**

## Check Your Understanding and Patterns of Organization

Based on the reading, Ferrante's "Life and Death in an Indian City," choose the best answer to each of the following multiple-choice questions.

1. Which of the following is the best topic for the reading?
   a. Bhopal, India: an example of urban growth, poverty, and disaster
   b. Compensation for victims of the accident at Bhopal, India
   c. The largest human exodus of the industrial age

2. Which of the following is the best statement of the main idea of the reading?
   a. On December 3, 1984, approximately 40 tons of methylisocyanate (MIC), a highly toxic, volatile, flammable chemical used in making pesticides, escaped from a Union Carbide storage tank and blanketed the densely populated city of Bhopal, India.

     b. Poor people who migrate to the cities in poor countries frequently end up living in slums, which sometimes, as in the case of Bhopal, India, has disastrous consequences.

     c. Very few victims (or their relatives) of the accident in Bhopal have received any compensation for the damage to their health or for the loss of lives.

3. This reading provides
   a. the medical causes of the problems resulting from the Bhopal spill.
   b. an extended example of the possible disastrous consequences of urban poverty in poor countries.
   c. the problems and possible solutions for urban poverty in poor countries.

4. What is the dominant pattern of organization for paragraph 1?
   a. Narration
   b. Cause and effect
   c. Comparison and contrast

5. What is the dominant pattern of organization for paragraph 2?
   a. Cause and effect
   b. Narration
   c. Problem and solution

6. What is the dominant pattern of organization for paragraph 3?
   a. Comparison and contrast
   b. Definition
   c. Cause and effect and chronological order

7. Which of the following sentences best expresses the main idea of paragraph 4?
   a. The victims of the Bhopal accident have not received fair compensation.
   b. The Indian government failed in its goal of providing vocational rehabilitation for the victims of the accident.
   c. Union Carbide agreed to pay $470 million to the Indian government as compensation to the victims and their families.

8. What is the dominant pattern of organization for paragraph 5?
   a. Exemplification
   b. Narration
   c. Cause and effect

9. Which of the following is the best main idea statement for paragraphs 5 and 6?
   a. One vivid and dramatic example concerns the city of Bhopal, India.
   b. What happened to the victims of the accident in Bhopal, India is an example of the consequences of poverty and the growth of slums in poor countries.
   c. Union Carbide should have provided greater compensation to the victims of the accident.

10. The author
   a. presents clear solutions to the problem of poverty and slums.
   b. probably sympathizes with the victims at Bhopal.
   c. probably sympathizes with the difficulties that Union Carbide faced because of the accident.

**Exercise 3**

Organize to Learn and Write a Summary

Review the reading and complete the following activities on a separate sheet of paper.

1. Organize the information in paragraph 4 in a way that demonstrates the dominant pattern of organization used in the paragraph as support for the main idea.

2. Write a summary of the reading.

**Exercise 4**

Reflect

Think about what you read in "Life and Death in an Indian City" and what you already know about the health consequences of different kinds of neighborhoods and living conditions. Then answer the following questions.

1. What kind of neighborhood do you live in? Are there any health dangers there? Explain.

_____

_____

_____

2. What do you think are some of the things that could have prevented the deaths and injuries in Bhopal, India? Explain your answer.

_____

_____

_____

# 6 Inferences and Reading Literature

## DEALING WITH GENDER

Evan Hurd/Sygma/Corbis

*The emotional, sexual, and psychological stereotyping of females begins when the doctor says, "It's a girl." —Shirley Chisholm*

1. How are the little girls in the picture dressed? Why do you think they are dressed this way?

2. What does the quotation mean?

3. Do you think the photo illustrates the ideas of the quotation? Why or why not?

4. Do you think the stereotyping of boys begins at birth? Why or why not?

# Prepare to Read

The little girls on page 227 are dressed as princesses or beauty queens. Their outfits are stereotypically feminine, and they are "made up" to look like women. Though much has changed in the last fifty years in terms of women's roles and their status in American society, there are still beauty pageants for women and girls. Women still do most of the housework even if they are also employed outside the home. Women continue to predominate in certain jobs, such as elementary school teachers, librarians, and nurses. Men outnumber women in other fields—for example, in construction, computer technology, and science. Do you think that certain careers are more appropriate for one sex or the other? Do you think girls and boys naturally want to dress differently and play with different toys? What role do parents play in teaching their children how girls and boys should dress, act, and talk?

In this chapter, you will read about gender from a variety of perspectives and learn to

- Infer meaning from text and illustrations
- Recognize connotative meanings of words
- Interpret irony and imagery
- Practice reading poetry and fiction

In the process of acquiring these skills, you will read about concepts of gender, how men and women communicate, and how conflicts arise due to gender-based power relationships.

Reading 1

# Sex and Gender*

— WILLIAM E. THOMPSON AND JOSEPH V. HICKEY

**TEXT BOOK** **William E. Thompson and Joseph V. Hickey discuss sex and gender in their sociology textbook, *Society in Focus*. They describe gender roles and how they have evolved.**

**innumerable**
uncountable

1    Women and men are different. This undeniable fact has contributed to innumerable myths, stereotypes, and arguments concerning precisely what these differences mean. How much of the difference is based on genetics, biology, and physiology and how much is based on cultural values and social practices? Sociologists pursue answers to these questions when they attempt to differentiate between *sex* and *gender*.

2    Much of the debate over the differences between women and men stems from people's confusing the terms *sex* and *gender*. *Sex* is based on biological and physical differences between females and males; *gender* refers to a cultural understanding of what

**constitutes**
makes up

constitutes masculinity and femininity in a society.

## SEX: BIOLOGICAL DIFFERENTIATION

3    While there is no scientific evidence to support claims that women are unfit for military combat or that men are biologically driven to hunt large animals, at least part of the difference between females and males must be attributed to genetics and biology. Humans have 23 pairs of chromosomes. Two of these are the sex chromosomes, X and Y. The normal chromosomal pattern in females is XX; in males it is XY. During prenatal development, different hormones trigger physical changes in the male and female genitalia and reproductive systems. . . .

4    Later in life, people develop sex-linked disparities in height, weight, body and facial hair, physical strength, and endurance. And, although research suggests that the brains of females and males may be both structurally and operationally different, most researchers acknowledge that women and men are far more alike than they are different (Phillips, 1990; Shapiro, 1990; Begley, 1995). Since we cannot see peoples' chromosomes, hormones, or brains, all sex-linked differences are of far less consequence than the cultural and social expectations linked to them. . . .

## GENDER: SOCIAL AND CULTURAL DIFFERENTIATION

5    A popular nineteenth-century nursery rhyme tells us that little girls are made of "sugar and spice and everything nice," while little boys are made of "frogs and snails and puppy dogs' tails." Newborn baby boys are often described as "bouncing," while baby girls are "beautiful." Why do we make these distinctions between boys and girls? Males and females are biologically and physiologically distinct at birth; these differences become more pronounced as humans develop to maturity, but they do not explain the important social and cultural distinctions that are made on the basis of sex. . . . The most important differences between the sexes are acquired through socialization as we all learn to fulfill our *gender roles*, the social and cultural expectations associated with a person's sex.

*"Sex and Gender," by William E. Thompson and Joseph V. Hickey, from SOCIETY IN FOCUS: INTRODUCTION SOCIOLOGY, pp. 305–31, ©2005 Pearson Education, Inc., published as Allyn and Bacon. Reproduced by permission of Pearson Education, Inc.

These gender roles affect virtually every aspect of our lives, from our eating behavior and the type of neighbor we are likely to be, to how long we live and our cause of death—in short, the way we think about and live life itself (Gilligan, 1982; Campbell and Lee, 1990; Morgan et al., 1990; Slevin and Aday, 1993; Lott, 1994; Walzer, 1994).

## MASCULINITY AND FEMININITY

**conform to**
fit into

6  *Masculinity* refers to attributes considered appropriate for males. In American society, these traditionally include being aggressive, athletic, physically active, logical, and dominant in social relationships with females. Conversely, *femininity* refers to attributes traditionally associated with appropriate behavior for females, which in America include passivity, docility, fragility, emotionality, and subordination to males. Research conducted by Carol Gilligan and her students at Harvard's Gender Studies Department indicate that children are acutely aware of and feel pressure to conform to these powerful gender stereotypes by the age of 4 (Kantrowitz and Kalb, 1998). Some people insist that gender traits such as male aggressiveness are innate characteristics linked to sex and do not depend on cultural definitions (Maccoby, 1980). However, the preponderance of research indicates that females and males can be equally aggressive under different social and cultural conditions and that levels of aggression vary as widely within the sexes as between them (e.g., Fry, 1988; Melson and Fogel, 1988; Butler, 1990). . . .

## ANDROGYNY: REDEFINING GENDER

7  Have you ever wondered why we place so much emphasis on distinctive gender identities and gender roles? Many people do, and in an effort to reduce social differentiation and inequality based on sex and gender some people advocate *androgyny*, a blending of masculine and feminine attributes. Androgyny is not role reversal, where boys are taught to act feminine and girls to behave more masculinely. It embraces the full range of human emotions and behaviors rather than only those traditionally considered appropriate to a specific sex. This involves redefining gender roles and attaching new meanings to the concepts of masculinity and femininity. Boys are taught that it is okay to cry and that it is perfectly natural to display their emotions and sensitivity when circumstances warrant. Likewise, girls are taught to be aggressive and assertive when social situations call for such behavior.

**chastised**
punished

8    In the world of androgyny, children are not  chastised for being tomboys or sissies, and there are no such things as "boys' toys" and "girls' toys." Similarly there is neither "women's work" nor "men's work"; whatever its nature, work is performed by whoever is capable, regardless of sex. Ideally, in a culture where androgyny is the norm, human potential would not be limited by narrow cultural stereotypes.

9    Despite more androgynous views of gender and the weakening of some gender stereotypes . . . powerful cultural distinctions between masculinity and femininity persist. Today, women must "prove" that they are capable of performing traditional "men's work" in the military and in the fields of law, medicine, science, and politics. Similarly, social and cultural attitudes often discourage or ridicule men who pursue "feminine roles" such as homemaker, secretary, nurse, flight attendant, and housekeeper. From a functionalist perspective, distinctive and complementary gender roles are important to preserving social structure and ensuring that society functions properly.

Exercise 1

## Recall and Discuss

Based on Reading 1, answer the following questions in your own words and prepare to discuss them with your classmates.

1. What is the difference between *sex* and *gender*?

   _____

   _____

   _____

2. From your own observations and experience, how do you think a child develops gender identity?

   _____

   _____

3. Do you think it's a good idea to teach children to be androgynous? Explain your answer.

   _____

   _____

4. What have been some of the major influences for your own identification of men's and women's roles in society?

   _____

   _____

# Inferences

**inference**
a reasonable
assumption based
on the information
we have

When we meet someone for the first time, we form much of our first impression about that person's adherence to conventional masculine or feminine roles, based on what we observe about his or her dress and appearance. We do this by making inferences based on our previous knowledge about how our culture understands "appropriate" gender roles; sometimes we do this based on stereotypes that are not always accurate. An **inference** is a reasonable assumption based on the information we have about an event, a person, or a written passage. Another way to think of making inferences, or inferring, is "reading between the lines." When reading, if you use the information you already have about the world (your previous knowledge) and the information provided to you by the author, you can often come to well-founded conclusions, which are probably accurate.

In your daily life, you make inferences from the signals you get from other people. Say, for example, that you are having a conversation with a friend, and your friend turns her back to you and opens a book. What can you infer from her action? You will probably infer that your friend does not want to talk to you anymore; she wants to end the conversation. You might also infer that your friend is not being sensitive to your feelings.

For another example, imagine that one day your boss, normally a very friendly guy, gets to work late and stomps into his office without talking to anybody. You know that he has been having trouble with his car, and you notice that he took a taxi to work. From these observations, you could reasonably infer that your boss had trouble with his car again this morning and that he is upset about the inconvenience, about being late for work, and perhaps about the expense of fixing it. You can also infer that he is most likely not directly angry at any of the people at work, even though his failure to greet people was impolite.

The inferences you make about your boss in this example would be based on a great deal of background information and accumulated experience. To correctly infer the cause of your boss's response would require that you already know him quite well. You would have worked with him for some time and would have seen his reactions under many conditions. You would, for example, know that he never treats his employees with anger, so he is unlikely to start now. Therefore, you can reason that his anger must be due to external events: having to take a taxi and his recent car trouble support your inference.

Inferences are *reasonable* assumptions and conclusions about what you see, hear, experience, or read. They are not immediate responses; you arrive at them after careful thought. The pictures and readings in this chapter, on the sometimes controversial issue of gender, will challenge you to exercise caution in drawing inferences.

## INFERENCES FROM VISUAL AIDS

Many inferences in everyday life and reading are based on visual clues. Visual aids provide a great deal of important information (see "Reading Visual Aids" in "A Reader's Toolkit," pages 425 through 433). They can also assist us in making inferences. For example, examine Figure 6.1, a 1924 German lithograph titled *Brot!* (*Bread!*) by Käthe Kollwitz. Now circle the inferences that are probably true based on what you observed in the picture. (You can choose more than one.)

a. The woman in the picture is the mother of the two children.
b. The children are hungry, but the mother doesn't have food for them.
c. The woman has no husband.
d. The woman is proud of her family and of their accomplishments.

You should have chosen "a" and "b" as reasonable inferences you can make based on the picture. The size of the children and their close, clinging appearance reasonably support assumption "a," that the woman is their mother. She seems to be responding to their pleas, and she is not sending them away for hanging on her. The title of the print, *Bread!*; the sad, imploring eyes of the younger child; the clinging of the bigger child; and the woman's humped form seem to support assumption "b," that she cannot give her children the bread they want.

On the other hand, we cannot reasonably infer assumption "c," "The woman has no husband." She could have a husband, but he could be unemployed, in prison, or off at war and not able to help his family. We do not have enough information to assume that she is not married. Also, answer "d" is clearly incorrect: The woman does not appear to be "proud of her family and of their accomplishments." Rather, she seems, from her hunched posture and hidden face, to be overwhelmed by her inability to feed her hungry children.

**Figure 6.1**  Brot! (Bread!).

| Exercise 2 | ## Make Inferences from Visual Clues |
|---|---|

Look at the following cartoons (Figures 6.2 and 6.3) and read the dialogue. Then circle the letters of all the inferences that are probably true. You can choose more than one inference for each cartoon.

**Figure 6.2**  "I don't suppose it occurred to you to simply agree to disagree?"

<br /><br /><br /><br /><br /><br />

1.  a. The woman in the cartoon is the man's sister.
    b. He got injured in a fight over a disagreement.
    c. She thinks he is very brave for standing up for his beliefs.
    d. She feels sorry for him.
    e. She thinks he acted stupidly.

**Figure 6.3** CATHY

2.  a. The two people having coffee have known one another a long time.
    b. The two people having coffee are just getting to know one another.
    c. They are both nervous and a little embarrassed.
    d. They don't know how to act with each other.
    e. They will definitely get together again.

## Exercise 3

### Make Inferences from Visual Clues

Look at the following photographs (Figures 6.4 and 6.5). They depict two people in relation to one another. Study their "body language"—what their poses, gestures, and facial expressions tell you about their relationship. Then circle the letters of all the inferences you can make that are probably true. You can choose more than one inference for each photograph.

Lisa Southwick

**Figure 6.4**

a. The two people in the picture have equal positions at work.
b. The two people teach in college.
c. The two people have known one another for a very long time.
d. The woman is interested in pleasing the man.
e. The man has more power in this relationship than the woman.

Lisa Southwick

**Figure 6.5**

a. The man has more power in this relationship than the woman.
b. The man and woman in the photo are married.
c. The woman has more power in this relationship than the man.
d. The man is interested in pleasing the woman.
e. The two people are brother and sister.

## INFERENCES IN TEXTBOOKS

Writers of textbooks use inference in at least two ways: (1) they report on their own inferences, or conclusions, about data and concepts, and (2) they provide data and insights from which readers can make further inferences. For example, read the following paragraph from a sociology textbook by William E. Thompson and Joseph V. Hickey. This is a concluding paragraph from their chapter on sex and gender, in which they draw some conclusions and make some predictions. (We have added the numbers appearing in parentheses.)

(1) Will there be increased freedom, equality, and tolerance for those who violate traditional gender roles? (2) Or will a conservative backlash and a renewed emphasis on genetics and biology attempt to reestablish traditional masculine and feminine roles? (3) While these questions cannot be answered with any certainty, a 1996 survey shows that attitudes about women's and men's roles have become much more flexible since the 1970s (Teegardin, 1996). (4) From a sociological perspective it is indisputable that changing attitudes toward sex and gender will continue to have an impact on people's daily lives—in America and throughout the world. (Thompson and Hickey, *Society in Focus*)

Sentences 1 and 2 ask questions about gender roles in the future. Readers are asked to speculate about what the changes of the twentieth century mean for gender roles in the twenty-first century. Then the authors provide more information: sentence 3 reports on a study about gender roles completed by researcher Teegardin in 1996. The authors end with sentence 4, their vision of the future. Now circle the inference(s) that you can reasonably make about the information you read in this paragraph.

a. There will definitely be more tolerance in the future for those who violate traditional gender roles.
b. We cannot predict the impact that changing attitudes toward sex and gender will have on the future.
c. Attitudes about men's and women's roles have become more flexible.

You should have chosen "b" as the only reasonable inference from this paragraph. Statement "a" assumes too positive a response to gender issues; this is only one possible response, raised as a question in sentence 1. Statement "c" is not an inference; it simply repeats the findings of Teegardin's 1996 study.

## INFERENCES IN AUTOBIOGRAPHIES

Another type of writing we will consider in our discussion of inferences is autobiographical writing, or personal narrative. An **autobiography** is the story of the author's life experience. Often, to make a point, a writer will tell a story, or narrative, about his or her experience that reveals an aspect of personality. The writer does not state this personality trait but expects you, the reader, to infer it. You make a reasonable assumption based on the information the author gives you.

**autobiography**
a story of
one's own life
experience

For example, read the following autobiographical paragraph from Carol Tavris's essay, "Love Story."

> As a child, I was nuts about cowboys, guns, and palomino ponies, and so when I first saw the musical *Annie Get Your Gun* I was in heaven. Annie Oakley was a woman who could ride, wear cowgirl outfits, and shoot. She became my hero at once. She sang, "Anything you can do, I can do better," and she outshot her rival, Frank Butler. I loved Annie Oakley so much that I entirely blocked out the end of the musical when she realizes that "You can't get a man with a gun." Annie deliberately blows her next competition with Butler, who of course then realizes he loves her after all. I couldn't understand why a woman would give up being the world's best sharpshooter (even for Frank Butler, who was definitely terrific), or why Frank Butler could love Annie only if she gave up sharpshooting. (Tavris, "Love Story")

Which of the following statements are reasonable inferences you can make from this paragraph?

a. Tavris admired Annie Oakley.
b. Tavris was later troubled by Annie's deliberate loss in the competition.
c. The sure way to get a man is to let him win; don't beat him in any competition, even if you are more skilled.

You should have chosen statements "a" and "b" as reasonable inferences. Annie Oakley was a hero in Tavris's eyes, and Tavris was disturbed by Oakley's method of winning Butler's affection. (Actually, Tavris goes on in her essay to report that, in real life, Butler was attracted to Annie Oakley precisely because she was such a good shot, and they were happily married for more than 50 years.) Statement "c" might be an assumption some people would make from viewing *Annie Get Your Gun*, but Tavris implies in her response to this story that we should definitely question this strategy.

| **Exercise 4** | Make Inferences in Passages from Written Texts |

Carefully read the following passages, and then circle the letters of all the reasonable inferences you can make from the stated information in the passage.

1. When I was a young boy—before puberty, before girls, before feeling embarrassed when seen with my parents—I thought of myself as strong and athletic. I never doubted my sex and never thought about my ability or inability to attract a mate. But let me tell you, things changed. As a teenager beginning high school, I started noticing the size of other boys around me. I started noticing that even though I was great at sports, I was smaller than most boys my age, in both height and breadth. I started believing I wasn't even a man and never would be at the rate I was going. So I stayed at the school gym late every day, working out, pumping iron. I invested in special protein shakes and powders. I overate. Soon I started to grow and found myself constantly flexing and posturing like a rooster about to get into a fight. Whenever I passed a mirror, I glanced at my reflection to make sure I wasn't that short, skinny boy any more. But even though I had grown thick and muscular, had gained over 50 pounds, I saw a puny runt in the mirror, and to this day, especially when my confidence gets shattered, I still do. (Wong, "The Runt")

   a. The author had questions about his sexual orientation.
   b. The author started to believe that to be a real man, he would need to increase in size.
   c. The author is a man by now looking back on his experience as a teen.

2. Mainstream American culture determines that there are only two genders. A person is either male or female and must behave according to his/her biological sex. However, not all cultures within the United States have the same gender regulations. In fact, this country along with others, has had a third gender. Many North American Indian tribes accepted and respected men and women known as *berdache*. The *berdache* mixed characteristics of both genders and were often regarded as blessed and holy. To have a *berdache* as a family member was often considered a sign of good fortune. European conquest and conversion of native peoples virtually annihilated the *berdache* or forced them to live underground. Today, though, many *berdache* do still live in the American Southwest and other regions of the world. (McDermott, "Third Gender")

   a. Mainstream American culture would not be very accepting of *berdache*.
   b. *Berdache* have always been revered within their own tribes.
   c. Settlers probably accepted the *berdache* shortly after the conquest and conversion of Native American peoples.

3. The controversy over the extent to which biological and physiological differences in the sexes determine gender differences continues to attract widespread attention. Sociobiological research in the field is likely to expand. An interesting technological development . . . is the ability of parents not only to know the sex of an infant before its birth but to choose the baby's sex. This choice is medically possible today. What if it were to become a widely accepted cultural practice in the future? The world of genetic engineering, human cloning, and other technological developments offers fascinating and even frightening possibilities. (Thompson and Hickey, *Society in Focus*)

    a. Genetic engineering will lead to frightening results.

    b. Parents' ability to choose a baby's sex could cause an imbalance of males and females in some cultures.

    c. Choosing your baby's sex will be a widely accepted practice in the future.

4. I lay in bed with my eyes closed. I visualize the make-up sitting on my dresser, and my mother lying in her bed visualizing the make-up and wishing it were on my face instead of the dresser. I open my eyes and see the square blue eye shadow box and the triangular tube of pink lipstick. My parents! They buy me a pink lipstick and think it will hide my sexual feelings toward other women if I put it on my lips.

    I lay back on my back glancing occasionally at the ceiling and the make-up. I really thought it would make my life easier if I told them how I was feeling. So instead of hiding my true self, I announced that I thought I might be a lesbian. I was grappling with this issue for four years and was wondering what my future would be like as a homosexual. What is life like when you are thirty, or forty? And what will my neighbors think? I hope they are not as hostile as my parents are; if so, I had better continue suppressing my feelings, I thought. (Watnick, "Triangular Tube of Pink Lipstick")

    a. Watnick's feelings were hurt by her parents' response to her revelation.

    b. Watnick's parents do not want to accept her sense of her sexual orientation.

    c. Wearing pink lipstick will change Watnick's sexual feelings toward other women.

5. For travelers in parts of the developing world, the sight is a familiar one: barefoot women trudging for miles with enormous loads of firewood or water balanced on their heads. Scientists at the University of Nairobi in Africa, studying human energy expenditure, recently recruited women from the Kikuyu and Luo tribes to carry heavy loads on their heads while walking on a motorized treadmill (*New York Times*, 1986). Since oxygen use accurately reflects energy use, the researchers prepared to monitor carefully the extra amounts of oxygen that carrying loads of various sizes would require.

    To the scientists' amazement, the women were able to carry loads weighing up to 20 percent of their body weights without any increase in their use of oxygen at all, which meant that loads of this size did not result in any increased expenditure of energy. Carrying an astounding 70 percent of their body weight increased the women's oxygen use by only 50 percent. In contrast, males carrying backpacks equaling 20 percent of their body weight increased their oxygen use by 13 percent; loads equal to 70 percent of the carrier's weight increased males' oxygen consumption by nearly 100 percent. (Hicks and Gwynne, *Cultural Anthropology*)

    a. The men who were tested were probably not in the habit of carrying weight in backpacks.

    b. The women who were tested were in excellent physical condition.

    c. African women are probably stronger than African men in other ways as well.

**Reading 2**

# Sex, Lies, and Conversation* — Deborah Tannen

**Deborah Tannen is a professor of linguistics at Georgetown University. She has published several books on the differences in communication styles between men and women. As you read, pay close attention to the misunderstandings that arise between men and women because each makes inferences based on wrong assumptions about the other.**

1   I was addressing a small gathering in a suburban Virginia living room—a women's group that had invited men to join them. Throughout the evening, one man had been particularly talkative, frequently offering ideas and anecdotes, while his wife sat silently beside him on the couch. Toward the end of the evening, I commented that women frequently complain that their husbands don't talk to them. This man quickly concurred. He gestured toward his wife and said, "She's the talker in our family." The room burst into laughter; the man looked puzzled and hurt. "It's true," he explained. "When I come home from work I have nothing to say. If she didn't keep the conversation going, we'd spend the whole evening in silence."

2      This episode crystallizes the irony that although American men tend to talk more than women in public situations, they often talk less at home. And this pattern is wreaking havoc with marriage.

3      The pattern was observed by political scientist Andrew Hacker in the late '70s. Sociologist Catherine Kohler Reissman reports in her new book *Divorce Talk* that most of the women she interviewed—but only a few of the men—gave lack of communication as the reason for their divorces. Given the current divorce rate of nearly 50 percent, that amounts to millions of cases in the United States every year—a virtual epidemic of failed conversation.

**tangible**
measurable

4      In my own research, complaints from women about their husbands most often focused not on tangible inequities such as having given up the chance for a career to accompany a husband to his, or doing far more than their share of daily life—support work like cleaning, cooking, social arrangements and errands. Instead, they focused on communication: "He doesn't listen to me," "He doesn't talk to me." I found, as Hacker observed years before, that most wives want their husbands to be, first and foremost, conversational partners, but few husbands share this expectation of their wives.

5      In short, the image that best represents the current crisis is the stereotypical cartoon scene of a man sitting at the breakfast table with a newspaper held up in front of his face while a woman glares at the back of it, wanting to talk.

## LINGUISTIC BATTLE OF THE SEXES

6   How can women and men have such different impressions of communication in marriage? Why the widespread imbalance in their interests and expectations?

7      In the April issue of *American Psychologist*, Stanford University's Eleanor Macoby reports the results of her own and others' research showing that children's development is most influenced by the social structure of peer interactions. Boys and girls tend to play with children of their own gender, and their sex-separate groups have different organizational structures and interactive norms.

8      I believe these systematic differences in childhood socialization make talk between women and men like cross-cultural communication, heir to all the attraction and pitfalls

* "Sex, Lies, and Conversation" by Deborah Tannen from THE WASHINGTON POST, June 24, 1990, copyright by Deborah Tannen. Reprinted by permission.

of that enticing but difficult enterprise. My research on men's and women's conversations uncovered patterns similar to those described for children's groups.

9    For women, as for girls, intimacy is the fabric of relationships, and talk is the thread from which it is woven. Little girls create and maintain friendships by exchanging secrets; similarly, women regard conversation as the cornerstone of friendship. So a woman expects her husband to be a new and improved version of a best friend. What is important is not the individual subjects that are discussed but the sense of closeness, of a life shared, that emerges when people tell their thoughts, feelings, and impressions.

10    Bonds between boys can be as intense as girls', but they are based less on talking, more on doing things together. Since they don't assume talk is the cement that binds a relationship, men don't know what kind of talk women want, and they don't miss it when it isn't there.

11    Boys' groups are larger, more inclusive, and more hierarchical, so boys must struggle to avoid the subordinate position in the group. This may play a role in women's complaints that men don't listen to them. Some men really don't like to listen, because being the listener makes them feel one-down, like a child listening to adults or an employee to a boss.

**misalignment**
out of line, badly arranged

12    But often when women tell men, "You aren't listening," and the men protest, "I am," the men are right. The impression of not listening results from misalignments in the mechanics of conversation. The misalignment begins as soon as a man and a woman take physical positions. This became clear when I studied videotapes made by psychologist Bruce Dorval of children and adults talking to their same-sex best friends. I found that at every age, the girls and women faced each other directly, their eyes anchored on each other's faces. At every age, the boys and men sat at angles to each other and looked elsewhere in the room, periodically glancing at each other. They were obviously attuned to each other, often mirroring each other's movements. But the tendency of men to face away can give women the impression they aren't listening even when they are. A young woman in college was frustrated: Whenever she told her boyfriend she wanted to talk to him, he would lie down on the floor, close his eyes, and put his arm over his face. This signaled to her "He's taking a nap." But he insisted he was listening extra-hard. Normally, he looks around the room, so he is easily distracted. Lying down and covering his eyes helped him concentrate on what she was saying.

**analogous**
similar, parallel

13    Analogous to the physical alignment that women and men take in conversation is their topical alignment. The girls in my study tended to talk at length about one topic, but the boys tended to jump from topic to topic. The second-grade girls exchanged stories about people they knew. The second-grade boys teased, told jokes, noticed things in the room and talked about finding games to play. The sixth-grade girls talked about problems with a mutual friend. The sixth-grade boys talked about 55 different topics, none of which extended over more than a few turns.

## LISTENING TO BODY LANGUAGE

14    Switching topics is another habit that gives women the impression men aren't listening, especially if they switch to a topic about themselves. But the evidence of the 10th-grade boys in my study indicates otherwise. The 10th-grade boys sprawled across their chairs with bodies parallel and eyes straight ahead, rarely looking at each other. They looked as if they were riding in a car, staring out the windshield. But they were talking about their feelings. One boy was upset because a girl had told him he had a drinking problem, and the other was feeling alienated from all his friends.

15    Now, when a girl told a friend about a problem, the friend responded by asking prob-
ing questions and expressing agreement and understanding. But the boys dismissed
each other's problems. Todd assured Richard that his drinking was "no big problem"
because "sometimes you're funny when you're off your butt." And when Todd said he felt
left out, Richard responded, "Why should you? You know more people than me."

16    Women perceive such responses as belittling and unsupportive. But the boys seemed
satisfied with them. Whereas women reassure each other by implying, "You shouldn't
feel bad because I've had similar experiences," men do so by implying, "You shouldn't
feel bad because your problems aren't so bad."

17    There are even simpler reasons for women's impression that men don't listen. Linguist
Lynette Hirschman found that women make more listener-noise, such as "mhm," "uhuh,"
and "yeah," to show "I'm with you." Men, she found, more often give silent attention.
Women who expect a stream of listener-noise interpret silent attention as no attention
at all.

18    Women's conversational habits are as frustrating to men as men's are to women. Men
who expect silent attention interpret a stream of listener-noise as overreaction or impatience. Also, when women talk to each other in a close, comfortable setting, they often
overlap, finish each other's sentences and anticipate what the other is about to say. This
practice, which I call "participatory listenership," is often perceived by men as interruption, intrusion, and lack of attention.

19    A parallel difference caused a man to complain about his wife, "She just wants to talk
about her own point of view. If I show her another view, she gets mad at me." When most
women talk to each other, they assume a conversationalist's job is to express agreement
and support. But many men see their conversational duty as pointing out the other side
of an argument. This is heard as disloyalty by women, and refusal to offer the requisite
support. It is not that women don't want to see other points of view, but that they prefer
them phrased as suggestions and inquiries rather than as direct challenges.

20    In his book *Fighting for Life*, Walter Ong points out that men use "agonistic" or warlike, oppositional formats to do almost anything; thus discussion becomes debate, and
conversation a competitive sport. In contrast, women see conversation as a ritual means
of establishing rapport. If Jane tells a problem and June says she has a similar one, they
walk away feeling closer to each other. But this attempt at establishing rapport can
backfire when used with men. Men take too literally women's ritual "troubles talk," just
as women mistake men's ritual challenges for real attack.

## THE SOUNDS OF SILENCE

21    These differences begin to clarify why women and men have such different expectations about communication in marriage. For women, talk creates intimacy. Marriage is
an orgy of closeness: you can tell your feelings and thoughts, and still be loved. Their
greatest fear is being pushed away. But men live in a hierarchical world, where talk maintains independence and status. They are on guard to protect themselves from being put
down and pushed around.

22    This explains the paradox of the talkative man who said of his silent wife, "She's the
talker." In the public setting of a guest lecture, he felt challenged to show his intelligence
and display his understanding of the lecture. But at home, where he has nothing to
prove and no one to defend against, he is free to remain silent. For his wife, being home
means she is free from the worry that something she says might offend someone, or
spark disagreement, or appear to be showing off; at home she is free to talk.

23     The communication problems that endanger marriage can't be fixed by mechanical engineering. They require a new conceptual framework about the role of talk in human relationships. Many of the psychological explanations that have become second nature may not be helpful, because they tend to blame either women (for not being assertive enough) or men (for not being in touch with their feelings). A sociolinguistic approach by which male-female conversation is seen as cross-cultural communication allows us to understand the problem and forge solutions without blaming either party.

24     Once the problem is understood, improvement comes naturally, as it did to the young woman and her boyfriend who seemed to want to go to sleep when she wanted to talk. Previously, she had accused him of not listening, and he had refused to change his behavior, since that would be admitting fault. But then she learned about and explained to him the differences in women's and men's habitual ways of aligning themselves in conversation. The next time she told him she wanted to talk, he began, as usual, by lying down and covering his eyes. When the familiar negative reaction bubbled up, she reassured herself that he really was listening. But then he sat up and looked at her. Thrilled, she asked why. He said, "You like me to look at you when we talk, so I'll try to do it." Once he saw their differences as cross-cultural rather than right and wrong, he independently altered his behavior.

25     Women who feel abandoned and deprived when their husbands won't listen to or report daily news may be happy to discover their husbands trying to adapt once they understand the place of small talk in women's relationships. But if their husbands don't adapt, the women may still be comforted that for men, this is not a failure of intimacy. Accepting the difference, the wives may look to their friends or family for that kind of talk. And husbands who can't provide it shouldn't feel their wives have made unreasonable demands. Some couples will still decide to divorce, but at least their decisions will be based on realistic expectations.

26     In these times of resurgent ethnic conflicts, the world desperately needs cross-cultural understanding. Like charity, successful cross-cultural communication should begin at home.

**Exercise 5**

## Work with Words

The following sentences appear in Reading 2. Use context clues, dictionary skills, and your knowledge of word parts to determine the meaning of each italicized word in the sentences. Write the meaning of the word on the lines provided. The paragraph number is provided in case you want to check the context.

1. Throughout the evening, one man had been particularly talkative, frequently offering ideas and anecdotes, while his wife sat silently beside him on the couch. Toward the end of the evening, I commented that women frequently complain that their husbands don't talk to them. This man quickly *concurred*. (par. 1)

   *Concurred*: _____

2. This episode crystallizes the *irony* that although American men tend to talk more than women in public situations, they often talk less at home. And this pattern is *wreaking havoc* with marriage. (par. 2)

   *Irony*: _____

3. *Wreaking havoc:* _____

4. Boys and girls tend to play with children of their own gender, and their sex-separate groups have different organizational structures and interactive *norms.* (par. 7)

   *Norms:* _____

5. Boys' groups are larger, more inclusive, and more hierarchical, so boys must struggle to avoid the *subordinate* position in the group. (par. 11)

   *Subordinate:* _____

6. Also, when women talk to each other in a close, comfortable setting, they often overlap, finish each other's sentences and anticipate what the other is about to say. This practice, which I call *"participatory listenership,"* is often perceived by men as interruption, *intrusion,* and lack of attention. (par. 18)

   *Participatory listenership:* _____

   _____

7. *Intrusion:* _____

8. In his book *Fighting for Life,* Walter Ong points out that men use *"agonistic"* or warlike, oppositional formats to do almost anything; thus discussion becomes debate, and conversation a competitive sport. (par. 20)

   *Agonistic:* _____

9. This explains the *paradox* of the talkative man who said of his silent wife, "She's the talker." (par. 22)

   *Paradox:* _____

10. Many of the psychological explanations that have become second nature may not be helpful, because they tend to blame either women (for not being *assertive* enough) or men (for not being in touch with their feelings). (par. 23)

    *Assertive:* _____

**Exercise 6**

## Check Your Understanding

Based on Reading 2, write your answers to the following questions.

1. According to Riessman's book *Divorce Talk,* what did most women say was the reason for their divorce?

   _____

2. According to Tannen, what is the cornerstone of a friendship for women?

_____

3. According to Tannen, what is the basis of friendship for men?

_____

4. What kind of physical misalignments impede communication between men and women?

_____

5. What solution does Tannen suggest for the problems men and women have in communicating with each other?

_____

_____

**Exercise 7**

### Evaluate Inferences

Based on Reading 2, put a check next to each of the following statements that is a reasonable inference.

_____  1. Tannen was invited to give a talk to the women's group because of her expertise in language.

_____  2. People laughed at the man who said that his wife was the "talker" because he was the one who was doing all the talking that evening.

_____  3. Men's body language proves that men are not listening to their wives.

_____  4. Poor communication is the only reason marriages don't last.

_____  5. For many women, men's responses to them in conversation seem unsatisfying and simplistic.

_____  6. If men and women just understood their different conversation styles, the divorce rate would go down drastically.

_____  7. Women's conversational habits are probably superior because they are more communicative.

_____  8. Men's conversational habits are more frustrating to women than women's conversational habits are to men.

_____  9. Finishing someone else's sentence is considered rude by both men and women.

_____  10. Tannen believes that ethnic conflicts could be more easily resolved with cross-cultural understanding.

**Exercise 8**

Organize to Learn: Create a Chart or Diagram

On a separate sheet of paper, design a chart or diagram that compares and contrasts men's and women's communication styles, based on Reading 2.

**Exercise 9**

Reflect and Write

Think about what you read in Reading 2 and what you already know about men's and women's conversation styles. Answer the following questions, and prepare to discuss them with your classmates.

1. Which of the points of analysis of men's and women's communication styles in Tannen's article were new to you?

   _____

   _____

   _____

2. What situations described in the reading are familiar to you? Explain.

   _____

   _____

   _____

3. Having read about differences in women's and men's conversational styles, will you now infer different meanings when you communicate with someone of the opposite sex? Explain and give examples.

   _____

   _____

   _____

4. On a separate piece of paper, write a short essay of three or four paragraphs about conversational styles. In your first paragraph, paraphrase Tannen's thesis regarding men's and women's conversational styles and their consequences for relationships. Then state whether your experience supports her thesis. In the next two or three paragraphs, explain the conversational styles of men and women that you have observed in your life; how they are similar or different from Tannen's assertions; and how these conversational styles affect your relationships. Remember to describe specific situations to support your statements. Give your essay a meaningful title.

# Inferences from Words

The assumptions you make about information given in textbooks or personal narratives presented in autobiographies are based on paragraphs or longer passages. But these inferences are influenced by the author's choice of words, so careful reading also requires paying attention to the inferences from words.

## CONNOTATIONS

**connotation**
positive or negative feelings suggested by a word

**denotation**
the dictionary or literal meaning of a word

Some words have many possible effects on the reader. The positive or negative feelings evoked by a word are its **connotations.** By contrast, the precise meaning of a word, its literal meaning, is its **denotation,** or dictionary definition. If, for example, you think only of the denotative meaning of the word *family,* you might think of "people related by blood or marriage" or "relatives." This definition of *family* is straightforward; it does not carry a lot of emotion. However, if you think of *family* as a group of caring and loving relatives, it has a positive connotation. Not all people have this reaction to the word *family.* Consider the saying, "You can choose your friends but not your family." Here the word *family* has a negative connotation, conveying the idea that there may be members of your family you would rather not associate with.

Good writers often use words that are rich in connotative meaning. As a reader, you need to be aware of the connotations of the words you (or others) use when discussing gender issues, because many people are particularly sensitive about it. Most writers try to use language that will not offend anyone.

Maya Angelou, prize-winning poet and author, addresses the issue of gender and language in her book *Wouldn't Take Nothing for My Journey Now.* Read the following passage and look for three adjectives that have strong connotations.

> In my young years I took pride in the fact that luck was called a lady. In fact, there were so few public acknowledgments of the female presence that I felt personally honored whenever nature and large ships were referred to as feminine. But as I matured, I began to resent being considered a sister to a changeling as fickle as luck, as aloof as an ocean, and as frivolous as nature. (Angelou, *Wouldn't Take Nothing for My Journey Now*)

Did you pick out *fickle, aloof,* and *frivolous*? These words have strong negative connotations. Something or someone who is *fickle* changes unpredictably; thus, fickle luck is not something you can depend on. *Aloof* means "removed or distant in interest or feeling." This definition is commonly extended to mean uncaring or unconcerned. And the definition of *frivolous,* "lacking in seriousness," usually has a negative connotation. Maya Angelou deliberately chose words with negative connotations to strengthen her criticism of the custom of referring to luck, ships, and nature as feminine.

**Exercise 10**

### Evaluate Connotations and Inferences

Listed in the following columns under "Masculine" and "Feminine" are a number of adjectives commonly used to describe characteristics of each gender. Add any adjectives you often hear used to describe men or women to the appropriate lists. Then, in the "Connotation" column, indicate what kind of connotation each adjective usually has, positive (+) or negative (−). The first pair has been done for you.

Remember that this is a list of generalizations and stereotypes of the traditional gender roles in our society. Clearly, this list of adjectives cannot be accurate for all men or for all women.

| Masculine | Connotation | Feminine | Connotation |
|---|---|---|---|
| strong | + | weak | − |
| decisive | _____ | indecisive | _____ |
| unemotional | _____ | emotional | _____ |
| distant | _____ | nurturing | _____ |
| hard | _____ | soft | _____ |
| direct | _____ | indirect | _____ |
| insensitive | _____ | sensitive | _____ |
| not gossipy | _____ | gossipy | _____ |
| mechanically inclined | _____ | not mechanically inclined | _____ |
| independent | _____ | dependent | _____ |
| _____ | _____ | _____ | _____ |
| _____ | _____ | _____ | _____ |

**Exercise 11**

## Reflect

Based on Exercise 10, answer the following questions in your own words.

1. How many positive or negative connotations are there for the words in each column? Which column has more negative connotations?

_____

2. Why do you think one side of a list of traditional gender roles has more negative connotations? What conclusions can you draw from this observation?

_____

_____

3. Do you think the connotations of a word might be different depending on who is interpreting the word and what the situation was at the time? Explain your answer.

_____

_____

# IRONY

**irony**
writer says one
thing and means
another

Sometimes a writer wants you, the reader, to infer the opposite of what he or she writes. The writer is then using a device called **irony**. This device should be familiar to you. For example, if you crawl out from under your car where you've been changing the oil on a hot and muggy day and your friend says, "You look terrific!" you know you actually look a mess.

Or a writer may write about an ironic situation. For example, after a devastating flood, people often have no water to drink. Even though there is too much water, it's contaminated. Ironically, there's not a drop to drink.

Irony can often be humorous. At the least, it alerts the reader to look for other layers of meaning in a message. In an ironic statement, things are not what they seem to be. That is because the writer has stepped back from the subject and views it from a distance.

**Exercise 12**

## Recognize Irony

Read the following scenarios, and choose the sentence that makes an ironic statement about or gives an ironic conclusion to the situation.

1. Johnny was voted the student "most likely to succeed" in his high school class.
   a. Now he has a nice family and a fulfilling job that pays well.
   b. Now he is divorced, unemployed, and lonely.
   c. Now he's cheerful and happy but definitely not wealthy.

2. At one time, Zimbabwe exported food to all of Africa.
   a. Today Zimbabwe has a famine and can't feed its own people.
   b. Today Zimbabwe is blaming its problems on the white former colonialists who still live there.
   c. Today Zimbabwe needs to reexamine its use of land.

3. Erica didn't respect her advanced placement biology teacher and ended up with an F in the class.
   a. None of the students passed the Advanced Placement Biology test because the teacher was bad.
   b. All of the students passed the Advanced Placement Biology test in spite of the teacher.
   c. Erica got the highest grade of all the students on the Advanced Placement Biology test.

4. The president of a wealthy country said that corruption would not be tolerated among top executives of corporations.
   a. The president himself had always been a crusader against corrupt practices of businesses, especially when he was on the board of directors.
   b. The president followed up on his position, saying that executives are responsible for what their corporations do and that if they do anything illegal, they should be sent to jail like any other criminal.
   c. The president himself had benefited from insider information and used it to make millions of dollars when he was on the board of directors of a corporation.

5. An American from one of the western states was visiting Denmark on New Year's Eve. When the family she was staying with prepared their fireworks for the evening's festivities, she told them, "Fireworks are illegal in my state

© 2013 Wadsworth, Cengage Learning

because they're too dangerous." The Danes asked her what people did instead. She responded:

a. "They go to big fireworks shows."
b. "They don't do anything."
c. "They shoot guns in the air."

# Reading Literature

Reading literature—a category that includes fiction, poetry, and drama, as well as essays and autobiography—requires considerable skill in making inferences. Sometimes inferences are based not only on the usual reasonable assumptions but also on the interpretation of imagery.

## IMAGERY

**image**
a "sense picture" that uses words to describe something in terms of sight, taste, hearing, touch, and smell

An **image** in literature is a "sense picture" made up of words that describe something in terms of sight, taste, hearing, touch, and smell. Images can be descriptions of what the author has observed. For example, Scott Russell Sanders, in his essay, "The Men We Carry in Our Minds" (Additional Mastery Test 6B), uses descriptive words to create images of the men he knew: "The bodies of the men I knew were twisted and maimed in ways visible and invisible. The nails of their hands were black and split, the hands tattooed with scars. Some had lost fingers." When you read this description, it is easy to form a picture of the men and to think about how they were twisted in visible and invisible ways.

**figurative language**
direct or implied comparisons made to create an image

An author may also use figurative language to create images. **Figurative language** usually creates images by making direct or implied comparisons between two unlike things. For example, Sanders describes the faces of the men he knew, with their skin "creased *like the leather of old work gloves.*" In other words, their faces had so many wrinkles and lines from hard work that their skin looked like the fabric of cracked, worn-out leather gloves. When writers use these kinds of comparisons, they can make us understand what they are trying to communicate more clearly, with more imagination and fewer words. They expect us, as readers, to use these creative images to make inferences about their meanings.

Although textbook authors and essay writers do use figurative language, writers of literature—fiction, poetry, drama, and autobiography—use it even more frequently. *Similes* and *metaphors*, two important examples of figurative language, are imaginative comparisons that convey a writer's attitude about characters, events, or ideas.

## SIMILES

**simile**
a comparison between unlike things, using *like* or *as*

A **simile** makes a comparison between two unlike things, using the words *like* or *as*. The phrase "like the leather of old work gloves" is an example of a simile. It provides an exceptionally vivid image of the skin of these old men who had worked hard all their lives. The film *Forrest Gump* included a memorable simile: "Mama always said, 'Life is like a box of chocolates. You never know what you're going to get.'" Here the unpredictability of life is compared to the chance selection of flavors—some you like, some you don't—in a box of chocolates.

Similes in literature are often a bit more complicated. For example: "Women are like pictures; of no value in the hands of a fool till he hears men of sense bid high for their purchase" (Farquhar, *The Beaux*, Act II, sc. 1). What can you infer from this statement? To understand this simile, you have to understand that the author is referring to an art auction, where people bid on paintings and other pieces. As long as someone is willing to pay more for the piece, the price continues to go up. Sometimes people go to an auction thinking that a particular picture is not very interesting and not worth much, but they may change their minds if other people are interested in it and are bidding high. Farquhar, then, is implying that some men (the "fools") do not value their women as highly as they should until they realize that other men are interested in them.

| Exercise 13 |
| --- |

## Identify Similes

Read the following well-known poem by Robert Burns, and notice how he uses similes. (Some words are spelled differently because the poem was written 200 years ago in a Scottish dialect.) Then list the similes Burns used in this poem, and explain what you can infer from them about his lover.

**My Luve Is Like a Red, Red Rose**
O, My Luve is like a red, red rose,
  That's newly sprung in June;
O My Luve is like a melodie
  That's sweetly play'd in tune.

As fair art thou, my bonnie lass,
  So deep in luve am I:
And I will luve thee still, my dear,
  Till a' the seas gang dry.

Till a' the seas gang dry, my dear,
  And the rocks melt wi' the sun:
O I will luve thee still, my dear,
  While the sands o' life shall run.

And fare thee weel, my only luve,
  And fare thee weel awhile!
And I will come again, my luve,
  Tho' it were ten thousand mile!

(Burns, "My Luve Is Like a Red, Red Rose")

|   | **Simile** | **Inference** |
| --- | --- | --- |
| 1. | _____ | _____ |
| 2. | _____ | _____ |

# METAPHORS

**metaphor**
an implied
comparison

A **metaphor** compares two things without using the words *like* or *as*. Often something unknown is compared to something known to make it easier to understand. For example, poet-songwriter Paul Simon wrote, in the song by the same name, "I am a rock." This line is a simple metaphor that compares the qualities of the singer—the narrator—to those of an inanimate object, a rock. Another metaphor is presented in the next line, "I am an island." Simon is explaining how the character in the song feels about his relationship to other people. He feels isolated and unable to make contact with others, "cold," distant, unbending, and inflexible. The song continues, "I touch no one/and no one touches me." These lines confirm the sense of isolation that the metaphors in the first two lines introduced.

**Exercise 14**

## Identify Metaphors

Read the following lyrics from the song "The Rose," by Amanda McBroom, and notice how she uses metaphors. Then list five metaphors that McBroom uses in this song and explain what you think she is inferring.

**The Rose**
Some say love it is a river that drowns the tender reed.
Some say love it is a razor that leaves your soul to bleed.
Some say love it is a hunger, an endless aching need.
I say love it is a flower and you its only seed.

(McBroom, "The Rose")

| **Metaphor** | **Inferences** |
|---|---|
| 1. _____ | _____ |
| 2. _____ | _____ |
| 3. _____ | _____ |
| 4. _____ | _____ |
| 5. _____ | _____ |

**Exercise 15**

## Recognize and Interpret Figurative Language

Read the following examples of figurative language. For each quotation, answer the questions that follow. Then write the meaning of the quotation in your own words.

1. They say love is a two-way street. But I don't believe it, because the one I've been on for the last two years was a dirt road. (McMillan, *Waiting to Exhale*)

   a. What is love compared to? _____

   _____

   b. Are the comparisons similes or metaphors? _____

c. Write the meaning of this quotation in your own words.

_____

_____

_____

2. Beauty without virtue is a flower without perfume. (Anonymous, French proverb)

  a. Is this a simile or a metaphor? _____

  b. What two things are being compared?

_____

_____

_____

  c. Write the meaning of this quotation in your own words.

_____

_____

3. Love is blind. (William Shakespeare, _Merchant of Venice_)

  a. What image does Shakespeare's words bring into your mind?

_____

_____

  b. What two things are being compared?

_____

  c. Write the meaning of this quotation in your own words.

_____

_____

_____

4. The prolonged slavery of women is the darkest page in human history. (Elizabeth Cady Stanton, _History of Woman Suffrage_)

  a. Is this a simile or a metaphor? _____

  b. What two things are being compared?

_____

_____

c. Write the meaning of this quotation in your own words.

_____

_____

5. Our hours in love have wings; in absence, crutches. (Colley Cibber, "Xerxes IV")

a. Is this a simile or a metaphor? _____

b. What two things are being compared?

_____

_____

c. Write the meaning of this quotation in your own words.

_____

_____

_____

6. Love comforteth like sunshine after rain. (William Shakespeare, _Venus and Adonis_)

a. Is this a simile or a metaphor? _____

b. What two things are being compared?

_____

c. Write the meaning of this quotation in your own words.

_____

_____

7. Marriage . . . a fever in reverse: it starts with heat and ends with cold. (Anonymous, German proverb)

a. Is this a simile or a metaphor? _____

b. What two things are being compared?

_____

c. Write the meaning of the quotation in your own words.

_____

_____

8. A woman needs a man like a fish needs a bicycle. (Feminist slogan often attributed to Gloria Steinem)

   a. Is this a simile or a metaphor? _____

   b. What two things are being compared?

   _____

   c. Write the meaning of the quotation in your own words.

   _____

   _____

9. He has a heart of stone. (Common English expression)

   a. Is this a simile or a metaphor? _____

   b. What two things are being compared?

   _____

   c. Write the meaning of the quotation in your own words.

   _____

10. Love is the master key that opens the gates of happiness, of hatred, of jealousy, and, most easily of all, the gate of fear. (Oliver Wendell Holmes, *The Autocrat of the Breakfast Table*)

   a. Is this a simile or a metaphor? _____

   b. What two things are being compared?

   _____

   _____

   _____

   c. Write the meaning of the quotation in your own words.

   _____

   _____

## POETRY

A poem is a combination of images, rhythm, and sometimes rhyme that creates meaning for the reader. Determining the meaning, or message, of a poem is similar to the process of selecting a thesis statement that you learned about in Chapter 3. But often the message is implied, not stated outright. As a reader, you need to add up the visual imagery, the way the poem sounds, and other impressions of the poem to infer the most accurate interpretation. Like making inferences, interpreting poetry requires you to reach reasonable conclusions about meaning based on the evidence provided.

To practice finding the meaning, read the following poem by Christine Huynh.

> The dryline between us
> Thickens every time we fight.
> We don't understand each other's needs,
> But the need to correct is stronger
> Than steel plates in heads
> And on torn up streets.
>
> (Huynh, "Corrections")

What metaphors does Huynh use in this poem, and what does each represent?

**The dryline represents the communication problem that happens when the speaker and her/his lover fight. When this dryline thickens, the communications get worse. The "steel plates in heads and on torn up streets" represent each person's need to correct the other, to be the person who is right, or who wins the argument. Steel plates are very hard, practically impossible to break or wear down.**

What is the message or meaning of the poem?

**The message is pessimistic because the comparisons of the dryline and steel plates to communication and the need to be right are not hopeful. There is a barrier to compromise.**

## Exercise 16

### Interpret Poetry

Read each of the following poems. Answer the questions that follow.

1. The summer came too fast,
   stayed too long,
   like an unwanted man
   you keep around
   because being alone
   makes you feel fatter than you really are.

   (Gómez, "Chocolate Confessions")

   a. What two things is Gómez comparing and why?

   _____

   _____

   b. Explain why Gómez writes "being alone makes you feel fatter than you really are." What does feeling fat represent?

   _____

   _____

   c. What is the message or meaning of the poem?

   _____

   _____

2.     Our lives shall not be sweated from birth until life closes.
       Hearts starve as well as bodies;
       Give us bread, but give us roses.

   (James Oppenheimer, lyrics to the song, "Bread and Roses,"
   inspired by the picket signs of women on strike at the
   mills in Lawrence, Massachusetts, in 1912)

   a. The writer uses four images—hearts, bodies, bread, roses—that can be grouped into two connected pairs. What are the two pairs of connected images?

   _____

   b. What does the writer mean with the words, "Hearts starve as well as bodies?"

   _____

   _____

   c. What is the message or meaning of the poem?

   _____

   _____

3.     For courting's a pleasure,
       But parting is grief,
       And a false-hearted lover,
       Is worse than a thief.

   (From "On Top of Old Smokey," author unknown)

   a. What two things are being compared in the last two lines?

   _____

   b. Is it a metaphor or a simile? _____

   c. What does the writer mean by making this comparison?

   _____

   _____

4.  Although I conquer all the earth,
    yet for me there is only one city.
    In that city there is for me only one house;
    And in that house, one room only;
    And in that room, a bed.
    And one woman sleeps there,
    The shining joy and jewel of all my kingdom.

(Sanskrit poem, "Although I Conquer All the Earth")

a.  What is the woman sleeping in the bed compared to? Does the author use a metaphor or a simile?

_____

_____

b.  How do the images progress from the beginning of the poem to the end?

_____

_____

c.  What is the message or meaning of the poem?

_____

## FICTION

Understanding inferences and the language of images is also important in reading the other forms of literature, such as short stories and novels. But imagery is only one element in fiction. Character, plot, setting, point of view, and theme are other elements. After you read a short story, ask yourself some of the questions in the Reader's Tip feature to help you understand and organize the information.

**characters**
the people
in a story

### Reader's Tip:
### Key Questions for Reading Fiction

**Characters—The People in the Story**

- Who is the main character in the story? That is, who is the story primarily about? Who do we learn the most about?
- How does the main character change from the beginning to the end of the story? What causes this character to change?
- Describe each of the important people in the story. What kind of person is he or she? Base your answer on what the people do, what they say, and what other people say about them in the story.

**plot**
the action
of a story

**setting**
the time
and place
of a story

**point of
view**
the perspective
from which
a story is told

**theme**
interpretation
of life
experience
based on the
outcome of a
story

---

### Plot—The Action of the Story

- What happens to the main character(s) in the story?
- What is the main conflict or turning point of the story?
- List or map the main events in the story in the order in which they happen.

### Setting—The Time and Place of the Story

- When does the story take place?
- Where does the story take place?
- What influence does the setting have on the other parts of the story?

### Point of View—The Perspective from Which the Story Is Told

- Through whose eyes do we see the action of the story?
- Does the point of view change in the story, or is it consistent?
- How would the story be different if it were seen through another character's eyes?

### Theme—An Interpretation of Life Experience Based on the Outcome of the Story

- What is the meaning of the story? Can we learn something about life from the story?
- What general statement can you make about human experience based on the experience of the characters in this story?

---

**Reading 3**

# Sally*

— SANDRA CISNEROS

**In her novel, *The House on Mango Street*, Sandra Cisneros paints a vivid picture of a young girl growing up in a Latino neighborhood in Chicago in the 1960s. The following three vignettes—short scenes or events—are about the same character, Sally. Taken together, these pieces tell a story about important experiences in Sally's life. They are also rich in figurative language. As you read, think about the author's use of imagery, similes, and metaphors and the effect that they have on you as a reader.**

**raven**
a large black
bird

**satin**
a shiny, soft
material

1  Sally is the girl with eyes like Egypt and nylons the color of smoke. The boys at school think she's beautiful because her hair is shiny black like raven feathers and when she laughs, she flicks her hair back like a satin shawl over her shoulders and laughs.

2  Her father says to be this beautiful is trouble. They are very strict in his religion. They are not supposed to dance. He remembers his sisters and is sad. Then she can't go out. Sally I mean.

3   Sally, who taught you to paint your eyes like Cleopatra? And if I roll the little brush with my tongue and chew it to a point and dip it in the muddy cake, the one in the little red box, will you teach me?

4   I like your black coat and those shoes you wear, where did you get them? My mother says to wear black so young is dangerous, but I want to buy shoes just like yours, like your black ones made out of suede, just like those. And one day, when my mother's in a good mood, maybe after my next birthday, I'm going to ask to buy the nylons too.

5   Cheryl, who is not your friend anymore, not since last Tuesday before Easter, not since the day you made her ear bleed, not since she called you that name and bit a hole in your arm and you looked as if you were going to cry and everyone was waiting and you didn't, you didn't, Sally, not since then, you don't have a best friend to lean against the schoolyard fence with, to laugh behind your hands at what the boys say. There is no one to lend you her hairbrush.

6   The stories the boys tell in the coatroom, they're not true. You lean against the schoolyard fence alone with your eyes closed as if no one was watching, as if no one could see you standing there, Sally. What do you think about when you close your eyes like that? And why do you always have to go straight home after school? You become a different Sally. You pull your skirt straight, you rub the blue paint off your eyelids. You don't laugh, Sally. You look at your feet and walk fast to the house you can't come out from.

7   Sally, do you sometimes wish you didn't have to go home? Do you wish your feet would one day keep walking and take you far away from Mango Street, far away and maybe your feet would stop in front of a house, a nice one with flowers and big windows and steps for you to climb up two by two upstairs to where a room is waiting for you. And if you opened the little window latch and gave it a shove, the windows would swing open, all the sky would.

## WHAT SALLY SAID

8   He never hits me hard. She said her mama rubs lard on all the places where it hurts. Then at school she'd say she fell. That's where all the blue places come from. That's why her skin is always scarred.

9   But who believes her. A girl that big, a girl who comes in with her pretty face all beaten and black can't be falling off the stairs. He never hits me hard.

10  But Sally doesn't tell about that time he hit her with his hands just like a dog, she said, like if I was an animal. He thinks I'm going to run away like his sisters who made the family ashamed. Just because I'm a daughter, and then she doesn't say.

11  Sally was going to get permission to stay with us a little and one Thursday she came finally with a sack full of clothes and a paper bag of sweetbread her mama sent. And would've stayed too except when the dark came her father, whose eyes were little from crying, knocked on the door and said please come back, this is the last time. And she said Daddy and went home.

12  Then we didn't need to worry. Until one day Sally's father catches her talking to a boy and the next day she doesn't come to school. And the next. Until the way Sally tells it, he just went crazy, he just forgot he was her father between the buckle and the belt.

13  You're not my daughter, you're not my daughter. And then he broke into his hands.

### LINOLEUM ROSES

**linoleum**
a floor covering
similar to vinyl

14    Sally got married like we knew she would, young and not ready but married just the same. She met a marshmallow salesman at a school bazaar, and she married him in another state where it's legal to get married before eighth grade. She has her husband and her house now, her pillowcases and her plates. She says she is in love, but I think she did it to escape.

15    Sally says she likes being married because now she gets to buy her own things when her husband gives her money. She is happy, except sometimes her husband gets angry and once he broke the door where his foot went through, though most days he is okay. Except he won't let her talk on the telephone. And he doesn't let her look out the window. And he doesn't like her friends, so nobody gets to visit her unless he is working.

16    She sits at home because she is afraid to go outside without his permission. She looks at all the things they own: the towels and the toaster, the alarm clock and the drapes. She likes looking at the walls, at how neatly their corners meet, the linoleum roses on the floor, the ceiling smooth as wedding cake.

| Exercise 17 |
|---|

## Check Your Understanding

Based on Reading 3, decide whether each of the following statements is true or false.

_____  1. The narrator of the story is another girl about Sally's age.

_____  2. The narrator's name is Cheryl.

_____  3. Sally wears makeup at home.

_____  4. Sally's father beats her up.

_____  5. Sally stays with the narrator's family for a week.

_____  6. Sally's father never hits her again after she comes back from the narrator's house.

_____  7. Sally runs away from home and stays at the narrator's house.

_____  8. As soon as Sally turns 18, she gets married.

_____  9. At the end of the story, Sally has her own house.

_____  10. The narrator is jealous of Sally's new life.

**Exercise 18**

## Organize to Learn: Analyze Fiction

Use the questions in the Reader's Tip (pages 257–258) to organize this story and understand it.

1. Character
   a. What kind of person is the narrator of the story (the "I" who is telling the story)?

   _____

   _____

   _____

   _____

   b. What kind of person is Sally?

   _____

   _____

   c. What kind of person is Sally's father?

   _____

   d. What kind of person is Sally's husband?

   _____

2. Plot: List the main events of Sally's story in order:
   a. _____

   b. _____

   _____

   c. _____

   d. _____

   e. _____

   f. _____

   g. _____

   h. _____

3. Setting
    a. Where and when does each section of the story take place?

_____

_____

_____

_____

    b. In paragraph 7, the narrator describes a house that she wants for Sally. In the final section, Sally has her own house. Does Sally's house match the dream that the narrator has for her?

_____

_____

_____

4. Point of View
    a. Through whose eyes is the story told?

_____

    b. How would the story be different if it were told through Sally's eyes? her father's eyes?

_____

_____

_____

_____

5. Theme
    a. Why did Sally get married so young?

_____

_____

    b. Why did Cisneros title the last vignette "Linoleum Roses?"

_____

_____

_____

_____

_____

_____

**Exercise 19**

Identify Images and Figurative Language

Based on Reading 3, answer the following questions.

1. In the first paragraph, Cisneros uses three similes to describe Sally. What are the similes, and what do they tell the reader about Sally?

   a. _____

   b. _____

   c. _____

   _____

   _____

   _____

2. In paragraph 7, what does Mango Street represent and what does the house symbolize? What two images does Cisneros connect in the final sentence of that paragraph? What is the meaning of those images?

   _____

   _____

   _____

   _____

   _____

   _____

3. What similes does Cisneros use in paragraph 10? What do these comparisons show?

   _____

   _____

   _____

**Exercise 20**

Reflect and Write

Think about what you read in Reading 3 and what you already know about difficult family relationships. Answer the following questions, and prepare to discuss them with your classmates.

1. Do you think Sally was happy at the end of the story? Why or why not?

_____

_____

_____

_____

_____

2. What would you have done if you had been in Sally's place, or what advice would you have given her?

_____

_____

_____

_____

_____

3. This story takes place in the 1960s. Would Sally's story be different if it took place in the 2010s? If not, why not? If so, how would it be different? Explain.

_____

_____

_____

_____

_____

4. In paragraphs 2 and 4 of this story, adults predict "trouble" and "danger" for Sally. Why did adults judge Sally in this way? Is it trouble to be beautiful? Is it dangerous to wear black? What stereotypes did Sally face, and was she able to break free of them? On a separate piece of paper, write a short essay describing how stereotypes and oppression based on gender affected Sally as well as other girls you have known. To what extent do gender stereotypes and gender-based power relationships influence women's lives today?

## Write About It

Find a women's magazine, such as *Elle* or *Cosmopolitan*, and a magazine for men, such as *GQ* or *Esquire* (or visit their websites). Compare the magazines (or websites). Write three to four paragraphs explaining how the magazines (or websites) are similar and how they are different in their portrayal of women and men. For your paragraphs, focus on gender roles as portrayed in one of the following: the advertisements, an article or story in each, or the photographs in each. Be sure to discuss what the reader can infer is being communicated about gender roles from the visual and written content of the magazines. Give your essay a good title. Attach a copy of the photos, advertisements, or articles that you are using for your essay.

# Chapter Review

| Put It Together: Inferences and Reading Literature | |
| --- | --- |
| Skills and Concepts | Explanation |
| **Inference** (see pages 231–232) | A reasonable assumption based on the information we have |
| **Autobiography** (see page 236) | A story of one's own life experience |
| **Connotation** (see page 246) | Positive or negative feelings suggested by a word |
| **Denotation** (see page 246) | The dictionary or literal meaning of a word |
| **Irony** (see page 248) | Saying one thing and meaning another |
| **Image** (see page 249) | A "sense picture" that uses words to describe something in terms of sight, taste, hearing, touch, and smell |
| **Figurative Language** (see page 249) | Direct or implied comparisons made to create an image |
| **Simile** (see pages 249–250) | A comparison between unlike things, using *like* or *as* |
| **Metaphor** (see page 251) | An implied comparison |
| **Characters** (see page 257) | The people in a story |
| **Plot** (see page 258) | The action of a story |

| Put It Together: Inferences and Reading Literature | |
|---|---|
| Skills and Concepts | Explanation |
| **Setting** (see page 258) | The time and place of a story |
| **Point of View** (see page 258) | The perspective from which a story is told |
| **Theme** (see page 258) | Interpretation of life experience based on the outcome of a story |

## CRITICAL REFLECTIONS IN THE CLASSROOM COMMUNITY

Answer the following questions, and prepare to discuss them with your classmates.

1. Describe relationships between men and women in your college or workplace.

   _____

   _____

   _____

   _____

2. List how you think relationships between men and women are different today from relationships in your parents' or grandparents' generations.

   _____

   _____

   _____

   _____

3. What stereotypes do you think people have about men and women and their roles?

   _____

   _____

   _____

   _____

   _____

## WORK THE WEB

As you have learned in Chapter 6, we use inferences to understand the meaning of a number of texts, including illustrations, poems, stories, and songs. The following exercise will give you further practice identifying imagery and figurative language and inferring meaning through analyzing song lyrics. A number of sites are devoted to providing the public with the lyrics of songs. For this exercise, find the lyrics to the following two songs, and then answer the questions below. (Go to any search engine, type in the name of the song and the songwriter(s), and you'll get links to many sites. You may also want to visit YouTube to see these songs performed.)

1. "Smoke Gets in Your Eyes," written by Jerome Kern and Otto Harbach and performed by the Platters and others

   a. What is love compared to in the song?

   _____

   b. Smoke is a central metaphor in this song. Explain the meaning of smoke and how it changes.

   _____

   _____

   _____

2. "A Boy Named Sue," written by Shel Silverstein and performed by Johnny Cash and others

   a. What do we learn about the narrator of "A Boy Named Sue," the way he views his father, and their relationship based on the images Shel Silverstein uses and the plot of the song?

   _____

   _____

   _____

   _____

   b. What is the significance of the name Sue to the narrator of the song, and how has that name made him the man he is today?

   _____

   _____

   _____

   _____

   _____

   _____

   _____

Name _____ Date _____

# Black Men and Public Space*

— BRENT STAPLES

**The following reading about how black men are perceived is based on the author's own experiences as a graduate student and as a journalist. The vocabulary he uses is quite difficult, but you will find that you can identify his thesis and supporting points even though you may not understand every word. As you read, compare Staples's experiences of being in public places to your own. Also, pay attention to his use of metaphors and descriptive language as he relates the incidents that support his thesis.**

1    My first victim was a woman—white, well dressed, probably in her early twenties. I came upon her late one evening on a deserted street in Hyde Park, a relatively affluent neighborhood in an otherwise mean, impoverished section of Chicago. As I swung onto the avenue behind her, there seemed to be a discreet, <u>uninflammatory</u> distance between us. Not so. She cast back a worried glance. To her, the youngish black man—a broad six feet two inches with a beard and billowing hair, both hands shoved into the pockets of a bulky military jacket—seemed <u>menacingly</u> close. After a few more quick glimpses, she picked up her pace and was soon running in earnest. Within seconds she disappeared into a cross street.

2    That was more than a decade ago, I was twenty-two years old, a graduate student newly arrived at the University of Chicago. It was in the echo of that terrified woman's footfalls that I first began to know the <u>unwieldy</u> inheritance I'd come into—the ability to alter public space in ugly ways. It was clear that she thought herself the <u>quarry</u> of a mugger, a rapist, or worse. Suffering a bout of insomnia, however, I was stalking sleep, not defenseless wayfarers. As a softy who is scarcely able to take a knife to a raw chicken—let alone hold one to a person's throat—I was surprised, embarrassed, and dismayed all at once. Her flight made me feel like an accomplice in tyranny. It also made it clear that I was indistinguishable from the muggers who occasionally seeped into the area from the surrounding ghetto. That first encounter, and those that followed, signified that a vast, unnerving gulf lay between nighttime pedestrians—particularly women—and me. And I soon gathered that being perceived as dangerous is a hazard in itself. I only needed to turn a corner into a dicey situation, or crowd some frightened, armed person in a foyer somewhere, or make an errant move after being pulled over by a policeman. Where fear and weapons meet—and they often do in urban America—there is always the possibility of death.

3    In that first year, my first away from my hometown, I was to become thoroughly familiar with the language of fear. At dark, shadowy intersections, I could cross in front of a car stopped at a traffic light and elicit the *thunk, thunk, thunk, thunk* of the driver—black, white, male, or female—hammering down the door locks. On less traveled streets after dark I grew accustomed to but never comfortable with people crossing to the other side of the street rather than pass me. Then there were the standard unpleasantries with policemen, doormen, bouncers, cabdrivers, and others whose business it is to screen out troublesome individuals *before* there is any nastiness. . . .

4    After dark, on the warrenlike streets of Brooklyn where I live, I often see women who fear the worst from me. They seem to have set their faces on neutral, and with their purse straps strung across their chests bandolier-style, they forged ahead as though

**alter**
change

**signified**
meant

**unnerving**
upsetting

**perceived**
considered

---

* "From "Black Men and Public Space" by Brent Staples. Reprinted by permission of Brent Staples.

bracing themselves against being tackled. I understand, of course, that the danger they perceive is not a hallucination. Women are particularly vulnerable to street violence, and young black males are drastically overrepresented among the perpetrators of that violence. Yet these truths are no <u>solace</u> against the kind of <u>alienation</u> that comes of being ever the suspect, a fearsome entity with whom pedestrians avoid making eye contact.

**entity**
thing

5     It is not altogether clear to me how I reached the ripe old age of twenty-two without being conscious of the lethality nighttime pedestrians <u>attributed</u> to me. Perhaps it was because in Chester, Pennsylvania, the small, angry industrial town where I came of age in the 1960s, I was scarcely noticeable against a backdrop of gang warfare, street knifings, and murders. I grew up one of the good boys, had perhaps a half-dozen fistfights. In retrospect, my shyness of combat has clear sources.

**lethality**
deadliness

**in retrospect**
looking back in time

6     As a boy, I saw countless tough guys locked away; I have since buried several, too. They were babies, really—a teenage cousin, a brother of twenty-two, a childhood friend in his mid-twenties—all gone down in episodes of bravado played out in the streets. I came to doubt the virtues of intimidation early on. I chose, perhaps unconsciously, to remain a shadow—timid, but a survivor.

**bravado**
false bravery

**perilous**
dangerous

7     The fearsomeness mistakenly <u>attributed</u> to me in public places often has a perilous flavor. The most frightening of these confusions occurred in the late 1970s and early 1980s, when I worked as a journalist in Chicago. One day, rushing into the office of a magazine I was writing for with a deadline story in hand, I was mistaken for a burglar. The office manager called security and, with an <u>ad hoc</u> posse, pursued me through the labyrinthine halls, nearly to my editor's door. I had no way of proving who I was. I could only move briskly toward the company of someone who knew me.

**pursued**
chased

8     Another time I was on assignment for a local paper and killing time before an interview. I entered a jewelry store on the city's affluent Near North Side. The proprietor excused herself and returned with an enormous red Doberman pinscher straining at the end of a leash. She stood, the dog extended toward me, silent to my questions, her eyes bulging nearly out of her head. I took a cursory look around, nodded, and bade her good night.

**proprietor**
owner

9     Relatively speaking, however, I never fared as badly as another black male journalist. He went to nearby Waukegan, Illinois, a couple of summers ago to work on a story about a murderer who was born there. Mistaking the reporter for the killer, police officers hauled him from his car at gunpoint and but for his press credentials would probably have tried to book him. Such episodes are not uncommon. Black men trade tales like this all the time.

10    Over the years, I learned to smother the rage I felt at so often being taken for a criminal. Not to do so would surely have led to madness. I now take precautions to make myself less threatening. I move about with care, particularly late in the evening. I give wide <u>berth</u> to nervous people on subway platforms during the wee hours, particularly when I have exchanged business clothes for jeans. If I happen to be entering a building behind some people who appear skittish, I may walk by, letting them clear the lobby before I return, so as not to seem to be following them. I have been calm and extremely congenial on those rare occasions when I've been pulled over by the police.

**skittish**
nervous

**employ**
use

11    And on late-evening <u>constitutionals</u> I employ what has proved to be an excellent tension-reducing measure: I whistle melodies from Beethoven and Vivaldi and the more popular classical composers. Even steely New Yorkers hunching toward nighttime destinations seem to relax, and occasionally they even join in the tune. Virtually everybody seems to sense that a mugger wouldn't be warbling bright, sunny selections from Vivaldi's *Four Seasons*. It is my equivalent of the cowbell that hikers wear when they know they are in bear country.

# Work with Words

Use context clues, your knowledge of word parts, and if necessary, your dictionary skills, to determine the meaning of the following words underlined in the reading. The paragraph number is provided in case you want to check the context.

1. *Uninflammatory* (par. 1)
   a. not causing excitement or anger
   b. not causing fire
   c. not causing inflammation

2. *Menacingly* (par. 1)
   a. in an extreme manner
   b. in a threatening manner
   c. in a comfortable manner

3. *Unwieldy* (par. 2)
   a. powerful
   b. predetermined
   c. difficult to manage

4. *Quarry* (par. 2)
   a. diamond-shaped pane of glass
   b. game hunted with hawks
   c. something or someone being hunted

5. *Solace* (par. 4)
   a. source of relief
   b. source of additional worry
   c. certainty

6. *Alienation* (par. 4)
   a. feeling of self-worth
   b. isolation
   c. self-esteem

7. *Attributed* (par. 5 and par. 7)
   a. thought of as characteristic
   b. thought of as distinct
   c. thought of indifferently

8. *Ad hoc* (par. 7)
   a. improvised
   b. planned
   c. terrifying

9. *Berth* (par. 10)
   a. a place to sleep on a boat or train
   b. safe distance
   c. normal distance

10. *Constitutionals* (par. 11)
    a. things related to the Constitution
    b. things related to the government principles
    c. walks taken for one's health

## Exercise 2

### Check Your Understanding

Based on the reading, Staples's "Black Men and Public Space," choose the best answer to the following multiple-choice questions.

1. Which of the following is the best topic for the reading?
    a. stereotypes about black men
    b. how best to exercise if you're a black man
    c. problems of black men

2. Which of the following sentences best states the main idea (thesis) of the reading?
    a. Black men are frequently guilty of crimes, and that's why people are afraid of them.
    b. Black men are frequently stereotyped as being criminals and dangerous.
    c. Educated black men are more likely to suffer from discrimination than any other group.

3. We can infer that Staples begins his essay by referring to his "first victim" to
    a. get our attention and recognition that he is seen as a criminal by people who don't know him.
    b. explain how he got into trouble with the law in the first place.
    c. make sure the reader knows that he is not a criminal.

4. When the author writes, "I was twenty-two years old, a graduate student newly arrived at the University of Chicago" we can infer that
    a. he was a poor student.
    b. he had a scholarship.
    c. he was not a criminal.

5. Staples supports his main idea (thesis) by
    a. providing personal examples and examples of acquaintances of people's fear of black men.
    b. demonstrating that he is a well-respected journalist and would therefore be a reliable source of information.
    c. explaining how it feels to be perceived as a dangerous person.

6. Although Staples had seen friends and family die young in the streets of Chester, Pennsylvania, he portrays himself as
    a. self-confident and tough.
    b. timid, but a survivor.
    c. a mere shadow.

7. Which of the following is *not* an example of Staples's "ability to alter public space in ugly ways"?
    a. People crossing the street when they see him.
    b. Shop owners getting their Doberman pinschers to scare him out of the store.
    c. Recognition he receives as an excellent journalist.

8. For Staples, knowing that he is perceived as a threat to others is
   a. not a major problem.
   b. extremely painful.
   c. simply a philosophical problem.

9. Why does Staples whistle melodies from classical music when he goes out at night?
   a. because he enjoys whistling.
   b. to make himself less threatening.
   c. to help him pace his walk.

10. In the last line of the essay, Staples writes that his whistling is his "equivalent of the cowbell that hikers wear when they know they are in bear country." We can infer that hikers wear cowbells
    a. so bears will hear them coming and stay out of their way.
    b. to make their hike more pleasant.
    c. so bears will come to them.

---

**Exercise 3**

### Interpret Figurative Language

Based on the reading, answer the following questions about Staples's use of figurative language.

1. In paragraph 2, Staples reacts to the frightened woman's running from him by writing, "Suffering a bout of insomnia, however, I was stalking sleep, not defenseless wayfarers." What does the word *stalking* usually refer to? How does Staples use it here, and what is the effect?

   _____

   _____

   _____

   _____

   _____

2. In paragraph 3, Staples writes about "the language of fear." He is referring to things that people do when they are afraid. What examples does he give in the paragraph?

   _____

   _____

   _____

   _____

3. Staples writes that women who are afraid of him "seem to have set their faces on neutral" (par. 4). What image does this create, and what is its effect?

_____

_____

_____

_____

4. Staples writes "I chose, perhaps unconsciously, to remain a shadow—timid, but a survivor." (par. 6) What associations do you make with the word *shadow* and how does his use of this word affect our understanding?

_____

_____

_____

_____

5. In paragraph 10, Staples writes, "Over the years, I learned to smother the rage I felt at so often being taken for a criminal." What does *smother* usually refer to? How does the use of *smother* make us understand his emotions?

_____

_____

_____

_____

**Exercise 4**

## Reflect

Think about what you read in "Black Men and Public Space" and what you already know about stereotypes. Then based on your reading and your previous knowledge answer the following questions.

1. In what ways do you think people's reactions would be different toward a black woman in a public space?

_____

_____

_____

2. How do you think a person's style of dress affects people's initial reactions? Explain your opinion with some examples.

_____

_____

_____

3. Have you ever been in a situation where you felt people made positive or negative assumptions about you on the basis of stereotypes of your gender or ethnicity?

_____

_____

_____

4. Have you ever avoided somebody you didn't know because of assumptions you made about that person? What were the circumstances, and what did you do? Why did you have those assumptions?

_____

_____

_____

LIVING IN A DIVERSE SOCIETY

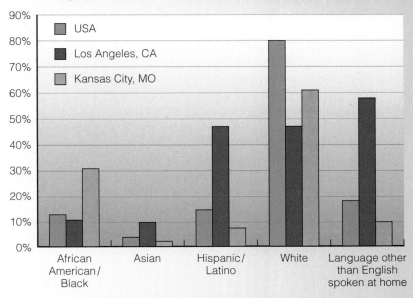

Demographic Data in the United States, Los Angeles, and Kansas City

Source: U.S. Census Bureau. USA data are from 2006; Los Angeles and Kansas City data are from the 2000 census.
"White" includes people of Hispanic descent as well as those who are not Hispanic.

*We must learn to live together as brothers, or we are going to perish together as fools. —Dr. Martin Luther King Jr.*

1. Compare Los Angeles and Kansas City to the United States as a whole and to each other in terms of ethnic and language background. Which statistics are most surprising? Explain.

2. What ethnic groups are represented at your college? What other types of diversity exist on your campus?

3. What does the quotation mean? How does it relate to the bar graph?

# Prepare to Read

Americans come from everywhere in the world. Even Native Americans are descendants of immigrants from Asia who crossed into North America some 20,000 years ago. After those immigrants came Europeans, Africans, and then Asians again, as well as people from Mexico and Central and South America. Today more than 11 percent of the U.S. population was born elsewhere, and about 18 percent of us speak a language other than English at home. We are diverse in many other ways as well. More than 50 million people in the United States have a disability. We also differ in age, religion, and sexual orientation.

How can those of us who live here—from so many different cultures and backgrounds—get along?

In this chapter, you will read about the diversity of people in the United States, and learn to

- Recognize fact and opinion
- Understand the use and sources of facts
- Recognize an author's worldview, point of view, and purpose for writing
- Identify bias and tone

In the process of acquiring these skills, you will read about how our identities are formed and how our perceptions of people who are different from us influence our lives and our society.

In Minneapolis, this predominantly Muslim Girl Scout troop gives girls from Somalia a chance to fit in.
Allen Brison-Smith/The New York Times/Redux Pictures

**Reading 1**

# Identity in Transformation*

—Yasmin Ahmed

**Yasmin Ahmed was a student at San Diego City College when she wrote this essay. She was taking advanced courses in sciences but volunteered to write something about her experiences for *A Community of Readers* because she wanted people to know what life is like for people like her—refugees from different parts of the world who have adopted the United States as their home.**

1   I spent the first years of my life growing up in East Africa. I was born in Somalia, but the civil war forced us to flee and live as refugees in Kenya and Ethiopia. When I was seven years old, I immigrated to the United States. At first, getting adjusted to a completely new culture was a shock, but I have since worked to integrate Western culture into the culture of my family and my heritage. I now lead a life with two different cultures wrapped around each other. But I am not the only one whose life is like this. There are many of us; we are East African Muslim girls struggling with the process of assimilation into American culture. Immigrating to the West has changed us for the better, but it has also introduced us to a puzzling, complex world.

**assimilation**
adaptation to the characteristics of another culture

2   Back home in East Africa, life for most young girls is much different from life for girls in the United States. The future of a girl in Somalia is determined by her family, culture, and religion. Girls are expected to grow up to fulfill their duties as mothers and wives and to remain disciplined, devout, respectful, and shy. From early childhood, girls are aware

---

*"Identity in Transformation" by Yasmin Ahmed.

that their primary goal is to get married, and they are usually married by the time they are sixteen. Families prepare their daughters for arranged marriages to older, already-established men, often men whom the girls have neither met nor seen. Once married, women are expected to cook, clean, bear children, and nurture the family, while men are expected to provide an income and the leadership for the family to survive. These roles limit the educational possibilities for girls. Education is scarce for most of the Somali population, especially those living in the countryside, but for citizens of the city, educational opportunities can, with effort, be pursued for boys. For girls, the paths are virtually closed.

**disparity**
difference

3    The disparity between the way women and girls are viewed in Somalia and the opportunities they have in the United States made me appreciate the chance to come to the United States and share in the experiences of real American girls. Immigration to the United States provided me and my family with a life that was very different from anything we had ever known. As they incorporated the cultural and social expectations of the United States, my family changed their expectations for me. Equal opportunities were presented to me in ways that I had never dreamed before. I went to the same schools as my brothers, and my parents accepted the idea that I could be educated and even successful in a career. Marriage no longer became the first concern for girls, and I am so happy that I'm not at the moment being pressured to get married even though I'm already eighteen.

**incorporated**
integrated

4    In spite of the changes in our families, though, we didn't forget who we are. Our social and cultural identity as Somali girls remained and at the same time was lost within the rushing of American crowds. We didn't picture ourselves different from anyone else, and in many ways we still don't. We watched the same television shows, listened to the same music, gossiped about the same celebrities, and bought magazines just to see the latest fashions. We led the same lives as other American children; nobody made us feel different. We were accepted as Somali Muslim girls living life with a Western flair. We were not discriminated against for who we were. At times we were asked curious questions, especially about how we dress, but nothing out of the ordinary.

5    Then, with the devastating attacks of September 11, everything changed for us, as well as for the country around us. Like our fellow Americans we lived life the next few days with our noses glued to the TV, fascinated by the reports, horror-struck by the death tolls. Like all Americans, we mourned for the innocent dead, hated the terrorists who killed them, and decried the effects of this tragic day on our country and on our lives. We were reminded of the civil war taking place back home in Somalia, and we remembered how tragedy can corrupt daily life.

6    Though we endured the sadness of September 11 just like all Americans, the weeks, months, and even years that followed were no longer the same for us Muslim girls. None of the terrorists was Somali, but we began experiencing prejudice and discrimination as we had never known existed. People who never cared to look twice at us were now staring at us. The scarf that each of us wore on her head as an expression of our religious beliefs became a center of attention and a symbol of terrorism. Our classmates began to whisper behind our backs, and some would go so far as to yell out "Terrorists!" or "Where is your Uncle Osama?" For those of us who wore black, kids would comment, "Here comes little Darth Vader." It was frustrating to hear such things out of the mouths of my friends and classmates; I can't even imagine where the idea of "Uncle Osama" or "little

Darth Vader" came from. The most unbelievable change was that our teachers excluded us from the discussion of current and world events and looked at us suspiciously. Suddenly, we were less American because we chose to cover our heads, because we dressed like the women in the countries that our country was at war with. We were easier to identify, at least on the street, than Muslim men and therefore more likely to be discriminated against.

7    The ridicule and disdain we experienced were so hurtful that some of my friends chose to stay home from school. Others became more conservative in covering themselves just to show they were proud of their religion. The effect of the prejudice we endured in some ways parallels what we faced in East Africa—this time not because of our gender, but because of our religious affiliation. Now we speculate what people might be thinking about us when they see us: do they think of us as a threat ("Could she be a sister of a terrorist?") or as a victim ("Her husband or family must force her to wear that scarf, poor little thing")? Before we felt like American girls from another country. Now we feel we're first seen as Muslims (read terrorist), then as women, and last as human beings.

**speculate**
guess

8    Muslim men have been more discriminated against by government agencies. Men older than sixteen from Muslim, Arab, and South Asian countries were required to report to the office of Immigration and Naturalization Services. Some were deported for visa violations, and some were detained for a long time, out of contact with the outside world, without knowing the charges against them and without having access to lawyers. Though the government has not revealed the total number of people detained since 9/11, the American Civil Liberties Union estimates that there were between three and five thousand Muslim, Arab, and South Asian detainees, none of whom had been charged with terrorist-related crimes.[1] It's just wrong to lump us all into one category. When Timothy McVeigh bombed the Oklahoma City Federal Building, nobody began rounding up white men or making stupid comments to their sisters. That would have been ridiculous, of course. So why don't people recognize that it's ridiculous to suspect all Muslims, or people who are Arab (and not necessarily Muslim), or people from South Asia?

9    At a time when Americans needed to lean on each other for support and comfort, we were leaning on empty space. We felt the pressure of being attacked from both sides: as Americans, we too had been attacked by the terrorists; as Muslims, we were now being attacked by our neighbors, harassed by people on the streets, and targeted by law enforcement agencies. In what is supposed to be a melting pot of various immigrant cultures that contributed to what is now America, we, as Muslims, are the ingredient that causes suspicion. It is only those people who know the truth about who we are, the Americans who get to know us as individuals, who can get through this wall of prejudice. But my identity as a Muslim American has changed forever since the attacks of September 11, 2001.

**Note**

1.  Many men from our mosque had to report to the immigration authorities, but not Somali men with refugee status in the United States. Other men have been interviewed by the Federal Bureau of Investigation.

**Exercise 1**

## Recall and Discuss

Based on Reading 1, answer the following questions and prepare to discuss them with your classmates.

1. In what ways was Ahmed's life transformed when she came to the United States? How was her life different from what it would have been like had she remained in Somalia?

   _____

   _____

   _____

   _____

2. How did Ahmed's life change after 9/11?

   _____

   _____

3. Why does Ahmed refer to Timothy McVeigh, the man convicted of bombing the Oklahoma City Federal Building?

   _____

   _____

   _____

4. At the end of her essay, what does Ahmed suggest would reduce the prejudice that she has experienced? Do you agree with her?

   _____

   _____

5. Now that you have read Ahmed's essay, look at the photograph of young Somali women on page 277. What do you think about the photo now that you know some of the experiences of these girls in the United States? How does the photo connect with the title of the reading?

   _____

   _____

   _____

# Fact and Opinion

As an active reader, you reflect on what you have read and you think critically about the information you have received. One important way to evaluate that information is by deciding whether it is based on fact or opinion—or both.

## FACT

**fact**
a piece of information that is verifiable

**verifiable**
can be checked

A **fact** is a piece of information that is verifiable, which means it can be checked. The easiest facts to identify are statements that include data such as dates, statistics, or numerical results of a study. Here is an example of a factual statement that includes data. "In 1905, the number of immigrants to the United States topped 1 million for the first time." If you read this sentence in an American history text-book, you would assume that it is correct because it is the kind of figure that could be obtained from immigration records. Statements of fact can also be easily checked for accuracy. For example, Yasmin Ahmed, in "Identity in Transformation" on pages 277 through 279, says that the civil war in Somalia "forced us to flee." We could verify information about the civil war and refugees leaving Somalia by checking in an encyclopedia or textbook or on a reputable site on the Web.

## OPINION

**opinion**
an interpretation of facts; an expression of beliefs or feelings

An **opinion** is an interpretation of information. It is also the expression of beliefs or feelings. Unlike statements of fact, statements of opinion do not usually provide data, or if they do, the data are used to support the opinion. The most obvious opinion statement includes language that acknowledges the opinion, such as "in my opinion," or "Ahmed thinks." An example of an opinion that Ahmed expresses in her essay is "Before we felt like American girls from another country. Now we feel we're first seen as Muslims (read terrorist), then as women, and last as human beings."

**value words**
words that indicate judgment

Another kind of opinion statement that is easy to recognize includes a value judgment, such as "Immigration is good for the United States" or Ahmed's statement "Immigrating to the West has changed us for the better, but it has also introduced us to a puzzling, complex world." **Value words** indicate judgment. Examples such as *good, bad, detrimental, positive, negative, terrific,* and *awful* are usually good indicators that an opinion is being expressed (see Table 7.1).

| Table 7.1    Facts and Opinions | |
|---|---|
| Facts | Opinions |
| Data | Interpretation of information |
| Statistics | Expression of beliefs, feelings, value judgments |
| Verifiable information | Language that acknowledges an opinion, value words |

**Exercise 2**

### Report Facts and Opinions

In the columns below, write three facts and three opinions about your family.

| Facts | Opinions |
|-------|----------|
| 1. | 1. |
| 2. | 2. |
| 3. | 3. |

## RECOGNIZING FACT AND OPINION

Often a writer mixes facts and opinions or uses facts to support opinions. For example, in the following excerpt from Reading 1, Ahmed uses a combination of factual statements and opinions. (We added the numbers in parentheses and the italics.)

> (1) Muslim men have been more discriminated against by government agencies. (2) Men older than age sixteen from Muslim, Arab, and South Asian countries were required to report to the office of Immigration and Naturalization Services. (3) Some were deported for visa violations, and some were detained for a long time, out of contact with the outside world, without knowing the charges against them and without having access to lawyers. (4) Though the government has not revealed the total number of people detained since 9/11, the American Civil Liberties Union estimates that there are between three and five thousand Muslim, Arab, and South Asian detainees, none of whom have been charged with terrorist-related crimes.[1] (5) It's just *wrong* to lump us all into one category. When Timothy McVeigh bombed the Oklahoma City Federal Building, nobody began rounding up white men or making stupid comments to their sisters. (6) That would have been *ridiculous*, of course. (7) So why don't people recognize that it's *ridiculous* to suspect all Muslims, or people who are Arab (and not necessarily Muslim), or people from South Asia? (Ahmed, "Identity in Transformation")

The words we've italicized in this paragraph—*wrong* and *ridiculous*—provide judgments or opinions about the topic. These particular words reflect how Ahmed felt about some events in the post-9/11 world. Sentences 3 and 4 are predominantly factual because the information could be checked in newspaper articles reporting on the activities of the Immigration and Naturalization Services or statements of the American Civil Liberties Union. Sentences 5, 6, and 7 are predominantly opinion because they express how the author interprets the facts. As you read, you should be going through a natural filtering process to distinguish between the facts and the opinions.

**Exercise 3**

## Recognize Fact and Opinion

Review these sentences from or based on Reading 1, and label them *F* if they are primarily factual and *O* if they are primarily opinion. Be aware of value words that influence your decision.

_____ 1. Back home in East Africa, life for most young girls is much different from life for girls in the United States.

_____ 2. Education is scarce for most of the Somali population, especially those living in the countryside, but for citizens of the city, educational opportunities can, with effort, be pursued for boys.

_____ 3. The opportunities women have in the United States made me appreciate the chance to come to the United States and share in the experiences of real American girls.

_____ 4. I am so happy that I'm not at the moment being pressured to get married, even though I'm already eighteen.

_____ 5. We didn't picture ourselves different from anyone else, and in many ways we still don't.

_____ 6. None of the terrorists was Somali.

_____ 7. Suddenly, we were less American because we chose to cover our heads, because we dressed like the women in the countries that our country was at war with.

_____ 8. Some of my friends chose to stay home from school.

_____ 9. No matter how anybody treated us, most of us became even more proud of our religion.

_____ 10. It is only those people who know the truth about who we are, the Americans who get to know us as individuals, who can get through this wall of prejudice.

**Exercise 4**

## Recognize Fact and Opinion

The following statements from four American history textbooks deal with issues central to the American colonies—immigration and slavery. Read each statement and indicate whether you think it is primarily fact or opinion.

_____ 1. Between 1700 and 1760 the colonial population mushroomed from 250,000 to 1.6 million persons—and 2.5 million by 1775. (Martin et al., *America and Its Peoples*)

_____ 2. "Pennsylvania, founded by the English, [will] become a colony of aliens, who will shortly be so numerous as to Germanize us, instead of our Anglifying them," since they "will never adopt our language or customs any more than they can acquire our complexion." (Benjamin Franklin, quoted in Martin et al., *America and Its Peoples*)

_____ 3. Many destitute Germans crossed the Atlantic as "redemptioners.". . . [F]amilies migrated together and shippers promised heads of households after a few days' time, upon arrival in America, to find some person or group to pay for the family's passage in return for a set number of years of labor (usually three to six years per family member). (Martin et al., *America and Its Peoples*)

_____ 4. Slaves and indentured servants made up most of the incoming human tide after 1713. The traffic in servants became a regular part of the commerce linking Europe and America. (Nash et al., *The American People*)

_____ 5. Shipboard conditions for servants worsened in the eighteenth century and were hardly better than aboard the slave ships. Crammed between decks in stifling air, servants suffered from smallpox and fevers, rotten food, impure water, cold, and lice. (Nash et al., *The American People*)

_____ 6. Carolina's demand for slaves was so great that Charleston became the major port of entry for Africans brought to the American mainland from Africa and the Caribbean. By the time of the American Revolution almost one hundred thousand slaves had entered through Charleston harbor, most of them bound for the rice-growing regions of the colony. (Horton and Horton, *Hard Road to Freedom*)

_____ 7. Slavery made possible the existence of a gracious and cultured upper class that, with its leisure, guarded the highest refinements of human achievement. (Conlin, *American Past*)

_____ 8. "Men who emigrate are from the nature of their circumstances, the most active, hardy, daring, bold and resolute spirits, and probably the most mischievous also." (An Englishman quoted in Nash et al., *The American People*)

_____ 9. All told, as many as 21 million people were captured in West Africa between 1700 and 1850: some 9 million among them entered the Americas as slaves, but millions died before or during the Atlantic crossing. (Davidson et al., *Nation of Nations*)

_____ 10. Charles Woodmason, an Anglican missionary in the Carolina backcountry, lamented the arrival of "5 or 6000 Ignorant, mean, worthless, beggarly Irish Presbyterians, the Scum of the Earth, the Refuse of Mankind," who "delighted in a low, lazy, sluttish, heathenish, hellish life." (Quoted in Davidson et al., *Nation of Nations*)

# Evaluating Facts

Although facts can be verified, they may not always tell the whole truth. The way facts are presented can sometimes distort the conclusions that you might draw from them. For example, public health officials know that the way risk statistics are presented makes a difference in how people react to them. Saying "0.7 percent of people will contract a certain disease" does not make an impact. But if the information is given as "7 out of 1,000 people will contract a certain disease," people regard the risk as much greater and take the warning more seriously—even though the information is the same.

Other questions to ask yourself in evaluating facts are: (1) What are the sources of the facts? and (2) Which facts are included and which are omitted?

## WHAT ARE THE SOURCES OF THE FACTS?

In many types of readings, especially in scholarly works, you will find the sources of information in endnotes or references that appear in parentheses after a statement. Sometimes this information will be in a bibliography or in a section of credits. In this textbook you can find the credits at the bottom of the first page of a reading to find out who gave permission to use this material.

Often the organization sponsoring the reading is a good indication of the source, and knowing its agenda can help you evaluate the facts. For example, when legislation is proposed to reduce greenhouse gases by improving the fuel efficiency of cars—important for reducing global warming—the auto industry responds by saying that the proposals are "costly and ineffective." An important question would be, "Costly to whom?" Increasing the fuel efficiency of cars, sport-utility vehicles, and trucks could very likely be a savings to owners, who would end up spending much less money on gas. These cars might be more costly, though, to manufacture (although some consumer advocates say that is not true), and higher prices might reduce sales. Because the auto industry perceives emission controls and fuel efficiency to be against its interests, it organizes its research and uses statistics to prove its position. Consumer advocacy groups, however, counter the auto industry by asserting that vehicles have already been developed that are more fuel efficient, safer, and even less expensive to produce than what is on the market today. And these groups also have studies and statistics to back up their assertions. As an alert and informed reader, it is up to you to evaluate the information you get. Recognizing the source of the information can be a clue to you that the facts are being presented to make you have a particular opinion—and only that opinion.

**Exercise 5**

### Consider the Source

Look through some newspapers and magazines. Select an advertisement that includes what appear to be statements of fact.

1. On a separate sheet of paper, make a list showing which facts are given and explaining how they might be presented in a certain way to influence your thinking.

2. Make a second list of what additional facts you might like to have.

3. Bring in the advertisement or a photocopy of it to share with classmates and to explain your lists.

## WHICH FACTS ARE INCLUDED?

Another important way to evaluate facts is to examine which facts are actually included. It is obviously impossible for an author to include every known detail about a specific topic. As a reader, you expect experts in various disciplines to select the most important information for you to learn. However, what information an author chooses to include, or exclude, strongly influences your understanding of what you read. **Inclusiveness** has become an important criteria for readers to consider when they begin to evaluate a text. Some school districts, for example, do not want evolution to be included in biology textbooks. On the other hand, many school districts require that textbooks include information about people with disabilities, a group that has frequently gone unmentioned in history and social studies texts.

**inclusiveness**
which facts are
included

**Exercise 6**

### Check for Inclusiveness

Read the following two excerpts from political science textbooks. Both cover U.S. population and immigration in roughly the same periods, but they do not present the same information. Examine what is included and what is excluded by each author. Then use the data supplied by each text to complete the table titled "The Origins of Immigrants" (page 287). After the dates given in the table, write the types of immigrants that came into the United States at that time. The first row of the table has been done for you.

### From *Government in America*

The United States has always been a nation of immigrants. As Lyndon Johnson said, America is "not merely a nation but a nation of nations." All Americans except for American Indians are either descended from immigrants or are immigrants themselves. Today federal law allows up to 630,000 new immigrants to be legally admitted every year. This is equivalent to adding a city with the population of Washington, D.C., every year.

There have been three great waves of immigration to the United States.

- Before the Civil War, northwestern Europeans (English, Irish, Germans, and Scandinavians) constituted the first wave of immigration.
- After the Civil War, southern and eastern Europeans (Italians, Jews, Poles, Russians, and others) made up the second wave. This immigration reached its high point in the first decade of the twentieth century, with almost all of these immigrants passing through Ellis Island in New York (now a popular museum) as their first stop in the new world.
- After World War II, Hispanics (from Cuba, Puerto Rico, Central America, and Mexico) and Asians (from Vietnam, Korea, the Philippines, and elsewhere) made up the third wave. The 1980s saw the second largest number of immigrants of any decade in American history. (Edwards et al., *Government in America*)

### From *The Struggle for Democracy*

Ours is an ethnically, religiously, and racially diverse society. The white European Protestants, black slaves, and Native Americans who made up the bulk of the U.S. population when the first census was taken in 1790 were joined by Catholic immigrants from Germany and Ireland in the 1840s and 1850s. In the 1870s, large numbers of Chinese migrated to America, drawn by jobs in railroad construction. Around the turn of the century, most immigration was from eastern, central, and southern Europe, with its diverse ethnic, language, and religious groups. Today, most immigration is from Asia and Latin America. The most recent immigration, like all the previous ones, has both added to the rich language, cultural, and religious diversity of our nation and created significant political and social tensions. (Greenberg and Page, *The Struggle for Democracy*)

| Table 7.2 The Origins of Immigrants | |
|---|---|
| *Government in America* | *The Struggle for Democracy* |
| Before Civil War (to 1861) Northwestern European: English, Irish, Germans, Scandinavians | 1790 census European Protestants, black slaves, and Native Americans |
| | 1840s and 1850s |
| After Civil War (1865–) | 1870s |
| First decade of the twentieth century (1900–1910) | Turn of century (1900) |
| After World War II (1946–) | Today |

**Exercise 7**

Reflect

Based on Exercise 6, answer the following questions and prepare to discuss them with your classmates.

1. In what ways do the two sets of information differ?

   _____

   _____

2. Are these differences important? Explain your answer.

   _____

   _____

   _____

3. Later in the same section, the authors of *Government in America* describe the African Americans in the United States by saying, "These are the descendants of reluctant immigrants, namely Africans who were brought to America by force as slaves." What do you think about calling slaves "reluctant immigrants"?

_____

_____

_____

**Reading 2**

# Colorblind: When Blacks and Whites Can See No Gray* —ALEX KOTLOWITZ

**The following reading first appeared in the *New York Times Magazine* on January 11, 1998. Alex Kotlowitz is the author of *The Other Side of the River: A Story of Two Towns, a Death and America's Dilemma,* a detailed account of the atmosphere of racial tensions surrounding a young boy's death in southwestern Michigan.**

1   One Christmas day seven years ago, I'd gone over to the Henry Horner Homes in Chicago to visit with Lafeyette and Pharoah, the subjects of my book *There Are No Children Here*. I had brought presents for the boys, as well as a gift for their friend Rickey, who lived on the other side of the housing complex, an area controlled by a rival gang. Lafeyette and Pharoah insisted on walking over with me. It was eerily quiet, since most everyone was inside, and so, bundled from the cold, we strolled toward the other end in silence. As we neared Damen Avenue, a kind of demilitarized zone, a uniformed police officer, a white woman, approached us. She looked first at the two boys, neither of whom reached my shoulder, and then directly at me. "Are you O.K.?" she asked.

2      About a year later, I was with Pharoah on the city's North Side, shopping for high-tops. We were walking down the busy street, my hand on Pharoah's shoulder, when a middle-aged black man approached. He looked at me, and then at Pharoah. "Son," he asked, "are you O.K.?"

3      Both this white police officer and middle-aged black man seemed certain of what they witnessed. The white woman saw a white man possibly in trouble; the black man saw a black boy possibly in trouble. It's all about perspective—which has everything to do with our personal and collective experiences, which are consistently informed by race. From those experiences, from our histories, we build myths, legends that both guide us and constrain us, legends that include both fact and fiction. This is not to say the truth doesn't matter. It does, in a big way. It's just that getting there may not be easy, in part because everyone is so quick to choose sides, to refute the other's myths and to pass on their own. . . .

*"Colorblind: When Blacks and Whites Can See No Gray" by Alex Kotlowitz. Originally published in the NEW YORK TIMES MAGAZINE, 1998. Used by permission of the author.

4    While myths help us make sense of the incomprehensible, they can also confine us, confuse us and leave us prey to historical laziness. Moreover, truth is not always easily discernible—and even when it is, the prism, depending on which side of the river you reside on, may create a wholly different illusion. . . . We—blacks and whites—need to examine and question our own perspectives. Only then can we grasp each other's myths and grapple with the truths.

5    In 1992, I came across the story of a 16-year-old black boy, Eric McGinnis, whose body had been found a year earlier floating in the St. Joseph River in southwestern Michigan. The river flows between Benton Harbor and St. Joseph, two small towns whose only connections are two bridges and a powerful undertow of contrasts.

6    St. Joseph is a town of 9,000, and, with its quaint downtown and brick-paved streets, resembles a New England tourist haunt. But for those in Benton Harbor, St. Joseph's most defining characteristic is its racial makeup: it is 95 percent white. Benton Harbor, a town of 12,000 on the other side of the river, is 92 percent black and dirt poor. For years, the municipality was so hurt for money that it could not afford to raze abandoned buildings.

**raze**
tear down

7    Eric, a high-school sophomore whose passion was dancing, was last seen at the Club, a teen-age nightspot in St. Joseph, where weeks earlier he had met and started dating a white girl. The night Eric disappeared, a white man said he caught the boy trying to break into his car and chased him—away from the river, past an off-duty white deputy sheriff. That was the last known moment he was seen alive, and it was then that the myths began.

8    I became obsessed with Eric's death, and so for five years moved in and out of these two communities, searching for answers to both Eric's disappearance and to matters of race. People would often ask which side of the river I was staying on, wanting to gauge my allegiance. And they would often ask about the secrets of those across the way or, looking for affirmation, repeat myths passed on from one generation to the next.

9    Once, during an unusually bitter effort by white school-board members to fire Benton Harbor's black superintendent, one black woman asked me: "How do you know how to do this? Do you take lessons? How do you all stick together the way you do?" Of course, we don't. Neither community is as unified or monolithic as the other believes. Indeed, contrary to the impression of those in St. Joseph, the black community itself was deeply divided in its support for the superintendent, who was eventually fired.

10    On occasion, whites in St. Joseph would regale me with tales of families migrating to Benton Harbor from nearby states for the high welfare benefits. It is, they would tell me, the reason for the town's economic decline. While some single mothers indeed moved to Benton Harbor and other Michigan cities in the early '80s to receive public assistance, the truth is that in the '30s and '40s, factories recruited blacks from the South, and when those factories shut down, unemployment, particularly among blacks, skyrocketed.

11    But the question most often asked was: "Why us? Why write about St. Joseph and Benton Harbor?" I would tell them that while the contrasts between the towns seem unusually stark, they are, I believe, typical of how most of us live: physically and spiritually isolated from one another.

12    It's not that I didn't find individuals who crossed the river to spend time with their neighbors. One St. Joseph woman, Amy Johnson, devotes her waking hours to a Benton Harbor community center. And Eric McGinnis himself was among a handful of black teen-agers who spent weekend nights at the Club in St. Joseph. Nor is it that I didn't find racial animosity. One St. Joseph resident informed me that Eric got what

**animosity**
hatred

he deserved: "That nigger came on the wrong side of the bridge," he said. And Benton Harbor's former schools superintendent, Sherwin Allen, made no effort to hide his contempt for the white power structure.

13    What I found in the main, though, were people who would like to do right but don't know where to begin. As was said of the South's politicians during Jim Crow, race diminishes us. It incites us to act as we wouldn't in other arenas: clumsily, cowardly and sometimes cruelly. We circle the wagons, watching out for our own.

14    That's what happened in the response to Eric's death. Most everyone in St. Joseph came to believe that Eric, knowing the police were looking for him, tried to swim the river to get home and drowned. Most everyone in Benton Harbor, with equal certitude, believes that Eric was killed—most likely by whites, most likely because he dated a white girl. I was struck by the disparity in perspective, the competing realities, but I was equally taken aback by the distance between the two towns—which, of course, accounts for the myths. Jim Reeves, the police lieutenant who headed the investigation into Eric's death, once confided that this teen-ager he'd never met had more impact on him than any other black person.

15    I'm often asked by whites, with some wonderment, how it is that I'm able to spend so much time in black communities without feeling misunderstood or unwelcomed or threatened. I find it much easier to talk to blacks about race than with fellow whites. While blacks often brave slights silently for fear that if they complain they won't be believed, when asked, they welcome the chance to relate their experiences. Among whites, there's a reluctance—or a lack of opportunity—to engage. Race for them poses no urgency; it does not impose on their daily routines. I once asked Ben Butzbaugh, a St. Joseph commissioner, how he felt the two towns got along. "I think we're pretty fair in this community," he said. "I don't know that I can say I know of any out-and-out racial-type things that occur. I just think people like their own better than others. I think that's pretty universal. Don't you? . . . We're not a bunch of racists. We're not anything America isn't." Butzbaugh proudly pointed to his friendship with Renée Williams, Benton Harbor's new schools superintendent. "Renée was in our home three, four, five days a week," he noted. "Nice gal. Put herself through school. We'd talk all the time." Williams used to clean for Butzbaugh's family.

16    As I learned during the years in and out of these towns, the room for day-to-day dialogue doesn't present itself. We become buried in our myths, certain of our truths—and refuse to acknowledge what the historian Allan Nevins calls "the grains of stony reality" embedded in most legends. A quarter-century ago, race was part of everyday public discourse; today it haunts us quietly, though on occasion—the Rodney King beating or the Simpson trial or Eric McGinnis's death—it erupts with jarring urgency. At these moments of crisis, during these squalls, we flail about, trying to find moral ballast. By then it is usually too late. The lines are drawn. Accusations are hurled across the river like cannon fire. And the cease-fires, when they occur, are just that, cease-fires, temporary and fragile. Even the best of people have already chosen sides.

**slights**
insults

**embedded**
included

**squalls**
storms

---

**Exercise 8**

## Work with Words

The following sentences appear in Reading 2. Use context clues, dictionary skills, and your knowledge of word parts to determine the meaning of each italicized word or phrase. Write the meaning of the word on the lines provided. The paragraph number is provided in case you want to check the context.

1. Both this white police officer and middle-aged black man seemed certain of what they witnessed. The white woman saw a white man possibly in trouble; the black man saw a black boy possibly in trouble. It's all about *perspective*—which has everything to do with our personal and collective experiences, which are consistently informed by race. (par. 3)

   *Perspective*: _____

2. From those experiences, from our histories, we build myths, legends that both guide us and *constrain* us, legends that include both fact and fiction. (par. 3)

   *Constrain*: _____

3. This is not to say the truth doesn't matter. It does, in a big way. It's just that getting there may not be easy, in part because everyone is so quick to choose sides, to *refute* the other's myths and to pass on their own. (par. 3)

   *Refute*: _____

4. While myths help us make sense of the incomprehensible, they can also confine us, confuse us and leave us *prey to* historical laziness. (par. 4)

   *Prey to*: _____

5. Moreover, truth is not always easily *discernible*—and even when it is, the *prism*, depending on which side of the river you reside on, may create a wholly different illusion. (par. 4)

   *Discernible*: _____

6. *Prism*: _____

   _____

7. And they would often ask about the secrets of those across the way or, looking for *affirmation*, repeat myths passed on from one generation to the next. (par. 8)

   *Affirmation*: _____

8. Neither community is as unified or *monolithic* as the other believes. (par. 9)

   *Monolithic*: _____

9. As was said of the South's politicians during *Jim Crow*, race diminishes us. (par. 13)

   *Jim Crow*: _____

10. Most everyone in Benton Harbor, with equal *certitude*, believes that Eric was killed—most likely by whites, most likely because he dated a white girl. (par. 14)

    *Certitude*: _____

**Exercise 9**

## Check Your Understanding

Based on Reading 2, answer the following questions in your own words.

1. Write the thesis of Reading 2.

   _____

   _____

   _____

2. Paragraphs 1 through 3 are organized around two examples. What are the examples, and what point is Kotlowitz making by using those examples?

   _____

   _____

   _____

   _____

   _____

   _____

3. How did people on each side of the river decide that Eric McGinnis died?

   _____

   _____

   _____

4. Why was Kotlowitz interested in writing about St. Joseph and Benton Harbor?

   _____

   _____

   _____

5. Why does Kotlowitz say that black people talk to him about race more than white people do?

   _____

   _____

   _____

**Exercise 10**

## Recognize Fact and Opinion

The following sentences appear in or are based on Reading 2. For each sentence, write *F* on the blank if the statement is primarily factual and *O* if it is primarily opinion.

_____    1. St. Joseph is a town of 9,000.

_____    2. But for those in Benton Harbor, St. Joseph's most defining charac-
              teristic is its racial makeup.

_____    3. Eric, a high-school sophomore whose passion was dancing, was last
              seen at the Club, a teen-age nightspot in St. Joseph, where weeks
              earlier he had met and started dating a white girl.

_____    4. Eric was trying to steal a car.

_____    5. A man "caught the boy trying to break into his car."

_____    6. Eric drowned because he tried to swim across the river to get away
              from the police.

_____    7. Eric was murdered because he was dating a white girl.

_____    8. Eric got what he deserved.

_____    9. Benton Harbor was in economic decline because families moved there
              for the generous welfare benefits.

_____   10. In the '30s and '40s, factories recruited blacks from the South, and
              when those factories shut down, unemployment, particularly among
              blacks, skyrocketed.

**Exercise 11**

### Recognize and Interpret Figurative Language

Answer the following questions in your own words.

1. In paragraph 5, Kotlowitz writes, "The river flows between Benton Harbor
   and St. Joseph, two small towns whose only connections are two bridges and
   a powerful undertow of contrasts." What is he comparing? What does he
   mean?

   _____

   _____

   _____

2. In paragraph 13, Kotlowitz writes, "We circle the wagons, watching out for
   our own." What is he comparing? What does he mean?

   _____

   _____

   _____

3. At the end of paragraph 16, Kotlowitz writes, "The lines are drawn. Accusations are hurled across the river like cannon fire. And the cease-fires, when they occur, are just that, cease-fires, temporary and fragile." Explain the metaphor. What does he mean?

_____

_____

_____

_____

**Exercise 12**

## Reflect and Write

Think about what you read in Reading 2 and what you already know about race relations in the United States. Answer the following questions, and prepare to discuss them with your classmates.

1. Why do you think Kotlowitz never tells us what really happened to Eric McGinnis?

_____

_____

_____

_____

2. On a separate piece of paper, write two or three paragraphs about a person you know whose background is different from your own. Explain who that person is and what your relationship is with him or her. Do you get along well? Give examples of your interactions. Are they similar to your interactions with other people? Or are they different? Explain. Pick a title for your paragraphs that reflects the content.

# Evaluating Opinions

Evaluating facts—knowing how to consider their source as well as what they include and what they omit—helps in understanding and eventually in evaluating opinions. If you recognize that the source of a set of facts has an agenda and that the facts have been selected to promote that agenda, then you are in a better position to place the author's opinions in the right context.

It is also important to recognize an author's worldview and point of view, purpose for writing, bias, and tone.

## WHAT ARE THE AUTHOR'S WORLDVIEW AND POINT OF VIEW?

In "Colorblind," Alex Kotlowitz describes two towns, each with its own perspective. The way the white people of St. Joseph view the world is different from the way the black people of Benton Harbor view the world—though only a river separates them. Race and economics make the difference.

**worldview**
perspective on the world

Each of us has a **worldview**, or perspective on the world. Like the people of St. Joseph and Benton Harbor, we interpret events based on that perspective. How are our worldviews formed? What influences our beliefs? Here are some of the factors that influence our belief systems or worldviews:

- Our economic position in society, such as wealthy, poor, middle class, on welfare, in a high tax bracket, or unemployed
- Our sex
- Where we come from: the inner city, the suburbs, a rural area, or another country
- Our ethnicity or religion, such as African American, Hispanic, or Anglo-Saxon, Catholic, Jewish, Hindu, Protestant, or Muslim
- Our experiences in life
- Our friends and families and their opinions
- The media we read, watch, or listen to

Authors, too, have worldviews that have been formed by background and experience. It is clear from the first paragraph of Yasmin Ahmed's essay on pages 277 through 279 that she is a young woman from Somalia, she is an immigrant to the United States, and she is Muslim. Clearly, each of these characteristics influence her worldview.

**point of view**
opinion about an issue or event

When we form an opinion about an issue or event, we express a **point of view**. Point of view refers to much more specific concerns, but our point of view is influenced by our worldview. Because of her worldview as a Somali girl and an immigrant, Ahmed believes that she and other Somalis have been unfairly discriminated against by Americans who, since September 11, have assumed they are terrorists.

**bias**
a "point of view" that has a negative connotation indicating that an author does not present differing opinions fairly

Another word for point of view is **bias**. This term has a negative connotation and is often used to indicate that an author is prejudiced and does not present differing opinions fairly.

## WHAT IS THE AUTHOR'S PURPOSE?

**purpose**
reason for writing

Related to the author's point of view is **purpose**—the reason for writing. Often, an author writes to inform or convince, usually with a specific group of readers in mind. This group of readers is called the **intended audience**. For example, since Ahmed wrote "Identity in Transformation" for this textbook, her purpose is to convince American college students that they must move beyond assumptions and stereotypes and get to know people as individuals.

**intended audience**
the specific group of readers the author has in mind when writing

A textbook author's purpose for writing is primarily to inform. How the writer approaches the task is influenced by his or her worldview. For example, one history book author might emphasize dates and devote a good deal of space to the "important people" in history about whom we have a written record. Another author might feel that history is more meaningful if it attempts to show what the life of an ordinary person was like at a specific time. Yet another author might decide to emphasize relationships between countries or diplomatic history. If you pick up four American history textbooks, you might find that one talks about the day-to-day lives of the slaves as well as about the plantation owners, one emphasizes women's roles in the family or in the economy, one has thorough coverage of the Native Americans, and one barely mentions minority groups or women but focuses on political campaigns, elections, and wars. In the latter book—the most common type of history textbook until the 1970s—the major focus would be on influential and powerful white men. Although the writers of all these textbooks might present what we consider to be facts, which facts they choose to present can make a lot of difference. You need to be aware that every writer makes these choices, and as a reader, you can form your own opinions about both the facts and the writer.

**Exercise 13**

## Check for Author's Worldview, Point of View, and Purpose

Read carefully the following paragraphs from the preface to the history text *Liberty, Equality, Power: A History of the American People,* by John M. Murrin and his coauthors. Then answer the questions that follow.

### Global Emphasis in Early and Most Recent Chapters

1  The focus is global in chapters covering the early and most recent periods; in between, it is continental. We begin where the human story began, with the Indian settlement of the Americas. The typical United States history textbook opens with a snapshot of Indian cultures on the East coast around 1600. This type of presentation suggests that these societies were stagnant and unchanging; that they are of more interest as curiosities than as participants in history; that history is something that Europeans did for themselves and to others; and that only their arrival brings focus and purposeful change to the Americas. We have rejected this formula. Native Americans had their own long and highly complex history before 1492, and much of that story is now being recovered. We incorporate it. We also alert readers to parallel or contrasting Canadian events, from the beginnings of New France through the adoption of Canadian Confederation in 1867. And, we have moved the Spanish borderlands much closer to the center of American history in the century and a half before the Mexican war.

### Integration of Social, Cultural, and Political History

2  Because of our desire to integrate social, cultural, and political history, we have made efforts not to isolate the concerns and achievements of women, Native Americans, African Americans, Hispanics, Asians, and other minorities. We believe that the larger story of what is now the United States simply will not make sense unless the potent influence of race and gender is made clear. To give a simple but important example, the rise of capitalism in the 18th and 19th centuries depended on specific assumptions about gender among European settlers. Women rarely owned property, but they lived in fixed households where goods could be accumulated, and an acquisitive ethic could take hold among both men and women. By contrast, most Native American women in the eastern

woodlands had to move twice a year. They had no interest in acquiring any more goods than they could carry on their backs. For them, an ethic of accumulation made no sense, even though their husbands, as hunters and trappers, played an active role as producers for a global market. (Murrin et al., *Liberty, Equality, Power*)

1. What perspective, or worldview, do the authors identify as their focus?

   _____

   _____

   _____

2. What is the authors' purpose for using their particular focus? Who is their intended audience?

   _____

   _____

   _____

   _____

   _____

3. When they state in paragraph 1, "We have rejected this formula," what formula are the authors referring to?

   _____

   _____

   _____

**Exercise 14**

Reflect

Based on the reading in Exercise 13, answer the following questions.

1. Murrin and his coauthors assert that their text is very different from other American history texts. Based on the history textbooks you have read, do you think the focus of their text would be very different? Why or why not?

   _____

   _____

   _____

2. Do you think you would like the focus that Murrin and his coauthors emphasize? Why or why not?

_____

_____

_____

3. What has the focus been of history textbooks you have read or are reading this semester?

_____

_____

_____

**Exercise 15**

## Work with Point of View

Pick two topics from the chart below and on page 299, or think of your own topics. Then, on a separate piece of paper, write two or three sentences about each topic from different points of view. Here is an example:

**Topic: Parking on campus**

**Student:** The campus needs to provide more parking places for students because buying a parking permit at this school is really just buying a hunting permit. There are 1,000 parking spaces and 12,000 students. It hurts our educational possibilities to have to spend so much time looking for parking every day.

**Administrator:** We are in a period of restricted financing, so, while we recognize the very serious parking problem on campus, it is important to look at the larger picture. First, there are not enough classrooms on campus, and construction of classroom space should have priority. Second, our part-time teachers and clerical employees don't have medical insurance. If we spend money on parking, these people will be justifiably upset. And finally, there is convenient public transportation to our campus that students should use.

| Possible Topics | Possible Points of View |
|---|---|
| Immigrant workers who do not have papers to be in the United States | Police officer<br>Auto insurance company spokesperson<br>Immigration official<br>Son or daughter of undocumented immigrants |
| High prices of college textbooks | Consumer advocate for cheaper textbooks<br>College bookstore manager<br>Public relations person for a textbook publishing company<br>Student |

| Possible Topics | Possible Points of View |
|---|---|
| Uniforms on a high school campus | High school student who opposes uniforms<br>High school student who supports uniforms<br>High school administrator<br>Parent |
| Establishment of police review board to review alleged incidents of police brutality | Public relations officer for the police department<br>Community member<br>Mother of a teenager beaten by the police |
| Health care for all | Parent of a child with cancer and no health insurance<br>Emergency room physician<br>Employer<br>Tax payer |
| A curfew at 10:00 PM for all people under 16 | Police officer<br>16-year-old<br>Parent of 16-year-old |

# Reader's Tip:
# What Is the Author's Tone?

**tone**
indication of the author's emotional response to a topic

An author's point of view and purpose for writing naturally affect the emotional content of the writing. The author's **tone**, or emotional response to the topic, reveals how he or she feels. Our understanding of tone is influenced by the inferences we can make from the author's choice of vocabulary (see Chapter 6). For example, about the problems of population growth, one author might write, "The rate of world population growth is a problem that needs to be addressed." Another author might write, "If we don't do something to stop the worldwide population explosion, we are surely doomed." The first writer's tone is concerned, and the word *growth* doesn't carry either a positive or negative connotation. The second writer's tone is alarmed and pessimistic. The words *explosion* and *doomed* carry heavy connotations—*explosion* makes us think of something that's very powerful and impossible to control, and *doomed* makes us think that there is no way to prevent the terrible things that will come to pass. Although this example is purposely extreme to show the differences in tone, it makes clear that recognizing the author's tone enhances our understanding.

The variety of tones authors can use is as wide ranging as human emotions. But an author usually uses a single, consistent tone throughout a piece of writing, based on the content of the piece. The tone can be matter-of-fact when the author simply provides factual information. Textbooks are usually written objectively, and the objective, matter-of-fact tone helps establish that the author is an expert. But tone can also be playful, and then the reader does not take the writer too seriously. A hopeful tone can keep the reader from becoming discouraged by negative or normally disheartening information. A sarcastic tone or irony lets the reader see that the writer is criticizing what is presented. Here is a list of just some of the many possible tones writers use:

| | | |
|---|---|---|
| alarmed | indifferent | positive |
| authoritative | ironic | regretful |
| cautious | matter-of-fact | resigned |
| concerned | moral | romantic |
| confessional | negative | sarcastic |
| dark | nostalgic | self-righteous |
| exuberant | objective | thoughtful |
| formal | optimistic | tongue-in-cheek |
| hopeful | pessimistic | |

**Exercise 16**   Work with Tone

Write one sentence about each of the topics below. Choose one of the tones in the parentheses to use in your sentence.

1. The need for the city to put a stop sign at a street corner where a child was killed on the way to school. (alarmed or pessimistic tone)

   _____

   _____

2. Congratulations to a newlywed couple. (positive or romantic tone)

   _____

   _____

3. Your friend got A's in all his classes. (exuberant or tongue-in-cheek tone)

   _____

   _____

4. Your instructor gives you extra homework at the last minute. (sarcastic or angry tone)

   _____

   _____

5. You are asking your boss for a raise. (humble or confident tone)

   _____

   _____

© 2013 Wadsworth, Cengage Learning

**Reading 3**

# Signing for a Revolution: Gallaudet University and Deaf Culture* —Heather Eudy

**Heather Eudy has a background in cultural studies and teaches English as a Second Language as well as English classes of all levels at various community colleges in Southern California. She has worked with an extremely diverse population of students. Her contact with deaf students in many of her classes led to her interest in deaf culture and the history of deaf education. As you read her article, think about her presentation of facts and opinions, her worldview, and her point of view.**

*"The problem is not that the students do not hear; the problem is that the hearing world does not listen."*

—Jesse Jackson

1    In March 1988, deaf students started a revolution. When yet another hearing person was chosen as president of Gallaudet University in Washington, DC, the first facility to offer college degrees for the deaf in the United States, the students had had enough. Since opening in 1864 the university had never had a deaf president. Yet there were qualified deaf candidates. The students marched, protested, organized rallies, pressured for better education, and demanded: first, that the newly picked hearing president be replaced with a deaf administrator; second, that the chair of the board resign; third, that deaf membership on the board rise to 51 percent; and finally, that there be no reprisals against the protesters. After days of rallying, media coverage, and nationwide support, the students' demands were met.

2    This was not the first battle deaf people have faced. The deaf have been discriminated against for centuries. Even religious leaders, philosophers, educators, and medical professionals have considered them inferior spiritually, mentally, intellectually, physically, and psychologically. The Greek philosopher Aristotle believed deaf people could not learn. The Christian leader Saint Augustine claimed deafness in a person was a sign of God's anger and served as punishment for sin. Struggles regarding how and what a deaf person should be taught continue today, as do the assumptions that deaf people are disabled or impaired.

3    The struggle over education methods for deaf students has lasted more than a century. The deaf community has fought to keep sign language in the schools, but it has not yet won. More than one hundred years ago, the Milan Conference endorsed oral education as opposed to education in sign, with the consequence that signing in the schools disappeared. Deaf students ended up leaving schools illiterate, with few opportunities available to them. This discrimination was one of the reasons that Gallaudet University was founded. The National Association of the Deaf also sought to keep sign language alive. Today bilingual education is provided in many states for students whose first language is not English, but American Sign Language (ASL) has not been granted the same status as Spanish, Vietnamese, or Navajo, even though as many as two million people use it.

**illiterate**
unable to read

---

*"Signing for a Revolution: Gallaudet University and Deaf Culture" by Heather Eudy. Reprinted with author's permission.

4      There are two ways to view deafness. The Medical Model sets up a framework in which hearing is the norm. That makes deaf people different or wrong. Deaf people are viewed as though they have a disability or an impairment that needs to be fixed. On the other hand, the Cultural Model recognizes that deaf people have their own distinct culture and common language.

5      Unfortunately, the Medical Model is predominant in the hearing world. The hearing world tends to stigmatize deaf people, defining them as physically defective. Because they cannot communicate orally, deaf people are assumed to be simpleminded. Hearing parents of a deaf child are often pressured by medical professionals into a "solution" for their child's "problem" that involves testing, hearing aids, and even surgery. In *The Mask of Benevolence*, Harlan Lane presents evidence of the ways in which psychiatrists and educators, in professional journals and academic studies, brand deaf people as mentally limited and lacking insight, as socially irresponsible and morally underdeveloped, as behaviorally aggressive and impulsive, and as emotionally disturbed. Lane calls these assessments symptomatic of "hearing paternalism" and "audism." Paternalism is evident in the assumption by hearing people that they should help deaf people be a part of hearing society. Audism is like racism but takes the form of hearing people's domination of the deaf community by enforcing the idea that the deaf are infirm, or ill, and by controlling deaf education.

6      The Cultural Model belongs to the deaf community. Here culture is not connected to ethnicity or race. If *culture* is defined as shared language, shared experiences, shared identifiable characteristics, and shared values and norms, then there is also a deaf culture. The deaf community has its own language, its own shared experiences, its own identifiable characteristics, and its own shared values and norms. Indeed, the deaf community sees itself as having a culture, distinct from any other and rightly so.

7      First, let's examine the deaf community's shared language. Be aware that language does not depend on the ability to speak or hear. The deaf community communicates through sign language, a manual and visual language with a distinct grammar. Not much is known about the development of sign language until the 1800s. However, we do know that in the 1500s Pedro Ponce de León of Spain created a system of gestures to educate the deaf, and in the late 1700s Jacob Rodríguez Pereira spread an adapted version of León's gestures across Europe. Soon after, Abbé de l'Épée founded the French institute for deaf students using Old French Sign Language (OFSL), followed by Ambroise Cucurron Sicard, who compiled a dictionary of signs. At the same time a very large deaf community on the island of Martha's Vineyard, in the United States, was using a version of sign language that contributed to modern day American Sign Language. In 1817 Laurent Clerc and Thomas Gallaudet founded the first permanent public American school for the deaf incorporating OFSL into the curriculum. OFSL constitutes 60 percent of today's American Sign Language. Sign Language is a language like other foreign languages, and it is estimated to be the fourth most used language in the United States today.

8      The deaf community also has its own literature. Deaf people have their own plays, poems, stories, newspapers, and magazines. They highly value mastery of their language and storytelling with clear communication. They excel in the arts, in mime, dance, sculpture, video, theater, television, and film. They engage in activities within cultural institutions such as residential schools, deaf clubs, political organizations, and athletic teams. They value deaf identity and see themselves as part of a unique heritage with

pride. They usually marry other deaf people. In fact, nine out of ten deaf people marry a deaf person and hope for deaf children. Other deaf people are viewed as family, so there is intense group loyalty. Some even consider those who choose to talk or think like hearing people to be traitors. Bobby Jo Duffy, a teacher's aide at the Lexington School for the Deaf in New York, says, "I value our own culture, our own language. It used to be that many people didn't realize that deaf people have a language. They felt sorry for deaf people. There's really no pity needed. Deaf people can do anything, except hear. That's all. . . . Everything that I am, how I express myself, my education, everything, it's with the deaf community."

9      Not all deaf people feel the same as Duffy, however. Some really do want to assimilate into the hearing mainstream and choose to invest in hearing aid technology and to learn to speak. The most recent technology that has stirred up controversy is the cochlear implant designed by Cochlear Corporation. This prosthesis puts electrodes into the inner ear, or cochlea, where sound waves get absorbed and interpreted. The controversy is twofold. First, are these implants effective enough to make them worth the risks? Second, are they even desirable for the deaf community? While some believe cochlear implants have enriched lives, others see the use of cochlear implants as another example of the assumption that deafness is an impairment in need of repair. Marvin Miller, a deaf man who is planning a town centered around deaf people's needs, expresses his view on these implants: "I do not want one for myself. I am very happy being deaf. To me, this is like asking a black or Asian person if he or she would take a pill to turn into a white person." Is this what we are asking of deaf people? To abandon their culture, their identity?

10     As the Gallaudet Revolution indicates, what's most important to the deaf community today is not finding ways to end deafness but finding ways to end educational and social injustice. Deaf culture wants the recognition and respect due every minority. Deaf people want equal rights.

**Sources**

Davey, Monica. "As Town for Deaf Takes Shape, Debate on Isolation Re-emerges." *New York Times*, March 21, 2005.

Lane, Harlan. *Masks of Benevolence*. San Diego, CA: DawnSign Press, 1999.

"Perspectives on Deaf People." Sign Media, Inc. http://www.signmedia.com/info/adc.htm

Public Broadcasting Service. "Sound and Fury." http://www.pbs.org/wnet/soundandfury/culture/index.html

Wilcox, Sherman, and Phyllis Wilcox. *Learning to See: American Sign Language as a Second Language*. Englewood Cliffs, NJ: Prentice-Hall, 1991.

© 2013 Wadsworth, Cengage Learning

**Exercise 17**

## Work with Words

The following sentences appear in Reading 3. Use context clues, dictionary skills, and your knowledge of word parts to determine the meaning of each italicized word. Write the meaning of the word on the lines provided. The paragraph number is provided in case you want to go back to the reading to check the context.

1. The students marched, protested, organized rallies, pressured for better education, and demanded: first, that the newly picked hearing president be replaced with a deaf administrator; second, that the chair of the board resign; third, that deaf membership on the board rise to 51 percent; and finally, that there be no *reprisals* against the protesters. (par. 1)

   *Reprisals*: _____

2. Struggles regarding how and what a deaf person should be taught continue today, as do the assumptions that deaf people are disabled or *impaired*. (par. 2)

   *Impaired*: _____

3. The *Medical Model* sets up a framework in which hearing is the norm. (par. 4)

   *Medical Model*: _____

   _____

4. On the other hand, the *Cultural Model* recognizes that deaf people have their own distinct culture and common language. (par. 4)

   *Cultural Model*: _____

   _____

5. The hearing world tends to *stigmatize* deaf people, defining them physically defective. (par. 5)

   *Stigmatize*: _____

6. In *The Mask of Benevolence*, Harlan Lane presents evidence of the ways in which psychiatrists and educators, in professional journals and academic studies, *brand* deaf people as mentally limited and lacking insight, as socially irresponsible and morally underdeveloped, as behaviorally aggressive and impulsive, and as emotionally disturbed. (par. 5)

   *Brand*: _____

7. *Paternalism* is evident in the assumption by hearing people that they should help deaf people be a part of hearing society. (par. 5)

   *Paternalism*: _____

8. *Audism* is like racism but takes the form of hearing people's domination of deaf community by enforcing the idea that the deaf are infirm, or ill, and by controlling deaf education. (par. 5)

   *Audism*: _____

   _____

9. The most recent technology that has stirred up controversy is the cochlear implant designed by Cochlear Corporation. This *prosthesis* puts electrodes into the inner ear, or *cochlea*, where sound waves get absorbed and interpreted. (par. 9)

*Prosthesis:* _____

_____

10. *Cochlea:* _____

**Exercise 18**

## Check Your Understanding

Based on Reading 3, answer the following questions in your own words.

1. What are some of the ways deaf people have been discriminated against?

_____

_____

_____

_____

2. What is the difference between the Medical Model and the Cultural Model, and who has typically followed each model?

_____

_____

_____

_____

3. What are some of the things that deaf people have in common and lead the author to state that they have their own culture?

_____

_____

_____

_____

**Exercise 19**

## Recognize Author's Point of View, Purpose, and Bias

Based on Reading 3, answer the following questions in your own words. Develop your answers as fully as possible.

1. What is Eudy's worldview or perspective that influences her opinion in this reading?

_____

_____

_____

_____

2. What do you think is Eudy's purpose for writing this article? What do you think she wants to achieve?

_____

_____

_____

3. Could you describe Eudy as "objective"? Explain your answer.

_____

_____

_____

_____

_____

**Exercise 20**

## Distinguish Fact from Opinion

List three sentences from Reading 3 that you think are clearly facts, and then list three opinions that Eudy presents.

### Facts

1. _____

_____

_____

_____

_____

2. _____

_____

_____

_____

_____

3. _____

_____

_____

_____

_____

_____

## Opinions

1. _____

_____

_____

_____

2. _____

_____

_____

3. _____

_____

_____

4. _____

_____

_____

**Exercise 21**

## Reflect and Write

Think about what you read in Reading 3 and what you already know about deaf people and deaf culture. Answer the following questions, and prepare to discuss them with your classmates.

1. Why does Eudy use the quotation from Jesse Jackson at the beginning of her essay?

   _____

   _____

   _____

   _____

   _____

   _____

2. Eudy quotes Marvin Miller as saying that he doesn't want a cochlear implant. "I am very happy being deaf. To me, this is like asking a black or Asian person if he or she would take a pill to turn into a white person." (par. 9) What does Miller mean by this statement? In what ways do you think the circumstances of deaf people are similar or different from the circumstances of black or Asian people in this country?

   _____

   _____

   _____

   _____

   _____

   _____

3. Imagine that you suddenly lost your sight, hearing, or the use of your legs. What would your life be like? What would you have to do to be able to take care of yourself? How do you think your relationships with other people might change? On a separate piece of paper, write a short essay about what you think your life would be like if you were blind or deaf, or unable to walk. Provide details in your writing to support your thesis. Give your essay an appropriate title.

## Write About It

What are the most important factors that influence your personal worldview? Look at page 295 and identify the two or three factors that are most important for how you view the world. On a separate sheet of paper, explain the factors that you chose, why you chose them, and how these elements of your life and background influence you and affect your life. Choose a title for your essay.

# Chapter Review

| Put It Together: Facts and Opinions | |
| --- | --- |
| Skills and Concepts | Explanation |
| **Fact** (see page 281) | A piece of information that is verifiable |
| **Opinion** (see page 281) | An interpretation of facts; an expression of beliefs or feelings |
| **Verifiable** (see page 281) | Can be checked |
| **Value Words** (see page 281) | Words that indicate judgment |
| **Inclusiveness** (see page 286) | Consideration of which facts are included and which are excluded |
| **Worldview** (see page 295) | Perspective on the world influenced by <br> • Economic position <br> • Sex and gender <br> • Where we come from <br> • Ethnicity, religion <br> • Experiences in life <br> • Friends, families <br> • Media we read, watch, or listen to |
| **Point of View** (see page 295) | An attitude or a position about an issue or event |
| **Author's Purpose** (see pages 295–296) | Author's reason for writing (that is, convince, inform, entertain) |

| Put It Together: Facts and Opinions | |
|---|---|
| Skills and Concepts | Explanation |
| **Intended Audience** (see page 295) | The specific group of readers the author has in mind when writing |
| **Bias** (see page 295) | A point of view that has a negative connotation and is often used to indicate that an author does not fairly represent both sides of an issue |
| **Tone** (see page 299) | Indication of the author's emotional response to a topic |

## CRITICAL REFLECTIONS IN THE CLASSROOM COMMUNITY

Answer the following questions, and prepare to discuss them with your classmates.

1. Do you think that racism and other forms of prejudice are problems in American society today? Give examples from your experience and reading to support your answer.

   _____

   _____

   _____

   _____

2. What have you learned from the readings in this chapter that you weren't aware of or hadn't thought about previously? What new perspective(s) have you gained?

   _____

   _____

   _____

   _____

3. Check your college catalog to find out what your college does to prevent discrimination on campus. What speech or behavior codes are in place to guarantee that students are respectful to one another? Present your results to your class group. Discuss the advantages and disadvantages of these codes.

   _____

   _____

   _____

   _____

4. Do you think that people who identify with each other because of a common culture or background should stay within their group (like deaf culture) or try to integrate into the wider culture (like the Somali girls)? Should the people from Benton Harbor and St. Joseph get to know each other, or stay on their own sides of the river?

_____

_____

_____

_____

 ## WORK THE WEB

Although you can discover useful resources on the Internet, you must also be careful not to believe everything you read there. To avoid being unduly persuaded by inaccurate or biased sites, you need to ask certain questions to determine the legitimacy of a site. Now that you have examined some issues concerning diversity in the United States, use the Internet to learn more.

1. Read pages 441 through 445 in the "Reader's Toolkit" to familiarize yourself with guidelines for evaluating a website.

2. Do an Internet search for the American Civil Liberties Union or Numbers USA. Write a website evaluation based on the instructions and the sample website evaluations (pages 444–445) for either website.

Name _____ Date _____

# Spanish at School Translates to Suspension*

—T. R. REID

**The following essay from the *Washington Post* was written by T. R. Reid, a staff writer for that newspaper. In this article, Reid reports on an incident that took place in Kansas City, Missouri, in 2005. As you read, consider the facts of the case, the opinions represented in the article, and what your own opinions are regarding the events described.**

1    Most of the time, 16-year-old Zach Rubio converses in clear, unaccented American teen-speak, a form of English in which the three most common words are "like," "whatever" and "totally." But Zach is also fluent in his dad's native language, Spanish—and that's what got him suspended from school. "It was, like, totally not in the classroom," the high school junior said, recalling the <u>infraction</u>. "We were in the, like, hall or whatever, on restroom break. This kid I know, he's like, 'Me prestas un dólar?' ['Will you lend me a dollar?'] Well, he asked in Spanish; it just seemed natural to answer that way. So I'm like, 'No problema.' "

2    But that conversation turned out to be a big problem for the staff at the Endeavor Alternative School, a small public high school in an ethnically mixed <u>blue-collar</u> neighborhood. A teacher who overheard the two boys sent Zach to the office, where Principal Jennifer Watts ordered him to call his father and leave the school. Watts, whom students describe as a disciplinarian, said she can't discuss the case. But in a written "discipline referral" explaining her decision to suspend Zach for 1 ½ days, she noted: "This is not the first time we have [asked] Zach and others to not speak Spanish at school."

3    Since then, the suspension of Zach Rubio has become the talk of the town in both English and Spanish newspapers and radio shows. The school district has officially <u>rescinded</u> his punishment and said that speaking a foreign language is not <u>grounds</u> for suspension. Meanwhile, the Rubio family has retained a lawyer who says a civil rights lawsuit may be in the offing.

4    The tension here surrounding that brief exchange in a high school hall reflects a broader national debate over the language Americans should speak amid a wave of Hispanic immigration. The National Council of La Raza, a Hispanic <u>advocacy</u> group, says that 20 percent of the U.S. school-age population is Latino. For half of those Latino students, the native language is Spanish.

5    Conflicts are bursting out nationwide over bilingual education, "English-only" laws, Spanish-language publications and advertising, and other linguistic collisions. Language concerns have been a key aspect of the growing political movement to reduce immigration. "There's a lot of <u>backlash</u> against the increasing Hispanic population," said D.C. school board member Victor A. Reinoso. "We've seen some of it in the D.C. schools. You see it in some cities, where people complain that their tax money shouldn't be used to print public notices in Spanish. And there have been cases where schools want to ban foreign languages."

6    Some advocates of an English-only policy in U.S. schools say that it is particularly important for students from immigrant families to use the nation's dominant language. California Gov. Arnold Schwarzenegger made that point this summer when he <u>vetoed</u> a bill authorizing various academic subjects to be tested in Spanish in the state's public

suspend
kick out of school
for a certain
number of days

offing
near future

---

*"Spanish at School Translates to Suspension" by T. R. Reid from THE WASHINGTON POST, December 9, 2005. Copyright © 2005 The Washington Post. Reprinted by permission.

schools. "As an immigrant," the Austrian-born governor said, "I know the importance of mastering English as quickly and as comprehensively as possible."

7    Hispanic groups generally agree with that, but they emphasize the value of a multilingual citizenry. "A fully bilingual young man like Zach Rubio should be considered an asset to the community," said Janet Murguia, national president of La Raza.

**asset**
advantage

8    The <u>influx</u> of immigrants has reached every corner of the country—even here in Kansas City, which is about as far as a U.S. town can be from a border. Along Southwest Boulevard, a main street through some of the older neighborhoods, there are blocks where almost every shop and restaurant has signs written in Spanish. "Most people, they don't care where you're from," said Zach's father, Lorenzo Rubio, a native of Veracruz, Mexico, who has lived in Kansas City for a quarter-century. "But sometimes, when they hear my accent, I get this, sort of, 'Why don't you go back home?'"

9    Rubio, a U.S. citizen, credits U.S. immigration law for his decision to fight his son's suspension. "You can't just walk in and become a citizen," he said. "They make you take this government test. I studied for that test, and I learned that in America, they can't punish you unless you violate a written policy." Rubio said he remembered that lesson . . . when he received a call from Endeavor Alternative saying his son had been suspended. "So I went to the principal and said, 'My son, he's not suspended for fighting, right? He's not suspended for disrespecting anyone. He's suspended for speaking Spanish in the hall?' So I asked her to show me the written policy about that. But they didn't have one."

10   Rubio then called the superintendent of the Turner Unified School District, which operates the school. The district immediately rescinded Zach's suspension, local media reported. The superintendent did not respond to several requests to comment for this article. Since then, the issue of speaking Spanish in the hall has not been raised at the school, Zach said. "I know it would be, like, disruptive if I answered in Spanish in the classroom. I totally don't do that. But outside of class now, the teachers are like, 'Whatever.'"

11   For Zach's father, and for the Hispanic organizations that have expressed concern, the suspension is not a closed case. "Obviously they've violated his <u>civil rights</u>," said Chuck Chionuma, a lawyer in Kansas City, Mo., who is representing the Rubio family. "We're studying what form of legal <u>redress</u> will correct the situation. . . . Punished for speaking Spanish? Somebody has to stand up and say: This is wrong."

## Exercise 1

### Work with Words

Use context clues, dictionary skills, and your knowledge of word parts to choose the best definition for each of the following words underlined in the reading. The paragraph number is provided in case you want to check the context.

1. *Infraction* (par. 1)
   a. agreement
   b. violation
   c. written regulation

2. *Blue-collar* (par. 2)
   a. working class
   b. upper class
   c. retired

3. *Rescinded* (par. 3)
   a. reinforced
   b. publicized
   c. cancelled

4. *Grounds* (par. 3)
   a. justification
   b. logical
   c. floor

5. *Advocacy* (par. 4)
   a. support
   b. only
   c. immigration

6. *Backlash* (par. 5)
   a. hospitable reaction
   b. whip
   c. hostile reaction

7. *Vetoed* (par. 6)
   a. encouraged
   b. stopped
   c. remained neutral to

8. *Influx* (par. 8)
   a. exit
   b. residence
   c. arrival

9. *Civil rights* (par. 11)
   a. liberties guaranteed by the Constitution
   b. polite exchanges
   c. having to do with war

10. *Redress* (par. 11)
    a. dress again
    b. review a situation to see if it is fair
    c. adjust a situation to make things fair

---

**Exercise 2**

## Check Your Understanding

Based on the reading, Reid's "Spanish at School Translates to Suspension," choose the best answer to each of the following multiple-choice questions.

1. Which of the following best states the topic of "Spanish at School Translates to Suspension"?
   a. bilingual education
   b. attitudes about language use in the United States
   c. suspension of a Mexican boy

2. Which of the following best states the main idea of "Spanish at School Translates to Suspension"?
   a. Zach's suspension for speaking Spanish in the hall reflects a national debate over when and where Americans should speak other languages.
   b. Zach's father is concerned with the civil liberties of all people who speak Spanish.
   c. A fully bilingual young man like Zach Rubio is an asset to the community.

3. What is the dominant pattern of organization for paragraphs 1 and 2?
   a. cause and effect
   b. comparison and contrast
   c. definition

4. What is the dominant pattern of organization for paragraphs 6 and 7?
   a. cause and effect
   b. comparison and contrast
   c. definition

5. In paragraph 4, the author states that, according to the National Council of La Raza, "20 percent of the U.S. school-age population is Latino" and "for half of those Latino students the native language is Spanish." From this statement, we can reasonably infer that

a. the author believes that Spanish should be spoken in the classroom.

b. the National Council of La Raza believes that the educational system needs to be sensitive to the needs of Spanish-speaking students.

c. the National Council of La Raza believes there should be special classes for students who speak other languages.

6. Although he sometimes encounters anti-immigrant feelings, Zach Rubio's father believes that

a. most people in Kansas City don't really care where he comes from.

b. people make racist remarks but are happy that immigrants have come to Kansas City.

c. only immigrants who have become citizens should be allowed to remain in the country.

7. According to Rubio's father,

a. the procedures required to become a U.S. citizen are unfair.

b. the test to become a U.S. citizen is easy.

c. it's not so simple to become a U.S. citizen.

8. In the process of preparing for the test to become a citizen, Rubio's father learned that

a. it is perfectly legal for children to speak Spanish at school.

b. school districts can establish any policy they want regarding languages spoken at school.

c. in the United States, you can't be punished unless you violate a written policy.

9. The tone of the entire article can be best described as

a. objective.

b. resigned.

c. alarmed.

10. The Hispanic organizations in Kansas City

a. believe the case of Zach's unfair suspension is no longer an issue because the school district rescinded the suspension.

b. believe that it is important to legally challenge Zach's initial suspension because it violated his civil rights.

c. believe that Zach's family should sue the school district or receive a monetary settlement for what happened.

**Exercise 3**

## Recognize Fact and Opinion

Based on your reading, indicate whether each of the following statements is fact or opinion.

_____ 1. The school district . . . officially rescinded Zach Rubio's punishment and said that speaking a foreign language is not grounds for suspension.

_____ 2. It is particularly important for students of immigrant families to use the nation's dominant language.

_____ 3. A fully bilingual young man like Zach Rubio should be considered an asset to the community.

_____ 4. Zach's father, who comes from Veracruz, Mexico, became a U.S. citizen.

_____ 5. Somebody has to stand up and say "This is wrong."

**Exercise 4**

## Recognize Worldview, Point of View

Based on the reading, briefly answer the following questions in your own words.

1. What factors influence Zach Rubio's worldview?

_____

_____

_____

_____

2. What factors influence Lorenzo Rubio's worldview?

_____

_____

_____

_____

3. What factors influence T. R. Reid's worldview?

_____

_____

_____

_____

4. What factors influence Arnold Schwarzenegger's worldview?

_____

_____

_____

_____

5. Discuss Zach Rubio, Lorenzo Rubio, T. R. Reid, and Arnold Schwarzenegger's points of view about "English-only" laws. Do you have enough information to determine each of their points of view?

_____

_____

_____

_____

_____

_____

**Exercise 5**

Reflect

Think about what you read in "Spanish at School Translates to Suspension" and what you already know about attitudes and policies regarding language use in schools. Then answer the following questions.

1. Why do you think the author of the article describes the way Zach speaks English in the first paragraph?

_____

_____

_____

_____

2. Why do you think the author quotes Arnold Schwarzenegger's opinions about learning language rather than a different public figure?

_____

_____

_____

_____

3. Do you think it's fair to require that students who haven't yet learned much English take exams in all their subjects in English?  Explain your answer.

_____

_____

_____

_____

_____

4. What experiences have you or someone you know had with learning a new language? Was that experience a positive one?  Explain your answers.

_____

_____

_____

_____

_____

5. Do you think it's a good idea for children and grandchildren of immigrants to learn to speak the language of their parents' or grandparents' home country? Explain your answer.

_____

_____

_____

_____

_____

_____

# Critical Thinking

## CRIME AND PUNISHMENT

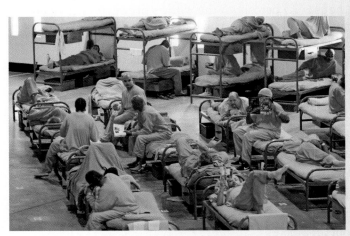

Brant Ward/San Francisco Chronicle/Corbis

*We are jammed up with this situation right now because we have fallen in love with one of the most undocumented beliefs: That somehow you get safer if you put more people in jail. —California State Senator Don Perata*

| Country Comparison: Prison Population and Incarceration Rate | | |
| --- | --- | --- |
| Country | Total Prison Population | Incarceration Rate per 100,000 Residents |
| United States | 2,293,157 | 756 |
| Russia | 891,738 | 691 |
| Rwanda | 58,598 | 604 |
| Iran | 158,351 | 222 |
| Mexico | 222,671 | 207 |
| England and Wales | 83,392 | 153 |
| Kenya | 47.036 | 130 |
| China | 1,565,771 | 119 |
| Germany | 73,203 | 89 |
| Japan | 81,255 | 63 |
| **World** | **9,800,000** | **145** |

Source: Roy Walmsey, *World Prison Population List*, 8th ed. (London: Kings College, January 2009).

1. Describe the picture. What does it show?

2. Describe the table. What does it show? How do the prison population and the incarceration rate in the United States compare with other countries? Which statistics surprise you? Why?

3. Restate the opinion expressed in the quotation. Do you agree with it? Why or why not?

4. Taken together, what do the picture, table, and quotation suggest about crime and punishment in the United States?

# Prepare to Read

The U.S. prison system has experienced a record expansion since the 1980s, with a greater than 400 percent rise in the prison population and a corresponding explosion in prison construction. At the end of 2008, 2.3 million adults were in state, local, or federal custody, with another 5.1 million on probation or parole. Although the United States only has five percent of the world's population, it houses 25 percent of the world's prisoners. Crime and punishment affect everyone in our society, whether as an offender, an ex-offender, a victim, a family member of an offender or a victim, or a taxpayer.

Why are so many people behind bars in the United States? Are there more criminals in our country than in other countries? Or is our definition of what constitutes a crime more strict? Are prisons the best way to reform behavior and protect society? Or would the taxpayer money spent for prisons be better directed toward education? What if the justice system fails and the wrong person is imprisoned? There are no easy answers to these questions.

In this chapter, you will read arguments from various perspectives about crime and punishment and learn to

- Identify and evaluate arguments
- Recognize fallacies
- Think critically about arguments
- Be an informed decision maker

In the process of acquiring these skills, you will read about ideas of crime and punishment in the nineteenth century, the consequences of legalizing marijuana, the costs to states of crowded prisons, and concerns about the death penalty.

## Reading 1

# Lizzie Borden, Murderer* — James Kirby Martin, Randy Roberts, Steven Mintz, Linda O. McMurry, and James H. Jones

**TEXT BOOK** The following reading is from a college American history textbook. It deals with a famous murder case and trial that took place in the late nineteenth century. As you read, consider the conclusions that people draw and how they are influenced by their worldviews. Also, think about the authors' purpose for including this case in an American history textbook. Are there any lessons from this incident that can be applied to life in the early twenty-first century?

**parsimonious**
stingy

**amassed**
gathered

1    Andrew Borden had, as the old Scotch saying goes, short arms and long pockets. He was cheap not because he had to be frugal but because he hated to spend money. He had dedicated his entire life to making and saving money, and talks of his unethical and parsimonious business behavior were legendary in his hometown of Fall River, Massachusetts. Local gossips maintained that as an undertaker he cut the feet off corpses so that he could fit them into undersized coffins that he had purchased at a very good price. Andrew, however, was not interested in rumors or the opinions of other people; he was more concerned with his own rising fortunes. By 1892, he had amassed over half a million dollars, he controlled the Fall River Union Savings Bank, and he served as the director of the Globe Yard Mill Company, the First National Bank, the Troy Cotton and Manufacturing Company, and the Merchants Manufacturing Company.

2    Andrew was rich, but he did not live like a wealthy man. Instead of living alongside the other prosperous Fall River citizens in the elite neighborhood known as the Hill, Andrew resided in an area near the business district called the Flats. He liked to save time as well as money, and from the Flats he could conveniently walk to work. For his daughters Lizzie and Emma, whose eyes and dreams focused on the Hill, life in the Flats was an intolerable embarrassment. Their house was a grim, boxlike structure lacking both comfort and privacy. Since Andrew believed that running water on each floor was a wasteful luxury, the only washing facilities were a cold-water faucet in the kitchen and a laundry room water tap in the cellar. Also in the cellar was the only toilet in the house. To make matters worse, the house was not connected to the Fall River gas main. Andrew preferred to use kerosene to light his house. Although it did not provide as good light or burn as cleanly as gas, it was less expensive. To save even more money, he and his family frequently sat in the dark.

**suitor**
a man who asks a woman to marry him

3    The Borden home was far from happy. Lizzie and Emma, ages 32 and 42 in 1892, strongly disliked their stepmother Abby and resented Andrew's penny-pinching ways. Lizzie especially felt alienated from the world around her. Although Fall River was the largest cotton-manufacturing town in America, it offered few opportunities for the unmarried daughter of a prosperous man. Society expected a woman of Lizzie's social position to marry, and while she waited for a proper suitor, her only respectable social outlets were church and community service. So Lizzie taught a Sunday school class and was active in the Woman's Christian Temperance Union [an organization that advocated making drinking alcohol illegal], the Ladies' Fruit and Flower Mission, and other organizations. She kept herself busy, but she was not happy.

*"Lizzie Borden, Murderer" by James Kirby Martin, Randy J. Roberts, Steven Mintz, Linda O. McMurry, and James H. Jones from AMERICA AND ITS PEOPLES: A MOSAIC IN THE MAKING, 5th Edition, © 2004, pp. 489–491. Reprinted by permission of Pearson Education, Inc., Upper Saddle River, NJ.

4    In August 1892, strange things started to happen in the Borden home—after Lizzie and Emma learned that Andrew had secretly changed his will. Abby became violently ill. In time so did the Borden maid Bridget Sullivan and Andrew himself. Abby told a neighborhood doctor that she had been poisoned, but Andrew refused to listen to her wild ideas. Shortly thereafter, Lizzie went shopping for prussic acid, a deadly poison, that she said she needed to clean her sealskin cape. When a Fall River druggist refused her request, she left the store in an agitated state. Later in the day, she told a friend that she feared an unknown enemy of her father's was after him. "I'm afraid somebody will do something," she said.

5    On August 4, 1892, Bridget awoke early and ill, but she still managed to prepare a large breakfast of johnnycakes, fresh-baked bread, ginger and oatmeal cookies with raisins, and some three-day-old mutton and hot mutton soup. After eating a hearty meal, Andrew left for work. Bridget also left to do some work outside. This left Abby and Lizzie in the house alone. Then somebody did something very grisly. As Abby was bent over making the bed in the guest room, someone moved into the room unobserved and killed her with an ax.

**grisly**
horrible

6    Andrew came home for lunch earlier than usual. He asked Lizzie where Abby was, and she said she did not know. Unconcerned, Andrew, who was not feeling well, lay down on the parlor sofa for a nap. He never awoke. Like Abby, he was slaughtered by someone with an ax. Lizzie "discovered" his body, still lying on the sofa. She called Bridget, who had taken the back stairs to her attic room: "Come down quick; father's dead; somebody came in and killed him."

7    Experts have examined and reexamined the crime, and most have reached the same conclusion: Lizzie killed her father and stepmother. In fact, Lizzie was tried for the gruesome murders. Despite a preponderance of evidence, however, an all-male jury found her not guilty, a verdict arrived at without debate or disagreement. A woman of Lizzie's social position, they affirmed, simply could not have committed such a terrible crime.

**affirmed**
agreed

8    Even before the trial began, newspaper and magazine writers had judged Lizzie innocent for the same reason. As historian Kathryn Allamong Jacob, an expert on the case, noted, "Americans were certain that well-brought-up daughters could not commit murder with a hatchet on sunny summery mornings." Criminal women, they believed, originated in the lower classes and even looked evil. A criminologist writing in the *North American Review* commented, "[The female criminal] has coarse black hair and a good deal of it. . . . She has often a long face, a receding forehead, overjutting brows, prominent cheek bones, an exaggerated frontal angle as seen in monkeys and savage races, and nearly always square jaws." They did not look like round-faced Lizzie and did not belong to the Ladies' Fruit and Flower Mission.

**preconceived**
opinion formed in advance based on little information or experience

9    Jurors and editorialists alike judged Lizzie Borden according to their preconceived notions of Victorian womanhood. They believed that such a woman was gentle, docile, and physically frail, short on analytical ability but long on nurturing instincts. "Women," wrote an editorialist for *Scribner's*, "are merely large babies. They are shortsighted, frivolous and occupy an intermediate state between children and men." Too uncoordinated and weak to accurately swing an ax and too gentle and unintelligent to coldly plan a double murder, a woman of Lizzie's background simply had to be innocent because of her basic innocence.

**frivolous**
silly, not serious

© 2013 Wadsworth, Cengage Learning

| Exercise 1 | Recall and Discuss |
| --- | --- |

Based on Reading 1, answer the following questions and prepare to discuss them with your classmates.

1. Write the main idea of this reading.

   _____

   _____

   _____

2. What facts support the main idea?

   _____

   _____

   _____

   _____

3. What reasonable inferences can you make about what was in the revised will?

   _____

   _____

   _____

4. What reasonable inferences can you make about Lizzie's guilt? What clues suggest she was the murderer?

   _____

   _____

   _____

   _____

5. From what you know from the reading, should she have been convicted? Was there enough evidence?

   _____

   _____

   _____

   _____

6. What ideas influenced the jurors' point of view about what kind of woman Lizzie Borden was?

_____

_____

_____

7. How do the authors of the textbook try to convince you that Lizzie was guilty? What is the purpose of paragraphs 1–3? What impression do the authors give of Andrew Borden and the Borden household? What words and phrases contribute to the tone?

_____

_____

_____

_____

_____

_____

_____

8. What was the authors' purpose in including the story of Lizzie Borden in an American history textbook?

_____

_____

_____

9. What can this case tell us about the nineteenth-century justice system?

_____

_____

_____

_____

10. What twenty-first century worldviews do you think are affecting the justice system today?

_____

_____

_____

_____

# Critical Thinking

© 2013 Wadsworth, Cengage Learning

**critical thinking**
ability to make an informed opinion about what you read

**Critical thinking** is the ability to make an informed opinion about what you read. It is more than understanding what you read. It means being able to apply reading skills and strategies and then go beyond them to decide what you think of the ideas and opinions the author has expressed.

## READING SKILLS

The reading skills that form the foundation for critical thinking include all those you have studied in this textbook.

- Identifying the author's main idea or thesis and supporting points
- Determining the structure and patterns of organization
- Making reasonable inferences
- Distinguishing facts from opinions
- Evaluating facts
- Considering the author's worldview and point of view
- Considering the author's purpose and the intended audience
- Recognizing the author's tone
- Reflecting about what you read and making connections to what you already know or have experienced

# Reader's Tip: Fallacies

**fallacies**
errors or weaknesses in reasoning in an argument

In studying facts and opinions (Chapter 7), you learned some skills for evaluating the author's worldview, point of view, bias, and purpose. Here are some weaknesses in an author's presentation that can also help you evaluate an argument. These **fallacies** are errors or weaknesses in reasoning in an argument that can lead to incorrect conclusions. When evaluating arguments, it is important to be aware of any and all fallacies. The following are common fallacies:

- **Ad hominem** involves attacking the opponent rather than the idea the opponent is discussing. For example, "Since you never fought in a war or experienced a terrorist attack, you don't have the right to criticize the military's interrogation techniques."

- **Appeal to emotions** takes advantage of the reader's emotions and sways the reader from evaluating the argument logically. For example, "If you have a heart, you will find the money to support this cause."
- **Bandwagon** attempts to convince the reader based on the popularity of the thing being proposed. Often you are meant to feel you will miss out on what everyone else is doing if you don't participate or believe. For example, "All the other parents have bought their kids cars, so why don't you?"
- **Overgeneralization** assumes that what is true under certain conditions is true under all conditions or what fits certain members of a group applies to all members. For example, "Drug rehabilitation programs are a waste of money. They never work."
- **Oversimplification** describes a complex idea or situation in terms that are so simple that they ignore the complexity and distort the idea or situation. For example, "If a child is having problems, the parent is to blame."
- **Slippery slope** claims that an action ought to be avoided because it will invariably lead to a series of unpleasant consequences for similar situations. For example, "Marijuana is a gateway drug. It always leads to using hard drugs, like meth and heroin."
- **Testimonial** uses famous people as representatives of authority on issues for which they have no expertise. Television commercials, for example, often hire well-known actors to promote services or products they do not use themselves.

### Exercise 2    Check for Fallacies

Examine the following statements and determine which fallacies are used. Circle the best answer.

1. How can you deny a human being the right to health and happiness?
   a. Slippery slope
   b. Ad hominem
   c. Appeal to emotions

2. My sister told me to take a self-defense class, but that's ridiculous. She went out every weekend and partied all night when she was my age. Nothing ever happened to her. Why should anybody listen to her advice?
   a. Oversimplification
   b. Bandwagon
   c. Ad hominem

3. If we reduce prison sentences, the next thing you know we'll be fighting the biggest crime wave in history.
   a. Slippery slope
   b. Testimonial
   c. Appeal to emotions

4. Poverty would end if people stopped having so many babies.
   a. Bandwagon
   b. Oversimplification
   c. Slippery slope

5. No one waits until they're 21 to try alcohol. Go ahead. Have a drink.
   a. Testimonial
   b. Bandwagon
   c. Appeal to emotions

6. Millions of people voted for President Obama in 2008 on Oprah Winfrey's recommendation.
   a. Slippery slope
   b. Testimonial
   c. Ad hominem

7. If you're not part of the solution, you're part of the problem.
   a. Appeal to emotions
   b. Slippery slope
   c. Oversimplification

8. My daughter would be alive today if the government had banned assault weapons.
   a. Bandwagon
   b. Appeal to emotions
   c. Overgeneralization

9. I would never go to that marriage counselor. She has been divorced twice already.
   a. Ad hominem
   b. Overgeneralization
   c. Testimonial

10. People who contract sexually transmitted diseases are irresponsible.
    a. Slippery slope
    b. Appeal to emotions
    c. Overgeneralization

# KEY QUESTIONS FOR CRITICAL THINKING

In addition to practicing reading skills and identifying fallacies in arguments, you will want to form your own opinion about what you read. Be aware of your own worldview and biases, and figure out where the ideas in what you read fit into what you already know and think. At the same time, be open to new points of view. Here are a series of questions that will help you think critically and form your own well-informed opinion.

## Identify the Argument

- What is the thesis?
- What is the structure and patterns of organization? How do they support or hinder the argument?
- What are the supporting points?
- What is the author's purpose, and who is the intended audience?

## Examine the Evidence

- Are the supporting points convincing?
- Are the sources reliable?
- Are all the appropriate facts included, or has some evidence been overlooked or excluded?
- Is the information current, or is it outdated? Does the date of publication matter?
- Does the author consider opposing viewpoints?

## Check for Fallacies

- Does the author attack people rather than issues?
- Does the author appeal to emotions without providing convincing evidence?
- Does the author attempt to sway the reader by focusing on the popularity of the subject or by using a testimonial from a celebrity rather than from an expert?
- Does the author oversimplify a complex issue or overgeneralize from just a few examples?
- Has the author attempted to convince the reader that something must be avoided by exaggerating the undesirable consequences?

## Form Your Own Opinion

- Have all potential benefits and risks been weighed? Have all effects been fully and fairly explored?
- What is the author's underlying worldview?
- On the basis of all your previous answers, is the argument valid?
- Has the writer convinced you to change your mind, or at least to be open to a different point of view?
- If you already agreed with the argument, has the author strengthened your belief through his or her support and evidence?

**Exercise 3**

## Evaluate the Argument and Think Critically

Read the following passage. It argues a particular point of view about an industrial disaster in Bhopal, India, in 1984. Modern technology, in the form of insecticides, was promoted in India to improve agricultural production. But in 1984, history's worst industrial disaster occurred when a deadly gas leaked from a Union Carbide insecticide plant. David Watson, in an article in *The Fifth Estate* in 1985, was critical of the people he saw as responsible for the tragedy. As you read, think about his argument, the evidence he uses, and any fallacies that are present. Then, decide what you think about his argument and whether you agree with him.

### We All Live in Bhopal

The cinders of the funeral pyres at Bhopal were still warm, and the mass graves still fresh, but the media prostitutes of the corporations have already begun their homilies in defense of industrialism and its uncounted horrors. Some 3,000 people were slaughtered in the wake of the deadly gas cloud, and 20,000 will remain permanently disabled. The poison gas left a 25-square-mile swath of dead and dying people and animals, as it drifted southeast away from the Union Carbide factory. "We thought it was a plague," said one victim. Indeed it was: a chemical plague, an *industrial plague.*

*Ashes, ashes, all fall down!*

A terrible, unfortunate "accident," we are assured by the propaganda apparatus for Progress, for History, for "Our Modern Way of Life." A price, of course, has to be paid—since the risks are necessary to ensure a Higher Standard of Living, a Better Way of Life. . . .

   The corporate vampires are guilty of greed, plunder, murder, slavery, extermination, and devastation. We should avoid any pangs of sentimentalism when the time comes for them to pay for their crimes against humanity and the natural world. . . . The Union Carbides, the Warren Andersons, the "optimistic experts" and the lying propagandists all must go, but with them must go the pesticides, the herbicides, the chemical factories and the chemical way of life which is nothing but death. (Watson, "We All Live in Bhopal")

**Warren Anderson** the CEO of the Union Carbide corporation at the time of the Bhopal disaster

1. What is the thesis or argument of this passage?

   _____

   _____

   _____

   _____

   _____

2. What is the evidence that Watson uses to support his argument?

   _____

   _____

   _____

3. How would you evaluate the evidence? Does he consider opposing viewpoints?

_____

_____

_____

_____

_____

_____

4. What fallacies are present in the passage?

_____

_____

_____

_____

5. Do you agree with Watson's point of view? Do you find his argument convincing? What would make his argument more convincing?

_____

_____

_____

_____

_____

_____

## Reading 2 | End the War on Pot* — NICHOLAS D. KRISTOFF

**In the following *New York Times* editorial, Nicholas D. Kristoff argues that it would be a good idea for California to legalize marijuana. The proposal was voted on and defeated in the November 2010 election. As you read, carefully consider Kristoff's support for his argument.**

1   I dropped in on a marijuana shop here [in Los Angeles] that proudly boasted that it sells "31 flavors." It also offered a loyalty program. For every 10 purchases of pot— supposedly for medical uses—you get one free packet. "There are five of these shops within a three-block radius," explained the proprietor, Edward J. Kim. He brimmed with pride at his inventory and sounded like any small businessman as he complained about onerous government regulation. Like, well, state and federal laws.

2   But those burdensome regulations are already evaporating in California, where anyone who can fake a headache already can buy pot. Now there's a significant chance that on Tuesday [November 2, 2010], California voters will choose to go further and broadly legalize marijuana. I hope so. Our nearly century-long experiment in banning marijuana has failed as abysmally as Prohibition did, and California may now be pioneering a saner approach. Sure, there are risks if California legalizes pot. But our present drug policy has three catastrophic consequences.

3   First, it squanders billions of dollars that might be better used for education. California now spends more money on prisons than on higher education. It spends about $216,000 per year on each juvenile detainee, and just $8,000 on each child in the troubled Oakland public school system. Each year, some 750,000 Americans are arrested for possession of small amounts of marijuana. Is that really the optimal use of our police force? In contrast, legalizing and taxing marijuana would bring in substantial sums that could be used to pay for schools, libraries, or early childhood education. A Harvard economist, Jeffrey A. Miron, calculates that marijuana could generate $8.7 billion in tax revenue each year if legalized nationally, while legalization would also save the same sum annually in enforcement costs. That's a $17 billion swing in the nation's finances—enough to send every 3- and 4-year-old in a poor family to a high-quality preschool. And that's an investment that would improve education outcomes and reduce crime and drug use in the future—with enough left over to pay for an extensive nationwide campaign to discourage drug use.

4   The second big problem with the drug war is that it has exacerbated poverty and devastated the family structure of African-Americans. Partly that's because drug laws are enforced inequitably. Black and Latino men are much more likely than whites to be stopped and searched and, when drugs are found, prosecuted. Here in Los Angeles, blacks are arrested for marijuana possession at seven times the rate whites are, according to a study by the Drug Policy Alliance, which favors legalization. Yet surveys consistently find that young whites use marijuana at higher rates than young blacks. Partly because of drug laws, a black man now has a one-in-three chance of serving time in prison at some point in his life, according to the Sentencing Project, a group that seeks reform in the criminal justice system. This makes it more difficult for black men to find jobs, more difficult for black

**Prohibition**
Period between 1920 and 1933 when making and selling alcohol was illegal in the United States. Criminal activity and organized gangster mobs became more widespread and violent. Drinking alcohol, though illegal, actually increased.

*"End the War on Pot" by Nicholas D. Kristoff. From THE NEW YORK TIMES, October 28, 2010 © 2010 The New York Times. All rights reserved. Used by permission and protected by the Copyright Laws of the United States. The printing, copying, redistribution, or retransmission of this Content without express written permission is prohibited.

women to find suitable husbands, and less common for black children to grow up in stable families with black male role models. So, sure, drugs have devastated black communities—but the remedy of criminal sentencing has made the situation worse.

5　The third problem with our drug policy is that it creates crime and empowers gangs. "The only groups that benefit from continuing to keep marijuana illegal are the violent gangs and cartels that control its distribution and reap immense profits from it through the black market," a group of current and former police officers, judges and prosecutors wrote last month in an open letter to voters in California.

6　I have no illusions about drugs. One of my childhood friends in Yamhill, Ore., pretty much squandered his life by dabbling with marijuana in ninth grade and then moving on to stronger stuff. And yes, there's some risk that legalization would make such dabbling more common. But that hasn't been a significant problem in Portugal, which decriminalized drug use in 2001. Likewise, medical marijuana laws approved in 1996 have in effect made pot accessible to any adult in California, without any large increase in usage. Special medical clinics abound where for about $45 you can see a doctor who is certain to give you the medical recommendation that you need to buy marijuana. Then you can visit Mr. Kim and choose one of his 31 varieties, topping out at a private "OG" brand that costs $75 for one-eighth of an ounce. "It's like a fine wine, cured, aged, dried," he boasted. Or browse the online offerings. One store advertises: "refer a friend, get free joint." And the world hasn't ended.

7　One advantage of our federal system is that when we have a failed policy, we can grope for improvements by experimenting at the state level. I hope California will lead the way on Tuesday by legalizing marijuana.

## Exercise 4　Work with Words

Identify words in Reading 2 that are unfamiliar to you and that are important for understanding the reading. Choose three to five of these words to add to your personal vocabulary. On a separate sheet of paper, or on 3 × 5 cards, write each word and its appropriate meaning, the original sentence in which it appeared, and your own sentence using the word.

## Exercise 5　Identify the Argument

Based on Reading 2, write answers to the following questions.

1. What is Kristoff's thesis or central argument? What does he want to convince the reader of?

_____

_____

_____

2. List the three major supporting points the author gives to support his argument. After each point, identify if it is a moral, economic, or social point.

   a. _____

   _____

   _____

   _____

   b. _____

   _____

   _____

   _____

   c. _____

   _____

   _____

   _____

3. Who is Kristoff's intended audience?

   _____

4. What can you infer Kristoff is trying to accomplish when he writes about a marijuana shop owner in Los Angeles in the first paragraph: "He brimmed with pride at his inventory and sounded like any small businessman as he complained about onerous government regulation"?

   _____

   _____

   _____

   _____

5. Why does Kristoff use Prohibition to support his argument?

   _____

   _____

   _____

6. What is the author's tone for most of the article? When does he change his tone, and why?

_____

_____

_____

_____

_____

_____

**Exercise 6**

## Examine the Evidence and Check for Fallacies

Based on Reading 2, answer the following questions and be prepared to discuss them with your classmates.

1. Check the facts.

   A. What facts does the author use for which he does not cite an outside source?

   1. _____

      _____

      _____

      _____

      _____

   2. _____

      _____

      _____

   3. _____

      _____

      _____

      _____

      _____

4. _____

_____

_____

_____

B. How can you check if these facts are accurate?

_____

_____

_____

C. What facts are attributed to an economist? Why might this economist be considered an "authority" on this subject?

_____

_____

_____

_____

_____

_____

_____

D. What facts are from the Drug Policy Alliance? What is its source of "authority"?

_____

_____

_____

_____

_____

_____

_____

E. Can you think of any information that you might want to research that is not included in this editorial?

_____

_____

_____

2. Does Kristoff anticipate and try to answer the concerns of people who disagree with him? How?

_____

_____

_____

_____

_____

_____

_____

3. Which of the following fallacies could Kristoff possibly be making: ad hominem, appeal to emotions, bandwagon, overgeneralization, oversimplification, slippery slope? Explain your reasons for your choices

_____

_____

_____

_____

_____

**Exercise 7**

### Reflect and Write: Form Your Own Opinion

Think about what you read in Reading 2, and what you already know about marijuana and its legality and use in your state, and what your own opinion is about legalizing marijuana.

1. If marijuana were legalized, who might lose and who might benefit? For each group listed below, indicate how you think each would benefit and/or lose. Explain your answers. _____

| | Possible Benefits | Possible Losses |
|---|---|---|
| Police departments | | |
| People who own marijuana shops now | | |
| Agricultural businesses | | |

|                                | Possible Benefits | Possible Losses |
|--------------------------------|-------------------|-----------------|
| The states                     |                   |                 |
| Schools and libraries          |                   |                 |
| Organized crime                |                   |                 |
| Recreational marijuana users   |                   |                 |

2. What is Kristoff's worldview? What does he value? Do you agree with his values? Explain why or why not.

_____

_____

_____

_____

_____

3. Think about Kristoff's argument and other arguments for or against the legalization of marijuana that you have read or heard about. How would you vote if legalization of marijuana were on the ballot in your state? On a separate sheet of paper, write two or three paragraphs stating your opinion, your reasons, and some examples. Give your paragraphs a title.

## Reading 3

# One in a Hundred* —THE PEW CHARITABLE TRUSTS

fiscally
financially

**This reading is a summary of a 2008 report on the dramatic increase in the numbers of people in jail and prison. It documents the cost to states and society generally of having so many people behind bars. The study was conducted by the Pew Center on the States' Public Safety Performance Project, which, according to its website, "seeks to help states advance fiscally sound, data-driven policies and practices in sentencing and corrections that protect public safety, hold offenders accountable, and control corrections costs." As you read, identify the argument, examine the evidence, check for fallacies, and evaluate the argument. Be sure to study the graphs.**

recidivism
returning
to criminal
behavior

1    Three decades of growth in America's prison population has quietly nudged the nation across a sobering threshold: for the first time, more than one in every 100 adults is now confined in an American jail or prison. According to figures gathered and analyzed by the Pew Public Safety Performance Project, the number of people behind bars in the United States continued to climb in 2007, saddling cash-strapped states with soaring costs they can ill afford and failing to have a clear impact either on recidivism or overall crime.

2    For some groups, the incarceration numbers are especially startling. While one in 30 men between the ages of 20 and 34 is behind bars, for black males in that age group the figure is one in nine. Gender adds another dimension to the picture. Men still are roughly 10 times more likely to be in jail or prison, but the female population is burgeoning at a far brisker pace. For black women in their mid- to late-30s, the incarceration rate also has hit the 1-in-100 mark. Growing older, meanwhile, continues to have a dramatic chilling effect on criminal behavior. While one in every 53 people in their 20s is behind bars, the rate for those over 55 falls to one in 837.

3    While the national incarceration trend remains on the rise, some states report a flattening of growth, or even a decline, figures from January 1 of this year [2008] show. Texas' count dropped slightly over the previous year, but with California's massive system dipping by 4,068 inmates, Texas has become the nation's imprisonment leader. New York and Michigan, also among the country's biggest systems, reported declines as well.

"There isn't a person in public office that's not sensitive to the accusation of being soft on crime. But you don't have to be soft on crime to be smart in dealing with criminals."

—OH Governor
Ted Strickland (D)
The Columbus
Dispatch
January 26, 2008

4    There is reason to suspect those states may soon have lots of company. Prison costs are blowing holes in state budgets but barely making a dent in recidivism rates. At the same time, policy makers are becoming increasingly aware of research-backed strategies for community corrections—better ways to identify which offenders need a prison cell and which can be safely handled in the community, new technologies to monitor their whereabouts and behavior, and more effective supervision and treatment programs to help them stay on the straight and narrow. Taken together, these trends are encouraging policy makers to diversify their states' array of criminal sanctions with options for low-risk offenders that save tax dollars but still hold offenders accountable for their actions.

* "One in a Hundred" by The Pew Charitable Trusts. Reprinted by permission of The Pew Charitable Trusts.

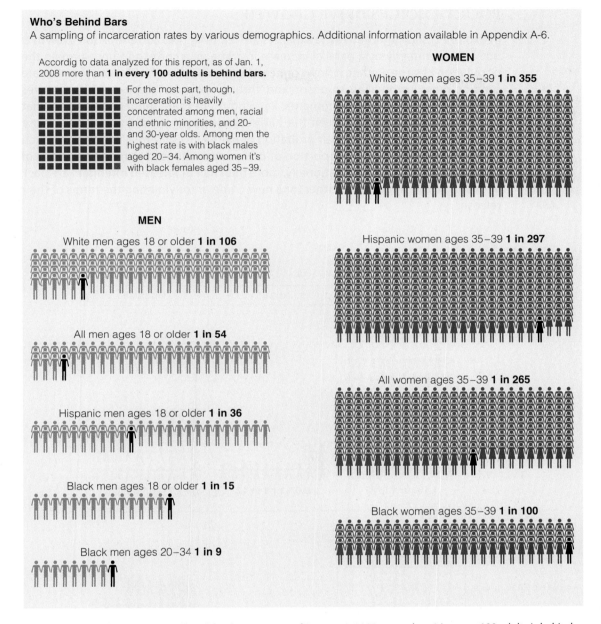

**Who's Behind Bars**

A sampling of incarceration rates by various demographics. Additional information available in Appendix A-6.

Accordig to data analyzed for this report, as of Jan. 1, 2008 more than **1 in every 100 adults is behind bars.**

For the most part, though, incarceration is heavily concentrated among men, racial and ethnic minorities, and 20- and 30-year olds. Among men the highest rate is with black males aged 20–34. Among women it's with black females aged 35–39.

**MEN**

White men ages 18 or older **1 in 106**

All men ages 18 or older **1 in 54**

Hispanic men ages 18 or older **1 in 36**

Black men ages 18 or older **1 in 15**

Black men ages 20–34 **1 in 9**

**WOMEN**

White women ages 35–39 **1 in 355**

Hispanic women ages 35–39 **1 in 297**

All women ages 35–39 **1 in 265**

Black women ages 35–39 **1 in 100**

**Figure 8.1** According to data analyzed for this report, as of January 1, 2008, more than 1 in every 100 adults is behind bars. For the most part, though, incarceration is heavily concentrated among men, racial and ethnic minorities, and 20- and 30-year-olds. Among men the highest rate is with black males aged 20–34. Among women it is with black females aged 35–39.

Source: Analysis of "Prison and Jail Inmates at Midyear 2006," published June 2007 by the U.S. Department of Justice, Bureau of Justice Statistics, printed in Pew Charitable Trusts, *One in 100: Behind Bars in America, 2008*, p. 6. All demographic statistics, with the exception of "1 in every 100 adults," are midyear 2006, not 2008 figures.

## POLICY CHOICES DRIVE GROWTH

> "There's a shift away from the mindset of lock them up and throw away the key. That cannot sustain itself."
>
> —*OH State Rep. John J. White (R)* Dayton Daily News *February 11, 2007*

5 In exploring such alternatives, lawmakers are learning that current prison growth is not driven primarily by a parallel increase in crime, or a corresponding surge in the population at large. Rather, it flows principally from a wave of policy choices that are sending more lawbreakers to prison and, through popular "three-strikes" measures and other sentencing enhancements, keeping them there longer. Overlaying that picture in some states has been the habitual use of prison stays to punish those who break rules governing their probation or parole. In California, for example, such violators make up a large proportion of prison admissions, churning in and out of badly overloaded facilities. Nationally, more than half of released offenders are back in prison within three years, either for a new crime or for violating the terms of their release.

**Working-Age Men Behind Bars:**
Rates of Incarceration by Race, Age, and Education, 2008

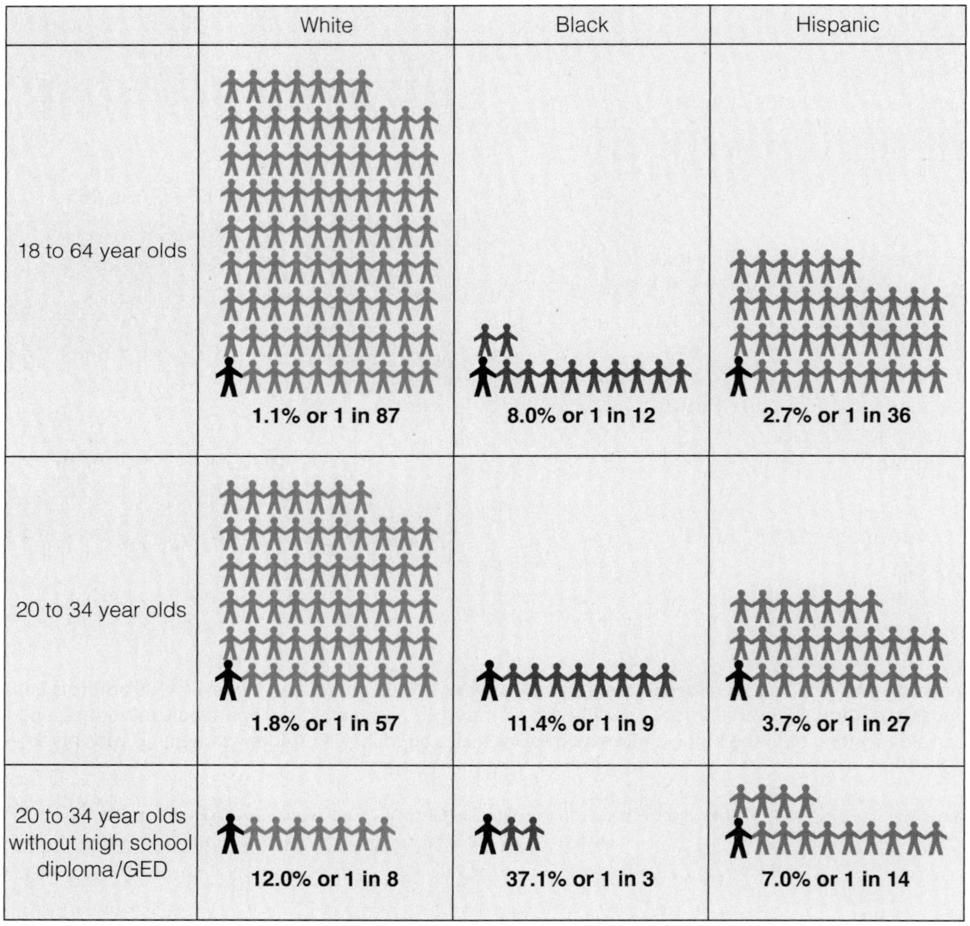
White
Black
Hispanic
18 to 64 year olds
1.1% or 1 in 87
8.0% or 1 in 12
2.7% or 1 in 36
20 to 34 year olds
1.8% or 1 in 57
11.4% or 1 in 9
3.7% or 1 in 27
20 to 34 year olds without high school diploma/GED
12.0% or 1 in 8
37.1% or 1 in 3
7.0% or 1 in 14

**Figure 8.2**

Note: These numbers differ from previous Pew reports primarily because they pertain to working-age men as opposed to all adults.

Source: Original analysis for the Pew Charitable Trusts by Bruce Western and Becky Pettit, 2009, printed in Pew Charitable Trusts, *Collateral Costs: Incarceration's Effect on Economic Mobility*, 2010, p. 8.

6    Few doubt the necessity of locking up violent criminals and those who repeatedly threaten community safety. And policy makers understandably are moved to act by especially heinous crimes or victims seeking justice in the name of a loved one.

**heinous**
atrocious,
monstrous

7    Increasingly, however, states are discovering that casting such a wide net for prisoners creates a vexing fiscal burden—especially in lean times. Finding enough dollars to house, feed, and provide a doctor's care to a low-risk inmate is a struggle besetting states from Arizona to Vermont. In the absence of tax hikes, lawmakers may find themselves forced to cut or limit other vital programs—from transportation to education and healthcare—to foot the incarceration tab.

**foot the . . . tab**
pay for

**State Expenditures on Corrections**

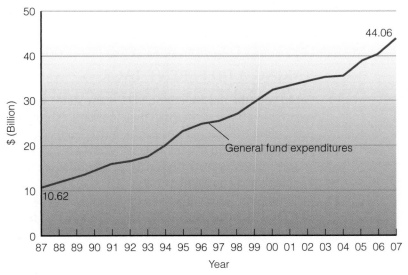

**Twenty Years of Rising Costs**
Between fiscal years 1987 and 2007, total state general fund
expenditures on corrections rose 315 percent.

**Figure 8.3**  Between fiscal years 1987 and 2007, total state general fund expenditures on corrections rose 315 percent.

Source: National Association of State Budget Officers, "State Expenditure Report" series, printed in Pew Charitable Trusts, *One in 100: Behind Bars in America, 2008*, p. 12.

8    That tab, meanwhile, is exploding, fueled in part by staff overtime expenses and a steep rise in healthcare costs. In 1987, the states collectively spent $10.6 billion of their general funds—their primary pool of discretionary tax dollars—on corrections. Last year [2007], they spent more than $44 billion, a 315 percent jump, data from the National Association of State Budget Officers show. Adjusted to 2007 dollars, the increase was 127 percent. Over the same period, adjusted spending on higher education rose just 21 percent.

**discretionary**
unrestricted, able
to be used for any
purpose

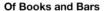

**Of Books and Bars**

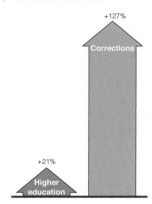

**Figure 8.4** Between 1987 and 2007, the amount states spent on corrections more than doubled, while the increase in higher education spending has been moderate.

Source: National Association of State Budget Officers, "State Expenditure Report" series, printed in Pew Charitable Trusts, *One in 100: Behind Bars in America, 2008*, p. 15.

## TAKING A DIFFERENT TACK

**tack**
approach

9    Faced with the mushrooming bills, many states are confronting agonizing choices and weathering bitter divisions in their legislatures. But lawmakers are by no means power-less before the budget onslaught. Indeed, a rising number of states already are diver-sifying their menu of sanctions with new approaches that save money but still ensure that the public is protected and that offenders are held accountable. And some already are reaping encouraging results.

10    Kansas and Texas are well on their way. Facing daunting projections of prison popula-tion growth, they have embraced a strategy that blends incentives for reduced recidi-vism with greater use of community supervision for lower-risk offenders. In addition, the two states increasingly are imposing sanctions other than prison for parole and pro-bation violators whose infractions are considered "technical," such as missing a counsel-ing session. The new approach, born of bipartisan leadership, is allowing the two states to ensure they have enough prison beds for violent offenders while helping less danger-ous lawbreakers become productive, taxpaying citizens.

**sanctions**
punishments

11    No policy maker would choose this path if it meant sacrificing public safety. But gradually, some states are proving that deploying a broad range of sanctions can protect commu-nities, punish lawbreakers, and conserve tax dollars for other pressing public needs.

**Exercise 8**

## Work with Words

Identify words in Reading 3 that are unfamiliar to you and that are important for understanding the reading. Choose three to five of these words to add to your per-sonal vocabulary. On a separate sheet of paper, or on 3 × 5 cards, write each word and its appropriate meaning, the original sentence in which it appeared, and your own sentence using the word.

**Exercise 9**

## Identify the Argument

Based on Reading 3, answer the following questions.

1. What is the thesis or central argument of "One in a Hundred"?

   _____

   _____

   _____

2. Briefly list the major supporting points.

   a. _____

   _____

   b. _____

   _____

   c. _____

   d. _____

   _____

3. Look at Figure 8.1, "Who's Behind Bars," on page 339.

   A. What is the main idea behind this visual aid?

   _____

   _____

   B. List four important supporting points.

   1. _____

   _____

   2. _____

   3. _____

   4. _____

4. Look at Figure 8.2, "Working-Age Men Behind Bars," on page 340. What new information does this visual aid provide?

   _____

   _____

   _____

   _____

   _____

5. Look at Figure 8.3, "Twenty Years of Rising Costs," on page 341.

   A. What is the main idea of this graph?

   _____

   _____

   B. List two important supporting points.

   1. _____

      _____

   2. _____

6. Look at Figure 8.4, "Of Books and Bars," on page 342. Why does the author include this graph?

   _____

   _____

   _____

   _____

7. Why are the visual aids included with the reading? In what way do they help convince the readers of the authors' argument?

   _____

   _____

   _____

8. Who is the primary intended audience for the study that this article discusses?

   _____

   _____

   _____

---

**Exercise 10**

### Examine the Evidence

Based on Reading 3, answer the following questions.

1. What is the source of information of each of the four graphs, and is the source reliable?

   A. Figure 8.1, "Who's Behind Bars"

   _____

   _____

B. Figure 8.2, "Working-Age Men Behind Bars"

_____

_____

C. Figure 8.3, "Twenty Years of Rising Costs"

_____

D. Figure 8.4, "Of Books and Bars"

_____

_____

2. What can you reasonably infer about the authors' point of view from Figure 8.4, "Of Books and Bars"?

_____

_____

_____

_____

_____

_____

3. In the reading itself, underline the two or three sentences that make it clear that the authors do not want anyone to think that they are soft on crime or too easy on criminals. Why is it important that they do so?

_____

_____

_____

_____

**Exercise 11**

### Reflect and Write: Form Your Own Opinion

Think about what you read in Reading 3 and what you already know about incarceration rates, the effectiveness of incarceration, and your opinion about the criminal justice system. Then answer the following questions.

1. From what you know, and from what you've read in this chapter (consider also Reading 2), why are black men, ages 20–34 incarcerated at such a high rate?

_____

_____

_____

_____

_____

2. Do you agree with the basic argument of the Pew Report, "One in a Hundred?" Why or why not? If you don't agree, how would you solve the problem of too many people incarcerated in this country? If you do agree, what new information did you learn to support your opinion?

_____

_____

_____

_____

_____

3. What do you think (or can you reasonably infer) are the effects of higher rates of incarceration for some groups than that of other groups? What would the consequences be for their families and communities? On a separate piece of paper, write a brief essay about the costs of incarceration to families and communities.

## Write About It

Find a recent editorial or argumentative essay about crime, offenders, a prison policy, sentencing, prison conditions, victims' concerns, or a released prisoner. Write a summary of the article and then respond to it by using the "Key Questions for Critical Thinking" (page 328).

# Chapter Review

| Put It Together: Critical Thinking | |
|---|---|
| Skills and Concepts | Explanation |
| **Critical Thinking** (see page 325) | Critical thinking is the ability to make an informed opinion about what you read. |
| **Reading Skills** (see page 325) | The reading skills that form the foundation for critical thinking include all those you have studied in this textbook. <br> • Identifying the author's main idea or thesis and supporting points <br> • Determining the structure and patterns of organization <br> • Making reasonable inferences <br> • Distinguishing facts from opinions <br> • Evaluating facts <br> • Considering the author's worldview and point of view <br> • Considering the author's purpose and the intended audience <br> • Recognizing the author's tone <br> • Reflecting about what you read and making connections to what you already know or have experienced |
| **Reader's Tip: Fallacies** (see pages 325–327) | Errors or weaknesses in reasoning in an argument include <br> • Ad hominem <br> • Appeal to emotions <br> • Bandwagon <br> • Overgeneralization <br> • Oversimplification <br> • Slippery slope <br> • Testimonial |
| **Key Questions for Critical Thinking** (see page 328) | Questions that help you think critically about a reading, including <br> • Identifying the argument <br> • Examining the evidence <br> • Checking for fallacies <br> • Forming your own opinion |

## CRITICAL REFLECTIONS IN THE CLASSROOM COMMUNITY

Answer the following questions, and prepare to discuss them with your classmates.

1. What do you think is the most serious challenge related to public safety? Identify the challenge, briefly explain your position, and be sure to give specific examples.

   _____

   _____

   _____

   _____

2. Do you think the government should invest money in prisons, in crime prevention and rehabilitation programs, or in education? What do you think makes our communities safer, spending more money on education or spending more money on incarceration? Evaluate what is best for individuals and for society.

   _____

   _____

   _____

   _____

3. In groups, choose one of the ethical issues listed below that are related to crime and punishment. Discuss and make a chart of the benefits, risks, and possible unintended consequences of each. Be prepared to share your list with your class and to turn the list in to your instructor.

   - Abolishing capital punishment (the death penalty)
   - Sentencing violent juvenile offenders the same as adult offenders
   - Legalizing marijuana
   - Legalizing prostitution
   - Releasing nonviolent offenders from prison in order to save money

 ## WORK THE WEB

Do an Internet search to find a nonprofit organization related to crime, sentencing, offenders' rights, crime prevention, or victims' rights. Some of these organizations include The Innocence Project, National Center for Victims of Crime, the Equal Justice Initiative, the Tariq Khamisa Foundation, and the National Coalition Against Domestic Violence. Using the critical thinking skills you have developed throughout this book, evaluate the website. Answer the following questions:

1. What position or point of view does the organization or group advocate? Who does it help or support? Who is the target audience for the website?

2. How is the position supported? What resources and information are available on the site? Are the sources sufficient and reliable?

3. Does the website use fallacies to persuade? If so, which ones? Are they effective?

4. What requests does the website make? What does the group want you to do?

5. Is the website visually appealing? Is the information presented clearly? What is the tone of the writing? Give examples.

6. Overall, how would you judge the effectiveness of the website? Would you consider supporting the organization (by donating money, volunteering, making phone calls, or writing letters)? Would you recommend that family members or friends visit the website? Why or why not?

Name _____ Date _____

# The Falsely Accused on Death Row* — Missy Gish

**TEXT BOOK** In this essay, first published in the textbook, *Sociology: A Global Perspective* by Joan Ferrante, Gish presents Illinois' struggles with the death penalty. She describes how and why Governor George Ryan suspended the death sentences of more than 167 men on death row from 1999 to 2003. The debate has continued in Illinois, and in 2011, the state Senate voted to abolish the death penalty. The future of the death penalty in Illinois is now up to Governor Pat Quinn. Some argue that reforms have been sufficient to remedy the past errors and that the state should continue to have the right to put violent offenders to death. Others claim that the system is still too flawed and innocent people may be put to death as a result. As you read, evaluate Gish's argument and the evidence she provides.

**stay of**
suspension of

1    In September 1998 Anthony Porter was within 50 hours of his scheduled execution for a double homicide when the Illinois Supreme Court granted him a stay of execution. Porter had been defended by a lawyer who fell asleep in court, assigned a judge who later left the bench over a financial scandal, and convicted by a jury prejudiced by a witness's false testimony. After his appeals had failed, a lawyer volunteered his services and had Porter's IQ tested. When the lawyer learned that Porter was borderline mentally retarded, a team of four other pro bono lawyers and journalism students agreed to take the case. The team interviewed two crime-scene witnesses.

2    One eyewitness, Inez Jackson, told the team that she had seen her then-husband, Alstory Simon, shoot both victims. Simon admitted his guilt, claiming that he killed one victim in self defense while fighting over a drug deal and that the other victim's death was an accident (Center on Wrongful Convictions 2003).

3    George Ryan had just been inaugurated governor of Illinois in early 1999 when he saw Simon's videotaped confession. A proponent of capital punishment when elected, Ryan said this case left him feeling "jolted into reexamining everything I believed in" (Shapiro 2001). Weeks later, Andrew Kokoraleis, another Illinois prisoner, was scheduled to die. After agonizing over the decision, Ryan chose to sign off on the execution.

**sign off**
approve

**DNA**
genetic

4    Later that year, Ryan learned that 13 death-row inmates, some convicted 25 years before, had been found innocent after DNA evidence was discovered. Among them was an inmate who was within days of a scheduled execution. Ryan's views on capital punishment changed drastically. While he never questioned the state's right to take a life, he argued that the sentencing process was so flawed that it must be shut down until it was repaired (*Christian Century* 2003). In January 2000 he ordered a moratorium on executions in Illinois.

5    Ryan then appointed a panel to investigate Illinois' capital punishment system. The panel recommended 85 changes, including videotaping all police questioning of capital suspects and revising the procedures for conducting lineups. Because the panel found that the death penalty was unevenly applied, they recommended that it should be applied only when the defendant had murdered two or more people, a police officer or firefighter, a prison officer or inmate, or a crime-scene witness. The panel also

suggested that the death penalty should not be a sentencing option when only eyewitness evidence existed (Governor's Commission on Capital Punishment 2002).

**slaying**
murder

6    In October 2002 Ryan pardoned four black men who, after serving 15 years on death row for the 1986 slaying and rape of a medical student, were <u>exonerated</u> by DNA evidence. Then in January 2003, after a three-year battle to reform the Illinois capital punishment system, Ryan announced that he was <u>commuting</u> the death sentences of another four black men tortured by Chicago police officers into confessing to crimes they did not commit. Ryan stated that these four men were "perfect examples of what is so terribly broken about our system" (Kelly 2003).

7    Two days before leaving office in January 2003, George Ryan commuted the death sentences of 167 inmates to life without parole. Because Illinois citizens were evenly divided on the issue of sparing prisoners and commuting death sentences to life (*The Economist* 2002), it should come as no surprise that Ryan's actions were both praised as courageous and <u>scorned</u> as irresponsible (Johnson 2003, p. 34). At a press conference, Ryan stated, "Our capital system is haunted by the demon of error—error in determining guilt, and error in determining who among the guilty deserve to die" (Ryan 2003).

8    Ryan's actions have raised public awareness about death penalty misuse and the <u>plight</u> of the wrongfully convicted. He has forced us to ask hard questions: How many of the 3,557 prisoners on death row in the United States were falsely convicted? How many of the 4,744 prisoners put to death since 1930 were innocent? (U.S. Department of Justice, 2004). Ryan has won many awards recognizing his courage and conviction, and he was nominated for the 2003 Nobel Peace Prize. Ryan's efforts run parallel to those of the Innocence Project, a not-for-profit legal clinic that "only handles cases where post-conviction DNA testing of evidence can yield <u>conclusive</u> proof of innocence" (Innocence Project 2004). Students, supervised by a team of attorneys and clinic staff, investigate and handle the cases. Of the 144 inmates the clinic has exonerated, 23 (16 percent) of them were convicted in Illinois.

## Sources

Center on Wrongful Convictions. 2003. "The Illinois Exonerated: Anthony Porter." Northwestern University School of Law. www.law.northwestern.edu/depts./clinic/wrongful/exonerations/porter.htm.

*Christian Century*. 2003. "Capital Offense: Can the Death Penalty Really Be Sufficiently Reformed?" (February 8): 5.

*Economist*. 2002. "The Tale of Two Ryans: Death and Politics in Illinois" (October 19). www.infotrac-college.com.

Governor's Commission on Capital Punishment, State of Illinois. 2002. *Report of the Governor's Commission on Capital Punishment* (April). www.idoc.state.il.us/ccp/ccp/reports/commission_report/summary_recommendations.pdf.

Innocence Project. 2004. "About the Innocence Project." http://innocenceproject.org/about/.

Kelly, Maura. 2003. "Illinois Governor Pardons 4 Inmates on Death Row." *Salt Lake Tribune* (January 11). www.sltrib.com.

Ryan, George H. 2003. Quoted in Jodi Wilgoren, "Two Days Left in Term, Governor Clears Out Death Row in Illinois" *New York Times* (January 11) A:1.

Shapiro, Bruce. 2001. "A Talk with Governor George Ryan." *Nation* (January 8): 17.

U.S. Department of Justice, Bureau of Justice Statistics. 2004. "Prison and Jail Inmates at Midyear, 2003." February 6. www.ojp.usdoj.gov/bjs/glance/tables/drtab.htm.

**Exercise 1**

## Work with Words

Use context clues, dictionary skills, and your knowledge of word parts to choose the best definition for each of the following words underlined in the reading. The paragraph number is provided in case you want to check the context.

1. *prejudiced* (par. 2)
    a. racist
    b. biased
    c. affected

2. *pro bono* (par. 1)
    a. free of charge
    b. highly qualified but expensive
    c. greedy

3. *proponent* (par. 3)
    a. critic
    b. supporter
    c. neutral observer

4. *a moratorium on* (par. 4)
    a. a revision of
    b. a new approach to
    c. a suspension of activity

5. *unevenly* (par. 5)
    a. fairly
    b. unintentionally
    c. inconsistently

6. *exonerated* (par. 6)
    a  confirmed
    b. cleared
    c. examined

7. *commuting* (par. 6)
    a. reducing the penalty
    b. extending the penalty
    c. reviewing the case

8. *scorned* (par. 7)
    a. rewarded
    b. labeled
    c. rejected

9. *plight* (par. 8)
    a. predicament
    b. numbers
    c. mission

10. *conclusive* (par. 8)
    a. questionable
    b. positive
    c. theoretical

**Exercise 2**

## Check Your Understanding and Identify the Argument

Based on the reading, Gish's "The Falsely Accused on Death Row,'" choose the best answer to the following multiple-choice questions.

1. This article was probably written for
   a. college students.
   b. sociology professors.
   c. opponents of the death penalty.

2. What is the main idea of the reading?
   a. The death penalty should be abolished.
   b. Illinois has the most corrupt and discriminatory legal system of all the fifty states.
   c. The number of innocent prisoners on death row raises serious questions about the death penalty.

3. What was Governor Ryan's position on the death penalty when he first came into office?
   a. He was in favor of it.
   b. He opposed it.
   c. He did not have a strong opinion about it.

4. What made Governor Ryan decide to stop executions in Illinois?
   a. DNA evidence made it clear that the state had made multiple errors in convicting offenders and sentencing them to death.
   b. The lawyers for Anthony Porter threatened to sue the state of Illinois, and given the evidence, they probably would have won.
   c. Ryan's tough-on-crime stance was going to make it difficult for him to get reelected since many voters in Illinois wanted to repeal the death penalty.

5. What is the dominant pattern of organization in paragraphs 1–7?
   a. classification and definition
   b. narration and exemplification
   c. compare and contrast

6. Anthony Porter was cleared of murder charges and freed because
   a. DNA evidence proved that he did not commit the crime.
   b. he was borderline mentally retarded.
   c. another man confessed to the murders.

7. Which of the following is the best main idea statement for paragraph 5?
   a. The death penalty should only be allowed when two or more people are murdered.
   b. The panel that investigated the death penalty in Illinois recommended that eyewitness testimony on its own would not be sufficient to sentence someone to death.
   c. Governor Ryan created a panel to investigate the death penalty in Illinois, and it recommended multiple reforms.

8. The sources for this essay
   a. do not include government documents.
   b. are mainly newspaper and journal articles.
   c. include transcripts from trials.

9. The overall tone of the reading is
   a. objective.
   b. alarming.
   c. hopeful.

10. We can reasonably infer that Gish
    a. disagrees with Ryan and feels that he should not have commuted the death sentences of all the inmates on death row.
    b. admires Ryan and believes that he made the right decision about the death-row prisoners in Illinois.
    c. thinks that Ryan was the best governor that Illinois ever had.

---

**Exercise 3**

## Examine the Evidence and Check for Fallacies

Answer the following questions as fully as you can in your own words.

1. In the case of Anthony Porter, what are some of the flaws in the justice system that affected the outcome of the case (his conviction) initially?

_____

_____

_____

_____

_____

2. The judge in the original Porter case later left the court because of a financial scandal. Is that relevant to Porter's case, or could it be considered a fallacy? Explain.

_____

_____

_____

_____

_____

_____

3. What inference can we make about the criminal justice system in Illinois? What evidence supports this inference?

_____

_____

_____

_____

_____

_____

4. The Governor's Commission on Capital Punishment in Illinois made two recommendations: (1) Capital punishment should be applied only when the defendant had murdered two or more people, a police officer or fire fighter, a prison officer or inmate, or a crime-scene witness. (2) The death penalty should not be applied based on only eyewitness evidence. What can you reasonably infer led to these recommendations?

_____

_____

_____

_____

5. When Governor Ryan decided to commute the death sentences of 167 inmates to life without parole, some people thought he was "courageous," while others thought he was "irresponsible." Why would he be seen as courageous? Why would he be seen as irresponsible? What are the two arguments?

_____

_____

_____

_____

_____

_____

6. What imagery does Ryan use in his statements about the death penalty? How does Ryan's use of figurative language affect his argument?

_____

_____

_____

_____

_____

_____

**Exercise 4**

## Reflect and Think Critically: Form Your Own Opinion

Think about what you read in "The Falsely Accused on Death Row" and what you already know about the justice system and capital punishment. Then answer the following questions.

1. According to this article and other sources you have read or seen, how do people get convicted of crimes they did not commit? Give at least three reasons with sufficient explanation or examples.

_____

_____

_____

_____

_____

_____

_____

_____

2. What is your position on the death penalty? Did this article alter or strengthen your position in any way? Explain.

_____

_____

_____

_____

_____

3. What is society's responsibility to people who have been wrongfully imprisoned? How can we compensate them?

_____

_____

_____

_____

4. Have you ever changed your mind about an issue, or were you able to change someone else's mind? What was the issue and what brought about the change? Explain fully.

_____

_____

_____

# Additional Mastery Tests

# 1B

## Mastery Test

**Exercise 1**

### Prepare to Read and Read Actively

Answer the following questions. They will help you prepare to read "What Is Collaborative Learning?" which begins on page 359.

1. Which of the following might you do as you prepare to read? (Circle all that apply.)
   a. Determine your purpose for reading.
   b. Carefully start reading, beginning with the first sentence.
   c. Preview the reading.
   d. Ask questions the reading might answer.
   e. Try to determine what words you need to know and look them up in the dictionary.
   f. Consider your previous knowledge about the subject.

2. What is your purpose for reading this text? (Circle all that apply.)
   a. To complete a homework assignment
   b. To answer your questions about remembering material better
   c. To demonstrate that you can read and understand a textbook excerpt and respond to questions within a limited time
   d. To remember the information for a future test
   e. To get some information because you are interested in the subject

3. What previous knowledge do you have about collaborative learning? Write what you already know about how collaborative learning works.

   _____

4. Very quickly, preview the reading. What did you notice in your preview?

   _____

   _____

   _____

5. Write two preview questions you predict might be answered in this reading.
   a. _____
   b. _____

6. As you read, write two questions or comments in the margins to monitor your understanding as an active reader.

   _____

# What Is Collaborative Learning?*

— TONI HARING-SMITH

**TEXT BOOK** **The following reading is from a college writing textbook by Toni Haring-Smith. In this section, the author explains how group work can benefit the class as a whole and each student individually by helping students become active learners. She explains how writers and readers work together, a process she calls collaborative learning.**

*We work together, whether together or apart.*

*Robert Frost*

1   When you think of writing, what do you visualize? Do you see a solitary individual like Emily Dickinson sitting alone in an attic room? Do you imagine F. Scott Fitzgerald lying drunk in his lonely study? Or, do you see people working together—the early leaders of this country huddled in candlelight, talking, writing, and revising the Declaration of Independence? Do you see a famous novelist like Hemingway leaning over the typescript of a new book with his editor? . . .

2   Although most of our familiar images of writers and students present them as <u>solitary</u>, in fact most writers and thinkers work together to share ideas with one another. Our historical and cultural mythology encourages us to think of great ideas, discoveries, and events as the product of individual effort when they usually result from group effort. We remember Alexander Graham Bell and his telephone, Marie Curie and radium, Aristotle and the definition of tragedy, or Martin Luther King, Jr., and the civil rights movement. But none of these people worked alone. Bell developed his invention with his associate, Thomas Watson; Curie performed most of her experiments with her husband or her daughter; Aristotle spent twenty years discussing ideas with thinkers in Plato's Academy and later with his friend Theophrastus; and Martin Luther King, Jr., had a small army of supporters surrounding him as he marched out of Selma. There are, of course, hermits and solitary geniuses in our society, but they are the exceptions—so exceptional, in fact, that we frequently <u>brand</u> them peculiar or even insane.

3   It is not surprising, then, that recent research in education, psychology, and business management shows us that people can accomplish more if they work together. Dozens of studies have revealed that people working as a group to solve mazes or number puzzles can outperform individuals working alone at the same task. And perhaps the most interesting, research demonstrates that groups even solve puzzles more accurately than the brightest individual in them could alone. . . .

4   The classroom in which collaborative learning is used looks quite different from a more traditional lecture or class discussion. You will work in pairs or small groups, you may move about the room rather than sit still, and you will find out answers for yourselves rather than wait for the teacher to give you the answer. In fact, in most of these exercises, there is no "right answer," so you and your groups will be developing and defending your own ideas, not just trying to figure out "what the teacher wants."

5   Have you been asked to work in groups before and thought, "What a waste of time. Why doesn't the teacher just lecture?" Have you ever waited patiently through a class discussion in order to find out what the teacher really thinks? If you have been asked to read and comment on another student's paper, have you wondered what you could possibly have to say? Have you assumed that your classmates wouldn't be able to help you write, and have you

*"What Is Collaborative Learning?" by Toni Haring-Smith from WRITING TOGETHER: COLLABORATIVE LEARNING IN THE WRITING CLASSROOM. Reprinted with permission.

wished that the teacher would read your essay drafts? Or maybe most of your teachers have spent class time presenting material to you, while you took notes or worked on homework.

6     If any of these experiences sounds familiar, you will find collaborative learning a new approach. Of course, it is not a new kind of learning—in fact, reading, talking, and learning together was the practice in most schools until the twentieth century. But collaborative learning is not very common in American schools now. The first rules that most students learn in school are

- Be quiet.
- Don't talk to other students.
- Do your own work.

Our school systems have become so concerned with testing individual comprehension of material that they have stopped students from learning together. This has had a very serious effect on how well students learn and it has warped our assumptions about teachers' and students' roles in the classroom. Let's look at how collaborative learning challenges the kind of schooling most Americans now receive.

7     In order to work together with your classmates, you will have to recognize the knowledge and experience that you and your classmates have. Why work with others if you don't think that they have anything worthwhile to share? Why ask someone to respond to your writing if you think that only the teacher can do that? Most students have gradually come to distrust the knowledge they and their classmates have. The American educational system teaches most students that they should listen to the teacher, memorize what she and the textbooks say, and then <u>regurgitate</u> that information on exams and in papers. In many cases, students find it easier to forget or ignore what they think and just concentrate on what the teacher thinks.

**existentialism**
a philosophy that emphasizes the independence and isolation of each individual

8     I know that when I was a student, I was often afraid to speak in class. It seemed safer to be quiet than to be wrong. I remember sitting in English class and thinking, "Where did the teacher get that interpretation of this text? I thought that the poem was about a flower and she says that it is about existentialism." I learned to keep quiet rather than reveal my ignorance. I think many students share my fear of being wrong. Consequently, it is not surprising that American educators today <u>bemoan</u> the fact that their students are <u>passive</u>. . . .

9     In most colleges and universities, teachers and students alike assume that students are empty <u>vessels</u>, waiting to be filled with the knowledge of calculus, Chinese history, modern American architecture, or whatever. The basic definition of a teacher is one who knows a subject, while a student is assumed to be ignorant of the subject. Now to some extent, this is true. You take a class in organic chemistry because you want to learn organic chemistry. If you already knew the subject, you would probably try to "test out" of the course and take a different one. Of course, you might take a diagnostic test at the beginning of a course to see how much American history or calculus you remember, but these random questions can't really tell teachers what you know about a subject. If you know that Washington was president before Lincoln, does this mean that you also understand different cultural or political <u>climates</u> in which these two men worked? . . .

10     Most of the time, you do know something about the subject of the courses you take. Your courses up to this point have prepared you for organic chemistry. You have learned methods for balancing chemical equations, and you understand the basic structure of chemical compounds. Similarly, although you may never have taken a course in Chinese history, you probably know something about it—that it involves many dynasties, that China was a great silk producer, that Chinese women used to bind their feet, that the Chinese built the Great Wall, that the Communist party has been crushing political

dissent, and so on. Some of the things you "know" about a subject may not be "true." For example, based on popular media, you might assume that the Chinese were especially

ruthless
cruel

ruthless warriors. You might also have memorized incorrect valences for certain chemical elements. In any case, your mind is not a blank slate.

11    Not only do you come into a course with knowledge and experience that is relevant to it, but, as you go along in the course, you gradually come to understand its content. You will be learning about the subject from the teacher, the texts, and the other students in the class. What you learn will shape the way you hear the teacher, argue with your classmates, or read the texts.

12    If we teachers treat you as if you know nothing about the subject, and if you are afraid to speak for fear of being wrong, then you will become passive. You will wait for us to tell you what you think, and then you will write it down, and tell it back to us in papers and on exams. In this kind of system, there is little reward for thinking on your own. There is also little reward for listening to other, apparently equally ignorant students. This is why students often complain about group work of any kind. They want to know why the teacher does not just give them the answer.

13    Collaborative learning asks that you

- Have the courage to recognize and speak your own ideas.
- Respect the ideas and knowledge that other students bring to the class.
- Trust the teacher to listen to you with respect and to care about your ideas.

Collaborative learning redefines your relationship to your teacher and to the other students in the class. Rather than assume that your mind is a blank slate, waiting to be written on by the teacher, collaborative learning focuses on the knowledge and experience that you bring to a classroom. It works by finding out what you know and then allowing the teacher to respond and give you exercises that will let you learn. The teacher does not digest all the knowledge and feed it to you like the predigested food fed to baby birds. The teacher does not report her learning. You learn for yourself, and the teacher is there as a kind of coach to guide your learning, to point you to important ideas and books, to give you exercises that will help you sharpen your skills.

| Exercise 2 |

## Check Your "Prepare to Read and Reading Actively"

Briefly answer the following questions about how you applied the active reading process as you read "What Is Collaborative Learning?"

1. Which of your preview questions were answered?

_____

2. What strategies did you use to be an active reader? In what ways did these strategies help you remain involved, interested, and attentive?

_____

_____

_____

3. List the important information in the reading that was new for you.

_____

**Exercise 3**

## Work with Words

Choose the best definition for each of the following words underlined in the reading. The paragraph number is provided in case you want to go back to the reading to check the context. Use a dictionary if necessary.

1. *Solitary* (par. 2)
   a. with other people
   b. with one other person
   c. by oneself, alone

2. *Brand* (par. 2)
   a. put a mark on (a person or animal) with a hot piece of metal
   b. put a name brand on (a person or an object)
   c. put a person or object into a category

3. *Regurgitate* (par. 7)
   a. spit something out of your mouth
   b. throw up
   c. give the same information back

4. *Bemoan* (par. 8)
   a. complain about
   b. moan when in pain
   c. groan

5. *Passive* (par. 8)
   a. uninvolved
   b. pacific
   c. involved

6. *Vessels* (par. 9)
   a. ships
   b. containers
   c. tanks

7. *Climates* (par. 9)
   a. temperatures
   b. atmospheres
   c. weather zones

8. *Dissent* (par. 10)
   a. agreement
   b. beliefs
   c. disagreement

9. *Blank slate* (par. 10)
   a. blackboard with nothing on it
   b. empty
   c. full of information already

10. *Redefines* (par. 13)
    a. gives a new definition of
    b. gives the same meaning to
    c. changes the quality of

**Exercise 4**

## Check Your Understanding

Based on the reading, Haring-Smith's "What Is Collaborative Learning?" choose the best answer to each of the multiple-choice questions.

1. The author chose the examples of Alexander Graham Bell, Madame Curie, Aristotle, and Martin Luther King, Jr., because
   a. they were all very famous, solitary geniuses.
   b. they were all very famous and they all worked with other people.
   c. they were all a part of history that we are familiar with.

2. According to the author, we frequently say that hermits and solitary geniuses are "peculiar" because
   a. they are strange people.
   b. they are exceptions.
   c. they are smarter than other people.

3. Research shows that
   a. the smartest person in a group can finish a task faster alone.
   b. groups work faster and more accurately than the brightest person in them could do alone.
   c. groups rarely outperform bright individuals working alone.

4. Research on working together has been done in
   a. education, psychology, and business management.
   b. religious studies.
   c. anthropological studies.

5. The collaborative classroom looks different from regular classrooms because
   a. people frequently move around.
   b. students are quieter and neater than usual.
   c. learning is taking place.

6. According to the author
   a. collaborative learning is not very commonly used in American colleges and universities.
   b. most teachers assume that their students already know a great deal about the subject they are studying.
   c. collaborative learning is a new approach to education that was introduced in the twentieth century.

7. The author believes that our schools
   a. are not concerned enough with testing individual comprehension.
   b. are doing a good job educating generations of Americans and should be supported.
   c. should encourage students to learn together.

8. To work with your classmates, you should
   a. not assert your opinion too strongly, just go along with the group.
   b. recognize that the teacher will give you the correct answers in the end.
   c. recognize that you and your classmates have knowledge and experience to contribute to the discussion.

9. For collaborative learning to work
   a. students need to be more involved in their own learning.
   b. teachers need to prepare their lecture notes more carefully than usual.
   c. teachers do not need to know their subject matter as well.

10. Collaborative learning
    a. relies on the teacher more than on the students themselves.
    b. changes your relationship to your teacher and to other students in the class.
    c. is very difficult for students who study on their own.

**Exercise 5**

## Reflect

Think about what you read in "What Is Collaborative Learning?" and what you already know about this topic. Then answer the following questions.

1. What experiences have you had working with groups of people to achieve a common goal?

   _____

   _____

   _____

2. What examples do you know of people who worked together and achieved a better result than they would have by working alone?

   _____

   _____

   _____

3. Why do you think that students do better when they study and work together in groups?

   _____

   _____

   _____

   _____

   _____

**2B**

**Mastery Test**

# A Ring Tone Meant to Fall on Deaf Ears*

—PAUL VITELLO

**The following reading, from the *New York Times*, discusses an invention that young people discovered and used for their own purposes. As you read, notice how you can understand many of the underlined words because of the context of the sentence around them. Also, consider when you think talking on a cell phone is appropriate and when it is not.**

1   In that old battle of the wills between young people and their keepers, the young have found a new weapon that could change the balance of power on the cellphone front: a ring tone that many adults cannot hear. In settings where cellphone use is forbidden—in class, for example—it is perfect for signaling the arrival of a text message without being <u>detected</u> by an <u>elder of the species</u>. "When I heard about it I didn't believe it at first," said Donna Lewis, a technology teacher at the Trinity School in Manhattan. "But one of the kids gave me a copy, and I sent it to a <u>colleague</u>. She played it for her first graders. All of them could hear it, and neither she nor I could."

2   The technology, which relies on the fact that most adults gradually lose the ability to hear high-pitched sounds, was developed in Britain but has only recently spread to America—by Internet, of course. Recently, in classes at Trinity and elsewhere, some students have begun testing the boundaries of their new technology. One place was Michelle Musorofiti's freshman honors math class at Roslyn High School on Long Island. At Roslyn, as at most schools, cellphones must be turned off during class. But one morning last week, a high-pitched ring tone went off that set teeth on edge for anyone who could hear it. To the students' surprise, that group included their teacher.

"Whose cellphone is that?" Miss Musorofiti demanded, demonstrating that at 28, her ears had not lost their sensitivity to strangely annoying, high-pitched, though virtually inaudible tones.

**inaudible**
unable to be heard

3   "You can hear that?" one of them asked.

4   "Adults are not supposed to be able to hear that," said another, according to the teacher's account. She had indeed heard that, Miss Musorofiti said, adding, "Now turn it off."

5   The cellphone ring tone that she heard was the offshoot of an invention called the Mosquito, developed last year by a Welsh security company to annoy teenagers and <u>gratify</u> adults, not the other way around. It was marketed as an ultrasonic teenager <u>repellent</u>, an ear-splitting 17-kilohertz buzzer designed to help shopkeepers disperse young people <u>loitering</u> in front of their stores while leaving adults unaffected. The principle behind it is a biological reality that hearing experts refer to as <u>presbycusis</u>, or aging ear. While Miss Musorofiti is not likely to have it, most adults over 40 or 50 seem to have some symptoms, scientists say.

6     While most human communication takes place in a frequency range between 200 and 8,000 hertz (a hertz being the scientific unit of frequency equal to one cycle per second), most adults' ability to hear frequencies higher than that begins to <u>deteriorate</u> in early middle age. "It's the most common sensory abnormality in the world," said Dr. Rick A. Friedman, an ear surgeon and research scientist at the House Ear Institute in Los Angeles.

7     But in a bit of techno-jujitsu, someone—a person unknown at this time, but probably not someone with presbycusis—realized that the Mosquito, which uses this common adult abnormality to adults' advantage, could be turned against them. The Mosquito noise was reinvented as a ring tone.

**hooligans**
troublemakers

8     "Our high-frequency buzzer was copied. It is not exactly what we developed, but it's a pretty good imitation," said Simon Morris, marketing director for Compound Security, the company behind the Mosquito. "You've got to give the kids credit for <u>ingenuity</u>." British newspapers described the first use of the high-frequency ring tone last month in some schools in Wales, where Compound Security's Mosquito device was introduced as a "yob-buster," a reference to the hooligans it was meant to disperse.

**disperse**
cause to leave
or scatter

9     Since then, Mr. Morris said his company has received so much attention—none of it profit-making because the ring tone was in effect pirated—that he and his partner, Howard Stapleton, the inventor, decided to start selling a ring tone of their own. It is called Mosquitotone, and it is now advertised as "the authentic Mosquito ring tone." David Herzka, a Roslyn High School freshman, said he researched the British phenomenon a few weeks ago on the Web, and managed to upload a version of the high-pitched sound into his cellphone.

10    He transferred the ring tone to the cellphones of two of his friends at a birthday party on June 3. Two days later, he said, about five students at school were using it, and by Tuesday the number was a couple of dozen. "I just made it for my friends. I don't use a cellphone during class at school," he said.

11    How, David was asked, did he think this new device would <u>alter</u> the balance of power between adults and teenagers? Or did he suppose it was a passing fad? "Well, probably it is," said David, who added after a moment's thought, "And if not, I guess the school will just have to hire a lot of young teachers."

**Exercise 1**

## Work with Words

Use context, dictionary skills, and your knowledge of word parts to choose the best definition for each of the following words underlined in the reading. The paragraph number is provided in case you want to check the context.

1. *Detected* (par. 1)
   a. discovered
   b. trusted
   c. eliminated

2. *Elder of the species* (par. 1)
   a. type of tree
   b. older human being
   c. younger human being

3. *Colleague* (par. 1)
   a. fellow worker, a teacher
   b. fellow worker, a computer analyst
   c. friend

4. *Gratify* (par. 5)
   a. annoy
   b. invite
   c. please

5. *Repellent* (par. 5)
   a. something that attracts
   b. something that is interesting
   c. something that drives away

6. *Loitering* (par. 5)
   a. constructively working in an area
   b. staying in an area for no obvious reason
   c. helping out when stores need an extra hand

7. *Presbycusis* (par. 5)
   a. strong ear
   b. young ear
   c. aging ear

8. *Deteriorate* (par. 6)
   a. decline
   b. harden
   c. elevate

9. *Ingenuity* (par. 8)
   a. deception
   b. attention
   c. inventiveness

10. *Alter* (par. 11)
    a. improve
    b. destroy
    c. change

**Exercise 2**

## Check Your Understanding

Based on the reading, Vitello's "A Ring Tone Meant to Fall on Deaf Ears," choose the best answer to each of the following multiple-choice questions.

1. At first the purpose of the high-pitched tone that adults couldn't hear was to
   a. disperse young people who were loitering.
   b. invent a new ring tone that could be used on cell phones.
   c. eliminate hooligans.

2. When a first grade teacher played the tone for her class,
   a. none of them could hear it.
   b. only she could hear it.
   c. only the children could hear it.

3. The high-pitched tone
    a. is pleasing to the ear.
    b. is very loud.
    c. sounds really bad.

4. Somebody—probably a young person—figured out that the tone could
   be used as a ring tone and was especially useful when they were
    a. watching a movie and it was important to be quiet.
    b. traveling by plane or by car.
    c. in class and cell phones were supposed to be turned off because
       the teacher couldn't hear it.

5. When the high-pitched ring tone went off in Michelle Musorofiti's freshman
   honors math class,
    a. nobody heard it.
    b. all the students heard it but not Ms. Musorofiti.
    c. everybody heard it including Ms. Musorofiti.

6. Most human communication takes place
    a. by cell phone or text messaging.
    b. in a range between 200 and 8,000 hertz.
    c. before the age of 50.

7. Adults' ability to hear frequencies higher than 8,000 hertz
    a. is better than that of younger people.
    b. begins to deteriorate in early middle age.
    c. never changes over their lifetime.

8. The company that designed the high-frequency buzzer,
   Compound Security,
    a. made a lot of money when it was turned into a ring tone.
    b. got a lot of attention when it was turned into a ring tone.
    c. decided to go out of business because of the negative publicity.

9. Students' using the ring tone on their cell phones in class is
    a. perfectly acceptable for their teachers.
    b. a funny twist since it was invented to help adults and to annoy young
       people.
    c. used as an example of how students are dishonest.

10. David said that if the new device catches on, the "school will just have to
    hire a lot of young teachers" because
    a. only young teachers would be able to hear the ring tone.
    b. he believes that young teachers are better than old ones.
    c. he is certain that the device will soon be very popular.

**Exercise 3**

Reflect

Think about what you read in "A Ring Tone Meant to Fall on Deaf Ears" and what you already know about this topic. Then answer the following questions.

1. Do you think that using annoying sounds that adults can't hear is a good way to keep teenagers from loitering? Explain your answer.

   _____

   _____

   _____

   _____

   _____

2. When do you think it's appropriate to talk on a cell phone? When is it inappropriate? Explain the reasons for your answers.

   _____

   _____

   _____

   _____

   _____

   _____

   _____

## 3B

### Mastery Test

# Eating: Why We Do It When We Do*

— Douglas A. Bernstein and Peggy W. Nash

**TEXT BOOK** This reading is from a popular psychology textbook, *Essentials of Psychology*. It challenges us to think about the many reasons we have for eating. By understanding why we eat, we may be able to develop healthier eating habits. The authors base their conclusions on brain research that is currently being done with animals and humans. As you read, note the topics, main ideas, and specific details.

1   You get hungry when you haven't eaten for a while. Much as a car needs gasoline, you need fuel from food, so you eat. But what bodily <u>mechanism</u> acts as a "gauge" to signal the need for fuel? What determines which foods you eat, and how do you know when to stop? The answers to these questions involve complex interactions between the brain and the rest of the body (Hill & Peters, 1998).

## SIGNALS FOR HUNGER AND SATIETY

underlie
account for

2   A variety of mechanisms underlie *hunger*, the general state of wanting to eat, and *satiety* . . . the general state of no longer wanting to eat.

### Signals from the Stomach

3   The stomach would seem to be a logical source of signals for hunger and satiety. You have probably felt "hunger pangs" from an "empty" stomach and felt "stuffed" after overeating. In fact, the stomach does <u>contract</u> during hunger pangs, and increased pressure within the stomach can reduce appetite (Cannon & Washburn, 1912; Houpt, 1994). But people who have lost their stomachs due to illness still get hungry, and they still eat normal amounts of food (Janowitz, 1967). So stomach cues can affect eating, but they appear to operate mainly when you are very hungry or very full.

### Signals from the Blood

4   The most important signals about the body's fuel level and nutrient needs are sent to the brain from the blood. The brain's ability to "read" blood-borne signals about the body's nutritional need was discovered when researchers <u>deprived</u> rats of food for a long period and then injected some of the rats with blood from rats that had just eaten. When offered food, the injected rats ate little or nothing (Davis et al., 1969). Something in the injected blood of the well-fed animals apparently signaled the hungry rats' brains that there was no need to eat. What was that satiety signal? Research has shown that the brain constantly monitors both the level of food *nutrients* absorbed into the

bloodstream from the stomach and the level of *hormones* released into the blood in response to those nutrients (Korner & Leibel, 2003).

5    The nutrients that the brain monitors include <u>glucose</u> (the main form of sugar used by body cells), *fatty acids* (from fat), and *amino acids* (from protein). When the level of blood glucose drops, eating increases sharply (Mogenson, 1976). The brain also monitors hormone levels to regulate hunger and satiety. For example, when glucose levels rise, the pancreas releases *insulin*, a hormone that most body cells need to use the glucose they receive. Insulin itself may also provide a satiety signal by acting directly on brain cells (Bruning et al., 2000; Schwartz et al., 2000).

**regulate**
control

6    Several brain regions and many brain chemicals regulate hunger and food selection. These internal regulatory processes are themselves affected by the physical environment (e.g., what foods are available), by learning experiences with particular foods, and, for humans, by social and cultural traditions about eating.

## FLAVOR, EXPERIENCE AND CULTURE

7    Eating is powerfully affected by the *flavor* of food—the combination of its taste and smell (Carlson, 2001). In general, people eat more when differently flavored foods are served, as in a <u>multicourse</u> meal than when only one food is served (Raynor & Epstein, 2001). Apparently the flavor of a food becomes less enjoyable as more of it is eaten (Swithers & Hall, 1994). In one study, people rated how much they liked four kinds of food; then they ate one of the foods and rated all four again. The food they had just eaten now got a lower rating, whereas liking increased for all the rest (Johnson & Vickers, 1993).

8    Eating is also affected by the appearance and smell of certain foods. These signals come to <u>elicit</u> conditioned physiological responses—including the secretion of saliva, digestive juices, and insulin—in anticipation of eating those foods. So merely seeing a pizza on television may prompt you to order one. And if you see a delicious-looking cookie, you don't have to be hungry to start eating it. In fact, many people who have just pronounced themselves "full" after a huge holiday meal still manage to find room for an appetizing dessert. In other words, humans eat not just to satisfy nutritional needs but also to experience enjoyment.

9    Eating is stimulated by other kinds of signals, too. Do you usually eat while reading or watching television? If so, you may find that merely settling down with a book or your favorite show can <u>trigger</u> the desire to have a snack, even if you just finished dinner! This happens partly because situations associated with eating in the past can become signals that stimulate eating in the future (Birch et al., 1989; Weingarten, 1983). People also learn social rules and cultural traditions that influence eating. In North American culture, having lunch at noon, munching popcorn at movies, and eating hot dogs at ball games are common examples of how certain social situations can stimulate eating particular items at particular times. How much you eat may also depend on what others do. Politeness or custom might prompt you to try foods you would otherwise have avoided. Generally, the mere presence of others, even strangers, tends to increase food consumption. Most people consume 60 to 75 percent more food when they are with others than when eating alone (Clendenen, Herman, & Polivy, 1995) and the same effect has been observed in other species, from monkeys to chickens (Galloway et al., 2005; Keeling & Hurink, 1996).

10    Celebrations, holidays, vacations, and even daily family interactions often revolve around food and what some call a food *culture* (Rozin, 1996). There are wide cultural variations in food use and selection. For example, chewing coca leaves is popular in the Bolivian highlands but illegal in the United States (Burchard, 1992). Insects called palm weevils, a <u>delicacy</u> for people in Papua New Guinea (Paoletti, 1995), are regarded by many Westerners as disgusting (Springer & Belk, 1994), and the beef enjoyed by

many Westerners is morally <u>repugnant</u> to devout Hindus in India. Even within the same culture, different groups may have sharply contrasting food traditions. Squirrel brains won't be found on most dinner tables in the United States, but some people in the rural South consider them to be a tasty treat. In short, eating serves functions beyond nutrition—functions that help to remind us of who we are and with whom we identify.

## Work with Words

Use context clues, dictionary skills, and your knowledge of word parts to choose the best definition for each of the following words underlined in the reading. The paragraph number is provided in case you want to check the context.

1. *Mechanism* (par. 1)
   a. a physical or mental process
   b. a machine or mechanical structure
   c. action or movement

2. *Satiety* (par. 2)
   a. the general state of wanting to eat
   b. the general state of no longer wanting to eat
   c. the feeling of being too full or stuffed

3. *Contract* (par. 3)
   a. get smaller or shrink
   b. make a business deal
   c. acquire or cause pain

4. *Deprived . . . of food* (par. 4)
   a. prevented from having food
   b. encouraged to continue eating
   c. stopped the desire for food

5. *Glucose* (par. 5)
   a. fat
   b. protein
   c. sugar

6. *Multicourse* (par. 7)
   a. requiring a lot of preparation
   b. consisting of many dishes
   c. lasting a long period of time

7. *Elicit* (par. 8)
   a. remove
   b. work against
   c. bring out

8. *Trigger* (par. 9)
   a. expand
   b. weaken
   c. stimulate

9. *Delicacy* (par. 10)
   a. main food
   b. special treat
   c. dessert

10. *Repugnant* (par. 10)
   a. indifferent
   b. offensive
   c. desirable

**Exercise 2**

## Check Your Understanding

Based on the reading, Bernstein and Nash's "Eating: Why We Do It When We Do," choose the best answer to each of the following multiple-choice questions.

1. Signals from the stomach occur primarily when you
   a. have not felt hunger pangs in a while.
   b. are either very hungry or very full.
   c. are not thinking logically.

2. The blood carries messages to your brain which indicate
   a. that you have stuffed yourself.
   b. nutritional needs and hormone levels.
   c. how flavors influence your food preferences.

3. In the experiment mentioned in paragraph 4, the researchers concluded that
   a. it is impossible to compare rat brains with human brains.
   b. blood transmits signals about whether it is time to eat.
   c. hungry rats will overeat after they have been without food for a long period of time.

4. Glucose, fatty acids, and amino acids are
   a. hormones that the brain regulates.
   b. indicators of satiety.
   c. nutrients that the brain monitors.

5. Insulin is a hormone that
   a. enables cells to use glucose.
   b. causes diabetes.
   c. releases fatty acids into cells.

6. According to the reading, people tend to enjoy eating more when
   a. there is a variety of food available.
   b. they have been given large amounts of their favorite dish.
   c. they are eating very sweet or salty foods.

7. According to the reading, wanting to eat as soon as you sit down in front of the TV is likely due to
   a. the high number of food and restaurant commercials.
   b. feelings of boredom or loneliness.
   c. having the habit of eating while watching TV.

8. According to the authors, animals and people tend to eat more
   a. at certain times of the day.
   b. when they are in social situations.
   c. when they are alone or feeling lonely.

9. Eating squirrel brains in the rural South is an example of
   a. social eating.
   b. a food trigger.
   c. a food culture.

10. The authors believe that
    a. laboratory research which uses animals is not really helpful in understanding human behavior.
    b. there is no way to completely understand why people eat what they eat.
    c. eating has to do with culture, social practices, and individual habits as well as nutrition.

**Exercise 3**

## Identify Topics, Main Ideas, and Thesis

For each of the following paragraphs from the reading, choose the best topic and main idea statement. Then write the main idea in your own words on the lines provided. In the last question, choose the best topic and thesis for the whole reading. Then rewrite the thesis in your own words.

1. Paragraph 3

   Topic:

   a. the stomach
   b. cues for eating
   c. empty stomachs compared to full stomachs

   Main idea:

   a. You have probably felt "hunger pangs" from an "empty" stomach and felt "stuffed" after overeating.
   b. People who have lost their stomachs due to illness still get hungry, and they still eat normal amounts of food.
   c. Stomach cues can affect eating, but they appear to operate mainly when you are very hungry or very full.

   The main idea in your own words: _____

   _____

   _____

2. Paragraph 4

   Topic:

   a. animal hunger
   b. studies about rats and hunger
   c. the brain reception of hunger signals from the blood

   Main idea:

   a. The most important signals about the body's fuel level and nutrient needs are sent to the brain from the blood.
   b. Something in the injected blood of the well-fed animals apparently signaled the hungry rats' brains that there was no need to eat.

c. The brain's ability to "read" blood-borne signals about the body's nutritional need was discovered when researchers deprived rats of food for a long period and then injected some of the rats with blood from rats that had just eaten.

The main idea in your own words: _____

_____

_____

3. Paragraph 8

Topic:

a. television advertisements and eating
b. eating for enjoyment, not just nutrition
c. overeating at holiday meals

Main idea:

a. Many people who have just pronounced themselves "full" after a huge holiday meal still manage to find room for an appetizing dessert.
b. Humans eat not just to satisfy nutritional needs but also to experience enjoyment.
c. Merely seeing a pizza on television may prompt you to order one.

The main idea in your own words: _____

_____

_____

4. Paragraph 9

Topic:

a. situational eating
b. snacking
c. eating with other people

Main idea:

a. When we eat and how much we eat is influenced by the situation or circumstances we are in.
b. How much you eat may depend on what others do.
c. Generally, the mere presence of others, even strangers, tends to increase food consumption.

The main idea in your own words: _____

_____

_____

5. Paragraphs 1–10

Topic:

a. when and why we eat
b. nutrition and eating
c. cultural influences on food

Thesis:

a. We eat because we need energy, just like a car needs gasoline.
b. Several brain regions and chemicals regulate hunger and food choices, and the blood sends the most important signals about the body's energy and food needs to the brain.
c. Interactions among the stomach, blood, and brain signal us to eat, but social, cultural, and individual factors also greatly influence our eating behaviors.

The thesis in your own words: _____

_____

_____

---

**Exercise 4**

### Reflect

Think about what you read in "Eating: Why We Do It When We Do" and what you already know about what influences eating habits. Then answer the following questions.

1. Are there any times when you tend to eat even if you are not hungry? When does it happen, and why do you think those particular situations make you want to eat? Explain your answer.

_____

_____

_____

_____

2. The authors discuss many reasons for eating. Which reason (other than nutrition) influences you the most in what, how, and when you eat? Give specific examples to support your answer.

_____

_____

_____

_____

_____

**4B**

**Mastery Test**

# A Personal Stress Survival Guide*

—Dianne Hales

**TEXT BOOK** The following reading from the textbook *An Invitation to Health* outlines some of the most important ways that people can deal with the stress in their lives. As you read, pay attention to how the main ideas are explained and developed with supporting points.

1   Although stress is a very real threat to emotional and physical well-being, its impact depends not just on what happens to you, but on how you handle it. . . .

2   In studying individuals who manage stress so well that they seem "stress-resistant," researchers have observed that these individuals share many of the following <u>traits</u>:

- They respond actively to challenges. If a problem comes up, they look for resources, do some reading or research, and try to find a solution rather than giving up and feeling helpless. Because they've faced numerous challenges, they have confidence in their abilities to cope.
- They have personal goals, such as getting a college degree or becoming a better parent.
- They rely on a combination of planning, goal setting, problem solving, and risk taking to control stress.
- They use a minimum of substances such as nicotine, caffeine, alcohol, or drugs.
- They regularly <u>engage in</u> some form of relaxation, from meditation to exercise to knitting, at least 15 minutes a day.
- They tend to seek out other people and become involved with them.

3   In order to achieve greater control over the stress in your life, start with some self-analysis: If you're feeling overwhelmed, ask yourself: Are you taking an extra course that's draining your last ounce of energy? Are you staying up late studying every night and missing morning classes? Are you living on black coffee and jelly doughnuts? While you may think that you don't have time to reduce the stress in your life, some simple changes can often ease the pressure you're under and help you achieve your long-term goals. . . .

4   Since the small ups and downs of daily life have an enormous <u>impact</u> on psychological and physical well-being, getting a handle on daily hassles will reduce your stress load.

## POSITIVE COPING MECHANISMS

5   After a perfectly miserable, aggravating day, a teacher comes home and yells at her children for making too much noise. Another individual, after an equally stressful day, jokes about what went wrong during the all-time most miserable moment of the month. Both

*"A Personal Stress Survival Guide" by Dianne Hales from INVITATION TO HEALTH (with Info Trac), 8th Edition. © 1999 Brooks/Cole, a part of Cengage Learning, Inc. Reproduced by permission. www.cengage.com/permissions.

---

### STRATEGIES FOR CHANGE
#### How to Cope with Stress

✔ Recognize your stress signals. Is your back bothering you more? Do you find yourself speeding or misplacing things? Force yourself to stop whenever you see these early warnings and say, "I'm under stress; I need to do something about it."

✔ Keep a stress journal. Focus on intense emotional experiences and "<u>autopsy</u>" them to try to understand why they affected you the way they did. Re-reading and thinking about your notes may reveal the underlying reasons for your response.

✔ Try "<u>stress-inoculation</u>." Rehearse everyday situations that you find stressful, such as speaking in class. Think of how you might handle the situation, perhaps by breathing deeply before you talk.

✔ Put things in proper perspective. Ask yourself: Will I remember what's made me so upset a month from now? If you had to rank this problem on a scale of 1 to 10, with worldwide catastrophe as 10, where would it rate?

✔ Think of one simple thing that could make your life easier. What if you put up a hook to hold your keys so that you didn't spend five minutes searching for them every morning?

---

6

of these people are using <u>defense mechanisms</u>—actions or behaviors that help protect their sense of self-worth. The first is displacing anger onto someone else; the second uses humor to vent frustration.

**alleviate**
relieve

7  Under great stress, we all may turn to negative defense mechanisms to alleviate anxiety and eliminate conflict. These can lead to maladaptive behavior, such as rationalizing overeating by explaining to yourself that you need the extra calories to cope with the extra stress in your life. <u>Coping mechanisms</u> are healthier, more mature and adaptive ways of dealing with stressful situations. While they also ward off unpleasant emotions, they usually are helpful rather than harmful. The most common are:

**ward off**
keep away

**drives**
urges

● <u>Sublimation</u>, the redirection of any drives considered unacceptable into socially acceptable channels. For example, someone who is furious with a friend or relative may go for a long run to sublimate anger.

● Religiosity, in which one comes to terms with a painful experience, such as a child's death, by experiencing it as being in accord with God's will.

**in accord**
in agreement

● Humor, which counters stress by focusing on comic aspects. Medical students, for instance, often make jokes in anatomy lab as a way of dealing with their anxieties about working with cadavers.

● Altruism, which takes a negative experience and turns it into a positive one. For example, an HIV-positive individual may talk to teenagers about AIDS prevention.

# MANAGING TIME

8     Every day you make dozens of decisions, and the choices you make about how to use your time directly affect your stress level. If you have a big test on Monday and a term paper due Tuesday, you may plan to study all weekend. Then, when you're invited to a party Saturday night, you go. Although you set the alarm for 7:00 A.M. on Sunday, you don't pull yourself out of bed until noon. By the time you start studying, it's 4:00 P.M., and anxiety is building inside you.

9     How can you tell if you've lost control of your time? The following are telltale symptoms of poor time management:

- Rushing.
- Chronic inability to make choices or decisions.
- Fatigue or listlessness.
- Constantly missed deadlines.
- Not enough time for rest or personal relationships.
- A sense of being overwhelmed by demands and details and having to do what you don't want to do most of the time.

10     One of the hard lessons of being on your own is that your choices and your actions have consequences. Stress is just one of them. But by thinking ahead, being realistic about your workload, and sticking to your plans, you can gain better control over your time and your stress levels.

# OVERCOMING PROCRASTINATION

11     Putting off until tomorrow what should be done today is a habit that creates a great deal of stress for many students. The three most common types of procrastination are: putting off unpleasant things, putting off difficult tasks, and putting off tough decisions. Procrastinators are most likely to delay by wishing they didn't have to do what they must or by telling themselves they "just can't get started," which means they never do.

12     People procrastinate, not because they're lazy, but to protect their self-esteem and make a favorable impression. "Procrastinators often perceive their worth as based solely on task ability, and their ability is determined only by how well they perform on completed tasks," notes psychologist Joseph Ferrari, Ph.D. "By never completing the tasks, they are never judged on their ability, thus allowing them to maintain an illusion of competence."[1]

13     To get out of a time trap, keep track of the tasks you're most likely to put off, and try to figure out why you don't want to tackle them. Think of alternative ways to get tasks done. If you put off library readings, for instance, figure out if the problem is getting to the library or the reading itself. If it's the trip to the library, arrange to walk over with a friend whose company you enjoy.

14     Develop daily time-management techniques, such as a "To Do" list. Rank items according to priorities: A, B, C, and schedule your days to make sure the A's get accomplished. Try not to fixate on half-completed projects. Divide large tasks, such as a term paper, into smaller ones, and reward yourself when you complete a part.

15     Do what you like least first. Once you have it out of the way, you can concentrate on the tasks you do enjoy. You also should build time into your schedule for interruptions, <u>unforeseen</u> problems, unexpected events, and so on, so you aren't constantly racing around. Establish ground rules for meeting your own needs (including getting enough sleep and making time for friends) before saying yes to any activity. Learn to live according to a three-word motto: Just do it!

## RELAXATION TECHNIQUES

16    Relaxation is the physical and mental state opposite that of stress. Rather than gearing up for a fight or flight, our bodies and minds grow calmer and work more smoothly. We're less likely to become frazzled and more capable of staying in control. The most effective relaxation techniques include progressive relaxation, visualization, meditation, mindfulness, and biofeedback.

17    *Progressive relaxation* works by intentionally increasing and then decreasing tension in the muscles. While sitting or lying down in a quiet, comfortable setting, you tense and release various muscles, beginning with those of the hand, for instance, and then proceeding to the arms, shoulders, neck, face, scalp, chest, stomach, buttocks, genitals, and so on, down each leg to the toes. Relaxing the muscles can quiet the mind and restore internal balance.[2]

18    *Visualization,* or *guided imagery*, involves creating mental pictures that calm you down and focus your mind. . . . Some people use this technique to promote healing when they are ill. The Glasser study showed that elderly residents of retirement homes in Ohio who learned progressive relaxation and guided imagery <u>enhanced</u> their immune function and reported better health than did the other residents. Visualization skills require practice and, in some cases, instruction by qualified health professionals.[3]

19    *Meditation* has been practiced in many forms over the ages, from the yogic techniques of the Far East to the Quaker silence of more modern times. Meditation helps a person reach a state of relaxation, but with the goal of achieving inner peace and harmony. There is no one right way to meditate, and many people have discovered how to meditate on their own, without even knowing what it is they are doing. Among college students, meditation has proven especially effective in increasing relaxation.[4] Most forms of meditation have common elements: sitting quietly for 15 to 20 minutes once or twice a day, concentrating on a word or image, and breathing slowly and rhythmically. If you wish to try meditation, it often helps to have someone guide you through your first sessions. Or try tape recording your own voice (with or without favorite music in the background) and playing it back to yourself, freeing yourself to concentrate on the goal of turning the attention within.

20    *Mindfulness* is a modern-day form of an ancient Asian technique that involves maintaining awareness in the present moment. You tune into each part of your body, scanning from head to toe, noting the slightest sensation. You allow whatever you experience—an itch, an ache, a feeling of warmth—to enter your awareness. Then you open yourself to focus on all the thoughts, sensations, sounds, and feelings that enter your awareness. Mindfulness keeps you in the here-and-now, thinking about what is rather than about "what if" or "if only."

21    *Biofeedback* . . . is a method of obtaining feedback, or information, about some physiological activity occurring in the body. An electronic monitoring device attached to a person's body detects a change in an internal function and communicates it back to the person through a tone, light, or meter. By paying attention to this feedback, most people can gain some control over functions previously thought to be beyond conscious control, such as body temperature, heart rate, muscle tension, and brain waves. Biofeedback training consists of three stages:

1.  Developing increased awareness of a body state or function.

2.  Gaining control over it.

3.  Transferring this control to everyday living without use of the electronic instrument.

22    The goal of biofeedback for stress reduction is a state of tranquility, usually associated with the brain's production of alpha waves (which are slower and more regular than

normal waking waves). After several training sessions, most people can produce alpha waves more or less at will.[5]

**Notes**

1. Joseph Ferrari, "Self-Destructive Motivation—Personality, Social, and Clinical Perspectives" (paper presented to the American Psychological Association, August 1992).

2. Herbert Benson and Michael McKee, "Relaxation and Other Alternative Therapies," *Patient Care* 27 (December 15, 1993).

3. Janice Kiecolt-Glaser and Ronald Glaser, "Stress and the Immune System: Human Studies," *Review of Psychiatry* 11 (1992).

4. John Janowiak, "The Effects of Meditation on College Students' Self-Actualization and Stress Management," *Dissertation Abstracts International* 53 (April 1993).

5. Benson and McKee, "Relaxation and Other Alternative Therapies."

**Exercise 1**

## Work with Words

Use context, clues, dictionary skills, and your knowledge of word parts to choose the best definition for each of the following words underlined in the reading. The paragraph number is provided in case you want to check the context.

1. *Traits* (par. 2)
   a. problems
   b. responses
   c. characteristics

2. *Engage in* (par. 2)
   a. participate in
   b. plan to get married
   c. indulge in

3. *Impact* (par. 4)
   a. collision
   b. increase
   c. effect

4. *Defense mechanisms* (par. 5)
   a. actions to defend oneself from attack
   b. tactics of self-defense
   c. actions or behaviors that help protect one's sense of self-worth

5. *Autopsy* (par. 6)
   a. study or review
   b. examine a body to determine cause of death
   c. reduce

6. *Stress-inoculation* (par. 6)
   a. advance preparation for stress
   b. vaccination for stress
   c. stressful shot

7. *Coping mechanisms* (par. 7)
   a. healthier, more mature, and adaptive ways of dealing with stressful situations
   b. ways of displacing anger onto someone else so that one feels better
   c. some of the most important forms of defense mechanisms

8. *Sublimation* (par. 7)
   a. recognition of the sublime or wonderful aspects of a mental condition
   b. the redirection of any drives considered unacceptable into socially acceptable channels
   c. going for a run as a way of dealing with anger with a friend

9. *Unforeseen* (par. 15)
   a. seen from before
   b. not expected
   c. seen in the past

10. *Enhanced* (par. 18)
   a. decreased
   b. improved
   c. immunized

## Exercise 2

### Check Your Understanding

Based on the reading, Hales's "A Personal Stress Survival Guide," choose the best answer to each of the following multiple-choice questions.

1. Although stress is a very real threat to emotional and physical well-being
   a. some individuals manage it better than others.
   b. everyone suffers from it equally.
   c. there is not much that can be done about it.

2. People who manage stress well
   a. abuse drugs.
   b. have personal goals.
   c. respond passively to challenges.

3. All the following are strategies for coping with stress except
   a. recognizing your stress signals.
   b. putting things in proper perspective.
   c. having a relaxing drink.

4. Yelling at your children after a miserable day at work is an example of
   a. physical child abuse.
   b. a positive defense mechanism.
   c. a negative defense mechanism.

5. Sublimation, religiosity, humor, and altruism are examples of
   a. negative defense mechanisms.
   b. coping mechanisms.
   c. redirecting drives considered unacceptable into socially acceptable channels.

6. If you don't have time for rest or personal relationships, and you feel overwhelmed by demands and details, the chances are
   a. you are using ineffective coping mechanisms.
   b. you are not managing your time well.
   c. you have a mature outlook on life.

7. According to Hales, some people procrastinate because they
   a. are lazy.
   b. don't like to do what they have to do.
   c. want to protect their self-esteem.

8. One suggestion for overcoming procrastination is
   a. do what you like least first.
   b. concentrate on enjoying everything that you do.
   c. fixate on half-completed projects.

9. Progressive relaxation is
   a. a way to progress from one form of relaxation to another.
   b. a method of intentionally increasing and then decreasing tension in the muscles.
   c. one of the ways to best apply visualization.

10. Mindfulness is a technique that helps you
   a. maintain and be aware of the present moment.
   b. get away from the stress of the moment.
   c. meditate for relaxation.

**Exercise 3**

## Organize to Learn: Outline and Summarize

Complete the following outline for the reading. Then, using your outline, write a brief summary of the reading on a separate sheet of paper. In the first sentence of your summary, put the main idea in your own words, and be sure to include the title and author of the reading.

### A Personal Stress Survival Guide

**Main Idea:** In "A Personal Stress Survival Guide," Dianne Hales emphasizes that although stress can threaten your emotional and physical health, how it affects you also depends on how you cope with it.

I. Common traits of people who manage stress well

  A. Respond actively to stress

    1. Look for resources

    2. _____

    3. _____

    4. Have confidence in their ability to cope

  B. _____

  C. Rely on combination of activities to control stress

    1. _____

    2. _____

    3. Problem solving

    4. _____

  D. Use a minimum of substances (nicotine, caffeine, alcohol, drugs)

  E. _____

  F. _____

II. How to cope with stress

   A. _____

   B. _____

   C. Think in advance about how you would handle a stressful situation

   D. _____

   E. _____

III. Positive coping mechanisms

   A. Sublimation (redirection of unacceptable drives into acceptable channels)

   B. _____

   C. _____

   D. _____

IV. Signs of poor time management

   A. _____

   B. Inability to make decisions

   C. _____

   D. _____

   E. _____

   F. Sense of being overwhelmed

V. Overcoming procrastination

   A. Three common forms of procrastination

      1. _____

      2. _____

      3. _____

   B. Reasons for procrastination

      1. _____

      2. _____

   C. Ways to stop procrastinating

      1. _____

      2. _____

      3. _____

VI. Relaxation techniques

A. _____

B. _____

C. _____

D. _____

E. _____

**Exercise 4**

## Reflect

Think about what you read in "A Personal Stress Survival Guide" and what you already know about stress. Then answer the following questions.

1. Which of the techniques for avoiding stress have you observed other people using? Give an example of someone you know and how that person uses or has used a technique mentioned in the reading.

    _____

    _____

    _____

2. Which of the techniques for avoiding stress do you think are most important for you to master? Explain.

    _____

    _____

    _____

**5B**

**Mastery Test**

# Sociological Perspectives on Urbanization and City Life* — ALEX THIO

**TEXT BOOK** The following reading from the textbook *Sociology: A Brief Introduction* explains the three basic approaches that sociologists use when analyzing social developments. In this reading, you will learn how sociologists analyze urbanization and city life using the functionalist perspective, conflict perspective, and symbolic interactionist perspective. As you read, try to identify the various patterns of organization used to present this information.

**beneficiary**
someone or something that benefits

1    Both the functionalist and conflict perspectives can be used to explain the forces behind the urbanization of U.S. society. To functionalists, the masses of ordinary people seek and benefit from urbanization as a way of adapting to their changing environment. To conflict theorists, the driving force and beneficiary of urbanization is really big business. Symbolic interactionists, however, are more interested in explaining city life by focusing on how people interact with one another in the city.

## FUNCTIONALIST PERSPECTIVE: URBANIZATION DRIVEN BY THE MASSES

2    According to the functionalist perspective, the masses of ordinary people are the primary driving force behind urbanization, or urbanization reflects what the masses want when faced with changes in their environment (Rybczynski, 1995). Let's take a close look at the role of the masses in urbanization.

3    First, technology increases agricultural production so much that considerably fewer people are needed to work on farms. So, seeking better job opportunities, throngs of people leave the farms for the cities, which leads to explosive urban growth. Since these former farmers are mostly manual laborers, their influx to the cities helps to expand the manufacturing industry, allowing the mass production of everything from shoes to clothes to cars and computers. Next, as cities become crowded, increasing numbers of people move to the outskirts to live. They can continue to work in the inner cities, however, thanks to the mass production of cars. Then, as the suburbs become increasingly populated, various businesses emerge to cater to the shopping needs of suburbanites, eventually leading to the proliferation of shopping malls. Finally, a

**cornucopia**
abundance

cornucopia of jobs is created in the suburbs, so that suburbanites do not need to commute to the central cities to work. At this late stage of urbanization, metropolises and megalopolises begin to emerge. Functionalists assume that all these social changes

*Alex Thio, SOCIOLOGY: BRIEF INTRODUCTION, "Sociological Perspectives on Urbanization and City Life" pp. 420–421, © 1997 Addison Wesley Longman, Inc. Reproduced by permission of Pearson Education, Inc.

| Urbanization and City Life | | |
|---|---|---|
| Perspective | Focus | Insights |
| Functionalist | How the masses drive urbanization | People leave farms to seek better opportunities and lives in the cities and then the suburbs. |
| Conflict | How big business fuels urbanization | Large corporations pursue profit by starting agri-business that forces farmers to leave for the cities and then building homes, factories, and businesses in urban and suburban areas. |
| Symbolic Interactionist | How city people interact | City people tend to interact superficially, with civil inattention but with tolerance for others' lifestyles. |

brought about by urbanization and suburbanization reflect what the masses need and seek to have a comfortable life.

## CONFLICT PERSPECTIVE: URBANIZATION FUELED BY BIG BUSINESS

4   The conflict perspective provides a different picture of urbanization, one that stresses the role played by big business in the growth and expansion of cities (Gottdiener, 1994, 1985).

5      First, in the pursuit of profit, large corporations bought up huge tracts of farmland and mass-produced food, driving many small family farms into bankruptcy and forcing huge numbers of farmers to leave for the city. In doing so, big business received considerable assistance from big government as a partner of the <u>ruling elite</u>. The assistance included direct <u>subsidies</u> to businesses, grants for research and development, low-interest loans, and support of farm-related education.

6      Second, the expansion of cities into suburbs has resulted from big business <u>making a killing</u> in the real estate, construction, and banking industries. Again, with considerable government subsidies and tax deductions, numerous single-family homes were built in the suburbs in the 1950s and 1960s. To <u>induce</u> people to buy these houses, the government guaranteed mortgages and provided tax deductions for interest payments. The result was massive suburbanization.

7      Third, from the 1970s to today, large corporations have helped turn many suburbs into edge cities by moving their businesses and factories there from central cities. This move has been motivated by profit. By building new plants in the suburbs, corporations have intended to avoid problems in central cities such as labor unrest, high city taxes, and other financial costs—or have expected to receive such benefits from the suburbs as cheap land, lower taxes, a local industry-friendly government, and the lack of organized labor.

unrest
conflict

## SYMBOLIC INTERACTIONIST PERSPECTIVE: HOW URBANITES INTERACT

8   We can learn much from symbolic interactionists about how strangers interact in cities (Karp et al., 1991).

9       First, city people tend to interact with one another in a superficial, impersonal way. Given the density of the urban population and hence the huge number of potential

interpersonal contacts, urbanites have learned to protect themselves from _psychic overload_ by shutting out as many sensations as possible, maybe even the call of a neighbor for help. Thus, most interactions with strangers are brief. An example is one person asking another for a street direction and the second person responding by pointing at a street and saying "over there."

10        Second, city people tend to interact through _civil inattention_ as a way of respecting others' desire for privacy in public places. This involves avoiding eye or physical contact in an elevator, a bus, or some other public place. Conversations with strangers do occur but often under unusual circumstances, as when people are stuck in a stalled elevator or a traffic jam.

11        Third, city people tend to be tolerant of others' lifestyles, such as different sexual orientations and religious practices. When such people interact, they usually <u>refrain</u> from <u>imposing</u> their values on others or showing disapproval of others' behavior.

| Exercise 1 |
| --- |

## Work with Words

Use context clues, dictionary skills, and your knowledge of word parts to choose the best definition for each of the following words underlined in the reading. The paragraph number is provided in case you want to go back to check the context.

1. _Urbanization_ (par. 1)
    a. growth and expansion of cities
    b. reflection of what the masses want
    c. driving force and beneficiary

2. _Proliferation_ (par. 3)
    a. rapid spread
    b. slow destruction
    c. regular renewal

3. _Ruling elite_ (par. 5)
    a. group of the most skilled
    b. group of the most powerful
    c. group of the most critical

4. _Subsidies_ (par. 5)
    a. complications
    b. financial assistance
    c. reductions

5. _Making a killing_ (par. 6)
    a. making huge profits
    b. murdering
    c. losing money

6. _Induce_ (par. 6)
    a. prevent
    b. infer
    c. influence

7. *Psychic overload* (par. 9)
   a. stressed mental condition caused by too many potential interpersonal contacts
   b. stressed mental condition caused by too much psychic power
   c. stressed mental condition caused by shutting down all sensations

8. *Civil inattention* (par. 10)
   a. pretending not to pay attention
   b. paying careful attention
   c. politely not paying attention

9. *Refrain* (par. 11)
   a. avoid
   b. insist on
   c. try to

10. *Imposing* (par. 11)
    a. reducing
    b. explaining
    c. forcing

**Exercise 2**

## Check Your Understanding and Patterns of Organization

Based on the reading, Thio's "Sociological Perspectives on Urbanization and City Life," choose the best answer to each of the following multiple-choice questions.

1. Which of the following is the best topic for the reading?
   a. causes of urbanization
   b. sociological perspectives on urbanization and city life
   c. functionalist, conflict, and symbolic interactionist perspectives on how urbanites relate to each other

2. Which of the following sentences best states the main idea for paragraphs 1 through 7?
   a. The functionalist perspective asserts that urbanization takes place to benefit people, while the conflict perspective argues that it has been driven by big businesses.
   b. The masses of ordinary people are the primary driving force behind urbanization, which reflects the changes that the people want.
   c. The conflict perspective, unlike the functionalist perspective, stresses the role played by big business in the growth and expansion of cities.

3. Which of the following is the best topic for paragraphs 2 and 3?
   a. technology and urbanization
   b. functionalist perspective: urbanization driven by the masses
   c. the role of business in urbanization

4. Which of the following is the best topic for paragraphs 8 through 11?
   a. how urbanites interact
   b. psychic overload
   c. civil inattention

5. Which of the following is the best main idea statement for paragraphs 8 through 11?
   a. City people tend to interact with one another in superficial ways.
   b. City people tend to be inattentive as a way to respect others' rights for privacy.
   c. City people tend to interact superficially, briefly, and with tolerance.

6. According to the conflict perspective, what is the fundamental motivation of big business?
   a. Serving the people
   b. Reducing costs
   c. Making profits

7. What is the dominant pattern of organization for paragraph 1?
   a. Chronological order
   b. Comparison and contrast
   c. Process

8. What is the dominant pattern of organization for paragraph 3?
   a. Process, and cause and effect
   b. Definition, and comparison and contrast
   c. Exemplification and definition

9. What is the dominant pattern of organization for paragraph 4?
   a. Definition
   b. Chronological order
   c. Exemplification

10. What is the dominant pattern of organization for paragraphs 5 through 7?
    a. Definition and chronological order
    b. Cause and effect, and chronological order
    c. Exemplification and narration

## Exercise 3

### Create an Outline or Map and Flowchart

Complete the following activities on a separate piece of paper.

1. Make a list of the ways that urbanites interact according to the symbolic interactionist perspective in paragraphs 8 through 11.

2. Create a map or a flowchart of the information in paragraphs 2 and 3.

3. Create an outline of the information in paragraphs 4 through 7.

4. Summarize the reading "Sociological Perspectives on Urbanization and City Life."

| Exercise 4 | Reflect |
|---|---|

Think about what you read in "Sociological Perspectives on Urbanization and City Life" and what you already know about the topic. Then answer the following questions.

1. How does the chart on page 387 assist you in understanding the text? Explain your answer.

_____

_____

_____

_____

_____

2. The reading presents the functionalist perspective, the conflict perspective, and the symbolic interactionist perspective. Which of the three perspectives do you agree with? Explain your reasons. You can agree with two of the perspectives.

_____

_____

_____

_____

_____

_____

_____

## 6B

**Mastery Test**

# The Men We Carry in Our Minds*

— SCOTT RUSSELL SANDERS

**In this essay, Scott Russell Sanders views relationships between men and women based on his childhood experiences of living in a poor, hardworking family. As you read, think about the differences between Sanders's background and assumptions, and how they compare to your own experiences.**

1 . . . When I was a boy growing up on the back roads of Tennessee and Ohio, the men I knew labored with their bodies. They were <u>marginal</u> farmers, just scraping by, or welders, steelworkers, carpenters; they swept floors, dug ditches, mined coal, or drove trucks, their forearms ropy with muscle; they trained horses, stoked furnaces, made tires, stood on assembly lines wrestling parts onto cars and refrigerators. They got up before light, worked all day long whatever the weather, and when they came home at night they looked as though somebody had been whipping them. In the evenings and on weekends they worked on their own places, <u>tilling</u> gardens that were lumpy with clay, fixing broken-down cars, hammering on houses that were always too drafty, too leaky, too small.

2 The bodies of the men I knew were twisted and <u>maimed</u> in ways visible and invisible. The nails of their hands were black and split, the hands tattooed with scars. Some had lost fingers. Heavy lifting had given many of them finicky backs and guts weak from hernias. Racing against conveyor belts had given them ulcers. Their ankles and knees ached from years of standing on concrete. Anyone who had worked for long around machines was hard of hearing. They squinted, and the skin of their faces was creased like the leather of old work gloves. There were times, studying them, when I dreaded growing up. Most of them coughed, from dust or cigarettes, and most of them drank cheap wine or whiskey, so their eyes looked bloodshot and bruised. The fathers of my friends always seemed older than the mothers. Men wore out sooner. Only women lived into old age.

3 As a boy I also knew another sort of men, who did not sweat and break down like mules. They were soldiers, and so far as I could tell they scarcely worked at all. But when the shooting started, many of them would die. This was what soldiers were *for*, just as a hammer was for driving nails.

4 Warriors and <u>toilers</u>; those seemed, in my boyhood vision, to be the chief destinies for men. They weren't the only destinies, as I learned from having a few male teachers, from reading books, and from watching television. But the men on television—the politicians, the astronauts, the generals, the savvy lawyers, the philosophical doctors, the bosses who gave orders to both soldiers and laborers—seemed as <u>remote</u> and unreal to me as the figures in Renaissance tapestries. I could no more imagine growing up to become one of these cool, potent creatures than I could imagine becoming a prince.

**potent**
powerful

*"The Men We Carry in Our Minds" by Scott Russell Sanders. Reprinted with permission.

5    A nearer and more hopeful example was that of my father, who had escaped from a red-dirt farm to a tire factory, and from the assembly line to the front office. Eventually he dressed in a white shirt and tie. He carried himself as if he had been born to work with his mind. But his body, remembering the earlier years of slogging work, began to give out on him in his fifties, and it quit on him entirely before he turned 65.

6    A scholarship <u>enabled</u> me not only to attend college, a rare enough <u>feat</u> in my circle, but even to study in a university meant for the children of the rich. Here I met for the first time young men who had assumed from birth that they would lead lives of comfort and power. And for the first time I met women who told me that men were guilty of having kept all the joys and privileges of the earth for themselves. I was baffled. What privileges? What joys? I thought about the maimed, <u>dismal</u> lives of most of the men back home. What had they stolen from their wives and daughters? The right to go five days a week, 12 months a year, for 30 or 40 years to a steel mill or a coal mine? The right to drop bombs and die in war? The right to feel every leak in the roof, every gap in the fence, every cough in the engine as a wound they must mend? The right to feel, when the layoff comes or the plant shuts down, not only afraid but ashamed?

**baffled**
confused

**grievances**
complaints

7    I was slow to understand the deep grievances of women. This was because, as a boy, I had envied them. Before college, the only people I had ever known who were interested in art or music or literature, the only ones who read books, the only ones who ever seemed to enjoy a sense of ease and grace were the mothers and daughters. Like the menfolk, they fretted about money, they scrimped and made do. But, when the pay stopped coming in, they were not the ones who had failed. Nor did they have to go to war, and that seemed to me a blessed fact. By comparison with the narrow, ironclad days of fathers, there was an expansiveness, I thought, in the days of mothers. They went to see neighbors, to shop in town, to run errands at school, at the library, at church. No doubt, had I looked harder at their lives, I would have envied them less. It was not my fate to become a woman, so it was easier for me to see the graces. I didn't see, then, what a prison a house could be, since houses seemed to me brighter, handsomer places than any factory. I did not realize—because such things were never spoken of—how often women suffered from men's bullying. Even then I could see how exhausting it was for a mother to <u>cater</u> all day to the needs of young children. But if I had been asked, as a boy, to choose between <u>tending</u> a baby and tending a machine, I think I would have chosen the baby. (Having now tended both, I know I would choose the baby.)

8    So I was baffled when the women at college accused me and my sex of having cornered the world's pleasures. I think something like my bafflement has been felt by other boys (and by girls as well) who grew up in dirt-poor farm country, in mining country, in black ghettos, in Hispanic barrios, in the shadows of factories, in Third World nations— any place where the fate of men is just as grim and bleak as the fate of women.

9    When the women I met at college thought about the joys and privileges of men, they did not carry in their minds the sort of men I had known in my childhood. They thought of their fathers, who were bankers, physicians, architects, stockbrokers, the big wheels of the big cities. They were never laid off, never short of cash at month's end, never lined up for welfare. These fathers made decisions that mattered. They ran the world.

10   The daughters of such men wanted to share in this power, this glory. So did I. They yearned for a say over their future, for jobs worthy of their abilities, for the right to live at peace, unmolested, whole. Yes, I thought, yes, yes. The difference between me and these daughters was that they saw me, because of my sex, as destined from birth to become like their fathers, and therefore as an enemy to their desires. But I knew better. I wasn't an enemy, in fact or in feeling. I was an ally. If I had known, then, how to tell them so, would they have believed me? Would they now?

**Exercise 1**

## Work with Words

Use context clues, dictionary skills, and your knowledge of word parts to choose the best definition for each of the following words underlined in the reading. The paragraph number is provided in case you want to check the context.

1. *Marginal* (par. 1)
   a  at the lower limits, poor
   b. situated on a border
   c. of or pertaining to the edge

2. *Tilling* (par. 1)
   a. breaking up the soil
   b. planting
   c. adding fertilizer

3. *Maimed* (par. 2)
   a. poorly copied
   b. wounded
   c. extremely strong

4. *Toilers* (par. 4)
   a. soldiers
   b. professionals
   c. workers

5. *Remote* (par. 4)
   a. close
   b. powerful
   c. distant

6. *Enabled* (par. 6)
   a. gave money
   b. made possible
   c. prevented

7. *Feat* (par. 6)
   a. great accomplishment
   b. grand plan
   c. ambitious goal

8. *Dismal* (par. 6)
   a. happy
   b. successful
   c. dreary

9. *Cater* (par. 7)
   a. provide for
   b. entertain
   c. discipline

10. *Tending* (par. 7)
    a. listening to
    b  taking care of
    c. fixing

**Exercise 2**

## Check Your Understanding

Based on the reading, Sanders's "The Men We Carry in Our Minds," choose the best answer to each of the following multiple-choice questions.

1. Which of the following sentences best states the main idea of the reading?
   a. Even though some women think that all men have a lot of power and an easy life, working-class men have very difficult lives.
   b. Women are the real victims of an unfair society.
   c. Women's lives, regardless of their social class, are actually quite pleasant compared with the lives of men.

2. When Scott Russell Sanders wrote this essay,
   a. he was a student.
   b. he was not a student.
   c. he may or may not have been a student.

3. The author grew up
   a. in the country.
   b. in the city.
   c. in the suburbs.

4. The author went to college because
   a. his parents scraped together enough money to send him.
   b. he worked his way through.
   c  he got a scholarship.

5. While growing up, Sanders believed that women's lives were
   a. better than men's lives.
   b. easy.
   c. more difficult than men's lives.

6. Sanders admits that
   a  he was slow to understand the grievances of women.
   b. taking care of children is harder than taking care of a machine.
   c. he never was interested in sharing the real power.

7. Sanders was confused when women at college accused him of being powerful because
   a. he didn't think there was anything wrong with being powerful.
   b. the men he had known in his life were not powerful.
   c. he thought that the really powerful people were educated women.

8. Because he came from a poor rural mining town, Sanders believes
   a. he has something in common with people from black ghettos and Hispanic barrios.
   b. that people of his background cannot succeed in college.
   c. that he would be unsuccessful in making friends with women from wealthy families.

9. Sanders feels that poor men are
   a. very different from women.
   b. in a position similar to women.
   c. in a position superior to women.

10. Sanders's essay, "The Men We Carry in Our Minds," discusses
    a. problems of social class.
    b. problems of power, gender, and social class.
    c. the problems of sexism for women who are trying to be successful.

**Exercise 3**  Evaluate Inferences

Based on the reading, put a check next to each of the following statements that is a reasonable inference.

_____ 1. Sanders wants to follow his father's career path.

_____ 2. The author's understanding of gender roles was framed by his experiences and observations while he was growing up.

_____ 3. Depending on their economic status, people carry different men in their minds.

_____ 4. Sanders resents women for having it easier than men.

_____ 5. Sanders does not think that soldiers have it better than laborers.

**Exercise 4**

Interpret Figurative Language

For each of the following sentences from "The Men We Carry in Our Minds," explain what Sanders is saying with his use of figurative language. Is he using a metaphor or a simile? How does the figurative language support the point the author wants to make?

1. As a boy I also knew another sort of men, who did not sweat and break down like mules. (par. 3)

_____

_____

2. But when the shooting started, many of them would die. This was what soldiers were *for*, just as a hammer was for driving nails. (par. 3)

_____

_____

3. The right to feel every leak in the roof, every gap in the fence, every cough in the engine as a wound they must mend? (par. 6)

_____

_____

4. I didn't see, then, what a prison a house could be. (par. 7)

_____

_____

5. They thought of their fathers, who were bankers, physicians, architects, stockbrokers, the big wheels of the cities. (par. 9)

_____

_____

_____

**Exercise 5**

Reflect

Think about what you read in "The Men We Carry in Our Minds" and what you already know about relationships and the lives of men and women. Then answer the following questions.

1. In your experience, who has more power, men or women? Give examples and explain what kind of power you mean (for example, in the home, in the world, in other ways).

   _____

   _____

   _____

2. How do you think power should be divided in the home? At work? In society as a whole?

   _____

   _____

   _____

   _____

3. Thinking about the lives of the men and women you know, who do you think has it better and why? Explain your answer.

   _____

   _____

   _____

   _____

# Rage* —Martín Espada

**Martín Espada is a prominent Puerto Rican poet. Formerly a lawyer, he eventually became a professor of literature at the University of Massachusetts–Amherst. Much of Espada's work deals with the lives and struggles of poor people and immigrants in the United States. In the following essay, he discusses some of the reasons that Latino men feel "rage," the different ways of handling anger, stereotypes of Latino men, his memories of his father, and his hopes for his son. As you read, think about Espada's point of view on anger.**

1    My father has good reason for rage. A brown-skinned man, he learned rage when he was arrested in Biloxi, Mississippi, in 1950, and spent a week in jail for refusing to go to the back of the bus. He learned rage when he was denied a college education and instead struggled for years working for an electrical contractor, hating his work and yearning for so much more. He learned rage as the political triumphs of the 1960s he helped to achieve were attacked from without and betrayed from within. My father externalized his rage. He raged at his enemies and he raged at us. A tremendous ethical and cultural influence for us nonetheless, he must have considered himself a failure by the male career-obsessed standards of the decade into which I was born: the 1950s.

2    By adolescence, I had learned to <u>internalize</u> my rage. I learned to do this, not so much in response to my father, but more in response to my own growing awareness of <u>bigotry</u>. Having left my Brooklyn birthplace for the town Valley Stream, Long Island, I was dubbed a <u>spic</u> in an endless torrent of taunting, bullying, and brawling. To defend myself against a few people would have been feasible; to defend my self against dozens and dozens of people deeply in love with their own racism was a practical impossibility. So I told no one, no parent or counselor or teacher or friend, about the constant racial hostility. Instead, I punched a lamp, not once but twice, and watched the blood ooze between my knuckles as if somehow I could leech the poison from my body. My evolving manhood was defined by how well I could take punishment, and <u>paradoxically</u> I punished myself for not being man enough to end my own humiliation. Later in life, I would <u>emulate</u> my father and rage openly. Rarely, however, was the real enemy within earshot, or even visible.

3    Someday, my son will be called a spic for the first time; this is as much a part of the Puerto Rican experience as the music he gleefully dances to. I hope he will tell me. I hope that I can help him handle the glowing toxic waste of his rage. I hope that I can explain clearly why there are those waiting for him to explode, to confirm their stereotypes of the hot-blooded, bad-tempered Latino male who has, without provocation, injured the Anglo innocents. His anger—and that anger must come—has to be controlled, directed, creatively channeled, <u>articulated</u>—but not all-consuming nor self-destructive. I keep it between the covers of the books I write.

**dubbed**
called

**brawling**
fighting

---

*From the *Puerto Rican Dummy* and the *Merciful Son* by Martín Espada. Copyright 1998 by Martín Espada. Reprinted by permission of the author.

4    The anger will continue to <u>manifest</u> itself as he matures and discovers the utter resourcefulness of bigotry, the ability of racism to change shape and survive all attempts to snuff it out. "<u>Spic</u>" is a crude expression of certain sentiments that become subtle and sophisticated and insidious at other levels. Speaking of crudity, I am reminded of a group organized by white ethnics in New York during the 1960s under the acronym of SPONGE: The Society for the Prevention of the Niggers Getting Everything. . . .

5    Violence is the first cousin to rage. If learning to confront rage is an important element of developing Latino manhood, then the question of violence must be addressed with equal urgency. Violence is terribly <u>seductive</u>; all of us, especially males, are trained to gaze upon violence until it becomes beautiful. Beautiful violence is not only the way to victory for armies and football teams; this becomes the solution to everyday problems as well. For many characters on the movie or television screen, problems are solved by *shooting* them. This is certainly the most emphatic way to win an argument.

6    Katherine and I try to minimize the seductiveness of violence for Clemente. No guns, no soldiers, and so on. But his dinosaurs still eat each other with great relish. His trains still crash, to their delight. He is experimenting with power and control, with action and reaction, which brings him to an imitation of violence. Needless to say, there is a vast difference between stegosaurus and Desert Storm [the U.S. military invasion of Iraq in 1990].

7    Again, all I can do is call upon my own experience as an example. I not only found violence seductive; at some point, I found myself enjoying it. I remember one brawl in Valley Stream when I snatched a chain away from an assailant, knocked him down, and needlessly lashed the chain across his knees as he lay sobbing in the street. That I was now the assailant with the chain did not occur to me.

**assailant**
attacker

8    I also remember the day I stopped enjoying the act of fistfighting. I was working as a bouncer in a bar, and found myself struggling with a man who was so drunk that he appeared numb to the blows bounding off his cranium. Suddenly, I heard my fist echo: *thok*. I was sickened by the sound. Later, I learned that I had broken my right ring finger with the punch, but all I could recall was the headache I must have caused him. I never had a fistfight again. Parenthetically, that job ended another romance: the one with alcohol. Too much of my job consisted of ministering to people who had passed out at the bar, finding their hats and coats, calling a cab, dragging them in their stupor down the stairs. Years later, I channeled those instincts cultivated as a bouncer into my work as a legal services lawyer, representing Latino tenants, finding landlords who forgot to heat buildings in winter or exterminate rats to be more deserving targets of my wrath. . . .

**bouncer**
security guard at a bar or club

9    Will I urge my son to be a <u>pacifist</u>, thereby gutting one of the foundations of traditional manhood, the pleasure taken in violence and the power <u>derived</u> from it? That is an ideal state. I hope that he lives a life that permits him pacifism. I hope that the world around him evolves in such a way that pacifism is a <u>viable</u> choice. Still, I would not deny him the option of physical self-defense. I would not deny him, on philosophical grounds, the right to resistance in any form that resistance must take to be effective. Nor would I have him deny that right to others, with the luxury of distance. Too many people in this world still need a revolution.

**derived**
gained

**viable**
possible

10    When he is old enough, Clemente and I will talk about matters of justification, which must be carefully and narrowly defined. He must understand that abstractions like "patriotism" and "country" are not reasons to fight on the battlefield. He must understand that violence against women is not acceptable, a message which will have to be somehow repeated every time another movie trailer blazes the art of <u>misogyny</u> across his subconscious mind. Rather than sloganizing, however, the best way I can communicate that message is by the way I treat his mother. How else will he know that jealousy is not love, that a lover is not property?

**movie trailer**
advertisement showing a clip of the movie

11        Clemente was born on December 28, 1991. This was a difficult birth. Katherine's coccyx, or tailbone, broken in childhood [by her abusive father], would break again during delivery. Yet only with the birth could we move from gesture to fulfillment, from generous moments to real giving. The extraordinary healing that took place was not only physical but emotional and spiritual as well. After years of constant pain, her coccyx bone set properly, as if a living metaphor for the new opportunity represented by the birth of this child. . . .

12        The behavior we collectively refer to as "macho" [usually thought of as a tough man] has deep historical roots, but the trigger is often a profound insecurity, a sense of being threatened. Clemente will be as secure as possible, and that security will stem in large part from self-knowledge. He will know the meaning of his name.

13        Clemente Soto Vélez was a great Puerto Rican poet, a fighter for the independence of Puerto Rico who spent years in prison as a result. He was also our good friend. The two Clementes met once, when the elder Clemente was eighty-seven years old and the younger Clemente was nine months. Fittingly, it was Columbus Day, 1992, the five-hundredth anniversary of the conquest. We passed the day with a man who devoted his life and his art to battling the very colonialism personified by Columbus. The two Clementes traced the topography of one another's faces. Even from his sickbed, the elder Clemente was gentle and generous. We took photographs, signed books. Clemente Soto Vélez died the following spring, and eventually my family and I visited the grave in the mountains of Puerto Rico. We found the grave unmarked but for a stick with a number and letter, so we bought a gravestone and gave the poet his name back. My son still asks to see the framed photograph of the two Clementes, still asks about the man with the long white hair who gave him *his* name. This will be family legend, family ritual, the origins of the name explained in greater and greater detail as the years pass, a source of knowledge and power as meaningful as the Book of Genesis.

**topography**
physical features

14        Thankfully, Clemente also has a literal meaning: "merciful." Every time my son asks about his name, an opportunity presents itself to teach the power of mercy, the power of compassion. When Clemente, in later years consciously acts out these qualities, he does so knowing that he is doing what his very name expects of him. His name gives him the beginnings of a moral code, a goal to which he can aspire. "Merciful": Not the first word scrawled on the mental blackboard next to the phrase "Puerto Rican male."

**scrawled**
written messily

## Exercise 1

## Work with Words

Use context clues, dictionary skills, and your knowledge of word parts to choose the best definition for each of the following words underlined in the reading. The paragraph number is provided in case you want to check the context.

1. *Internalize* (par. 2)
   a. control
   b. keep inside
   c. deal with

2. *Bigotry* (par. 2)
   a. objectivity
   b. disillusionment
   c. prejudice

3. *"Spic"* (pars. 2, 3, and 4)
   a. crude expression for Puerto Rican
   b. an objective expression for Puerto Rican
   c. a term only used by Puerto Ricans among themselves

4. *Paradoxically* (par. 2)
   a. surprisingly
   b. logically
   c. indifferently

5. *Emulate* (par. 2)
   a. accept
   b. respect
   c. copy

6. *Articulated* (par. 3)
   a. suppressed
   b. restricted
   c. expressed

7. *Manifest* (par. 4)
   a. show
   b. multiply
   c. fortify

8. *Seductive* (par. 5)
   a. tempting
   b. irritating
   c. pathetic and compulsive

9. *Pacifist* (par. 9)
   a. someone who promotes war
   b. someone who promotes peace
   c. someone who promotes violence

10. *Misogyny* (par. 10)
   a. self-love
   b. violent response
   c. hatred of women

## Exercise 2

### Check Your Understanding

Based on the reading, Espada's "Rage," choose the best answer to each of the following multiple-choice questions.

1. Which of the following best states the topic of "Rage"?
   a. relationships between men and women in Latino culture
   b. rage, violence, and hope for alternatives for Puerto Rican men
   c. poetry, revolution, and the Puerto Rican independence movement

2. Which of the following best states the thesis of "Rage"?
   a. We can only hope that future generations of Latino (Puerto Rican) men will live in a world where violence is not necessary for self-defense or to feel good about oneself.
   b. We can only hope that future generations of Puerto Rican men will fight for the respect they deserve.
   c. It is never right for men to allow their anger—their rage—to take the form of violence against anyone.

3. In paragraph 2, Espada mentions moving to a town called Valley Stream, where he became aware of bigotry. From this paragraph, we can reasonably infer that
   a. the family was doing well so they moved to a more comfortable neighborhood.
   b. the new neighborhood was predominantly white.
   c. he was dubbed a spic and faced taunting, bullying, and brawling.

4. Espada writes in paragraph 2, "By adolescence, I had learned to internalize my rage." We can infer that Espada thinks that internalizing rage
   a. is probably not a good way to deal with anger.
   b. is a good solution and a healthy approach to anger management.
   c. is wrong and that it is much better to rage openly as his father did.

5. In paragraph 5, Espada assumes that his son will be tempted to be violent when he faces racism, but he hopes his son
   a. will respond to force with force.
   b. will live up to the reputation of the hot-blooded Latino man.
   c. will be able to channel and articulate his anger without resorting to violence.

6. According to Espada, violence is "terribly seductive." To support this statement, he gives examples of
   a. not buying toy guns or soldiers for his son.
   b. his own acts of violence, how he enjoyed it.
   c. how he learned to leave violence behind.

7. In which of the following cases does Espada say violence may be justified?
   a. For self-defense
   b. To defend one's respect and honor
   c. For patriotic reasons

8. In this essay, it is clear that Espada wanted to be a father who
   a. maintained a certain manly distance from his son.
   b. did not reveal his emotions to his son.
   c. was close to his son and able to discuss many things with him.

9. Espada believes that the best way to teach his son that violence against women is not acceptable is by
   a. not taking him to misogynistic movies.
   b. explaining to him that one must never be violent toward women.
   c. always treating Clemente's mother with respect.

10. Which of the following is not a reason that Espada named his son Clemente?
    a. He was named after Clemente Soto Vélez.
    b. *Clemente* means "merciful" in Spanish.
    c. His wife, Katherine, had always loved that name.

---

**Exercise 3**

Recognize Figurative Language and
Author's Worldview, Point of View, and Tone

Based on the reading, briefly answer the following questions in your own words.

1. In paragraph 2, Espada writes, "Instead, I punched a lamp, not once but twice, and watched the blood ooze between my knuckles as if somehow I could leech the poison from my body." What does *poison* represent in this sentence? What does it mean to "leech the poison" out of his body? What is the impression that this metaphor establishes?

   _____

   _____

   _____

   _____

2. Espada writes in paragraph 3, "I hope that I can help him [Clemente, his son] handle the glowing toxic waste of his rage." What two things are being compared? What impression does this comparison make?

_____

_____

3. How would you describe the tone of paragraph 3? Use two or three adjectives.

_____

_____

4. What are some of the things you know from reading this essay and the introduction that shaped Espada's worldview?

_____

_____

_____

5. How would you characterize Espada's point of view toward rage and violence in your own words?

_____

_____

_____

**Exercise 4**

Reflect

Think about what you read in "Rage" and what you already know about bigotry and racial violence. Then answer the following questions.

1. In paragraph 14, Espada writes, "His name gives him the beginnings of a moral code, a goal to which he can aspire. 'Merciful': Not the first word scrawled on the mental blackboard next to the phrase 'Puerto Rican male.'" What do you think this passage means? Why is the passage so important to this essay?

_____

_____

_____

_____

2. What kinds of prejudices have you observed or become aware of in your life? (Remember, people are prejudiced about many different things, not only race or ethnicity.) Explain your experiences.

_____

_____

_____

_____

_____

3. Have you ever felt discriminated against? How did you react? Do you think you acted in a "directed, creatively channeled" way? What could you have done to improve the way you reacted?

_____

_____

_____

_____

_____

## 8B

### Mastery Test

# Drug-Abusing Mothers-To-Be: Are They Criminals?* —DANUTA BUKATKO AND MARVIN W. DAEHLER

**TEXT BOOK** **In recent years, many reports have documented the harmful and persistent effects of illegal substances on babies born to drug-abusing mothers. In response to this problem, some lawmakers have proposed that drug-abusing expectant mothers should be prosecuted as child abusers. This reading, adapted from the textbook *Child Development: A Thematic Approach*, reviews the evidence regarding the effects of prenatal drug use and explores concerns about the effectiveness and legality of treating drug-abusing expectant mothers as criminals.**

**fetus**
unborn child, after eight weeks of development

**chaotic**
disordered, confused

1    The effects of illegal drugs such as marijuana, heroin, and cocaine on the development of the fetus are difficult to untangle. Drug users are rarely certain of the contents or concentrations of the drugs they consume. There are wide variations in frequency of use. There is also the possibility of interactions from exposure to multiple drugs, poor nutritional status, and inadequate or no prenatal care. All of these factors can <u>compound</u> the problem of isolating the harmful effects of drugs on the fetus. Finally, the lifestyles of many illegal-drug users can be described as essentially chaotic, so that conclusions about the impact of the drug itself are often difficult to make.

2    The effects of heroin and morphine became a public concern as early as the late 1800s when doctors reported withdrawal symptoms in newborns whose mothers used these substances. By the early 1900s, heroin and morphine were known to be <u>transmitted</u> through the placenta, as well as through the mother's milk. Today an estimated nine thousand infants born in the United States each year are exposed to heroin or methadone, a pharmacologically similar product. Often given as a prescribed and monitored heroin substitute, methadone's effects on fetal development are just as powerful as heroin's. So, too, may be the effects of a newer <u>synthetic</u> form of heroin, OxyContin, a prescribed painkiller that has recently achieved the status of a widely sought after street drug.

**crack**
especially strong and addictive variation of cocaine

**postnatal**
referring to the time after a child has been born

3    Each year in the United States alone, the National Institute on Drug Abuse estimates that more than 200,000 infants are born to mothers who use illegal drugs. However, probably none of these drugs has received more widespread attention than cocaine. Cocaine in its many forms, including crack, readily crosses the placenta. Once it reaches the fetus, it stays longer than in adults because the immature organs of the fetus have difficulty breaking it down. Cocaine also can continue to influence the baby after birth through the mother's milk.

4    The media have widely publicized the <u>dire</u> effects for the fetus and postnatal development as a result of exposure to cocaine. Indeed, evidence exists that cocaine

*"Drug-Abusing Mothers-to-be: Are they Criminals?" by Danuta Bukatko and Marvin W. Daehler from CHILD DEVELOPMENT: A Thematic Approach, 5th Edition, pp. 122–24. Reprinted by permission of Houghton Mifflin Company.

**motor**
muscle movement

may be associated with premature birth, low birth weight, attention and motor difficulties as well as some emotional, behavioral, or learning complications. However, researchers today tend to agree that these problems for newborns and young children can be explained by the lifestyle and parenting habits of someone who uses cocaine, rather than the direct physical effects of the pregnant mother's cocaine use. These other, higher-risk factors that are harmful to infants and young children include (1) increased exposure to tobacco and alcohol, (2) poor nutrition, (3) diminished parental responsiveness, (4) abuse and neglect, (5) social isolation of the family, and (6) the increased stress typically accompanying poverty.

### SHOULD A DRUG-ABUSING EXPECTANT MOTHER BE CHARGED WITH CHILD ABUSE?

5    Consider the circumstances surrounding the prosecution of Cornelia Whitner of South Carolina. Her son was born with cocaine in his system. In 1992 Cornelia pled guilty to a charge of child neglect after admitting to the use of cocaine in her third trimester of pregnancy. She was sentenced to eight years in prison.

### WHAT IS THE CONTROVERSY?

6    Although the conviction of Cornelia Whitner has since been <u>overturned</u>, the issues surrounding this and similar cases deeply divide law enforcement, medical, and social service agencies. Since the mid-1980s, more than two hundred American women in thirty states have been prosecuted for allegedly harming their children through prenatal exposure to cocaine or other illegal drugs. The charges have ranged from child abuse and neglect, to delivery of drugs to a minor, to assault with a deadly weapon. There are many court cases with policy <u>implications</u> for whether a woman can or should be arrested if she exposes a fetus to illegal drugs. In fact, these types of cases are continuing to be debated at the highest judicial levels, including the Supreme Court in the United States. Is this an effective way to reduce the *likelihood* of drug use and any of its accompanying risks for the fetus?

### WHAT ARE THE OPPOSING ARGUMENTS?

7    Some say a concerned society should impose criminal or other charges on a pregnant woman who uses a drug that may be dangerous to the fetus. A number of jurisdictions in the United States and provinces in Canada have implemented laws permitting a newborn to be removed from a parent on the grounds of child abuse or neglect because of drug exposure during pregnancy. In some cases, judges have ordered that women be confined to a drug-treatment facility during pregnancy. After all, anyone found to provide such illegal substances to a child would certainly expect to face criminal or other charges. Are the circumstances that much different in the case of a pregnant woman and her fetus?

**counterproductive**
doing more harm while trying to correct a problem

8    Others believe the situation is vastly different and further claim that criminal charges, imprisonment, or mandatory treatment are counterproductive. Legislation specifically targeted to pregnant drug users might actually drive prospective mothers—out of fear of being prosecuted—away from the care and treatment needed for both themselves and their fetuses. Moreover, the tendency to rely on criminal procedures could limit the funds available for the establishment of innovative, well-funded public health efforts to prevent and treat addiction in the first place.

# WHAT ANSWERS EXIST? WHAT QUESTIONS REMAIN?

9   Currently no research has been done on whether threats of criminal procedures or other forms of punishment <u>dissuade</u> a woman from using drugs during her pregnancy. If studies demonstrated that criminal punishment or mandatory treatment was effective in reducing drug use, perhaps it would be a good idea to use these methods against pregnant illegal drug abusers. But recent findings demonstrate that the negative consequences for the fetus often stem less from the illegal drugs themselves than from multiple other factors that are associated with drug use. If that is the case, would criminal punishment be helpful? In other words, what are the primary <u>culprits</u> in poor fetal development?  Are poor nutrition and other social and economic factors mainly responsible? What about the chaotic lifestyle that often accompanies drug use and over which a woman may not always have control? If these factors have a greater influence on the developing fetus than illegal drugs, then intervention must take place at the public health level. Do your views about how to address this issue change when you consider that alcohol and tobacco have been shown to have more serious consequences for fetal development than many illegal drugs? Shouldn't any fetus protection laws also apply to women who use legal, readily available and heavily advertised drugs that are proven to be more damaging to the fetus? Research has begun to shed light on some of these issues by providing knowledge about the effects of drug exposure on fetal development. What other kinds of research would be useful in helping to resolve these competing views? Are there alternatives that might be proposed to help solve this very complex problem? How can we ensure an <u>optimal</u> start for every child at birth?

**Exercise 1**

## Work with Words

Use context clues, dictionary skills, and your knowledge of word parts to choose the best definition for each italicized word from the reading. The paragraph number is provided in case you want to check the context.

1. *Compound* (par. 1)
   a. complicate
   b. combine
   c. make up

2. *Transmitted* (par. 2)
   a. communicated
   b. spread
   c. broadcast

3. *Synthetic* (par. 2)
   a. man-made
   b. more harmful
   c. current

4. *Dire* (par. 4)
   a. serious
   b. deadly
   c. mild

5. *Overturned* (par. 6)
   a. confirmed
   b. placed upside down
   c. reversed

6. *Implications* (par. 6)
   a. issues
   b. orders
   c. consequences

7. *Likelihood* (par. 6)
   a. probability
   b. likeability
   c. community

8. *Dissuade* (par. 9)
   a. distract
   b. discourage
   c. protect

9. *Culprits* (par. 9)
   a. participants
   b. offenders
   c. bodies

10. *Optimal* (par. 9)
    a. average
    b. unequal
    c. best possible

**Exercise 2**

## Check Your Understanding

Based on the reading, Bukatko and Daehler's "Drug-Abusing Mothers-To-Be: Are They Criminals?" choose the best answer to each of the following multiple-choice questions.

1. What is the main idea of this reading?
   a. Since expectant mothers who use drugs harm their baby's mental and physical development, they should be prosecuted as criminals and punished.
   b. There are many unanswered questions about the effects of prenatal drug use on a fetus and how to effectively treat expectant mothers who use drugs.
   c. Since alcohol and cigarettes do more damage to the fetus than illegal drugs, we should create laws to punish expectant mothers who abuse alcohol or smoke cigarettes first.

2. What is the main purpose of paragraph 1?
   a. To tell a story to get the readers' interest in the problem of expectant mothers who abuse illegal drugs
   b. To argue that drug-abusing mothers-to-be should be seen as criminals
   c. To list reasons why it is difficult to make direct connections about the effect of a mother's drug use on the fetus

3. Which of the following is the best main idea statement for paragraph 2?
   a. Methadone's effects on fetal development are just as powerful as heroin's.
   b. OxyContin, a synthetic form of heroin and a prescribed painkiller, has become a widely sought after street drug.
   c. Doctor-prescribed medications as well as heroin seem to produce withdrawal effects in newborns whose mothers take these drugs.

4. When did doctors first report that newborns had withdrawal symptoms?
   a. In the late 1980s
   b. In the late 1800s
   c. In the early 1990s

5. In paragraph 4, which of the following is not discussed as a factor that can harm fetal development?
   a. Stress due to financial problems
   b. Poor nutrition
   c. Lack of educational achievement

6. What is the primary pattern of organization in paragraphs 7 and 8?
   a. Process
   b. Comparison and contrast
   c. Exemplification

7. Based on the information in paragraph 9, we can reasonably infer that the authors think that
   a. it is a mistake to treat drug-abusing expectant mothers as criminals.
   b. the creation of stronger laws to protect the fetus must be done sooner rather than later.
   c. the problem of drug-abusing expectant mothers can be solved through education.

8. Which of the following statements from the reading is primarily a statement of opinion or interpretation of facts?
   a. Legislation specifically targeted to pregnant drug users might actually drive prospective mothers—out of fear of being prosecuted—away from the care and treatment needed for both themselves and their fetuses.
   b. Currently, no research has been carried out on whether threats of criminal procedures or other forms of punishment dissuade a woman from using drugs during her pregnancy.
   c. Each year in the United States alone, the National Institute on Drug Abuse estimates that more than 200,000 infants are born to mothers who use illegal drugs.

9. Which of the following statements from or related to the reading is primarily a statement of fact?
   a. A concerned society should impose criminal or other charges on a pregnant woman who uses a drug that may be dangerous to the fetus.
   b. By the early 1900s, heroin and morphine were known to be transmitted through the placenta, as well as through the mother's milk.
   c. Criminal charges, imprisonment, or mandatory treatment are counterproductive.

10. What is the primary tone of this reading?
    a. Pessimistic
    b. Subjective
    c. Objective

---

**Exercise 3**

## Reflect, Think Critically, and Form Your Own Opinion

Answer the following questions as fully as you can in your own words.

1. According to the authors, what are the arguments for and against charging drug-abusing expectant mothers with child abuse?

   a. _____

   _____

   _____

b. _____

_____

_____

_____

_____

_____

2. Which argument on whether or not to charge drug-abusing expectant mothers with a crime do you agree with? (Consider your own experience or that of others, and what you know about people who abuse drugs. Is criminal punishment effective for drug abusers?)

_____

_____

_____

_____

3. What was the authors' purpose in concluding the article with a series of questions? Consider the intended audience in your response.

_____

_____

_____

_____

4. What, in your opinion, can be done to reduce expectant mothers' drug abuse? Explain your answer.

_____

_____

_____

_____

_____

# Cumulative Mastery Tests

**A**

# The Pill*

—PAUL S. BOYER, CLIFFORD E. CLARK, JR., JOSEPH F. KETT, NEAL SALISBURY, HARVARD SITKOFF, AND NANCY WOLOCH

**TEXT BOOK** The following reading about the invention and introduction of the birth control pill is from the U.S. history textbook *The Enduring Vision*. It appears in a special feature of the book titled "Technology and Culture". As you read, try to understand what life would have been like before birth control. Also, focus on the reasons that people wanted to make a contraceptive pill available to women. What problems did they think would be solved?

1  The pill to prevent conception had many fathers and at least two mothers. Most of them were initially concerned with world overpopulation, not women's sexual freedom. In Margaret Sanger and Katherine McCormick, <u>heir</u> to the International Harvest Company fortune, the goals of the movements for birth control and for population control <u>meshed</u>. The two women wanted a safe, inexpensive contraceptive that would be easy to use in the poverty-stricken slums of the world. In the postwar [after World War II] climate that favored technological solutions to social problems, they recruited Gregory Pincus, a pharmaceutical scientist working in a small Massachusetts laboratory grandly called the Worcester Foundation for Experimental Biology. Pincus desperately needed money to keep his lab afloat. Assured of McCormick's support to the tune of $2 million, he went to work in 1950 on Sanger's request for an oral contraceptive that would be as simple to use and as plentiful as aspirin.

2  Like most scientists, Pincus drew heavily on the earlier work of others. Chemists in the 1930s had synthesized estrogen, the female hormone that prevents <u>ovulation</u> (stopping the female body from forming and releasing an egg). Others had worked on <u>progestin</u>, the hormone in the ovaries that keeps sperm from fertilizing an egg. Pincus utilized their experiments with rabbits, as well as Carl Djerassi's synthesis of steroids and the work of gynecologist Dr. John Rock. None of these scientists had birth control on their minds. Indeed, Rock, a Catholic, was seeking an effective hormonal pill to help women get pregnant.

dubiously
questionably

3  After years of experimenting with hundreds of combinations of substances, Pincus and his collaborator, Dr. M. C. Chiang, synthesized a mixture of estrogen and progestin that they believed safe and effective in suppressing ovulation in most women. In dubiously ethical practices, Pincus set up field trials with psychiatric patients and male prisoners (thinking it might work on men). Puerto Rico was the site for his first large-scale clinical trial of the oral contraceptive—because he could "attempt in Puerto Rico certain experiments which would be very difficult in this country." He followed that with tests in Haiti. Called Enovid, and produced by the G. D. Searle drug company, the pills were approved by the Food and Drug Administration (FDA) in 1957, but for gynecological disorders—not as a contraceptive.

*"The Pill" by Paul S. Boyer, Clifford E. Clark, Jr., Joseph F. Kett, Neal Salisbury, Harvard Sitkoff, and Nancy Woloch from THE ENDURING VISION, pp. 880–881. Reprinted by permission of Houghton Mifflin Company.

4      At the time, thirty states still had laws banning or restricting contraceptive use, and most drug companies feared the controversy such a pill would <u>arouse</u>. The other drug companies left it to G. D. Searle to ask the FDA to approve the drug as a contraceptive. In May 1960 the FDA approved Enovid for contraceptive use. It did so, in large part, because of widening concern about overpopulation and the threat of communism. Many feared that a teeming nonwhite underclass was tailor-made for a communist takeover, and thought the likelihood of that threat could be minimized by controlling population and thus reducing hunger, poverty, and disease in the world.

**teeming**
overflowing

5      Many American women <u>embraced</u> the new technology with enthusiasm, and Enovid unexpectedly helped to <u>foster</u> a sexual revolution in the United States. By 1965, despite being condemned as immoral by the Catholic Church and denounced as a technology of <u>genocide</u> by African-American militants, "the Pill" (as it was commonly called) had become the most popular form of birth control in the United States, used by 6.5 million married women (unmarried women were not counted in official reports). In 1968 Americans spent as much on the Pill as on all other contraceptive methods combined. By 1970 more than 10 million American women were "on the Pill."

6      Pincus was <u>deluged</u> with fan letters. A grateful user in St. Paul kissed his picture in the newspaper, "for this is the first year in her eight years of marriage that she has not been pregnant." And in a song named "The Pill," Loretta Lynn sang, "All these years I've stayed at home while you had all your fun/And ev'ry year that's gone by another baby's come/There's gonna be some changes made right here on Nurs'ry Hill/You've set this chicken your last time, 'cause now I've got the Pill."

7      Although widespread use of the Pill and the sexual revolution occurred together, the former did not cause the latter. Primarily married women consumed the Pill in the 1960s. It would take larger social changes in the United States before doctors would readily prescribe it for unmarried women, before the young would claim sexual pleasure as a right, and before a women's liberation movement would be strong enough to insist on a woman's right to control her own sexuality. Permissiveness resulted more from affluence and mobility, from changed attitudes and laws, than from the Pill. Still, the Pill disconnected fears of pregnancy from the pursuit of sexual pleasure, and breaking reproductive shackles made sexual freedom more likely. The greater degree of <u>autonomy</u> and choice in women's sexual-reproductive lives changed the experience and meaning of sex, in and out of marriage. . . .

**affluence**
wealth

**shackles**
chains

8      To date, the Pill has neither significantly limited population growth in the Third World nor ended the . . . unwanted pregnancies in the United States. It has changed the dynamics of women's health care and altered gender relations. The first medicine produced for a social, rather than therapeutic, purpose, it remains the pharmaceutical swallowed as a daily routine by more humans than any other prescribed medication in the world.

## Exercise 1

## Work with Words

Use context clues, dictionary skills, and your knowledge of word parts to choose the appropriate definition for each italicized word from the reading. The paragraph number is provided in case you want to check the context.

1. *Heir* (par. 1)
   a.  person who grants property to another
   b.  person who inherits property or money
   c.  person who manages money

2. *Meshed* (par. 1)
   a. came together
   b. became tangled
   c. engaged the gears

3. *Ovulation* (par. 2)
   a. combining hormones to prevent pregnancy
   b. producing the hormone that assists fertilization
   c. the forming and releasing of an egg

4. *Progestin* (par. 2)
   a. the hormone in the ovaries that keeps sperm from fertilizing an egg
   b. the male hormone essential for fertilization
   c. another word for estrogen

5. *Arouse* (par. 4)
   a. sexually excite
   b. cause
   c. dampen

6. *Embraced* (par. 5)
   a. used
   b. rejected
   c. hugged

7. *Foster* (par. 5)
   a. feel
   b. entertain
   c. encourage

8. *Genocide* (par. 5)
   a. birth control
   b. systematic killing of a people based on race, religion, or ethnicity
   c. systematic adoption of immoral values

9. *Deluged* (par. 6)
   a. flooded
   b. criticized
   c. deprived of

10. *Autonomy* (par. 7)
    a. self-government
    b. dependence
    c. independence

**Exercise 2**

## Check Your Understanding

Based on the reading, Boyer and his co-authors' "The Pill," choose the best answer to the following multiple-choice questions.

1. Which of the following is the best main idea statement for paragraph 2?
   a. Chemists in the 1930s synthesized estrogen, the female hormone that prevents ovulation.

    b. Some scientists worked on progestin, the hormone in the ovaries that keeps sperm from fertilizing an egg.

    c. Pincus learned from the work of scientists who did hormone research before him.

2. The main pattern of organization of paragraphs 2 and 3 is
    a. cause and effect.
    b. chronological order and process.
    c. problem and solution.

3. Which of the following is a reasonable inference?
    a. Pincus and Dr. Chiang did tests on prisoners, psychiatric patients, Puerto Ricans, and Haitians that they would probably not have done on mainstream Americans.
    b. Enovid was approved by the Food and Drug Administration in 1957.
    c. Dr. Chiang did more of the work to discover the birth control pill than Pincus.

4. Which of the following, from or based on the reading, is a statement of a biased opinion?
    a. Pincus went to work in 1950 on Sanger's request for an oral contraceptive that would be simple to use.
    b. The teeming nonwhite underclass was tailor-made for a Communist takeover but that could be minimized by controlling population.
    c. By 1970 more than 10 million American women were "on the Pill."

5. The early scientists whose work contributed to the development of the pill
    a. were well compensated by drug companies who knew there would be a lot of interest in using it.
    b. had no idea whatsoever of what the possible practical uses of their research would be.
    c. were not looking for a form of birth control.

6. In paragraph 6, the author provides
    a. statistics that demonstrate how widespread the use of the pill became.
    b. examples in American culture of how the pill changed women's lives.
    c. an explanation of how the pill affects women's hormones.

7. What is the primary pattern of organization for paragraph 7?
    a. Cause and effect
    b. Definition
    c. Exemplification

8. According to the author, the pill
    a. caused the sexual revolution.
    b. had nothing to do with the sexual revolution.
    c. was one of the factors that changed attitudes about sex.

9. Only one drug company chose to produce the pill probably because other companies
    a. believed it was morally wrong.
    b. knew it was controversial and didn't look like a good business deal.
    c. decided they were already making enough drugs.

10. Which paragraph sums up the consequences of "the Pill"?
    a. Paragraph 1
    b. Paragraph 3
    c. Paragraph 8

**Exercise 3**

## Reflect and Think Critically

Think about what you read in "The Pill" and what you already know about medicines, birth control, and their effects on people's lives. Then answer the following questions in your own words.

1. Why do you think that contraception was banned or limited in thirty states in the 1950s?

   _____

   _____

   _____

   _____

2. Explain how the original goals of the creators of the pill contrast with the effects of the availability of birth control pills on women's lives.

   _____

   _____

   _____

   _____

3. Why do you think that trials of the medicine could be done on psychiatric patients, prisoners, and citizens of Puerto Rico and Haiti would have been "very difficult in this country"? Explain your answers.

   _____

   _____

   _____

   _____

4. Before the introduction of contraceptive medicines and devices, women had to worry about getting pregnant whenever they had sex. What concerns do both men and women have today about sexual relationships? Or what concerns should they have? Explain your answer.

   _____

   _____

   _____

   _____

**B**

**Cumulative Mastery Test**

# The National Eating Disorder*

— JAMAL JACKSON

**The following reading summarizes the studies of Michael Pollan, a best-selling author and professor at University of California, Berkeley. His research focuses on U.S. eating habits and attitudes toward food. As you read, keep in mind your own eating habits as well as those of your family and other people you know. Consider whether you agree with Pollan's main points about Americans and our food.**

1   Michael Pollan is a journalist and professor at the University of California, Berkeley, who writes articles and books about food and eating. In his book *The Omnivore's Dilemma,* he explains the difficulties that humans face because we are <u>omnivores</u>.[1] Because we can eat so many different things, we are constantly facing the question, "What should I eat?" Compared to other parts of the world, the United States is a young nation composed of many different immigrant groups with different cultural traditions. Although the United States draws something from many of these traditions, this country has never had a stable, unifying culture of food. So there is no clear answer to the eternal question, "What should I eat for dinner?"

2   The cultural practices of most immigrant communities have also been diluted or weakened with time. This <u>phenomenon</u> can be seen in families where the children no longer speak the native language of their grandparents, and they usually don't eat like their grandparents either. A national cuisine or <u>culture of food</u> is not just the assortment of dishes and ingredients but the rules and cultural practices surrounding eating. Our immigrant grandparents' culture of food did not just tell them what to eat, it also told them how much to eat, when to eat, where to eat, and how to serve the food. Saying grace before meals is an example of a food tradition that gives meaning to the act of eating. Saying grace and eating meals together as a family are the kinds of food traditions that are being lost.

3   Pollan suggests that the lack of a stabilizing food culture in the United States has led to a "national eating disorder."[2] Because we do not have meaningful cultural guidelines that tell us when, what, why, and with whom to eat, we are often confused and worried about eating. Food anxiety, eating disorders, and <u>antisocial</u> eating are all results of this problem. Fewer families eat together. Many of us eat while doing other things, such as driving a car or watching television. Rates of anorexia, obesity, and other diet-related illnesses are increasing. People are always talking and worrying about what we *should* and *shouldn't* eat.

4   Although it is a problem for most Americans, the national eating disorder is a perfect opportunity for the food industry. In fact, Pollan argues that the food industry has helped to create the disorder.[3] The food industry takes advantage of the lack of a steadying food culture and plays on our confusion, anxiety, and trust of supposed "experts." Food companies do this because they are faced with a particular business problem. Unlike clothes or music, which we can always buy more of, we can only consume

*"The National Eating Disorder" by Jamal Jackson. Reprinted by permission of the author.

a certain amount of food before our stomachs are stuffed to <u>capacity</u>. Even if food gets cheaper, we can only eat so much. This means that the food industry has two options: it can either grow at the same rate as population growth in the United States, or it can get people to eat more food. The population grows at about 1 percent every year, a growth rate that is ridiculously small from a business perspective, so the main job of the food industry has been trying to get Americans to eat more and more and more. In addition, by maintaining a cloud of confusion around food choices, the food industry can keep us buying new and "improved" food products.

5    Adding to the confusion created by the food industry are the thousands of nutritional scientists and food <u>gurus</u> in the United States. These so-called "food experts" come up with countless <u>contradictory</u> studies, diet suggestions, diet books, and weight-loss and <u>eternal</u> youth programs. The government gets involved, too, with national health recommendations. Whom should we believe? Often, new studies contradict old studies. Eggs used to be seen as healthy; then, for a while they had too much cholesterol; then, they were considered healthy choices again; and now we're told it's only the yolks that are bad for us! Today, in light of the new wisdom about eggs, we can go to a restaurant and get an omelet made just from the egg whites.

6    The most dramatic examples of the cloud of confusion and expert advice surrounding food in the United States are the great carbohydrate debates. For centuries, bread, rice, tortillas, and other grain-based foods have been central in food traditions around the world. These foods were seen as <u>wholesome</u> and healthy, and in many places, a meal without rice or bread was not considered a complete meal. Then, in 2002, a wave of diet books, scientific studies, and articles came out referring to the work of the formerly discredited Dr. Robert Atkins. Contrary to common sense, Atkins's theory proposed that it was not actually eating fat that made you fat, but eating foods with lots of carbohydrates. All of a sudden, people in the United States were looking at pasta, potatoes, bread, and even some kinds of fruits and vegetables with a carb-counting suspicion. Across the country, people changed their eating and their way of looking at food. People started ordering hamburgers without the buns, menus changed, bakeries went out of business, and a wave of new food products hit the market. Pollan argues that such a *dramatic* change in the eating habits of Americans is proof of the national eating disorder. Such a diet fad could not have had the same impact in a country with a strong food culture. Would the French suddenly stop eating bread because some nutritionists said that they could lose weight that way? Would millions of Mexicans and Central Americans stop eating rice and tortillas with their meals? The answer to these questions is no. Such advice would be considered ridiculous.

**carbohydrates**
starches and sugars

7    In the United States, we think of food as either bad for us or good for us. We are obsessed with nutrition and weight, but ironically, we are the most obese nation in the world. It seems that worrying about the healthiness of our food is not helping us eat a healthy diet. So what can we do about the national eating disorder? Pollan says we should definitely not look to nutritional scientists, diet gurus, the government, or the food industry to tell us what we should eat. Instead of these supposed experts, who are actually benefiting from our confusion, we should look to our history, traditions, and cultures. People have been choosing, eating, and enjoying food without expert help for thousands of years. The parts of the world where people still eat according to a traditional cuisine don't have all the diet-related anxiety, disorders, and diseases that we do in the United States. In an interview for the *New York Times Magazine*, Pollan said that we can eat this way, too, and end up being more healthy and happy. "The goal should just be eating well for pleasure, for community, and all the other reasons people eat."[3] Enjoying the preparation of real

food, using family recipes, eating together as a family, and observing small details like saying grace before eating are all ways that we can cure the national eating disorder.

**Notes**

1. Michael Pollan. *The Omnivore's Dilemma: A Natural History of Four Meals* (New York: Penguin Press, 2006).

2. *New York Times.* http://well.blogs.nytimes.com/2008/01/17/an-omnivore-defends-real-food/?emc=eta1 (accessed March 9, 2008).

3. *New York Times.* http://www.nytimes.com/2007/01/28/magazine/28nutritionism.t.html?_r=1&ref=health&pagewanted=all (accessed October 17, 2008).

**Exercise 1**

## Work with Words

Use context clues, dictionary skills, and your knowledge of word parts to choose the best definition for each italicized word in the following sentences from the reading. The paragraph number is provided in case you want to check the context.

1. *Omnivores* (par. 1)
   a. animals that will eat any type of food
   b. people who only eat processed food
   c. animals that eat vegetables only

2. *Phenomenon* (par. 2)
   a. incident
   b. event
   c. trend

3. *Culture of food* (par. 2)
   a. the kinds of food people eat
   b. when, where, how much, and how food is served and eaten
   c. the assortment of dishes and ingredients traditionally used in certain cultures

4. *Antisocial* (par. 3)
   a. together with others
   b. while driving a car
   c. alone

5. *Capacity* (par. 4)
   a. ability
   b. competence
   c. the limit

6. *Gurus* (par. 5)
   a. so-called experts
   b. religious leaders
   c. influential experts

7. *Contradictory* (par. 5)
   a. consistent
   b. inconsistent
   c. advisory

8. *Eternal* (par. 5)
   a. temporary
   b. sound
   c. never-ending

9. *Wholesome* (par. 6)
   a. nutritious
   b. delicious
   c. inexpensive

10. *Dramatic* (par. 6)
    a. emotional
    b. impressive
    c. theatrical

---

**Exercise 2**

## Check Your Understanding

Based on the reading, Jackson's "The National Eating Disorder," choose the best answer to each of the following multiple-choice questions.

1. Which of the following sentences best states the main idea of the reading?
   a. People in the United States generally have what Pollan calls an "eating disorder" because we don't have strong cultural traditions for eating, and the food industry, aided by contradictory nutritional studies and food fads, makes that disorder even worse.
   b. Enjoying the preparation of real food, using family recipes, eating together as a family, and observing small details such as saying grace before eating are all things we can do to cure the national eating disorder.
   c. Contrary to common sense, Atkins's theory proposed that it was not actually eating fat that made you fat, but eating foods with lots of carbohydrates.

2. In paragraph 2, Jackson uses the example of grandchildren of immigrants not speaking the language of their grandparents to illustrate the idea that
   a. old traditions are not important to immigrants any more.
   b. language use really has nothing to do with food consumption.
   c. old traditions are being diluted or lost.

3. What is the dominant pattern of organization of paragraph 3?
   a. chronological order and description
   b. cause and effect and exemplification
   c. definition and comparison and contrast

4. Which of the following sentences best states the main idea of paragraph 4?
   a. Egg yolks are unhealthy because of the high levels of cholesterol in them.
   b. The food industry takes advantage of the lack of a steadying food culture by encouraging Americans to eat more so that it can increase its profits.
   c. The food industry has two options: it can either grow at the same rate as population growth in the United States, or it can get people to eat more food.

5. Which of the following sentences best states the main idea of paragraph 6?
   a. Mexicans and Central Americans would never decide to stop eating tortillas and rice.
   b. It has been confirmed that the low- and no-carbohydrate diet is the best eating habit to follow.
   c. The low- and no-carbohydrate diet craze is an example of the confusion about food in the United States.

6. What is the dominant pattern of organization of paragraph 6?
   a. cause and effect
   b. description
   c. chronological order

7. Jackson believes it is ironic that we are obsessed with nutrition and weight, but
   a. we are the most obese nation in the world.
   b. we constantly read about diets and health.
   c. we simply follow the rules of our family traditions even though there are many cultures in this country.

8. What is the dominant pattern of organization for paragraph 7?
   a. cause and effect
   b. description and chronological order
   c. problem and solution

9. Pollan repeatedly mentions "saying grace" before meals because
   a. it is an important Christian practice that helps to hold a family together.
   b. it is an example of following a tradition of eating that he believes Americans need to have.
   c. it is an example of the national eating disorder.

10. The recommendation that Michael Pollan suggests to deal with our national eating disorder is to
    a. eat well for pleasure, for community, and all the other reasons people eat.
    b. follow the eating guidelines made by the federal government.
    c. study the scientific evidence for the best nutritional practices.

---

**Exercise 3**

### Reflect, Think Critically, and Evaluate the Argument

Think about what you read in Jackson's "The National Eating Disorder" and what you already know about diet and eating. Then answer the following questions in your own words.

1. What is the author's purpose for writing this article?

   _____

   _____

   _____

   _____

2. After examining the evidence, checking for fallacies, and considering your own world view and experiences, do you find the argument in the reading convincing and will you think about changing your eating habits? Explain your answers.

_____

_____

_____

_____

3. What are some examples of processed foods sold in supermarkets that advertise that they are "good for you" (nutritious) or "new and improved?" Explain your examples.

_____

_____

_____

_____

4. Can you think of some reasons that Jackson doesn't discuss that lead to people eating by themselves, in their cars, or while doing other things?

_____

_____

_____

5. Do you know of anyone (or a family) who has the type of eating disorder described in this reading? Describe this person's (or family's) concerns and behaviors about food and eating. Explain why you consider these concerns and behaviors signals of an eating disorder.

_____

_____

_____

_____

PART II

# A Reader's Toolkit

# 1. Reading Visual Aids

Visual aids are images that assist the reader in understanding text, whether that text is on a book page or a computer screen. A visual aid can be a picture, map, cartoon, graph, table, pie chart, flow chart, or diagram as well as a figure, time line, or illustration in a story, article, or text selection. This brief section offers you further instruction and practice interpreting these aids. The answers to the practices are on pages 432–433.

When you read a chapter in a textbook, an article in a newspaper, or a page on a website, always look at the visual aids as you prepare to read. Study them again while you are reading. You will need to "read" each visual aid actively.

- *Decide* what you think is the purpose of the visual aid. Why is this visual aid included? What does it mean in relation to the reading?
- *Compare* items in different parts of the visual aid. What is the relationship between the parts? What is being compared? What is the result of the comparison?
- *Think* about what conclusions you can reach or what trends you can predict based on the information the visual aid provides. In some ways, you can consider this step as finding the *main idea* of the visual aid.

When you examine a visual aid, especially one in a textbook, be sure to read the title, the caption, and the credit line. The caption, a brief explanation that appears immediately above or below the image, will help you determine the purpose of the visual aid and reach some conclusions about the information it provides. The credit line identifies who created or supplied the image. Together they will help you understand and evaluate the image.

## MAPS

Maps convey geographical information and can help you understand distance relationships (through mileage legends) and the influence of physical features such as rivers, oceans, and mountains. Often maps show the location of specific populations or trends related to them. For example, as the title for Figure II.1

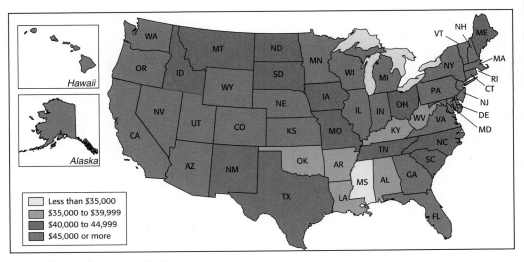

**median income**
the middle of the income range; just as many people earn more as earn less

**Figure II.1**  Median Income by State

What factors contribute to the uneven distribution of income in the United States?

Source: U.S. Census Bureau, 2007, in Diana Kendall, *Sociology in Our Times*, 8th ed. (Belmont, Calif.: Wadsworth/Cengage, 2011), p. 260.

indicates, it shows median income by state. The color of each state corresponds with one of the colors in the boxes that indicate the category of median income. In this way, it is graphically very easy to identify where people tend to earn more or less income. Notice that the caption at the bottom of the map asks, "What factors contribute to the uneven distribution of income in the United States?" The author wants you to think critically about the answer to this question. Look at the color of your state. Does its placement based on median income seem correct to you? Where do you or people you know fall in relation to the median income in your state?

**Practice II.1**

## Interpret a Map

Study the map in Figure II.2. Then answer the following questions.

1. Briefly summarize the income distribution information on this map.

   _____

   _____

   _____

2. What is the difference between "median income" and "average per capita" income?

   _____

   _____

   _____

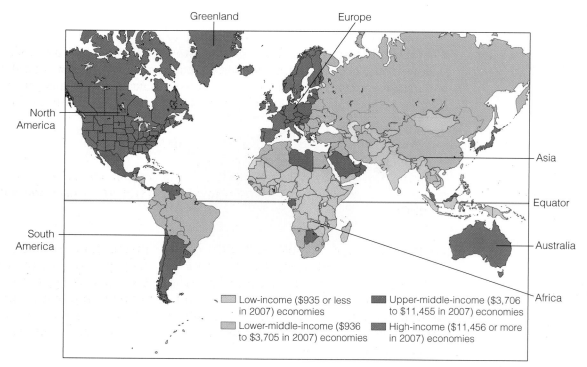

**Figure II.2**  High-, Middle-, and Low-Income Economies in Global Perspective, by average per capita (per person) income

Source: World Bank, 2009, in Diana Kendall, *Sociology in Our Times*, 8th ed. (Belmont, Calif.: Wadsworth/Cengage, 2011). p. 287.

3. What information is missing in "average" per capita income data?

_____

_____

_____

4. What might be some explanations for the extremely uneven distribution of income around the world?

_____

_____

_____

5. What kind of life do you think the people have in the various regions of this map? How might it be different from yours?

_____

_____

_____

(See answers on pages 432–433.)

## GRAPHS

Graphs are diagrams that present data using dots, lines, or bars to show the relationship between two things. Often one element is time, shown on the horizontal line, and the other element is a figure that changes with time, such as the number of people in poverty. To understand graphs, ask yourself the following questions:

- What does the horizontal line or bar indicate?
- What does the vertical line or bar indicate?
- What is the relationship between the information on each line or bar?
- What does the overall graph demonstrate? (In other words, what is the main idea?)

**Line Graphs**  For example, as its title suggests, Figure II.3 is a line graph that shows the number of people living in poverty and the poverty rate (percentage of people living in poverty) between 1959 and 2009. The graph gives the reader a visual representation of the increases and decreases in poverty. It allows us to understand that a much higher percentage of Americans were poor in 1959 (22 percent) than in 2009 (14.3 percent). However, in actual numbers, more people were poor in 2009 (43.6 million).

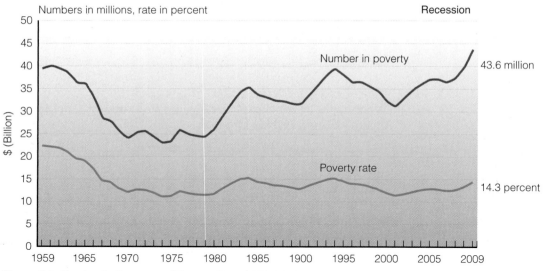

**Figure II.3** Number in Poverty and Poverty Rate, 1959–2009

Note: The data points are placed at the midpoints of the respective years.

Source: U.S. Census Bureau, Current Population Survey, 1960 to 2010 Annual Social and Economic Supplements.

**Practice II.2**

## Interpret a Line Graph

Study the graph in Figure II.4. Then answer the following questions.

1. Is the percentage of men or of women in poverty greater? Why do you think that is the case?

   _____

   _____

   _____

   _____

2. What group shown on this graph has the highest percentage in poverty? How has the percentage changed over the past fifty years? What do you think might explain the changes?

   _____

   _____

   _____

   _____

3. What additional information would be good to know to better understand poverty in the United States?

   _____

   _____

   _____

   _____

(See answers on page 433.)

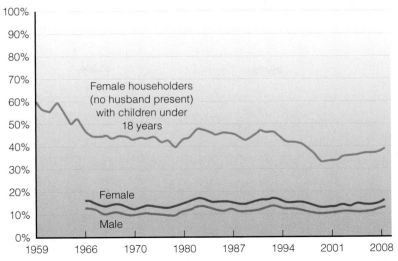

**Figure II.4**  Percent of Women and Men in Poverty, percent of each group with incomes below poverty line, 1959–2009

Source: U.S. Department of Commerce, Economics and Statistics Administration, and Executive Office of the President, Office of Management and Budget, in cooperation with the U.S. Census Bureau and others, *Women in American: Indicators of Social and Economic Well-Being*, March 2011.

**Bar Graphs** Another type of graph is a bar graph. Bar graphs are especially useful for showing comparisons among different categories. The title of the graph and the labeling of each bar, as well as the length of the bar make these graphs easily understandable. In Figure II.5, for example, it is clear by looking at both bar graphs that people who have the most education (a doctoral or professional degree) earn much more money per week ($1,532 and $1,529 median weekly earnings) and have far lower unemployment rates (2.5 percent and 2.3 percent) than people who have less education. The pattern continues downward for those with the least education.

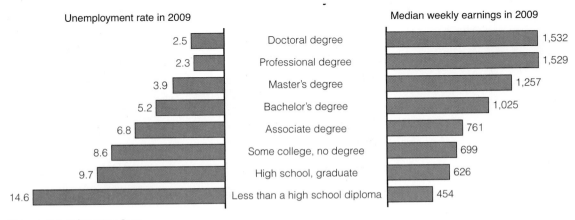

**Figure II.5**  Education Pays

Note: Data are 2009 annual averages for persons age 25 and over. Earnings are for full-time wage and salary workers.

Source: U.S. Bureau of Labor Statistics, Current Population Survey, 2010.

**Practice II.3**

## Interpret a Bar Graph

Study the graph in Figure II.6. Then answer the following questions.

1. Approximately how much after-tax family income did the bottom fifth of U.S. families have in 2006?

_____

2. Approximately how much after-tax income did the top 1 percent of U.S. families have in 2006?

_____

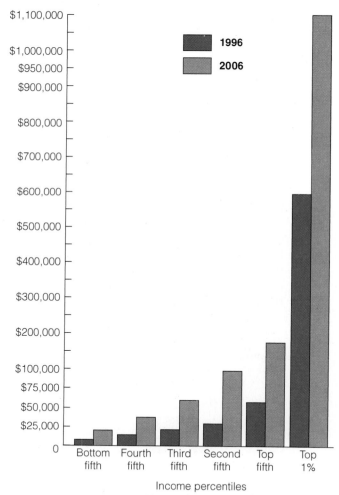

**Figure II.6**  Average Family Income in the United States, 1996 and 2006.

This chart shows the distribution of after-tax family income in the United States.

Source: U.S. Census Bureau, 2009, in Diana Kendall, *Sociology in Our Times*, 8th ed. (Belmont, Calif.: Wadsworth/Cengage, 2011), p. 261.

3. What are some different ways that people make income?

_____

_____

_____

4. What does this difference in income tell us about our society? What different worldviews or points of view do you think those in the bottom fifth and those in the top 1 percent might have about what is fair or good for the economy? What is your opinion?

_____

_____

_____

_____

(See answers on page 433.)

## PIE CHARTS

A pie chart shows the relationships of parts to a whole. The whole is the contents of a circle, or a pie, and divisions are appropriately sized portions, or slices. For example, look at Figure II.7. One circle represents the U.S. population in 1999, and the divisions of the pie or circle indicate the racial distribution of that population. The other circle shows the same information as it is projected for 2050. You can readily see that the most notable change will be in the proportion of the population that is of Hispanic origin: up from 11.5 percent in 1999 to 24 percent in 2050.

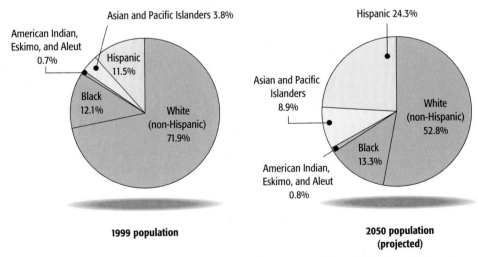

**1999 population**

**2050 population (projected)**

**Figure II.7** Percentage Distribution of Population by Race and Hispanic Origin, 1999 and 2050, projected

Note: Racial categories exclude those of Hispanic origin.

Source: U.S. Census Bureau, News Release, March 21, 2001.

**Practice II.4**

## Interpret a Pie Chart

Study the pie chart in Figure II.8. Then answer the following questions.

1. What are the two areas where households spend most of their money?

   _____

   _____

2. List two or three facts that you find interesting or even surprising about this pie chart.

   _____

   _____

   _____

   _____

3. What percentages in this pie chart correspond to your household expenditures? What percentages are very different from yours? Explain your answers.

   _____

   _____

   _____

   _____

(See answers on page 433.)

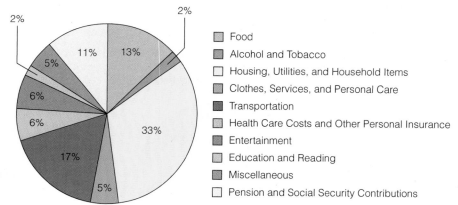

**Figure II.8**   Average Household Expenditures in the United States, 2008

In 2008, average household expenditures totaled $50,489. Households included families, single people living alone, and individuals sharing living expenses in a household.

Source: U.S. Census Bureau, *The 2011 Statistical Abstract: The National Data Book.*

## PRACTICE ANSWERS

### Practice II.1 Interpret a Map

1. (A) Highest median incomes: North America, Western Europe, and Australia ($11,456 or more in 2007.) (B) Lowest: Most of Sub-Saharan Africa, most of South and Southeast Asia, some of China ($935 or less.) (C) Lower-middle:

Much of South America, North Africa, and Asia ($936–$3,705) (D) Upper-middle income: Parts of Latin America (Mexico, Venezuela, Panama, Chile, and Argentina) and some parts of North Africa, Saudi Arabia, and some parts of Eastern Europe ($3,706–$11,455).

2. Median income is the number that falls in the middle of the range of incomes. Average per capita means the average income of every child, man, and woman in a country.

3. These kinds of data based on averages can hide the fact that millions of people are extremely poor, and a very few are extremely rich. Just because a country is listed as an "upper middle income" country, such as Mexico, does not mean that most people have income in the range that is given.

4. Answers will vary. Some possible answers: Some countries get income from natural resources, some countries are more developed, some countries may have a small group of extremely rich people.

5. Answers will vary. Some possible answers: In the poorest countries people probably don't have a lot of things we take for granted like easily available water, enough food, and decent housing.

### Practice II.2 Interpret a Line Graph

1. The percentage of women in poverty is greater, probably because women do not receive equal pay with men, women miss more work to raise children, and single women who are heads of households are especially poor.

2. Female heads of households with no husband present have the highest percentage in poverty. The percentage has gone down approximately 20 percent between 1959 and 2009. Perhaps there has been more government assistance (since 1959) for these women, such as paying for childcare so that they can go to work.

3. Answers will vary. Possible answers: It would be good to know how many households are headed by single women, and how many children live in those households, how many children generally live in poverty, and the ethnic, and geographic breakdown of poverty.

### Practice II.3 Interpret a Bar Graph

1. Less than $25,000
2. About $1,100,000
3. Answers will vary. Most people make income by working at jobs. Wealthy people may make additional income from their investments, companies they own, property, or even interest on their money.
4. Answers will vary.

### Practice II.4 Interpret a Pie Chart

1. Housing (33 percent) and transportation (17 percent)
2. Answers will vary. Possible answers: (1) It appears that, on average, American households spend as much money (2 percent) on alcohol and tobacco as they do on education and reading. (2) Households spend 13 percent on food. (3) Eleven percent of average household expenditures go toward pensions and social security.
3. Answers will vary.

# 2. Note Taking: The Cornell Note-Taking System

One of the most important ways college students acquire knowledge is through the process of taking notes during lectures. Although collaborative learning, discussion groups, and individualized learning are important sources of information, lectures by scholars and experts will continue to be a major means of instruction. Even if innovations such as distance learning and multimedia computer/video presentations enhance these lectures in the future, you will still need some basic note-taking techniques to organize and use the information you receive.

The **Cornell Note-Taking System,** which originated at Cornell University in New York, is one of the most popular note-taking systems among college students. To make the system easy to remember, it breaks the process into steps, called the **5Rs:**

1. **R**ecord
2. **R**educe
3. **R**eflect
4. **R**ecite
5. **R**eview

To begin the Cornell Note-Taking System, you need to draw a new left margin on a standard 8½ by 11 piece of notebook paper. Draw the left margin about 3 inches from the left edge of the paper. This space is for the *reduce* column, which you will fill in after recording your notes in the space at the right. Leave about a 2-inch space at the bottom of the page to record your reflections on the lecture sometime after the class session. (To see what this setup looks like, turn to the example on page 436.) You can buy notebooks at some college bookstores that already have the correct margins printed for the Cornell Note-Taking System.

## RECORD

Before you begin recording notes for a class lecture, write the date at the top of the paper. Keep the notes for each course in a separate notebook, or at least in a clearly divided portion of a notebook.

Be on time for the lecture, or even a little early, so you don't miss introductory comments or directions. *Read* assigned textbook material. Before you get to class, *review* the reading as well as your lecture notes from recent classes. This review process enables you to easily recognize the context, or framework, of this day's lecture presentation.

*Record all the essential information* you need to remember from the lecture. How do you choose the right information? First, you need to *listen* carefully and *select* the important points. Don't try to be a human tape recorder, writing down every word that the lecturer says. You will be frustrated, and you won't have time to think about what is being said. Record points such as the following:

- Main ideas, major supporting points
- Patterns of organization (recognizing the pattern of the lecturer's organization will help you to order your notes accordingly)

- Major transitions (to help you recognize the relationships between ideas)
- Information written on the board or presented on an overhead or with computer graphics
- Points that the lecturer obviously stresses by introducing with phrases such as "you need to know," "this will be on the test," "remember this point," and "it is most important to consider"
- Emphasized information (watch for lecturer's style: raising or lowering the voice, gesturing, pacing, or other movements may indicate emphasis)
- Repeated information

Check your notes at the end of class for any errors. If you missed an important point and didn't have a chance to ask about it during the lecture, ask the instructor or a classmate as soon as you can after class so you don't forget it.

## REDUCE

As soon as you have a chance to study your notes, you can *reduce* them. Read over the notes you have recorded in the right column. Select key words and phrases that summarize the main points of the lecture. List these points in the left-hand column.

## REFLECT

You already know that thinking about what you read is an important part of active reading. *Reflecting* on what you learn in lectures is also important. Consider how the concepts, facts, and interpretations you learned in the lecture relate to what you've read, what you've experienced, and what you already know about the topic. Does this information reinforce what you already know? Does it add new information or understanding? Does it contradict your previous knowledge? If so, how can you resolve the differences? What new questions or problems are raised that you need to explore? Record your reflections at the bottom of your notes.

## RECITE

As you already know from the PRO system, *recite* means to test yourself. In the Cornell Note-Taking System, you use the key words and phrases identified in the *reduce* section of your notes to assist you. Cover the recorded notes, and use the reduced notes to form questions. See if you can provide detailed definitions, explanations, comparisons, and so on, without looking back. Uncover the detailed notes to check your answers.

## REVIEW

The process of *reviewing* your notes is actually the same as reviewing your selected points in reading. Repeat the recite step periodically—within 24 hours, two to three days, a week, two to three weeks, and over increasingly spaced intervals—to retain the essential information and understanding you will need for tests and for work.

You can take notes from what you read as well as from lectures. You could then use the Cornell Note-Taking System to organize these reading notes for reciting and review.

# USE THE CORNELL METHOD

If you had used the Cornell Note-Taking System to take notes on the information you just read, it would look something like the following. First the important ideas are recorded on the right. Then that information is reduced to key terms in the left-hand column. At the end are some reflections on the information.

### The Cornell Note-Taking System       January 5, 2013

| Reduce | Record |
|---|---|
| Set up | Set up paper with 3-inch margin from left side of the paper and a 2-inch margin at the bottom. |
| Record | Record all essential information on the right side of the paper. |
| | Listen carefully and select important points, main ideas, patterns, information on the board, and emphasized information. If you missed something, ask a classmate or the professor. |
| Reduce key words and phrases | After the lecture, select key words and phrases that summarize main points. List these in the left column. |
| Reflect | Think about how concepts, facts, and information from the lecture relate to what you know and to your reading. What observations can you make? What questions can you ask? |
| | Write your thoughts at the bottom of the paper as soon as you can at the end of the lecture. |
| Recite | Test yourself. Ask yourself questions from the key words and phrases in the left column, and try to fill in the rest of the information, keeping the right column covered. Uncover your detailed notes to check your answers. |
| Review | Repeat the recite step periodically—after one day, a few days later, two to three weeks later. |
| Reflections | This seems like a good method of note taking. The hardest part will be to take the time to reduce my notes, write my reflections, and then recite and review them. If I do all these things on a regular basis, studying from my notes for tests will be pretty easy. |

© 2013 Wadsworth, Cengage Learning

# 3. Test Taking

Being confident and well prepared are the basic essentials for successful test taking. Regular exams are part of the requirements of college courses. Some employers give new or potential employees tests to measure knowledge and aptitude. Entry into certain professions, such as nursing, cosmetology, accounting, insurance, and teaching, require special tests for certification or licensing. Whatever the testing situation, careful preparation is the key to confidence.

## OVERCOME TEST ANXIETY

Preparing for tests in college courses is simplified by using a system for reading and studying such as PRO. With conscientious study and review, test taking becomes a less anxious experience. If you tend to be overly stressed about tests, try *overlearning* the material—learning it so well that you could "recite it in your sleep." Even when you are confident about what you know, test taking is still a challenge, but you should be able to approach it positively. Your stress at this point should be *eustress*, which helps you to do your very best, instead of *distress*. Visualize yourself arriving for the test a little early, with time to relax, and then calmly and confidently answering even the most difficult questions. Know that you are well prepared and can answer any objective or essay questions that arise.

## ANTICIPATE TEST QUESTIONS

A helpful way to prepare for tests is to anticipate what the questions will be and then *recite*, to test yourself on those questions. Use your knowledge of the course objectives from the syllabus, the professor's suggestions and clues in lectures, and your own identification of what is important in both the textbook and in lectures through the application of the PRO Reading System and the Cornell Note-Taking System. Ask yourself, "What are the essential pieces of information, relationships among data, and understandings I have mastered so far in the course?" Ask your professor what kinds of questions will be on the test—objective questions, essay questions, or a combination of both?

Write possible test items. Practice answering them yourself and in study groups. If you review in a study group, you might divide writing and answering the practice questions. The advantages of a study group, of course, are that together you have a better chance of covering all the essentials, you can cover them more quickly and completely, and you can test each other.

## FOLLOW DIRECTIONS

Students and job applicants frequently lose points on tests because they simply don't follow directions. Read *all* the directions on a test before you do anything else. Take note of any changes in directions or corrections to test items that the professor may announce or write on the board at the beginning of class. Be sure you know how many points each portion of the test is worth, decide how much time you will spend on each section accordingly, and *budget your time* so you can complete the entire test.

# UNDERSTAND THE TYPES OF QUESTIONS

**Objective Questions** Objective questions on tests are usually multiple choice, true/false, or matching. Objective questions may be perceived as relatively easy because they don't appear to require complete recall of the content, only recognition of a correct answer. However, it is possible to be overconfident when approaching objective tests and thus lose points unnecessarily. Read carefully the directions for the scoring of objective questions. Sometimes there is a definite penalty for guessing; you may, for example, lose double points for a wrong answer. Here are some additional hints that can help you become more accurate in answering objective questions.

- In matching exercises, how many choices will be used? How useful will the process of elimination be in making your choices?
- Watch for qualifying words and negative words that will strongly influence your answer.
- For multiple-choice questions, always read all the choices before making a decision. Check each choice as if it were a true/false statement. Then choose the best answer for the question. Remember that "none of the above" or "all of the above" is sometimes the right answer. Again, read the directions carefully; you may be asked to choose all the correct answers, not just one.

**Essay Questions** Essay test questions require answers of various lengths, from one paragraph to two or three pages or more. The first requirement for answering an essay question effectively is to read the question carefully. Be sure you understand the requirements. What exactly is the question asking you to do? Essay directions usually include terms that you should now associate with patterns of organization (as discussed in Chapter 5). You may, for example, be asked to *define, compare and contrast, analyze, give examples,* or *explain causes or effects.* Each of these directions gives you a specific task. See page 439 for more vocabulary clues for essay questions.

Before you begin writing an essay exam, take a few minutes to outline your answer. This step helps you organize your ideas. Begin with a thesis statement that answers the question directly. List all the supporting points you want to include; that way, you won't forget any of them, and you'll be able to present them in the best possible order.

Begin your essay by answering the question directly. Choose key words from the question itself to begin your answer so it is obvious that you are answering the question and not straying. For example, if a question on a history test is "Discuss the immediate cause for the beginning of the American Revolutionary War," your answer might begin something like this: "Although many incidents led up to the outbreak of the Revolutionary War, *the immediate cause for the beginning of the American Revolutionary War was* the firing of arms at Lexington and Concord." The italicized words show that you have answered the question at the very beginning and that you will go on to develop the points to support your answer.

Divide the time allowed for the test to be sure you can include all the supporting points you noted in your preliminary outline. Your goal in an essay test is to let the instructor know how much you know about the topic and how well you can organize and express your knowledge in a limited amount of time.

# VOCABULARY CLUES FOR TEST TAKING

There are a number of ways that your vocabulary skills can assist you in successful test taking.

**In Objective Questions** For true/false questions, identify the *qualifying words* used, such as *most, some, all, none,* and *few.* These words often make the difference between a true and a false statement. Obviously, absolutes such as *all* or *none* seldom exist, so statements containing them may well be false. For example, in the sentence "All dogs have fleas," the word *all* obviously makes the statement false.

For both true/false and multiple-choice questions, be aware of *negative words,* such as *no, not, never;* one word can reverse the meaning of the entire sentence. Always be careful of *except.* Sometimes a multiple-choice question is worded something like, "all of the following are true, except." In this case, you are looking for the choice that is *not* true.

**In Essay Questions** Read the directions for essay questions very carefully, and distinguish between the various parts of answers required. Use the following key words in the directions to help you plan an answer.

- *Discuss:* Write about various aspects of the topic; you decide how to limit the scope or provide a focus.
- *Define:* Provide a definition; that is, place an item in a category and then explain the specific characteristics that distinguish it from other items in that category.
- *Effect:* Write about the consequences or the results of a previous action or event.
- *Compare:* Write about the similarities and differences between two items, persons, concepts, and so on.
- *Contrast:* Write about the differences between two items, persons, concepts, and so on.
- *Cause:* Write about the reasons why something is the way it is. You may be asked to identify and analyze both immediate causes and underlying causes.
- *Analyze:* Write about the parts of a whole and discuss how the parts are related to each other. You might be asked to analyze a process, a cause-effect relationship, a character in literature, or any complex concept.
- *Summarize:* State concisely, usually in a paragraph or essay, the main ideas and major supporting points in the original reading or lecture.
- *Evaluate:* Write a reasoned response about the effectiveness or worth of a process, solution, argument, or product. Evaluating goes beyond stating an opinion—a simple like or dislike. It is based on thorough knowledge and careful analysis.

# 4. Writing Tips for Readers

Many college writing assignments ask you to write about what you have read. These assignments vary from short answers on tests to longer critiques, reflections, essays, and research papers. In this text, for example, each chapter ends with a writing activity that asks you to write a paragraph or short essay. Here are some tips on how to complete such assignments.

- *Read* thoroughly all the information on which the assignment is based. As you read, think about the question(s) you will be writing about.
- Carefully *read* the directions for your writing assignment and be sure you understand and follow the directions.
- *Write* notes for your answer to the question.
- *Decide* what the main point is you want to make about the topic. In one sentence, state your answer to the question. (This is similar to finding the main idea as a reader. Now, as a writer, you are deciding what the main idea will be for your readers. Clearly answering the question will make it easier for your readers to comprehend what you write.)
- *Organize* what you want to say in an outline so you don't forget any points you want to include and your points will be presented in a clear and logical order.
- *Write* a rough draft of your answer.
- *Get feedback* on what you have written. Have classmates or friends read your paper, and see what questions they have about what you have written. If your campus has a writing center, ask a writing tutor to review your paper with you.
- *Revise* what you have written, and write your final draft. (As you review what you wrote, check to see if you have answered all parts of the question. Did you include enough supporting points to fully explain your ideas? Then proofread to ensure that all your sentences make sense and all words are spelled correctly.)
- *Keep your completed writing assignments* for the semester in a portfolio. Your instructor may want to evaluate your semester's progress by reviewing your work in this format. Many students find it useful to save what they have learned and to monitor their own writing and learning from semester to semester by keeping a portfolio. Some colleges ask for a portfolio of student work for admission into certain programs.

# 5. Evaluating and Navigating Websites

You can find all kinds of information on the Internet. It can be an invaluable resource for researching topics ranging from diseases, drugs, and diets to history, literature, and technological advances. But the web also has lots of inaccurate, misleading, and even slanderous "information." So it is essential for you to develop the ability to evaluate websites. To use the information on a website, you should familiarize yourself with ways to judge its reliability. How do you judge whether the information on a website is true and reliable? To do so effectively, you will use many of the skills you've learned: prereading (scanning the site home page), reading, organizing, and critical thinking. To provide a structure for your evaluation, you should answer the following questions.

## SOURCE

**Who Is Giving You the Information? Should You Trust the Author?** One way to evaluate a site's author is by looking at the address, or URL (uniform resource locator). Part of the URL, called the domain name, tells you who originated the site. For instance, the URL for the website for this book is www.cengagebrain.com. The domain name for this URL is .com. As shown in Table II.3, the .com domain name indicates that the main purpose of the site is to sell products—in this case, books. The table lists other common domain names and what they mean.

Many sites have an "About" section that gives you a little background information on the author and/or the purpose of the site so you can judge his or her qualifications as well as the agenda of the site. Is this person an expert? Is his or her resumé on the site? Is there a list of the author's print media publications?

If the website includes information from outside printed sources, such as newspapers or magazines, does it properly document them? A website author who makes it easy for you to check sources and get background information is probably more reliable than one who states "facts" without saying where they come from.

Finally, take into account who can put information on the site. To post a comment on some websites, such as discussion boards, a person need only register an e-mail address. The authors of these posts are not held responsible for the information they contain, and the website owners usually put a disclaimer that they are not liable for any misinformation. Avoid using this sort of website in your research.

## CURRENCY

**How Current Is the Site—That Is, Is the Information Kept Up-To-Date?** Many sites tell you when the last update occurred, and articles are usually dated. If there isn't a date on the page, try going to the View menu in your browser and selecting Page Info, Source, or whatever option is available to provide the information you need.

| Table II.3 Domain Names and Reliability | | |
|---|---|---|
| **Domain Name** | **Reliability of Sponsor** | **Possible Purposes** |
| .edu | Educational institution (college, university, or research institution). Information found here is usually reliable. But a person affiliated with the institution (a student, for example) may have a page on the site that reflects only that individual's viewpoint. The URL for this kind of Web page usually ends with the person's name in the form of http://www.university.edu/~name. | • Disseminate information about the institution<br>• Disseminate research<br>• Make useful information available to the public |
| .com | Anyone can buy a .com Web address, and there are few or no restrictions on the content that can go on the site. Usually, the purpose of a .com site is to sell things. Most businesses have .com sites. | • Sell a product<br>• Promote the public image of a private company |
| .org | Like .com, the .org domain name is available for anyone to purchase. Most nonprofit organizations have .org addresses. While the information is probably reliable, it usually has a bias. Many .org addresses promote a particular viewpoint. | • Promote a position (e.g., defending the rights of children, protecting the environment)<br>• Advocate that readers do something to support the position of the group<br>• Announce events<br>• Disseminate information |
| .gov | Official site maintained by the U.S. government. This kind of site should be reliable but can be political, reflecting and promoting the views of the politicians or party that controls the particular government agency. | • Provide information (e.g., regulations, statistics reports)<br>• Provide resources for the public (e.g., how to apply for unemployment insurance)<br>• Promote the political position of the current administration |

## USEFULNESS

**How Useful Is the Site?** Even reliable information is useless if you can't find it. An established, reliable website usually has a home page, which is the first document you see when you enter the site and serves as an introduction to the site. A home page includes links to other parts of the site and frequently links to other websites that have related information. Sometimes the home pages are well organized, but sometimes they are not. In any case, "reading" a home page is not a linear process.

You do not necessarily start at the top of the page and read down. Often you will find yourself "looking all around" the page to get an idea of what is available. You will need to scan the page, not read it word for word. You are acting as a detective, searching until you find what you want and using clues to guide your search.

## THE ELEMENTS OF A WEBSITE

For practice, examine Figure II.9, the home page for the U.S. Department of Labor's website (http://www.dol.gov) under the Bush administration. If you examine the Find It! column on the left, you will see that you can look for information by topic. If you have a specific question about wages, for example, you can click on Wages. You can also look for information by audience. Here you can find information important to workers or employers. For example, if you are looking for a job, you would first click on Workers. This takes you to a new web page with several sections, including one titled Information for Job Seekers.

**Figure II.9**    U.S. Department of Labor Home Page

Source: http://www.dol.gov

There are many other interesting features on this website, and you could easily spend hours exploring them all. For example, the In Focus section of the homepage includes recent news items or bulletins that the Department of Labor would like you to see, and the right column of the home page lists more topics you might want to check.

It is important to remember that most active websites do not remain the same. They are constantly updated and even the home page may change, so the picture you see here and the information you find for the Department of Labor website dated November 4, 2008, will not be the same when you go to the site yourself. Government websites tend to change when a different president is elected to office. In fact, this website changed significantly when President Obama came into office.

**Practice II.5**

## Evaluate a Website

Go to the website for the Centers for Disease Control and Prevention (http://www.cdc.gov), and then fill out the following evaluation form. (Answers for Practice II.5 are on pages 445–446.)

1. Site address:_____ Date accessed:_____

2. Who created the site? What are the qualifications and affiliations of the site? For whom is the site written? What is the purpose of the site?.

   _____

   _____

   _____

3. When was the site last updated?

   _____

4. What is the content of the site?

   _____

   _____

   _____

5. Where can you find the information you need from this site?

   _____

   _____

   _____

   _____

6. How can you use the information on this site? Would you recommend this site to another student? Remember to use your reading and critical thinking skills to evaluate the content of the site. (See the discussions in Chapter 7 on worldview, point of view, and bias on pages 295 through 296, and in Chapter 8 on evaluating arguments, including the Reader's Tip on pages 325–328)

_____

_____

_____

_____

_____

## PRACTICE ANSWERS

### Practice II.5

1. Site address: _____ Date accessed: _____

2. Who created the site? What are the qualifications and affiliations of the site? For whom is the site written? What is the purpose of the site? This site is created by the Centers for Disease Control and Prevention, an agency of the U.S. Department of Health and Human Services. Because it is a government site (with a .gov domain name), the information is probably accurate, although it is possible that it reflects the political bias of the current administration. The site is written for health professionals but also for anybody who wants to research health issues. The site's purpose is to make information about health widely available.

3. When was the site last updated? _____

4. What is the content of the site? The site has interesting information on a lot of topics such as diseases and conditions, emergency preparedness, environmental health, and workplace safety and health. It also has links to healthy living, and a section on data and statistics about health in the United States.

5. Where can you find the information you need from this site? The home page includes links to several sections of the site that provide specific information, including an A–Z index of health topics and a search box.

6. How can you use the information on this site? Would you recommend this site to another student? Remember to use your reading and critical thinking skills to evaluate the content of the site. (See the discussions in Chapter 7 on world-view, point of view, and bias on pages 295 through 296 and in Chapter 8 on evaluating arguments, including the Reader's Tip, on pages 325 through 328.)

This site is a good source for information on health issues in the United States. It

has lots of well-documented data, and the CDC itself is an authoritative source.

The information in this site can be used in a research paper about various health

subjects. It can also be used by people who might be interested in going into a

health-related career or by somebody who just wants to find out more about a

specific disease or health condition. The links it provides are also excellent for

finding additional information about specific subjects.

# 6. Reader Response Journals

Often readers are asked to reflect on what they have read. Throughout this text, you have been asked to answer questions about your reflections on readings from all types of sources. Sometimes instructors ask students to organize their reflections in a *reader response journal*. Reader response journals are assigned in various kinds of courses, from math and biology to philosophy and English literature. If you read an additional book, besides your text, for this reading course, a reader response journal would be a good way to record your reflections on what you read.

The most common kind of reader response journal is organized like the one shown on the opposite page, with a quotation from the text recorded on the left and the reader's reflections recorded on the right. Other times, the quotation is simply recorded first and the reflections follow. Regardless of the format, instructors are usually looking for certain types of responses in journal entries. They will probably request some of the following types of entries:

- Connections between new knowledge and previously acquired understandings
- Responses to the ease or difficulty of mastering new concepts or processes
- Evaluations of the significance of new concepts
- Personal responses to new concepts; comments on the value of the reading to your own life
- Questions that arise from the new ideas
- Ethical considerations that need to be added
- Comments on logical fallacies or other errors in reasoning
- New ideas that the recently learned information stimulated
- Recognition of relationships between ideas
- Applications of new concepts to other areas of knowledge
- Specific assignments, such as a list of quotations and reflections that lead to an analysis of a character in a literary text

| Quote from Text | Response |
|---|---|
| **Computer Science** | |
| "Artificial intelligence is the branch of computer science that explores the use of computers in tasks that require intelligence, imagination, and insight— tasks that have traditionally been performed by people rather than machines." (Beekman, Computer Confluence) | What kinds of "human" activities can be done by machines? How could a computer possibly show imagination? This seems like a uniquely human trait. Perhaps Beekman defines imagination differently than I do! |
| **Sociology** | |
| "Paycheck inequality has grown so much that the top 4 percent of Americans make more in wages and salaries than the entire bottom half." (Sklar, Chaos or Community?) | Wow! That isn't fair! How can they even spend all that money? I'm working 40 hours a week besides going to school and barely making it. Maybe there should be laws that regulate how much profit individuals can take out of a company. |
| **Psychology** | |
| "Although machines are likely to break down, humans will continue to work even when they are overloaded." (Smither, The Psychology of Work and Human Performance) | This idea of human advantage contradicts what we read in computer science by Beekman. I'm not sure that working when you're "overloaded" is really an advantage though. Consider all the injuries studies that show what happens when workers are fatigued. |
| **Literature** | |
| "Sally, do you sometimes wish you didn't have to go home? Do you wish your feet would one day keep walking and take you far away from Mango Street, far away and maybe your feet would stop in front of a house, a nice one with flowers and big windows and steps for you to climb up two by two upstairs to where a room is waiting for you. And if you opened the little window latch and gave it a shove, the windows would swing open, all the sky would. (Sandra Cisneros, A House on Mango Street) | This passage makes me feel sorry for Sally, because we know that Sally is in trouble and her home is not happy. It makes me hope that Sally could be free, that Sally's feet (not under Sally's control, like an outside force) could take her away from her sad circumstances and set her free, free because the windows would swing open, and the sky and all its possibilities would open up for Sally. |

# 7. Reading Circles

Reading circles provide a student-centered format that empowers students to work in groups independently of direct instructor involvement. At the same time, reading circles provide a system that enables the instructor to know exactly who is doing the work and what each member is contributing to the group. The following guidelines are adapted from Harvey Daniels's *Literature Circles* (1994), where the technique was first explained. They will help you make your reading circle a success.

## GET ORGANIZED

1. In class, preview and choose a book you wish to read from a list of about four to six books your instructor provides.
2. Form a reading circle with other students who chose the same book you chose. Your instructor will help in this process to ensure that the groups are about the right size. Usually, each reading circle has three to five students.
3. Groups meet during class time to get organized. At the first meeting, members of your reading group should
   a. introduce yourselves and exchange contact information.
   b. decide how you will divide up reading the book. If your group has four meetings, for example, and your chosen book has 16 chapters, you might decide to prepare 4 chapters for each meeting.
   c. Develop a calendar. If your instructor has assigned a presentation at the end of the reading circle project, plan on using your last meeting or two, and possibly a meeting scheduled outside of class time, to prepare and practice the presentation.
   d. Assign each member a role for the next meeting. (See the role guidelines on the assignment sheets that follow.) If you don't have enough members to fill all the roles, some people can fill more than one. The assignments for the first three roles must be done each time you meet, however. The roles are summarizer, discussion leader, passage selector, researcher/connector, illustrator, and vocabulary finder.

## READING CIRCLE MEETINGS

1. Read the assignment ahead of time and complete your role assignment sheet. Bring the book and *two copies* of the role assignment sheet to the meeting.
2. Turn in one copy of the completed assignment sheet to your instructor.
3. Share your role assignment preparations, starting with the summarizer. *Everyone* is expected to participate in all parts of the discussion.
4. Assign new roles for the next meeting, paying attention to what would be best for your book and for the interests of the members.
5. Anonymously, each member of the reading circle evaluates the group's work, answering the questions on page 457 (Anonymous Reading Circle Evaluation).

## FINAL PRESENTATION (OPTIONAL)

Your presentation should communicate to the class important information about your book without "giving everything away."

1. Everyone in the reading circle needs to be involved in the presentation and to speak. The presentation should stay within the time allotted by your instructor (usually 5 to 10 minutes).

2. As a group, decide what you want to present about your book. You might decide to summarize the most important information or to give a few highlights about the best and most interesting parts of your book. You might also present some of the research done by some members of your group. Or you could even act out a scene from the book. Your presentation should have a beginning, or introduction, a middle, and an end, or conclusion.

3. Use visual aids to reinforce the content of your presentation. They can be realia (stuff), a poster (see pages 458–460 for suggestions on how to prepare a poster), a video clip, music, or even food. But make sure that all the aids you use relate to the content of your presentation.

4. In your group, practice your presentation. Help each other with presentation skills (see pages 459–460 for suggestions). Make sure your presentation is clearly coordinated and flows well.

## ROLE ASSIGNMENT SHEETS

The following role assignment sheets will help you think about, organize, and record your assignments for your reading circle meetings.

# SUMMARIZER

Name: _____     Meeting Date: _____

Book: _____     Assignment:   Page _____ to _____

Summarize the reading for today's meeting. The group discussion will start with your statement, covering the main ideas and/or key points of today's reading assignment. Use the spaces below or a separate piece of paper to write your summary and list the key points. Be prepared to read them to the group.

Summary:

_____

_____

_____

_____

_____

_____

_____

_____

_____

_____

_____

_____

_____

_____

_____

_____

_____

Key Points:

1. _____

2. _____

3. _____

4. _____

# DISCUSSION LEADER

Name: _____     Meeting Date: _____

Book: _____     Assignment:   Page _____ to _____

Develop five or six discussion questions (not short answer or yes/no questions) that will stimulate discussion in your group. To write good questions, try answering your question yourself. Is there a correct answer? If there is, then it's not a good discussion question. To answer the question, do you have to think and organize your thoughts? If so, then it's a good discussion question. Use a separate piece of paper if necessary.

Discussion questions:

1. _____

   _____

   _____

2. _____

   _____

   _____

3. _____

   _____

   _____

4. _____

   _____

   _____

5. _____

   _____

   _____

6. _____

   _____

   _____

Sample questions:

   Why do you think the author _____?

   What is/are the central theme(s) of the book so far? Why do you think so?

   Did you find anything disturbing about _____? Why?

   What questions did you have about _____?

Remember: Apply your questions to the assigned portion of the book.

# PASSAGE SELECTOR

Name: _____          Meeting Date: _____

Book: _____          Assignment:   Page _____ to _____

Find and record four to six especially important passages from the reading assignment. You can pick passages for many different reasons: (1) the writing is particularly beautiful or has powerful language; (2) it's funny; (3) it's a turning point in the plot; (4) it reveals how a character really thinks; (5) it captures the theme of the reading.

Use the chart below or create a chart on a separate piece of paper to record your passages. At the meeting, you will read your passages out loud to your reading group (members of your group might choose to follow along in their books), explain why you picked them, and get other members' ideas about them.

| Page and paragraph | The passage | Reason for picking |
|---|---|---|
|  |  |  |
|  |  |  |
|  |  |  |
|  |  |  |
|  |  |  |
|  |  |  |

# RESEARCHER/CONNECTOR

Name: _____          Meeting Date: _____

Book: _____          Assignment:  Page _____ to _____

Research background information on the author and other relevant information such as (1) the historical period dealt with in the book; (2) the geographical location; or (3) some of the issues or events in the
book. You may do your research on the web, but don't just download information. Rather, choose information to share that will be helpful for understanding the book. Record the information below or on a
separate piece of paper, and record where the information came from—the name of the website or the
book title and author. Finally, make connections between the reading assignment and what you already
know—your life experiences, other books you are familiar with, or other events and issues.

Author's background:

_____

_____

_____

Source(s):

_____

Other relevant information:

_____

_____

_____

Source(s):

_____

Connections:

_____

_____

_____

# ILLUSTRATOR

Name: _____  Meeting Date: _____

Book: _____  Assignment: Page _____ to _____

Illustrate an important event or idea in the reading assignment by drawing and/or finding a photo or other image that relates to it. You can make a sketch or a diagram or flowchart, or even draw stick figures. You can also do research in the library or on the Internet for a photo, drawing, or other type of illustration. Be sure to *give credit* to the source of your illustration. Put your illustration in the box below or on a separate piece of paper. When you share the illustration with your group, explain how it relates to the reading.

Source(s): _____

_____

# VOCABULARY FINDER

Name: _____     Meeting Date: _____

Book: _____     Assignment:  Page _____ to _____

Choose about five terms or vocabulary words from the reading assignment to discuss with your group. You can pick words that are particularly interesting, appear often, or are not familiar to you but seem important. Use the chart below or a separate piece of paper to record the words, where you found them in the book, and why you picked them. If it's a word you don't know, write down the definition that is most appropriate for its context.

| Word | Page # | Definition and/or why you picked it |
|------|--------|-------------------------------------|
| 1. | | |
| 2. | | |
| 3. | | |
| 4. | | |
| 5. | | |

# ANONYMOUS READING CIRCLE EVALUATIONS (SAMPLE)

Answer the following questions, and be sure to *explain* your answers.

1.  How did your reading circle work at this meeting?

    _____

    _____

    _____

2.  Was everyone in your reading circle prepared? Did everyone do his or her role assignments?

    _____

    _____

    _____

3.  Did you participate constructively in the group? Did you talk enough? Did you talk too much?

    _____

    _____

    _____

4.  Did everyone participate in the discussion? Were quiet students encouraged to speak up?

    _____

    _____

    _____

5.  What can you do to improve how your group functions?

    _____

    _____

    _____

6.  What can the instructor do to improve how your group functions?

    _____

    _____

    _____

# 8. Poster Sessions

A poster session allows you to make a presentation in a comfortable environment that encourages the "listeners" to be active. Poster sessions can be used for book reports or other reading projects that you do independently.

Your instructor will set aside at least one day for poster sessions. Each student will prepare a poster and an oral presentation. At the beginning of class, about one-third or one-half of the students (depending on the class size and time available) will set up their posters around the room. The other students and your instructor will circulate around the room, visiting each presenter.

For your presentation, you will give a prepared talk (usually 3 to 5 minutes) about the book or reading for which you prepared the poster. During your talk, you will refer to various parts of the poster as a visual aid for your oral presentation. Your classmates will ask you questions, and a lively interchange of ideas will probably take place.

Students observing your presentation will fill out an evaluation sheet and move on to the next presentation until they've seen them all. Then another group of students will set up their posters, and the process will continue until all students make their presentations.

The following guidelines will help you make your poster presentation a success.

## PREPARING YOUR TOPIC

To make a presentation about an article, research you have done, or a book you have read, follow these steps:

1. Complete your reading carefully, giving yourself enough time to finish your reading and research well in advance. Allow several days to prepare the entire poster session.
2. Decide on the most important points or information you want to share with your audience. Remember, you have a limited amount of time. If you are presenting a book you have read, you need to distill the story or information to make it understandable for your listeners. You may be able to prepare a brief summary or just give some highlights.
3. Make an outline of what you want to "say."
4. Think about the best way to put what you want to "say" in a visual format.

## PREPARING YOUR POSTER

**Content** When you know what you want to "say" in the poster, you need to decide how to handle its three major components.

1. *Title.* Decide on a title that is catchy and will attract the attention of your audience as well as accurately represent the information in your poster. If your poster is about a book you have read, the title of the book with the author's name is satisfactory.
2. *Visual elements.* Remember, your poster is above all supposed to explain your information *visually*, so decide what the visual aids will be. They can include graphs, charts, maps, photos, or art.

3. *Text*. Decide what written information you want to include on your poster. Keep the amount of text very small because the people in your audience will not have time to read a lot of information on your poster. Their role is to listen to your presentation and look at the poster to better understand what you say.

Remember! This is *your* poster project. Everything you write on your poster must be *your own ideas and your own words*. If you use *anything* written by somebody else, you *must* give credit to the author and use quotation marks.

## VISUAL APPEARANCE

1. *Neatness*. Make your poster neat to demonstrate the thought and care you put into it.
2. *Visibility*. Everything on your poster should be large enough for observers to see 4 to 8 feet away.
3. *Organization*. Think about how people will be looking at your poster. Do you need arrows to show cause-and-effect relationships or to direct people's eyes as they look at your poster? Do you need to number its various parts?
4. *Lettering and written text*. Here you have a choice. Some people can write the title very well by hand, but if you use a computer, follow these suggestions:
   a. Use only one font style for your poster. A standard font like Times or Times New Roman is best.
   b. Make the title a very large font (at least 72 points). The subtitles can be smaller (36 points). Any other text can be smaller, but still should be easy to read (14 to 18 point).
5. *Color*. Using color will improve the visual impact. Some experts recommend that light items be mounted on darker contrasting colors and dark items be mounted on lighter paper. Leave a border of ¼ to 1 inch around any artwork or text.
6. *Sources*. If you get any visual aids from the Internet or from a published book, be sure to provide the name of the website or the title and author of the book at the bottom of the visual aid itself. For this you can use a small font.

## PREPARING YOUR ORAL PRESENTATION

1. Decide what you want to say. Organize your presentation into three sections:
   a. A brief *introduction*, in which you explain the purpose of your presentation and get your audience's attention.
   b. A *body* in which you make the points that you have decided are most important for others to know about your book, reading, or research.
   c. A *conclusion*, in which you sum up what you have said, with a recommendation about the topic or book you are presenting.
2. Make notes on 3 × 5 cards or on a piece of paper so you can remember what you want to say.
3. Practice your presentation by delivering your talk just as if students were listening to you. (It's a good idea to get a friend to listen to your presentation.)
   a. Time yourself. You don't want to be too long or too brief. Be sure you stay within the time limits that your instructor gives you.

b. Remember to refer to your poster. You want your listeners to look at the poster for at least part of the time during your presentation. You also want them to understand the relation between the poster and your talk.

## GIVING YOUR PRESENTATION

1. Be on time, and be prepared.
2. Dress appropriately.
3. Make eye contact.
4. Speak clearly and slowly enough so people can easily understand you. Speak loudly enough so people can hear you.
5. Finally, be enthusiastic about your subject.

# POSTER SESSION PEER EVALUATIONS

Name of the Presenter: _____

Title of the Presentation: _____

Poster

1. What I liked best:

   _____

   _____

   _____

   _____

2. Suggestions for improvement:

   _____

   _____

   _____

   _____

Oral Presentation

1. What I liked best:

   _____

   _____

   _____

   _____

2. Suggestions for improvement:

   _____

   _____

   _____

   _____

# HOW POSTER SESSIONS ARE GRADED

These are the things your instructor will consider in grading your poster presentation.

1. Reading assignment
   a. Completeness
   b. Evidence that you've read and understood the assignment (the entire book or all the articles)
   c. Evidence that you've done the appropriate research
2. Poster
   a. Thoughtfulness
   b. Illustration helpful for oral presentation
   c. Neatness
   d. Creativity
   e. Appropriate size of art and lettering
   f. Clarity
3. Oral presentation
   a. Evidence of preparation and practice
   b. Good organization and appropriate level of information
   c. Within the time limit
   d. Good eye contact
   e. Clear speech, appropriate speed of speech
   f. Good use of poster to support points

# 9. Suggested Reading for Book Projects

Increasing your reading skills as quickly as possible requires considerable practice. Many teachers assign an extra book for students to read and discuss along with their text. This section lists books that relate to the themes presented in this textbook; other books in the list were chosen by students and teachers. You have already read excerpts from some of the books as you completed your work in this textbook. The list includes books of various lengths and levels of difficulty. After each author and title is a short description of the book.

Alvarez, Julia. *How the García Girls Lost Their Accents.* Yolanda and her three sisters tell their family's story after they emigrated from the Dominican Republic to the United States.

Asimov, Isaac. *I, Robot.* In this classic science fiction novel, Asimov sets up the three principles for creating, living with, and controlling robots.

Baca, Jimmy Santiago. *A Place to Stand.* This memoir details Baca's struggles with poverty, abuse, and illiteracy. It shows his transformation from convict to poet while serving a sentence in a maximum-security prison.

Baldacci, David. *Wish You Well.* This legal thriller, set in rural Appalachia, is a coming-of-age novel dealing with the struggles of the people of Appalachia during the Great Depression.

Boothe, DeMico. *Why Are So Many Black Men in Prison?* The author relates his own incarceration, release, and re-incarceration, and explains the historical forces that have led to the high rates of incarceration and disenfranchisement of African American men. He also discusses the effect on the black community of having so many men behind bars and provides some solutions to this crisis.

Bortner, M. A., and Linda M. Williams. *Youth in Prison: We the People of Unit Four.* This book deals with crime, youth, drugs, schools, gangs, and violence by looking at the lives of young people before, during, and after their incarceration.

Brumbert, Joan Jacobs. *The Body Project: An Intimate History of American Girls.* This book explores the issues of appearance for teenage girls and how insecurity is exploited for profit.

Butler, Octavia. *Kindred.* In this story of time travel, a woman from the twentieth century is repeatedly pulled back in time by her slave-owning ancestor, Rufus, when his life is endangered. She chooses to save him because she discovers that one of his slaves will eventually become her grandmother.

Canada, Geoffrey. *Fist Stick Knife Gun.* The author tells his own story of growing up in a violent South Bronx neighborhood. Canada has spent most of his life working with young people and communities at risk.

Cisneros, Sandra. *The House on Mango Street.* This exquisitely written novel describes a girl's childhood and adolescence among family, friends, and neighbors in a Spanish-speaking neighborhood of Chicago.

Cofer, Judy Ortiz. *The Latin Deli.* This anthology presents short stories about Puerto Rican life in New Jersey, by an important contemporary writer.

Cook, Robin. *Contagion.* Cook's novel is a medical thriller about three extremely rare diseases that start killing patients at a New York hospital. A pathologist suspects that the deaths may have been caused deliberately.

Courtenay, Bryce. *Power of One.* This is the moving story of struggle and triumph of an orphaned boy of English descent growing up in racially and ethnically torn South Africa.

Daniel Tatum, Beverly, PhD. *Why Are All the Black Kids Sitting Together in the Cafeteria? And Other Conversations about Race.* Students and adults segregate ourselves based on racial and ethnic identity. This book, written by a clinical psychologist, honestly and openly discusses the impulses that cause self-segregation, and whether it is a problem that needs to be fixed or a positive coping mechanism for dealing with complex social interactions.

Davis, Sampson, George Jenkins, Rameck Hunt, with Lisa Frazier Page. *The Pact.* This book describes the experiences of three African American friends who grew up in a rough New Jersey neighborhood. Two of them went on to become doctors and the third became a dentist.

Ehrenreich, Barbara. *Nickel and Dimed.* Essayist and cultural critic Ehrenreich sets out to determine whether it is possible to support herself as an unskilled worker. She recounts her experiences with jobs in restaurants, retail stores, and hotels in different parts of the country.

Erdrich, Louise. *Love Medicine.* This magical novel weaves together the stories of two families, one Native American (Chippewa) and one white, in rural North Dakota. Its themes include love, alcoholism, and healing.

Gardner, Chris, and Quincy Troupe. *The Pursuit of Happyness.* This book tells the true story of Chris Gardner, who grew up in inner city Milwaukee with a violent stepfather. He became a successful stockbroker but later faced homelessness as a single father.

Gray, John. *Men Are from Mars, Women Are from Venus.* A relationship counselor focuses on the differences between men and women so each can better understand and improve their relationships with the opposite sex.

Grealy, Lucy. *Autobiography of a Face.* At age 9, Lucy Grealy had a third of her jaw removed because of bone cancer. She then underwent years of treatment and operations, as well as cruel taunts from her classmates because of her appearance.

Haddon, Mark. *The Curious Incident of the Dog in the Night-Time.* This mystery has an unusual detective, a 15-year-old autistic boy who has been accused of killing his neighbor's dog. As he investigates the crime, he discovers many things about his family and himself.

Haley, Alex. *The Autobiography of Malcolm X.* Based on a series of interviews the author did with Malcolm X, this book relates the story of Malcolm's childhood, youth, trouble with the law, and conversion to Islam.

Hayden, Torey. *Murphy's Boy.* Hayden tells the moving story of a young boy who must struggle to overcome his disabilities.

Hillerman, Tony. *Talking God.* This suspenseful story of a grave robber and a corpse features Officer Jim Chee, who solves the mystery surrounding the two.

Hosseini, Khaled. *The Kite Runner.* This novel tells the story of Amir, the son of a wealthy Afghan businessman, and Hassan, the son of his father's servant. It is a story of friendship and tragedy set during the political upheavals of twentieth-century Afghanistan.

Houston, Jeanne Wakatsuki. *Farewell to Manzanar.* This is a true story of one spirited Japanese American family's survival of the indignities of forced detention at Manzanar internment camp during World War II.

Humes, Edward. No *Matter How Loud I Shout: A Year in the Life of Juvenile Court.* The author relates stories of individual kids and many of the alarming details of how the juvenile justice system works.

Kaufman, Moises. *The Laramie Project.* This play documents the effect that the brutal killing of Matthew Shepard, a young gay man, had on his community, as told by both friends and strangers. This incident has become a symbol for America's struggle against intolerance.

Keller, Helen. *The Story of My Life.* Helen Keller became deaf and blind at 19 months due to scarlet fever. She learned to read (in several languages) and even speak, eventually graduating with honors from Radcliffe College in 1904. She wrote this autobiography while she was a student.

Kessler, David A., MD. *The End of Overeating.* The author explains the science of the human appetite; how the food industry uses this information to get us to buy and eat more food; and simple measures we can take to take charge of our own eating habits.

Keyes, Daniel. *Flowers for Algernon.* This science fiction novel tells the story of a semiliterate young man with a limited IQ who undergoes experimental brain surgery and becomes a genius.

Kingsolver, Barbara. *The Bean Trees.* Kingsolver's novel tells the story of a spirited young woman who grew up poor in rural Kentucky and headed west to escape. It is a story of love and friendship, abandonment and belonging.

Kotlowitz, Alex. *The Other Side of the River: A Story of Two Towns,* a *Death, and America's Dilemma.* Exploring how two towns—one mostly black, the other white—react to the death of an African American teenaged boy, Kotlowitz reveals a deep understanding of the racial divide in this country.

Krakauer, John. *Into Thin Air: A Personal Account of the Mount Everest Disaster.* In 1996, journalist John Krakauer joined an expedition to Mount Everest in which eight people died. This book describes the adventure and tragedy in vivid detail.

Martel, Yann. *The Life of Pi.* This is the story of how a boy, stranded on a lifeboat with a tiger, crosses the Pacific Ocean—facing storms, hunger, and all manner of disasters. In the end, he becomes comfortable with himself, the tiger, and the ocean.

McBride, James. *The Color of Water.* A black man, McBride, tells the story of his white mother's remarkable battle against racism and poverty to raise twelve children.

Medina, John. *Brain Rules.* The author, a molecular biologist, explains the best ways to get the most out of our brains.

Mohr, Nicholasa. *In Nueva York.* This book is a collection of stories of New York's Puerto Rican immigrants growing up in the South Bronx from 1946 to 1956.

Morrison, Toni. *The Bluest Eye.* This is the story of an 11-year-old black girl who is abused by her father. Because of the difficult conditions of her life, she yearns to be her exact opposite: a blonde, blue-eyed white girl.

Mortensen, Greg, and David Oliver Relin. *Three Cups of Tea: One Man's Mission to Promote Peace One School at a Time.* Greg Mortensen was a nurse and enthusiastic mountaineer. After a fateful experience climbing in the Himalayas, he dedicated his life to building schools—especially for girls—in Pakistan and Afghanistan.

Nazario, Sonia. *Enrique's Journey.* Journalist Sonia Nazario writes about the experiences of Enrique and other young Central Americans who travel north to find a parent who had left them to work in the United States. They face hunger, bandits, and even death as they ride north on the top of trains.

Nguyen, Kien. *The Unwanted: A Memoir of Childhood.* This book tells the story of a mixed-race child in Vietnam (American and Vietnamese) who endures rejection and war but finally escapes. Through the process, he comes to understand and accept his identity.

Obama, Barack. *Dreams from My Father: A Story of Race and Inheritance.* President Obama deals with his childhood experiences as well as his experiences as a young adult. The book explores in detail what it's like to be a mixed-race child: his father was African, his mother white American.

Peltzer, David J. *A Child Called It.* This book is an autobiographical account of a boy who suffered severe abuse from his mother.

Pollan, Michael. *In Defense of Food.* This well-written and accessible book explains the problems of the American diet and proposes some simple rules to healthy eating: "Eat food. Not too much. Mostly plants."

Rodriguez, Luis. *Always Running: La Vida Loca: Gang Days in LA.* This book explores the motivation of gang life and cautions against the death and destruction that inevitably claim its participants. Rodriguez himself is a veteran of East L.A. gang warfare, but he successfully broke free and became an award-winning Chicano poet.

Santiago, Esmeralda. *When I Was Puerto Rican.* Essentially autobiographical, this book recounts the struggles of a teenage girl whose family moves to New York from Puerto Rico when she is 14 years old, her determination to succeed against the odds in her new environment, and her successes.

Schlosser, Eric. *Fast Food Nation.* Investigative reporter Schlosser relates the story behind the fast-food industry: the history, the raw materials (potatoes and cattle), the processing, the food, the workers, the problems, and some of the consequences—cultural, environmental, and economic—of the global popularity of fast food.

Tan, Amy. *The Joy Luck Club.* Four mothers and four daughters tell their family stories as Chinese immigrants living in San Francisco.

Tannen, Deborah. *You Just Don't Understand: Women and Men in Conversation.* Tannen explains the different conversational styles of women and men and some of the problems of misunderstanding that these styles create.

Viramontes, Helena María. *Under the Feet of Jesus.* This novel tells about the dangers and challenges Estrella and her Mexican American migrant family face during a summer working in the fields.

Waitley, Denis. *The Psychology of Winning.* Waitley is one of this country's best-known and respected motivational psychologists. In this book, he emphasizes that being a winner is an attitude, a way of life, a self-concept.

Walker, Alice. *In Love and Trouble: Stories of Black Women.* Through 13 powerful stories, Walker explores the struggles and joys of black women in the South.

Weisel, Eli. *Night.* A Jewish teenager struggles with the guilt he feels at surviving the Holocaust in which the rest of his family died. Although fictional, the story strongly parallels Weisel's experiences in the death camps.

Weiss, Elaine. *Surviving Domestic Violence: Voices of Women Who Broke Free.* This life-affirming book tells the stories of 12 women who are survivors of domestic violence and who have reclaimed their dignity, restructured their lives, and found peace.

Welch, James. *Winter in the Blood.* This novel is about a young Native American in Montana coming to terms with his heritage and his dreams.

YenMah, Adeline. *Falling Leaves.* The author tells her own story of growing up in China, where she suffers nonstop emotional abuse from her wealthy father and his cruel second wife. She escapes to America, where she begins a medical career and enters a happy marriage.

# Index